DATE DUE

The Unbroken Chain

CHINESE LITERATURE IN TRANSLATION

Editors

Irving Yucheng Lo
Joseph S. M. Lau
Leo Ou-fan Lee
Eugene Chen Eoyang

The Unbroken Chain

An Anthology of
Taiwan Fiction since 1926

EDITED BY
Joseph S. M. Lau

INDIANA UNIVERSITY PRESS / Bloomington

Library of Congress Cataloging in Publication Data
Main entry under title:

The Unbroken chain.

(Chinese literature in translation)
Includes index.
1. Chinese fiction—Taiwan—Translations into English.
2. Chinese fiction—20th century—Translations into
English. 3. English fiction—Translations from Chinese.
I. Lau, Joseph S. M., 1934–   . II. Series.
PL2658.E8U52   1983   895.1′35′080951249   83-47904
ISBN 0-253-36162-1
1 2 3 4 5 87 86 85 84 83

For Yu-shan Lau

Contents

PREFACE

Much progress has been made toward acquainting the Western reader with the richness and genius of Taiwan fiction since the appearance of Chi Pang-yüan's *Anthology of Contemporary Chinese Literature* in 1975 and my *Chinese Stories from Taiwan: 1960-1970* in 1976.[1] On February 23–24, 1979, a symposium on Taiwan fiction was convened at the University of Texas at Austin, the first undertaking of this nature sponsored by a major American university. The papers delivered on that occasion are now published in the collection entitled *Chinese Fiction from Taiwan: Critical Perspectives.*[2] Another measure of the vitality of the field is demonstrated by the fact that some of the more prominent writers represented in the two anthologies cited above are now published in individual volumes.[3] Indeed, Taiwan fiction in English translation has not only increased in quantity over the years, it has also become diversified enough to accommodate the particular needs of some specialists. One case in point is *Born of the Same Roots: Stories of Modern Chinese Women,*[4] which includes six selections by Taiwan writers on the basis of their "feminine sensibility."

However, as far as chronological representation is concerned, our translation of Taiwan literature has been heavily lopsided. No existing anthology has included works dating earlier than the fifties.[5] Such lopsidedness will certainly create the unfortunate impression that Taiwan was a literary wasteland prior to its retrocession to China in 1945.

This is not the case. If we take Lai Ho (1894–1943) as the father of Taiwan literature and his "Busy Over Nothing" *(Tou nao-je,* 1926) as the first vernacular story published by a major Taiwan writer, then it is clear that Taiwan had over twenty years of literary activity before its return to the motherland.[6]

In all fairness, it must be pointed out that the exclusion of the Japanese Occupation Period (1895—1945) is due neither to political prejudice nor to the caprices of literary taste. Quite simply, the omission results from the insufficiency of source material. Until the publication of the monumental *Taiwan Literature under the Japanese Occupation* in 1979,[7] nearly all the writers of Lai Ho's generation, such as Wu Cho-liu (1900–1976), Yang K'uei (1905–), and Lung Ying-tsung (1911–), have remained names more often encountered in memoirs than seen on library shelves. Compounded with the unavailability of texts is the barrier of language. With few exceptions, most of the writers who flourished in the decades from the twenties to the forties wrote in Japanese. Had their writings not been translated, or, as in the case of Yang K'uei, rewritten in Chinese, it is likely that our knowledge of Taiwan fiction would go back no further than the fifties. Obviously enough, it would not have been possible for me to put together an anthology of this fiction since the Japanese period without the assistance of my colleagues in Taiwan, who have provided me with expertly edited collections of basic texts.

Admittedly, the fiction of Lai Ho and his contemporaries makes rewarding reading only from a historical perspective: as records of a people under foreign domination. While police corruption and bribe-taking on the part of a hospital administrator may seem to us too commonplace to warrant reporting in a story, in the contexts of Lai Ho's "The Steelyard" and Yang K'uei's "Mother Goose Gets Married," such practices are to be understood not so much as violations of law but as evidences of humiliation suffered by a subjugated race.

Similar strains of nationalism are heard in Wu Cho-liu's "The Doctor's Mother" and Chu Tien-jen's "Autumn Note." In contrast to "Steelyard" and "Mother Goose," however, those who appear abominable in these two stories are not the Japanese conquerors but their Taiwanese vassals who are only too eager to surrender their Chinese identity, including their names, to qualify them to enjoy the special privileges of a naturalized Japanese citizen. A dramatic foil to these social climbers is the doctor's mother, who refuses to eat her dinner squatting on the tatami, and the Confucian scholar who passes his days chanting the utopian rhymes of T'ao Ch'ien's "Peach Blossom Spring" (*T'ao-hua yüan chi*). Though their resistance against Japanization is passive, and perhaps foolhardy, they have through their spiritual defiance bequeathed to Taiwan literature a moral legacy of self-respect and a consciousness of national pride. Literature for the writers of the Japanese period is a *sui juris* means of protest as much as it is a form of self-expression. In this light, the four writers represented in Part I of this anthology are not only precursors of Taiwan fiction: they are vital links to the great chain of May Fourth literature precisely because the engagé spirit they espouse has constantly been reasserted in later writing.

After the Communists took over China in 1949, the Nationalist Government and hundreds of thousands of refugees loyal to Chiang Kai-shek retreated to Taiwan. No literature worthy of serious attention was produced in the period of settlement until the late fifties. The reason, as I have explained elsewhere, is that the government's "Recover the Mainland" slogan had been read by refugee Chinese "not so much as an indication of determination 'to go home' as an unrelenting personal reminder that Taiwan was not their home. For this reason, they looked upon themselves more or less as 'transit passengers' in an airport even though they had not the slightest idea just when, if ever, they could board the next home-bound plane."[8]

This transit-passenger mentality is sensitively described in Lin Hai-yin's "Lunar New Year's Feast." Since this story deals only with the experience of the mainlanders and their pipedreams, it is only fitting that life in Taiwan during the early fifties should be mirrored from another angle. Nominally an autobiographical love story, Chung Li-ho's "Together through Thick and Thin" is no less realistic for its description of Taiwan's rural poverty and hardship before the island was transformed into an "economic miracle" in the seventies. The rural change in Taiwan during the last twenty years can be gauged by comparing Chung's story with Cheng Ch'ing-wen's "Betel Palm Village."

By consensus, the decade of the sixties was a period of experiment and growth. While the main current stayed close to the course of social realism, some writers occasionally took a detour to the realms of surrealism and personal *agonia*. Li Ch'iao's "The Spheric Man," which bears the unmistakable "anxiety of influence" from Kafka, is a noted example of the former. Ou-yang Tzu's "The Net," punctuated at almost every other sentence by a muffled cry of existential loss, is an early instance of Taiwan women's futile efforts to disentangle themselves from the "net" of traditional expectations in being a wife and a mother. Feminine aspiration is also the concern of "The Story of Three Springs," though presented from a vastly different point of view. Sexually aggresive, Wang Chen-ho's heroine exudes animalistic energies; her self-confidence and purposiveness make a mockery of the anguish and the dilemmas experienced by Ou-yang Tzu's intellectual woman.

However, much as they are varied in narrative technique and in their interpretations of reality, the above three selections have one common characteristic: self-sufficiency as a literary entity. Unlike the stories in Part I, or the *hsiang-t'u* morality tales in the seventies,[9] the fortunes of the individuals in "The Spheric Man," "The Net," and "Three Springs" bear no particular relation to the society in which they live. In other words, they are not intended to be an immediate reflection of metropolitan Taiwan in the sixties, and they are refreshingly free from any burden of ideological or moralistic predispositions.

The situation is quite different in the fiction of the seventies, in which personal destinies are often affected by political exigencies. Published in 1970, Liu Ta-jen's story can in this respect be read as a transitional piece in that the individual is still allowed the freedom to vacillate between courses of action and retirement. At once compassionate and ironic, "Chrysalis" is a sad commentary on the guilt-ridden scholarly bureaucrats of the Kuomintang regime who have expatriated to California in hopes of burying their past—only to find that a life in exile is emptied of meaning unless the past is recalled to redress the drabness of the present.

But the ruminations of "Chrysalis" are soon drowned out by the on- slaught of larger realities in the arena of international politics. On April 9, 1971, the U.S. State Department announced its decision to return the Chien-kuo (Senkaku in Japanese) Islands, about 100 kilometers northeast of Keelung, Taiwan, to the jurisdiction of Japan in 1972. Tiao Yü T'ai is the largest of this group of islands. This decision set off violent chain protests by Chinese students in the United States, Hong Kong, and eventually Taiwan. The vicissitudes of this student demonstration, known as the "Protect Tiao Yü T'ai Movement," are the subject of Chang Hsi-kuo's "Red Boy," who is a political activist.

The Tiao Yü T'ai incident is but one of a series of political setbacks for the Nationalist Government. In 1971, Taiwan was expelled from the United Nations. A year later, President Nixon made his pilgrimage to Peking. The image of America as a reliable friend and a staunch ally was soon discolored. Both Huang Ch'un-ming's "I Love Mary" and Ch'en Ying-chen's "Night Freight" are products of this era, echoing the passions and concerns of the Japanese Period writers. It would be naïve, however, to regard the resentment seething in Huang's and Ch'en's stories merely as an impulsive reaction to what the Japanese call the "Nixon *shokku*." In point of fact, the American presence, and later the Japanese as well, had long been resented before Nixon's trip. There was, for instance, the Liu Tzu-jan incident in 1957, which culminated in the destruction of the U.S. Embassy and the Information Service headquarters by an angry mob. But as far as the writers are concerned, open denunciation of American and Japanese economic domination erupted only after they had witnessed the desertion of their government by its allies one after another.[10] Viewed in this light, "I Love Mary" and "Night Freight" can be taken as a cumulative story: the experience recorded at hand is but a symptomatic expression of a nation's long and bitter memory of compromises and mortification.

To be sure, not every writer active in the seventies is likewise politi- cally oriented. Li Yung-p'ing, for one, draws material from his Sarawak experience to enrich his parable of human depravity. "The Rain from the Sun" is one of the most ambitious undertakings in mythopoesis in modern Chinese fiction. Some, like Tung Nien, have sought to interpret Taiwan's social ills in sociological rather than ideological terms. As with most societies, industrialization has brought to the island concomitant prob- lems such as the disintegration of cohesive kinship, glaring differences in the standards of living, juvenile delinquency, and, as dramatized in "Fire," the loneliness and alienation of dislocated individuals who have moved from the countryside to the big cities. In this context, perhaps we can understand why the college graduate in "Betel Palm Village" has chosen to make his fortune in farming rather than taking a job in Taipei.

Loneliness once again pervades the mood of Chang Ta-ch'un's "Birds of a Feather." Those soldiers who followed the government to Taiwan when they were in their teens are now well past middle age. Unlike the host and his guests in "Lunar New Year's Feast," the old soldier in "Birds of a Feather" cherishes no illusion of returning to China. After all, even the government has abandoned such slogans as "Recover the Mainland, Liberate our Compatriots." Homesickness, however, transcends the pettiness of politics. The old soldier still longs for his old home in Shantung. To relieve his nostalgia, he names each of the chickens he raises after his kin—to the taunts and mockery of his fellow armymen, who are either Taiwanese or Taiwan-born descendants of mainlander parents. His sorrows and grief are private because it is difficult for his comrades-in-arms to understand why he should choose to sleep in the chicken coop whenever he has an opportunity, just as it is impossible to explain to them why his chickens are not commodities to be sold for a profit. He kills all the birds and buries them with traditional rites befitting a human being after his squadron has received orders to decamp. In observing the personal anguish of this Shantungnese veteran, Chang Ta-ch'un has at the same time confided to us the fate of the aging *ta-lu-jen* (mainlander Chinese) in Taiwan: solitary outsiders crippled by their anachronist sense of value and their distant memories.

The summary presented above is by no means a survey of Taiwan fiction over the past fifty years. What is intended in this preface is an editorial statement regarding the organization of this volume and the rationale for the selections. Due to the limit of space, I was compelled to give up a number of stories originally commissioned for this book. I would have liked to see Lung Ying-tsung's "The Huangs" and Lü He-jo's "All Is Well in the Family" represented in Part I for the sake of variety. While Lai Ho and his peers are notable for their patriotic sentiments, the works of Lung and Lü should not be denied their place in history just because they happened to practice their craft as if they had never seen a Japanese policeman in occupied Taiwan. Similarly, one or two authors whose views are in line with the Nationalist Government should also be included, if only for the sake of offsetting the cynicism seeping through the pages of "Lunar New Year's Feast."

But even a modest attempt at expansion would require more space than is realistically available. As it stands, however, this volume is the only anthology of Taiwan fiction comprehensive enough to contain half a century of achievements and diversified enough to offer various examples demonstrating a graduating degree of narrative sophistication. *The Un-*

broken Chain is a self-sufficient text for an introductory course in Taiwan fiction from the earliest times to the present.

In addition to the anthologies and reference works cited earlier, I have consulted Huang Wu-chung's *Brief Biographies of Taiwan Writers during the Japanese Period* (*Jih-chü shih-tai T'ai-wan hsin wen-hsüeh tso-chia hsiao-chüan*, Taipei, 1980) in preparing the biographical sketches that accompany the stories. Due to space considerations, the notes on the authors are kept to a minimum, providing no more information than is necessary to identify the particular qualities of their art or the significance of their works in sociohistorical perspectives.

The present volume is an outgrowth of a grant (1979–1980) from the Social Science Research Council, for which I would like to extend my gratitude. Thanks are also due to the Graduate School of the University of Wisconsin, Madison, for providing me with summer support that year. Publication of this book has been timely assisted by a grant from the Pacific Cultural Foundation, and I wish to thank its president, Dr. Jeanne Tchong Koei Li, for her speedy processing of my application. An undertaking of this nature is necessarily a collaborative effort, involving the generous contributions of many individuals. I am grateful to the authors or their descendants who have given me written permission to translate their works into English.

To the translators, whose names appear with their selections, I owe more than a perfunctory note of thanks. It is their skills and labor that have enabled the Chinese stories to live a double life in English. Apologies, along with thanks, must be offered to a number of friends whose efforts have not materialized in printed form for reasons explained earlier: to Tsai-fa Cheng, for translating Lung Ying-tsung's "The Huangs" from the Japanese; to David T. W. Wang, for Lü He-jo's "All Is Well in the Family"; to Michael Duke, for Chu Hsi-ning's "The General and I"; to Vivian Ling Hsu, for Chiang Hsiao-yün's "Mountain Joy." I would also like to thank C. H. Wang, who has been most unstinting with his advice and suggestions during the planning stage of this work. My sincere appreciation is expressed to Nancy Ing, editor of *Chinese P.E.N.*, for kind permission to reprint Li Yung-p'ing's "The Rain from the Sun" (Summer 1981, pp. 65–93), and for her much needed encouragement throughout the various stages of my undertaking. Last but not least, a word of thanks is due to Christopher Lupke for helping me read the proofs, and to Jason C. S. Wang, whose calligraphy has graced the index of authors and titles.

NOTES

1. Chi Pang-yüan et al., eds., *An Anthology of Contemporary Chinese Literature—Taiwan: 1949–1974*, 2 vols. (Taipei: National Institute for Compilation and Translation, 1975). *Chinese Stories from Taiwan: 1960–1970* is edited by Joseph

S. M. Lau with the assistance of Timothy A. Ross (New York: Columbia University Press, 1976). The latest anthology of Taiwan fiction in English translation is *Winter Plum: Contemporary Chinese Fiction,* edited by Nancy Ing (Taipei: Chinese Materials Center, 1982).

2. Edited by Jeannette L. Faurot, it was published by Indiana University Press, 1980. In addition to its essays on individual authors and its general studies on literary trends and movements, this volume is also valuable for its extensive bibliographical information on contemporary Taiwan fiction. Divided into four parts, the bibliography lists works in English and Chinese under the categories of (1) anthologies, (2) journals and literary magazines, (3) general studies, and (4) studies on individual writers. Additional information regarding the availability of Taiwan fiction in English translation can be found in *Modern Chinese Fiction: A Guide to Its Study and Appreciation: Essays and Bibliographies,* edited by Winston L. Y. Yang and Nathan K. Mao (Boston: G. K. Hall, 1981).

3. Since the appearance of Chen Jo-hsi's *The Execution of Mayor Yin and Other Stories from the Great Proletarian Cultural Revolution* in 1978, Indiana University Press has published the works of two prominent Taiwan fiction writers: Huang Ch'un-ming's *The Drowning of an Old Cat and Other Stories* (1980) and Pai Hsien-yung's *Wandering in the Garden, Waking from a Dream* (1982).

4. Edited by Vivian Ling Hsu and published by Indiana University Press in 1981, this anthology includes six Taiwan authors: Pai Hsien-yung, Yü Li-hua, Ch'en Ying-chen, Yang Ch'ing-ch'û, Wang T'o, and Chen Jo-hsi.

5. In the early sixties, Taipei's Heritage Press launched an ambitious translation project to represent the literary efforts of the fifties. Some of the titles include: Nancy Chang Ing, ed., *New Voices: Stories and Poems by Young Chinese Writers* (1961); Lucian Wu, ed., *New Chinese Stories* (1960), and *New Chinese Writing* (1962); Nieh Hua-ling, ed., *Eight Stories by Chinese Women* (1962). The last cited work makes a useful supplement to Vivian Hsu's *Born of the Same Roots.* I am grateful to C. T. Hsia for this information.

6. According to Chung Chao-cheng and Yeh Shih-t'ao, editors of *Taiwan Literature under the Japanese Occupation (Kuang-fu-ch'ien T'ai-wan wen-hsüeh ch'uan-chi),* 8 vols. (Taipei: Yüan-ching, 1979), the first vernacular story, entitled "Where Does She Want to Go?" *("T'a-yao wang ho-ch'u ch'ü?"),* was written by Chui Feng and was published in 1922. See Chung and Yeh's sectional preface to this story in Vol. 1, p. 1. However, since Chui Feng is the author of only one story, it is customary for the literary historians to begin their discussion of Taiwan fiction with Lai Ho ("Father of Taiwan fiction"), who has written fourteen stories and a number of poems and essays. For an evaluation of Lai Ho's importance in the development of Taiwan literature, see Jane Parish Yang, "The Evolution of the Taiwanese New Literature Movement from 1920–1937," Dissertation, University of Wisconsin, 1981. Of related interest is Hyman Kublin's "Taiwan's Japanese Interlude, 1895–1945," in *Taiwan in Modern Time,* edited by Paul K. T. Shih (New York: St. John's University Press, 1973), pp. 317–356.

7. In addition to this collection, referred to above, Taiwan writing during the Japanese period is also well represented in *Taiwan New Literature Under the Japanese Occupation (Jih-chü-hsia T'ai-wan hsin wen-hsüeh: Ming chi),* 5 vols., edited by Li Nan-heng (Taipei: Ming-t'an, 1979). This set contains a number of hitherto unpublished literary as well as historical documents that are of great interest to literary historians. In China, there has developed a steady interest in Taiwan literature since the death of Mao Tse-tung in 1976 and the fall of the Gang of Four in the same year. Works by Taiwan writers have been sporadically re-

printed in leading journals. In 1979, Peking's Renmin Wenxue chubanshe published a 602-page volume of Taiwan short fiction *(T'ai-wan hsiao-shuo-hsüan)* with selections from the Japanese period down to the present time. Research projects are now underway at universities in the Canton and Amoy areas to bring out a history of Taiwan literature as well as a handbook on this subject within three years.

8. See Joseph S. M. Lau, "'How Much Truth Can a Blade of Grass Carry?': Ch'en Ying-chen and the Emergence of Native Taiwan Writers," *Journal of Asian Studies*, Vol 32, No. 4 (Aug. 1973), p. 624.

9. Taiwan fiction of the *hsiang-t'u* variety is discussed in Jing Wang's "Taiwan *Hsiang-t'u* Literature: Perspectives in the Evolution of a Literary Movement," in *Chinese Fiction from Taiwan: Critical Perspectives*, pp. 43–70.

10. The response of Taiwan writers to the "Nixon *shokku*" (Nixon shock) and subsequently to Japan's severance of diplomatic ties with Taiwan in 1973 is treated in my essays: (1) "Echoes of the May Fourth Movement in Taiwan *Hsiang-t'u* Fiction," in *Mainland China, Taiwan, and U.S. Policy*, edited by Hung-mao Tien (Cambridge, Mass.: OG&H Publishers, 1983), pp. 135–150; and (2) "The Tropics Mythopoetized: The Extraterritorial Writing of Li Yung-p'ing in the Context of the *Hsiang-t'u* Movement," *Tamkang Review*, Vol. 12, No. 1 (Fall 1981), pp. 1–26.

The Unbroken Chain

Part One

Taiwan Fiction during the Japanese Period (1895–1945)

LAI HO

(1894–1943)

Two years after his graduation from Taipei Medical School in 1914, Lai Ho opened a hospital in his hometown, Changhua. In 1917, he went to China and offered his service to Amoy's Po-ai Hospital. He returned to the island in 1919, at a time when echoes of the May Fourth Movement, initiated by the students at Peking University, were reverberating over the country. His China experience affected his intellectual outlook immensely, so much so that he was no longer content to practice medicine alone. Following Lu Hsün's (1881–1936) example, he took up writing, hoping to rouse his compatriots from their sloth, apathy, and intellectual sterility in the face of Japanese barbarity. His spirit of defiance in this respect is sufficiently represented in "The Steelyard", selected for this volume. Though he has written a number of poems in classical Chinese, he is best remembered as the author of fourteen stories in the vernacular—a medium that provided him with the most leverage in his battles against feudalism, ignorance, and cowardice. When, on the day after the Japanese bombed Pearl Harbor (December 7, 1941), Lai Ho was jailed for the second time, his health rapidly deteriorated. He died of a heart attack on January 31, 1943. His complete works can be found in the first volume of Taiwan New Literature under the Japanese Occupation (Jih-chü-hsia T'ai-wan hsin wen-hsüeh).

The Steelyard

Translated by Jane Parish Yang

Most of the inhabitants in Wei-li Village of Chen-nan County were hard-working, steadfast, peaceful, and submissive farmers. Except for a few powerful families who managed the governmental affairs of the area and several families of low ranking clerks, the majority of the villagers were poor.

Ch'in Te-ts'an's family was especially poverty-stricken, since his father died before he was born. Though the father had rented several mou of farmland, after his death his wife and son were left with nothing. If the landlord had sympathized with them and continued to rent to them, they could have hired laborers to work the land. That way they could have

3

made a little profit to sustain themselves. But who among the wealthy would be willing to let someone else profit from the land? Such a person wouldn't have become wealthy in the first place. And so it was in this case: the landlord got a few more pecks of rice by renting the land out to someone else. The money the father had earned with his blood and sweat was carried into the ground with him. The situation of mother and son seemed hopeless.

The neighbors felt sorry for them. Some of the older people took it upon themselves to help keep Chin Te-ts'an's family from starving. With a neighbor acting as matchmaker, the mother was remarried to a man willing to bear her family name. But not only is it true that a stepfather seldom shows affection for the son of a previous husband: he also treats the son's mother like some kind of machine. In the case of Te-ts'an this was more than true, for he was cursed and beaten by his stepfather, and because of this, his mother was unable to get along with her second husband.

Fortunately, his mother was hard-working and was able to plan ahead. She wove grass sandals, raised ducks, chickens, and pigs, and, in spite of great hardship, managed to muddle through the hard days. When Te-ts'an was nine years old, she sent him off to herd cows and work as a farmhand. By that time, the stepfather wasn't paying much attention to household affairs. Even so, mother and son were able to avoid the threat of starvation only by their own efforts.

When Te-ts'an was sixteen, his mother had him quit his job as a farm-hand and return home. She wanted him to rent several mou of farmland, but at that time rented land was hard to come by. The Sugar Processing Company earned great profits from its operations. The farmers, badly exploited by the company, were unwilling to plant sugarcane. Thus, to compete with the farmers for rented lands, the company gave the land-lords most attractive offers. Now, if a landlord could bring himself more profit, why should he care about the farmers' difficulties? In this way land was grabbed up by the company for sugarcane production. There were several landlords who could be said to have had a conscience, because they were willing to rent to the farmers, but the rent was set at the same high price the sugar company paid. Thus Te-ts'an couldn't afford to farm, and working as a laborer for the sugar company was like being treated like a draft animal. His mother refused to allow him to do that, and so he remained at home and occasionally worked odd jobs. Because he was strong and hard-working, he was sent for every day and earned more with less effort than if he had hired out as a full-time laborer. His mother was thrifty, and they gradually saved up some money.

Three years swiftly passed. When Te-ts'an turned eighteen, his mother's one remaining wish was to see him married. The money she had saved up by her hard work was enough for a wedding, and he married a daughter of a farmer in the village. Fortunately, after they were married, the wife helped Te-ts'an work in the fields, her strength the equal of any man's. The harvests were good and the young couple were, for the time being, at least self-sufficient.

When Te-ts'an was twenty-one, he presented his mother with a grand-son, and from that time on a smile lit up her withered face. The satisfac-tion she felt in her heart allowed her gradually to lay down her burden of responsibility, because her duties as a mother were already fulfilled. But her frail body was unable to sustain itself after twenty years of hardship. Since she had now eased up on her responsibilities, she did not take care of herself as she used to. Illness struck. After several days in bed, satisfac-tion and joy spread over her features, and she passed away. At that time Te-ts'an's stepfather was husband to her in name only. With her death, Te-ts'an had nothing more to do with him. Poor Te-ts'an! His happiness vanished with the death of his kind mother.

The next year a daughter was born. With his mother now gone, Te-ts'an's wife had to take care of the house. Since she was unable to work outside because of her young children, their income was reduced by half, and Te-ts'an had to work twice as much as before. Under these difficult circumstances four years passed. Finally, he too became ill. At the begin-ning of harvest time, malaria struck. After four or five days without any signs of recovery, Te-ts'an saw a doctor of Western medicine. He spent more than two dollars. But, though he felt a little better, he was still weak.

At a busy time like this, however, the industrious Te-ts'an didn't dare sit idly at home. So, enduring the pain, he went back to the fields. When he returned that night, he felt a little sick. He woke up in the middle of the night with chills and hot spells. The next day he was unable to get out of bed. This time he didn't dare send for the doctor of Western medicine. Three days' work won't even pay for one treatment, he thought to him-self. Where is the money to come from? But he couldn't ignore his illness either. He would either brew some green herbs—that didn't cost any-thing—or take some relatively inexpensive Chinese medicine. Although this was somewhat effective, he still had hot spells and chills every two or three days. Only after many months did they stop recurring. His belly, however, had become bloated. Some said that eating too much of the green herbs caused it. Others said it was called swelling of the spleen and was caused by taking Western medicine. Te-ts'an didn't care what it was called or what caused it, but inasmuch as it prevented him from working, it became a great problem.

When Te-ts'an became ill, his wife had to go back to work and leave the children unattended at home. Their cries kept time with Te-ts'an's moans from his sickbed. Though they didn't starve to death, they got only one or two meals a day if they were lucky, and the whole family became malnourished, especially the children. Luckily, his wife did not become pregnant again.

At the end of the year, Te-ts'an was finally able to do a little work, but with the year-end banquet[1] approaching, he had yet to find a suitable job. Because everything came to a halt at Lunar New Year, and there would be no opportunity to work then, he would have to store up food for this half-month period. Te'ts'an became especially worried and upset.

In the end, having heard that selling vegetables in town was profitable, he decided to try it. But he lacked capital, and being an honest person, he felt uncomfortable asking people for a loan. Finally, having no alternative, he was forced to ask his wife to turn to her family for help.

It stood to reason that the wife of a poor farmer could hardly have come from a wealthy family, and so one couldn't expect much help from them. Her sister-in-law treated her well, however, and gave her the only jewelry she owned, a gold pin, to pawn for a few dollars to serve as capital. Pawning the pin was risky, but since there was no other solution, Te-ts'an's wife could only go along with it.

One morning Te-ts'an brought back a load of vegetables, hoping to go to town right after breakfast. It was then that his wife discovered that he didn't have a steelyard. "How can we get one?" Te-ts'an thought. "Steelyards are sold exclusively by the government, and they're not cheap either. Where can we get the money?" Finally, his wife hurried over to a neighbor's house to borrow a steelyard. The neighbor was kind and lent them a fairly new one. Because the police were bent on finding picayune faults with the common people in order to accumulate merit on their record for fast promotion—the ones who rooted out the most cases were promoted the fastest—there were countless crimes that were literally fabricated by the police. And, seeing that they had no chance to win these cases, the people, though wronged, wouldn't dare to speak out. Transportation bans, travel rules, scale and measurement regulations—anything to do with daily life was within the scope of the law and could be controlled or prohibited. Te-ts'an's wife, worried that something like that would happen, decided to borrow the new steelyard.

Business that day wasn't bad. By the end of the day, Te-ts'an had earned over a dollar. He first bought some rice for the New Year. After several days, when he had put aside enough food, he began to think, "Our luck this year was just awful. Next year first thing we have to do is buy a new picture of Bodhisattva Kuan-yin for the living room altar. The couplets along the door have to be replaced, too. And we have to have gold-colored sacrificial money to burn for the gods and silver-colored for the spirits. And then there's the joss sticks and candles." After several more days of fairly good business, he then thought of steaming some rice cakes, the traditional New Year treats. When he brought the rice home, his wife couldn't hold back and chided him, "We should save the extra money to get the gold pin back from the pawn shop. Isn't that more important?" Te-ts'an answered, "I haven't forgotten about it. But today is only the twenty-fifth. I'm not worried about earning the money to get it back. But even if I don't, we still have the capital. No matter when you redeem it, you still have to pay a full month's interest."

One evening when he was getting ready to go home, he remembered his children. He felt he wouldn't be fulfilling his duties as a father if he didn't buy them new outfits for the New Year. He may not have been able to provide a good life for his children, but he should at least bring them a little happiness. He bought several feet of patterned cloth for them, and in doing so he spent the profit from the last several days.

The next day at noon, a low-ranking policeman strolled over and stood in front of him, his eyes riveted on the load of cabbage. Te-ts'an asked politely, "Ta-lang,[2] is there something you want?" "Your produce seems fresher than the others'," the policeman said. Te-ts'an replied, saying, "That's right. People in the city know how to live better than country folk. If it's not the best, they don't want it."

"How much for a catty?"

"Since it is Ta-lang who wants it, don't bother about the price. I feel honored simply because you ask for it." He selected several of the cabbages, tied them up with a length of straw and respectfully offered them to the officer.

"No, weigh it." The policeman made a show of declining the offer several times. Unsuspecting, Te'ts'an did as he was told. Then he said: "Ta-lang, you're too polite. It's only one catty and fourteen ounces." Usually, requesting an item's weight was an indication of agreement to buy, rather than taking it for nothing as a present. "You're sure about that?" the policeman asked. "Well, actually it's two catties, but since it's you who wants it . . ." Te-ts'an answered in his usual business tone, giving no hint that it was to be taken as a present.

"Your steelyard's not accurate, then. Two catties should count as two catties. Why one catty and fourteen ounces?" The policeman's face hardened. "No, it's still new," Te-ts'an replied with composure. "Give it to me!" the policeman demanded angrily. "You can still see the lines," Te-ts'an said as he handed it over calmly. The policeman held it in his hand, examined it for a moment and said, "It's worthless. I'm taking you to the station." "What for? Can't it be fixed?" "Oh, so you don't want to go, eh?" The policeman ranted, "We'll see if you won't go, pig!" With a snap he broke the weighing rod in two and tossed it aside. Then, taking a small notebook out of his breast pocket, he recorded Te-ts'an's name and address. He returned to the police station in a rage.

Te-ts'an stood dumbly in front of his load of vegetables, vainly seething with anger from this unexpected insult. When the officer had gone some distance, several bystanders drew near. An older one said, "You dummy! You come to the market but don't even understand this rule? You think you're going to do business with him? So many catties of this and that? You really meant to take his money?" "Why should we give him things free of charge?" Te-ts'an protested. "You don't realize how much power he has! You don't know what green herb ointment feels like,"[3] the older man smiled sarcastically. "What? An official can insult the people as he pleases?" Te-ts'an asked. "What a blockhead!" someone in the crowd commented. The bystanders discussed the meaning of the incident for a while before they dispersed.

Te-ts'an returned home, but he had lost his appetite for dinner. He just sat glumly, in silence. After his wife gently prodded him several times, he finally told her what had happened that day. "Don't worry," she said, comforting him. "You can buy a new steelyard with what you've earned the past few days. The rest is still enough to redeem the gold pin. Take a rest. You don't need to go out tomorrow. We've got about everything we need for the New Year. Our luck has been rotten this year, and perhaps that explains why we got in trouble with the authorities. But since we've had bad luck this year, we might have better luck next year."

Te-ts'an stayed home the next day. No move was made against him, and since the next day was New Year's Eve, he had only one day left to do business before the long holidays started, and then, he decided, he could take a good rest. He got up early the next day and took a load of vegetables to the market. It was still dark when he arrived. The shouts of the people in the market sprang up out of the early morning mist, a sad reminder on this day of the year of the swift passage of time. Shortly after dawn, the produce in the market was almost gone. Some people had already begun packing up their baskets, eager to go home and gather around the table with their families and enjoy the New Year's Eve banquet as a reward for their hard work over the past year. It was then that Te-ts'an encountered the officer again.

"You pig! Where were you hiding yesterday?" the policeman roared.

"What? How could you curse me for no reason?" Te-ts'an retorted.

"I'll give you a reason at the yamen. Move, pig!"[4]

"If I've got to go, I'll go. Just stop calling me 'pig.' "

The policeman glared at him and led him off.

"Are you Ch'in Te-ts'an?" asked the judge at the yamen.

"Yes, I am," Te-ts'an, kneeling on the floor, answered.

"So you've committed a crime, huh?"

"I'm thirty years old and I've never committed a crime."

"I'm not interested in your past. I'm only telling you that you've violated the standard measurement regulation."

"I've been wronged, your Honor."

"What? You mean you've been falsely accused?"

"Yes, your Honor."

"But it's clearly stated in the policeman's report that you've violated the law, and a policeman can't be wrong!"

"But, in fact, I've been unjustly charged."

"Well, since it's reported that you committed this crime, I can't let you off lightly. However, I'll only fine you three dollars. Do consider that a special favor."

"I don't have any money."

"In that case, stay in jail for three days. Once again, do you have money to pay the fine?"

"No, your Honor." He figured that three dollars was certainly worth more than being jailed for three days during New Year's holidays.

Te-ts'an's wife had planned to redeem the gold pin from the pawn shop right after she finished doing the laundry. But before she got out of the house she heard the bad news. Immediately she asked herself: "Who can I turn to? Who can help me out?" She could think of no one. The more she thought about it, the more distressed she felt. She burst into tears, as if she could release her pent-up emotions only by crying. Finally, a neighbor suggested that she take the money she had planned to redeem the pin with and go to the yamen to find out what this was all about.

Country folk are frightened enough just by the thought of encountering a policeman, not to mention going to the yamen. Besides, she was just an ignorant woman. Her anxiety was not difficult to imagine. As she entered the building, she was stopped by a policeman shouting to her: "What're you doing here?"

She immediately stepped outside in terror. Fortunately, a young janitor came out to make inquiry about her, and she entreated him to help her out. What was even more fortunate was that the boy still had the innocence of youth with him. He sincerely offered her advice and volunteered to go in her behalf to pay the three dollars to the judge.

"I was locked up only a while ago. How come I'm released so soon?" Te-ts'an asked himself suspiciously before he came out of the yamen and saw his wife waiting outside.

"How come you are here?" he asked her dutifully.

"I heard . . . that you'd been locked up," she replied, sobbing.

. "Nothing to be excited about. I haven't done anything serious enough for them to chop off my head," Te-ts'an grumbled dispiritedly.

By the time they reached the market, it had already closed. The sound of firecrackers sending off the old year could be heard all around.

"Did you redeem the gold pin?"

"I hadn't even left the house when I heard about what had happened to you. So I hurried over to the yamen and gave them three dollars. What's left isn't enough now.

"Humph," Te-ts'an grunted. He took out the three dollars he earned that morning and handed it to her, saying: "I'll take the load home. You'd better run to the pawnshop before it closes. Come home as soon as you can."

No sooner had the children finished their dinner than they retired to bed, dreaming their sweet dreams. They wanted to get up early the next morning to welcome the New Year. The father paced back and forth in the room without heeding the call of his wife urging him to go to bed. His thoughts were tempered with unutterable sadness. Between sighs, he mumbled to himself: "People are treated just like animals. What kind of world is this that makes life more miserable than death?"

He recalled the look of contentment on his mother's face as she was about to depart from this world. Suddenly, he came to a final recognition of what he had to do.

On New Year's day, screams, followed by pleading and moaning, suddenly erupted from Te-ts'an's house. Then a short exchange was heard: "Is that all you've got?" "Yes, unless you want the sacrificial paper money."[5]

Around the same time a rumor spread through town that a night patrolman had been killed in the street.

AUTHOR'S END NOTE

I have witnessed this kind of tragedy many times and wanted to write it down. But on recollection, sorrow filled my breast and I couldn't take up my pen. Recently, having read Anatole France's (1844–1924) "Crainquebille" (1904), I have realized that incidents such as the above did not take place only in underdeveloped countries. It happens in any place subjugated by authoritarian force. For this reason, I have disregarded my own crudeness of style and committed this story to writing.

NOTES

This story was originally published under Lai Ho's pen name, Lan Yün ("idle clouds").

1. Given on the sixteenth day of the twelfth lunar month in celebration of the local god of the earth.
2. "Master." Polite address by Taiwanese to Japanese policemen during the Japanese occupation of Taiwan, from 1894–1945.
3. Ointment administered after a beating.
4. Yamen: Local government administrative offices.
5. The ending of this story is rather cryptic. We have no idea whether the exchange is between husband and wife, or between Te-ts'an and the policeman. The ambiguity might be deliberate in view of the nature of the story.

WU CHO-LIU (1900–1976)

Wu Cho-liu (pen name of Wu Chien-t'ien) was a graduate of Taipei Normal School in the Japanese system. For this reason, he was among those veteran writers, such as Yang K'uei and Lung Ying-tsung, who had to reeducate themselves in modern Chinese in order to resume their literary career after Taiwan was returned to China in 1945. His first story, "The Moon in the Water" (1936), was written in Japanese (the Chinese translation, "Shui yüeh," appeared in 1961). His Japanese training, however, has not blunted his nationalistic propensities, as can be seen in the present selection, "The Doctor's Mother." Author of a number of stories, novellas, and essays, Wu is best known for a novel he surreptitiously began in 1943, when the island was still under Japanese rule. First published in Japanese in 1946, and later translated into Chinese in 1962, The Orphan of Asia (Ya-hsi-ya ti ku-erh) *is one of the most ambitious attempts in Taiwan fiction to offer a kaleidoscopic view of the island under Japanese occupation. In his own words: "All the dregs of society, be they Japanese or Chinese, are represented in this novel: school teachers, government officials, doctors, businessmen, ordinary citizens, community security heads, 'model youths,' running dogs and what not" (quoted in Huang,* Brief Biographies, *p. 45). After the war, Wu worked for some time as a reporter for* Hsin-sheng Daily, *and in 1964 he founded the literary journal* Taiwan Wen-i. Wu Cho-liu tso-p'in-chi *(Taipei, 1977) contains his major works, in six volumes.*

The Doctor's Mother

Translated by Jane Parish Yang

The door to the back gate creaked open. Out came a respectable-looking old woman wearing tiny pointed shoes. Behind her, her maid carried a bamboo basket filled with meat, gold and silver paper, and joss sticks for the sacrifices.

The old beggar outside the gate stretched out his neck to look around, secretly surveying the activity within the gate and awaiting the old woman's arrival. He knew that she went to the temple to offer sacrifices on the fifteenth of every month. His greatest fear was that his fellow beggars would find this out, so he had taken great pains to keep this fact a secret. On the same day every month, he furtively made his way to this back gate to wait for her exit. He had done so for the past ten years without fail.

As soon as the lady was in sight, he approached her respectfully, as if meeting a living immortal. His white hair was in disarray, his clothing was patched and ragged; only his bamboo cane had a brilliant sheen to it. He walked up to her, calling in a pitiful voice: "Venerable Madam, have mercy! Have mercy on this old beggar."

The old woman responded by handing the beggar's sack over to the maid with these instructions: "Bring him two pecks of rice."

The maid hesitated and didn't move. Growing impatient, the old woman raised her voice: "What are you afraid of? Isn't Ch'ien Hsin-fa my son? Such a trifling matter, there's nothing to fear. Just go on now, and hurry up!"

"Madame is right, of course, but I don't have the courage. Every time I see the master, I'm scared speechless."

The maid crept back into the house as she spoke. Seeing no one around, she quickly opened the rice bin and measured the rice out into the sack, then dashed out of the kitchen and ran over to the old lady. She rubbed her hand over her chest to calm her thumping heart. The kitchen was next to Ch'ien Hsin-fa's room. If he caught her taking the rice out, he would be sure to scold her. Whenever he cursed someone, he would do it to his heart's content, never giving any thought to another's self-respect.

Once when the maid was measuring out the rice, Ch'ien Hsin-fa suddenly came charging in. He flew into a rage, screaming at her: "You're the real culprit! If you didn't do it, how would the beggar get anything? If the old lady says a peck, just give him one-tenth of it. Do you understand?"

The maid had no choice but to follow his order. When the old lady found this out, she shouted angrily: "That idiot!" Grabbing the beggar's staff, she rushed inside in a savage mood.

"What nonsense!" her son fumed. "The most a beggar should ever get is a cupful of rice, never one, not to mention two pecks!"

The old woman overheard what he said, and, without warning, she lashed out at him with the beggar's staff, roundly cursing him: "Hsin-fa! Your rent from the fields is more than three thousand bushels, but you aren't willing to part with even one single peck to the poor. You despise the poor, but if some district magistrate or section chief comes around, you busy yourself preparing meat and liquor. You wouldn't wince at spending a thousand ounces of gold on entertaining them. You're not human. You're just a running dog for the Japanese masters."

As she cursed him she took up the beggar's staff and beat Ch'ien Hsin-fa. The family was thrown into chaos. Finally, she was pacified and

calmed down. Ch'ien Hsin-fa was angry but dared not talk back to his
mother; he could only swallow his rage, blaming everything on the maid.
But it was hard for the maid to act correctly. On the one hand, she didn't
dare go against the old woman's orders. On the other, she couldn't afford
to offend her master. Thus, on the fifteenth day of every month, she
would stealthily measure out the rice to give to the beggar.

Later, when the war situation worsened, grain, including rice, was
rationed, so the old lady could not give out any more rice even if she
wanted to. Money was used as a substitute. Not until then was the maid's
anxiety over the fifteenth of every month relieved.

Ch'ien Hsin-fa was the public health physician for K Street. He liked to
be seen in his uniform whenever he went out, whether it was on business
or at a funeral. His neighbors had never seen him in casual clothes. His
uniform was always pressed neatly like that of a high-ranking government
official, for his uniform represented his prestige. There was nothing unusual about his medical skill, yet his reputation was known far and wide.
The simple reason was that he was good at putting on a show of concern
and friendliness toward his patients. The people in his area were all
honest, simple folk, and they had no way of knowing his hidden motive.
They all misjudged him. Thus the good word about him spread from one
patient to another, and his reputation was established. Fame contributed
to his wealth, and before fourteen or fifteen years had passed, he had
accumulated a fortune worth more than three thousand piculs.

Ch'ien Hsin-fa came from a poor family. When he was a student, his
school uniform had been patched and mended again and again. The students all jeered at him, saying that what he wore was not a uniform but a
judo outfit. The truth was that his uniform had been patched to such an
extent that it did look like a judo outfit. This kind of ridicule made him so
angry and ashamed that he was unable to answer. But there was nothing
he could do about it, so he had to take things as they came. During his
school years, his family could afford his tuition only because his father
worked as a laborer during the day and his mother knitted hats at night.
He passed the five years to graduation in extreme hardship.

Ch'ien Hsin-fa married a rich man's daughter and, with the assistance
of her uncles, opened a private clinic. When it first opened, he again
relied on the influence of his wife's uncles to hold a huge reception for the
officials, gentry, merchants, and prominent local figures, hoping that they
would help advertise his medical skills. And he received unexpectedly
good results. From then on he became even more cautious, treating all
his patients warmheartedly, unlike most practicing physicians who
merely treated them in a routine way. When the patients came in, he
would chat with them on various subjects. Though this kind of idle talk
was unrelated to their illnesses, the patients were always pleased with his

concern. When rural folk came in, he tried to flatter them by praising their children.

"Your son is so well-behaved and cultivated. He'll surely grow up to be an official."

He often used flattery. But sometimes he would adopt a considerate and understanding pose, such as: "This illness may be hard to cure. I'm afraid he's contracted pneumonia. I think I should give him shots. But they're expensive, and I don't dare make the decision without first consulting you. What is your opinion?" He discussed the problem so sweetly and agreeably that when country folk heard that their child's illness was serious, they were willing to empty their pockets to pay for the shots, no matter how expensive.

This wasn't Ch'ien Hsin-fa's only public relations scheme. Whenever he made house calls, he bowed politely to whomever he met, child or adult. Whenever he was traveling by sedan chair and came across rough mountainous terrain, he would get out and walk. This also won him the goodwill of the sedan chair bearers and rural folk.

In his leisure time at home, he would make use of fortune-tellers and friendly busybodies for his propanganda purposes. And his self-advertising was not limited to this. If he went out on private business, he did not neglect to advertise—he would certainly take his doctor's briefcase as a reminder of his prestige. Thus, his business flourished.

And what did Ch'ien Hsin-fa care about most? His bank book. His balance rose from one thousand to two thousand dollars, then, without his realizing it, from two thousand to three thousand dollars. His wealth increased daily. His pulse quickened as he counted with his fingers the time it would take for his account to reach ten thousand. After making this calculation, he worked even harder, giving more patients more shots. When he reached ten thousand dollars, he went to a broker to buy land and property. He continued to do this almost every year, and finally he became one of the richest men in town.

Perhaps because Ch'ien Hsin-fa had experienced poverty in his youth, he had developed a kind of obsession with money, above and beyond the virtue of frugality. His interference with his mother's rice-giving was perhaps a symptom of this obsession. Yet he also had a generous side to him. He would donate money without second thoughts to almost any cause concerned with his reputation and status. Although this kind of donation was merely for the sake of his practice and never for the sake of charity, he nevertheless won the approval of the people and became an influential member of the local gentry. He almost monopolized the ranks of local celebrities. He was public health physician, and concurrently chairman of the Social Reformation Society, member of the Coordination Council, and chairman of the local Elders Society. In short, his name appeared among the membership of every reputable organization, and he thus became a leading force on K Street. Because of his initiative and personal example, the local officials also came to trust him. He was a leader in the movement to have Japanese spoken at home and to have Chinese names changed to Japanese.

But he was never satisfied with his mother and often counseled her: "Mother, those who understand the times become the rulers of others. In times like these, shouldn't you learn to speak Japanese?"

His mother ignored him, and so he went on: "I'll get Chin-ying to teach you. How does that sound?"

"Fool! I'm old enough. Don't worry about me, I won't live much longer and won't be a bother to you."

Ch'ien Hsin-fa could only let the subject drop, for he did not dare risk speaking up again. He merely became more upset.

His concern was not just about this one thing. When his mother saw guests coming, she always came out to greet them in the parlor. Wearing Taiwanese dress, speaking nothing but Taiwanese in a loud high-pitched voice, she was the quintessential country hick. Whether it was the district magistrate or the administrative head of the local district, she treated them all alike. Every time a guest of some importance came to visit and was treated by his mother in this way, Ch'ien Hsin-fa became nervous, surreptitiously begging her, "Don't say anything, just hurry up and go back to your room." But the old woman would pay no attention to him. She would still chat away with the guest loudly in Taiwanese. Ch'ien Hsin-fa would get so angry that he could hardly speak, but since she was his mother, there was nothing he could do but keep his anguish to himself. The Ch'iens were a Japanese-speaking family—except for his mother, who did not understand Japanese and had no one to talk to at home. When Taiwanese friends or relatives came to visit, they didn't dare ignore her, so they would chat with her in Taiwanese, making her as happy as a child. When Japanese came to visit, they would speak to her politely and she would smile and respond in Taiwanese. Every time Ch'ien Hsin-fa saw his mother act this way, he was distressed, for he was afraid that he might lose his social prestige because of this, or that his Japanese friends would think lightly of him. Besides, he was also annoyed at his mother for wearing Taiwanese dress.

One day Ch'ien Hsin-fa said in the presence of his guests, "Mother, the guests have arrived. Will you please go inside?" When his mother heard that, she immediately flared up and shouted, "What kind of talk is this? 'The guests have come! The guests have come!' Am I such a pain in the neck? Go inside where? Isn't this my home too?"

She cursed him, making him feel so ashamed that he could not face anyone, his face blushing and paling in rapid succession. If a hole opened up in the ground, he would have crawled right into it. After that, he never attempted to stop his mother from coming into the parlor again. Nevertheless, his anxiety about losing face because of his mother never subsided.

When Japanese was being promoted as the "all-family" language, Ch'ien Hsin-fa lied to the investigators that his mother was able to handle at least some conversational Japanese. For this reason, the Ch'iens met the requirements for the "all-Japanese" family, and he considered this the highest honor ever bestowed on him. He immediately remodeled his house in Japanese style, installing new tatami mats and rice paper sliding doors. The lighting was good and everyone who saw it expressed approval. But before ten days had passed, this kind of genuine Japanese style of living had made his mother angry. She didn't like Japanese miso soup for breakfast for one thing, and she couldn't bear the pain of sitting cross-legged on the straw mats. When his mother ate her meals, she had to force her stiffened legs to bend to sit down. In less than ten minutes, her legs became so numb that not only wasn't she able to swallow her food, she couldn't even stand up.

The old woman had a midday nap habit for years. In Japanese style houses, one had to hang up mosquito nets. This became extremely troublesome for her, since she had to put hers up and down twice a day. On the ninth day of their all-Japanese family life, the old woman took more time than usual to eat her dinner and her legs became too numb to move. Even massaging them had no effect. Her son had no choice but to change his mother's room and the dining area back to the way they had been. He was extremely upset about this, but as usual, he could only sigh to himself, even though the very thought of his mother clouded his mind. He had hoped to put his views into practice, but could find no way of avoiding conflict with his own mother. A very stubborn old woman, she wouldn't change her ways for his sake, no matter how haggard or restless he looked. Whenever he tried to force a change, he invariably became the object of his mother's curses.

But, for his part, he did not want to give up so easily either. He always did his best to do whatever was within his power so as not to fall behind other all-Japanese families. For example, when the Taiwanese were allowed by the Japanese authorities to adopt Japanese names, he was among the first to apply and changed his name to Kanai Shinsuke. After putting up a new office sign bearing his new name, the next thing he did was to order his family to wear kimonos, the traditional Japanese clothing. To set a good example, he even gave up his public health department uniform, which he had been so fond of wearing for so long. At the same time, he built a new house in strict accordance to Japanese style house requirements. When it was finished, he was ecstatic and wanted to have a

photograph taken to commemorate the occasion. The only disappointment was that his mother refused to wear a kimono; she wore what she
had always worn—Taiwanese dress. The regret Kanai Shinsuke felt was
comparable to the feeling one has upon seeing jade and stone displayed
on the same shelf. But, as usual, frustrated as he was, he didn't dare
protest openly. After the photograph was taken, the old woman hacked
the kimono which had been prepared for her into pieces with a cleaver.
All the friends and acquaintances who had come for the occasion were
shocked, thinking the old woman had gone insane.

"If I don't destroy it now, they'll put it on me when I die. And if I were
to wear this kind of thing, I wouldn't have the face to meet my ancestors."
She hacked away at the garment as she spoke, slashing it to ribbons. The
bystanders then began to understand the old woman's feelings, and were
moved by her outspokenness.

Besides Kanai Shinsuke, there was only one other Taiwanese who immediately took advantage of the new law and adopted a Japanese name.
He was Ōyama Kinkichi, who was as influential as he was wealthy. The
two often got together to study the Japanese style of living and practice
the Japanese spirit. Ōyama Kinkichi had no parents to stand in his way, so
he did everything he wanted. Seeing Ōyama improving so rapidly, Kanai
Shinsuke was afraid he would fall behind, and he became very anxious.
He thought of his mother's stubbornness and became upset again.

The second time the authorities announced the list of those who had
been permitted to change their name, he found five families from his
district on the list. But they were all families of less prominence in terms
of wealth and influence in the community. When Kanai Shinsuke saw the
news, he nearly fainted, feeling deprived of his self-esteem and his sense
of superiority. He hurriedly contacted his colleague by phone. Before
long, Ōyama Kinkichi appeared in the parlor wearing a newly sewn
kimono, a yellow persimmon wood cane in hand, paulownia wooden
sandals on his feet.

"Mr. Ōyama, have you seen the news?"

"No, what's the news?"

"Bizarre! Lai Lang-ma changed his name. What qualifications do they
have?"

"What nonsense! Hsu Fa-hsin, Kuan Chung-shan, Lai Lang-ma, blah,
they're all rats. Fancy those kind of monkeys and rats wanting to copy
people!"

Kanai Shinsuke suddenly thumped the table in anger, shouting, "It
doesn't matter if they can copy people or not. In the first place, well, they
don't even have a tatami, not to mention a Japanese bath."

"Let me tell you frankly: no matter what they do, they're still cheap
counterfeits!"

"Humph!"

"The authorities are just too insensitive."

But they were unable to dispel their anger by just airing their opinions. A painful silence followed. Kanai Shinsuke, unable to stop himself, smoked one cigarette after another, exhaling the smoke along with his sighs. Ōyama played with his cane, and couldn't help saying in sad self-mockery, "Oh well, let's drop the subject."

"I bought another tea cabinet, made entirely out of black sandalwood. I don't think even the Japanese in the countryside have such a thing."

"I'd like to see it sometime. I also bought a Japanese koto harp made from an old paulownia tree five or six hundred years old. Guess how much it cost? Twelve hundred dollars!"

When Ōyama heard this, he went over to take a look at the koto that was used in decorating the bedroom area. He picked it up and played it.

When the district magistrate's post was handed over to a new official, the new magistrate came to the area for inspection. It happened that the administrative head of the local district was absent, so an assistant took over his job and reported on local activities and developments. When the welcoming ceremonies were over, the new magistrate chatted with the gentry. Kanai Shinsuke was also present. He wore a new kimono made of brocade from Ōshima. His bearing was so impressive that no one could tell by just looking that he was Taiwanese. The new magistrate was a loquacious but courteous person who liked to ask questions. At this time the assistant introduced each of the gentry to him and unwittingly called Kanai Shinsuke by his old name. Shinsuke immediately changed color. He cursed the assistant in his heart, "You bastard!" His hatred boiled inside him, but none of the gentry seated with him had any idea of what was going through his mind. He did his best to control his emotions, reasoning that a fight with the assistant would do his business no good. It was better to laugh it off, he concluded. Having so decided, he acted humbly as he spoke, with a broad grin on his face. Though the assistant also brought up Kanai's good points, it was still difficult to soothe his hurt feelings.

The third time name changes were announced, he became even more upset than before. Not only had the number increased considerably, but the social positions of those people were even more inferior than those of the earlier ones. Though indignant, he managed to keep his mouth shut. But by the time the fourth list was published, Kanai Shinsuke could hold it no longer. He walked outside and found himself heading toward Ōyama's house. As soon as Ōyama was in sight, Kanai shouted, "Mr. Ōyama, the strangest thing has happened. There's never been anything like it. Even the barber has changed his name!"

Ōyama took a look at Kanai's newspaper and choked, unable to speak. Finally, he managed to utter a heavy sigh. Kanai Shinsuke responded by cursing in Taiwanese: "I just can't believe it. Even scum are allowed to change names." He thought that changing one's name was the highest honor for a Taiwanese, as the household was then no different from that of a Japanese. Yet the barber, the shoe repairman, and the roving flute musician were all permitted to change their names! The effort he had expended up to now had vanished like a bubble. He felt his status had dropped drastically, as if he had fallen into a muddy swamp with no way to pull himself out. He mulled over this a long time, then said to Ōyama contemptuously:

"It's going downhill. You can't count on anything. If I had known this earlier, I . . ." His true feelings unconsciously slipped out. His heart was like a social gathering place for the gentry which had been stormed by disheveled beggars.

One day, in the yard of the elementary school, Kanai Ryōkichi and Ishida Saburō were running too quickly and bumped against each other. Ryōkichi immediately clenched his fists and without finding out the cause, began punching Saburō. Saburō yelled:

"You simpleton! My family's changed its name, too. We're not afraid of you." As he yelled, he advanced to exchange blows.

Ryōkichi retorted: "The name you've changed to is phoney!"

Saburō kept to his place and cursed Ryōkichi: "Yours is the one that's phoney."

Having cursed at each other by turn, they began to exchange blows again.

Saburō was the stronger of the two, and in no time he had Ryōkichi sprawled on the ground. Saburō straddled him and kept on hitting. At that moment some sixth grade students happened to see them. They yelled at them, "You're not supposed to fight in school!" and pulled the two apart. Ryōkichi cried and screamed at Saburō: "You stupid ass! Your family isn't equipped with a Japanese bath and you took a Japanese name. What a phoney!"

"Let's see if you've got the guts to try again!"

The two continued to curse each other, eyes gleaming with hatred. Then they made a fresh start and rushed at each other, but were held back by the sixth graders. Still fuming, Ryōkichi shouted: "My father said that a barber is the scum of society. Trash, simple pure trash!" After this, he walked away.

Kanai Ryōkichi was the youngest son of the public health physician. Ishida Saburō was the barber's son. The two were third-grade classmates at the elementary school. Two or three days after the incident, the barber's wife made a secret visit to see Kanai Shinsuke's mother.

"Venerable Madam, I have to tell you something. When your grandson is at school, he curses whenever he opens his mouth, calling my son 'trash' this and that. Because of this, my son no longer has the courage to face other people. Venerable Madam, would you put in a good word with your son for our sake?" The barber's wife spoke humbly and took leave.

After dinner, when the family customarily met together, the household centered on Kanai Shinsuke and his wife. In addition to the immediate members of the family, which included a son and a daughter, there were also a nurse and a pharmacist who were often seen in their company. It was usually during this "family hour" that Kanai Shinsuke would preach his understanding of the Japanese spirit—from how they washed their face, drank tea, and walked, to how they conducted their social activities. He would spare no details, in each case giving a demonstration from beginning to end with the express intent of instructing his family on how to act Japanese. After he spoke, his wife would then begin to praise the beauty of koto music and dwell on the difficulty of perfecting the art of flower arrangement. Of course, in the end she wouldn't forget to mention her own accomplishments in these fields. The pharmacist was a movie fan, and would often relate some amusing episodes from the movies for their entertainment. Their oldest son, a college graduate, had learned a little English and would occasionally drop a few phrases which he barely understood himself. After everyone had played his or her part, the daughter would then pick up the koto and start to play, strumming away vigorously. The evening would usually conclude with a chorus of Japanese folk songs. Among the singers, the highest pitched voice belonged to the nurse. This kind of entertainment went on without fail every evening.

Only the old woman refused to join them. After dinner she would just stay in her room by herself. In the summer, she had to suffer mosquito bites; in the winter, she had to endure the cold in her unheated room by staying in bed, covering her feet with blankets. Sometimes she would venture into the family to take a look, but since everyone was speaking in Japanese, she couldn't work up enough interest to join them. The activities they were engaged in were for her more like pandemonium than a family get-together.

But this evening she didn't go back to her room after dinner. She waited till everyone had gathered together before she spoke up harshly:

"Hsin-fa, why did you teach Ryōkichi to call the barber trash?"

Shinsuke sputtered and tried his best to explain himself, but his mother shook her head in disbelief. As proof, she told him about the fighting between Ryōkichi and the barber's son at school. After pointing this out she upbraided him: "You don't have any idea about how things were with us in the past, do you? Let me tell you, your father had worked both as a coolie and a sedan carrier. If a barber is 'trash' to you, then what is a coolie and a sedan carrier?"

At this, Shinsuke appeared a bit contrite, and he nodded his head frequently as if admitting his fault. But after only a few days, his earlier sentiments returned to claim him.

On the morning of the fifteenth, the old woman had a cough, but did not want to give up her habit of going to the temple to offer sacrifices. The old beggar was waiting as usual at the back gate. When he saw her, he was somewhat taken aback by her appearance. He asked hastily: "Madam, you seem to have lost your vitality. Aren't you feeling well?"

The old woman casually dismissed his question, saying: "I'm just show-ing my age, that's all." She then took out some money to give to the beggar.

The next day, however, the old woman was feeling very sick, and her condition worsened day by day. Signs of improvement would appear one day, only to be followed by more serious relapses the next day. Her illness was beyond cure. The old beggar did not know about any of this, so on the fifteenth of the next month he waited as usual at the back gate. But no one came out. He became more and more anxious, finally craning his neck to take a look inside. It wasn't until almost noon that the maid came out.

"The old woman has taken ill and forgot today was the fifteenth. She remembered just now and asked me to bring this to you."

The maid gave the beggar twenty dollars and turned to leave. When the beggar took the money and saw how much it was, he suddenly realized that the old woman's illness must be very serious, because she normally gave him five dollars. He immediately approached the maid and begged her to let him inside to see the old woman. The maid was moved by his concern and secretly took him in. Once inside the old woman's room, he stood respectfully at the foot of her bed. The old woman was delighted to see him and strained all her energy to sit up.

"You've come just in time, for I don't think I will be able to see you again!"

She greeted him and invited him to sit down. The beggar, however, was too conscious of his position and ragged clothes to dare sit on the shiny lacquered stool. After he declined several times, the old woman finally ordered him to take a seat, for only then would she feel relaxed enough to chat with him. She talked happily and uninhibitedly, as if she had accidentally run into an old friend. At the end of their conversation, she told the beggar:

"Old friend, my days in this world are numbered. I don't want anything in particular right now, but I'd really like to have a taste of some yu-t'iao[1] again before I die."

The old woman recalled the fragrance of the yu-t'iao she had eaten when she was poor, and she longed to eat one again. She had asked her son to buy some for her but he refused because his was a Japanese household. They drank miso soup, and did not eat yu-t'iao.

The next day the beggar bought some yu-t'iao for her. She ate happily, chewing with gusto and praising the flavor. "Old friend," she said with a long sigh, "you know that I used to be very poor. My husband worked as a coolie and every night I knitted hats until midnight to help make ends meet. There were days when we ate nothing but sweet potato greens. But I think I was happier then. What's the use of money? What's the use of having a son, a college-educated son, if he can't make his mother happy?"

The old beggar was deeply affected by her story. The desolation and loneliness of her later years filled her heart and she broke into tears. Doing his best to comfort her, the beggar said: "Madam, don't take it so hard. You'll get well in no time."

"I won't get well, because there's no point in getting well." The old woman muttered bitterly to herself, then searched under her pillow for some more money to give to the beggar. After he left, she had Shinsuke come to her and gave him instructions for her funeral.

"I don't understand Japanese, so don't hire Japanese monks for my funeral." Those were her last words.

On the third day she took a turn for the worse and breathed her last. But since Shinsuke was chairman of the Social Reformation Society, he couldn't afford to obey his mother's dying wish. The funeral was held in Japanese style. Many people came to the funeral, including the county magistrate, the administrative head of the local district, and other distinguished figures from the area. Yet at this pompous funeral, there was no one who truly mourned for the old woman, not even her own son. The funeral was only a formality. But there was one exception: the beggar. On the day of the funeral, not daring to get close to the coffin, he stood far away from the crowd and cried. Afterwards, on the fifteenth of every month, the old beggar never failed to prepare some joss sticks to burn in front of the old woman's grave. Watching the smoke floating over the grave, in tears he would tell his friend: "Madam, now you're as lonely as I am."

NOTE

1. Deep-fried fritters of twisted dough.

CHU TIEN-JEN (1903–1947)

*Compared with Wu Cho-liu, Chu Tien-jen (pen name of Chu Shih-t'ou)
lived a rather short and uneventful life. Not much is known about him.
Following the example of Lai Ho, he chose to write in Chinese, which is
only natural in view of the sentiments expressed in the story selected here.
Though sharply different in educational background, the scholar in "Autumn Note" is a spiritual kin to the illiterate old woman in the previous
selection, "The Doctor's Mother," in that they both cling to the memory of
the old country as an assertion of their pride and their Chinese identity.
To be sure, as a symbol of patriotic nobility the old scholar is over-
shadowed by the street hawker in "The Steelyard," who resorts to violence
as a means of defiance. But as the editors of* Taiwan Literature under the
Japanese Occupation *(Kuang-fu-ch'ien T'ai-wan wen-hsüeh ch'uan-chi)
rightly observe: "At a time when the Japanese were in firm control of the
island, the fact that Chu Tien-jen dared to subject his overlords to such
relentless mockery and ridicule bespeaks uncommon courage. His fiction
has therefore become a part of our valuable cultural heritage" (vol. 4, p.
33). His works are gathered in the afore-cited anthologies.*

Autumn Note

Translated by James C. T. Shu

Master[1] Tou-wen concentrated his thought, held his breath, and practiced calligraphy by copying Wen T'ien'hsiang's "The Song of Righteousness."[2] The tip of his pen danced blithely on the paper, balancing the firm
strokes with soft strokes. Every time his imitation approximated the calligraphy in the stone rubbings, he would put down the pen and spend
some time comparing his work with the rubbings.

A while later, he moved on to reading. He read aloud "Peach Blossom
Spring"[3] in a sing-song chant. Although he was over sixty years of age, his
voice did not show the wear and tear of years: the clear, resounding
recitation lingered and vibrated in the quiet of the morning.

This was Master Tou-wen's daily work, and it had gone uninterrupted
for the past decades. As soon as he finished his work, he made his way
across the yard where the unhulled rice was sunned. With a bamboo pipe

in his mouth, he carried in his hand the *National News Weekly,* mailed to him from Shanghai by his grandson. He read as he walked.

It was just getting light in the east. The morning sun had yet to reveal itself; for the time being, it only sent a diffusion of pink hue across the sky above the hilltop in front of him.

A flock of ducks huddled beside the fence. As soon as they noticed some human movement, they stood up and quacked. A red-faced duck walked on its clumsy feet, its tail waggling, its neck stretching back and forth, until it came near his feet. It pecked aimlessly.

"Little beasts! Want to go out?" He opened the gate; the ducks started quacking again, and jostled their way out. He too went out through the open gate and sat under an old ch'ieh-tung tree[4] near the gate, smoking.

The sky over the eastern hill changed from pink to bright red. The fog that had been shrouding the earth was thinning out and, without his noticing it, finally vanished. The rice stalks, their clusters of grains having just been picked, were already half dried up and yellowed. The dew on the grass by the fields glittered like silver beads.

He smoked leisurely. The wisps of smoke coming out of his mouth flitted past the back of his head. He closed his left eye and looked at the chimney smoke rising from inside the hedge of bamboos ahead.

From the hedge of bamboos three people appeared, each carrying a small bundle. As they skirted a field and got to another hedge of bamboos closer by, another three people happened to emerge from it. Both parties paused, exchanged a few words, and then, making a turn together, walked along the edge of fields toward him.

"Aren't you Hsiu-ts'ai[5] Ch'en?" the leader asked. "Out early for some good air, eh?"

Since they were still some distance away, Master Tou-wen could not make out who they were. When he heard the greeting, he recognized it was from Wu Hsiang of the bamboo hedge farther back.

"You were up early, too!" By the time he made his answer, they were already close by. As he noticed that they were dressed in their New Year's best, he had the feeling that they were on a trip. "Hey, Hsiang. You're going to Taipei, aren't you?"

"Right. To see the Exhibit. Hsiu-ts'ai Ch'en, you should go, too. Come with us!"

"I don't want to go."

"It's really a shame not to go. I don't know about other villages, but in our village every family has someone going to see it. I heard that there are many tourist groups today. Maybe the train is going to be all jammed again. Hsiu-ts'ai Ch'en, life is short, and you're quite old. If you don't see it now, when are you going to see it? Come on, let's go. Isn't it nice to see something different?"

"I don't want to go."

"You don't? Then, wait until we're back to tell you what it's like. Wow! It's late! We've got to hurry to get on the train."

Before the exhibit opened, the government[6] had done its best to propagandize for it. The press on the island also followed suit to give it good publicity. Railroad officials were even sent to the rural areas to promote it. And thus a very ordinary exhibit was transformed, through the magic of advertisement, into a raging sensation.

"Let's go! Go see the Exhibit in Metropolitan Taipei!" Everyone living outside Taipei had the idea that to go see it was a must in one's life, and a real pleasure at that.

"Grandpa! A policeman's coming!"

It was in an evening of early autumn, and Master Tou-wen was reading newspapers in his study when he heard his third grandson report, who rushed in all excited.

"Why didn't you tell him I've no time for visitors?"

"I did, but he wouldn't listen. He said something like he had to see you on business. Grandpa, what is 'on business'?"

"Very nice of him! Bothering you all the time! What damn business for today?"

Master Tou-wen came out, upset. He saw the old Japanese policeman Sasaki sitting in the living room, all smiles.

"You again."

"Hsiu-ts'ai Ch'en! Sorry, I know you're a busy man. Please sit down. I've something to tell you."

He had been working as a policeman for many years, a real old hand, and as he spoke, his Taiwanese was almost indistinguishable from that of a native of Taiwan.

"If you've something to tell me please hurry up."

"I'm taking the census today, and I'm just doing something extra on the side."

"Yes?"

"When will your grandson studying abroad in China be back?"

"No such thing! What's he coming back for?"

"Taiwan is having an exhibit. How can he not come back to take a look?"

"That's something I don't know."

"Well, so you don't know?" Sasaki paused at this point and changed his topic: "The Promotion Committee of the exhibit is recruiting members. A regular member is supposed to pay . . . five dollars. . . ."

"Wait a minute. I've nothing to do with the Promotion Committee. What are you coming to talk to me for ?"

"Ha—ha, Hsiu-ts'ai Ch'en! You don't pay for anything. If you're a member, the committee will give you a membership card and a memorial badge. During the entire period of the exhibit you can drop in any time you want, and you can count on being entertained. . ."

"So you want me to join?"

"You got it. Come on, join in. Come along and take a look at Taipei. How about taking a look at Japanese culture and your—no, Ch'ing dynasty culture."

"Ch'ing dynasty!" Upon hearing the two words "Ch'ing dynasty," Master Tou-wen felt as if his body had been hit with a jolt of electricity. Shivering all over, he stared blankly at the sky light, lost.

The exhibit had been open more than a dozen days now. The plowshare-wielding country people, who would consider such trivial things as two hens fighting each other a fit topic for conversation, were as jubilant about their visit to the island's capital and the exhibit as they would be about a visit to the moon. After their return, they lavished praise on it, making themselves the envy of those who could not go. Even though Master Tou-wen was not impressed, he would listen intently every time they praised. But what was surprising and disappointing was that most Taipei streets, as they mouthed them, were no longer under their old names.

"That's strange. Can Taipei change so fast?" Sometimes he would wonder, and felt the urge to go to Taipei. But Taipei was no longer the same city that used to fascinate him! So, he dropped the idea every time he thought of going. Then, more recently, he unexpectedly received a letter from a classmate of his grandson. It read as follows:

October 25

Dear Master Tou-wen:

As the summer was gone, I returned to this southern country with the autumn. My reasons for returning were first, to see my family and second, to see the Exhibit. Your grandson was so preoccupied with his study he didn't want to come, but he asked me to insist that you go to Taipei to take a look at the Exhibit.

Respectfully yours,
Wang Pei-fang

The few words helped Master Tou-wen make up his mind to go north. But he made no fuss over it; he did not even tell his family. Because he did not want to meet any of his acquaintances, he quietly took an unusual route to get on the 9 A.M. train from Station A.

It happened to be Sunday, and the train had long been packed with mixed crowds. As Master Tou-wen stepped into the car, somehow all the eyes were spontaneously trained on him. Into the atmosphere of modern dress in the car—kimonos, Taiwanese tunics, Western clothes—Master Tou-wen's old-fashioned dress made its surprise inroad. He wore a black bowl-shaped cap, a black gown, and black cloth shoes—this, together with the bamboo pipe in his mouth and the pigtail that hung from the back of his head, made him look like a stork joining a flock of chickens.

He took the people's stares as an affront. For a short while he felt very upset. But pretty soon he got over it, and defiantly, he gave the people a going-over. He then sat down with composure.

Time for departure. As the station master began to blow his whistle, Master Tou-wen hurried to cover both his ears to shut out the noise of the siren of the train. This caused an uproar of laughter in the car.

The train began to move slowly. The village, where Master Tou-wen felt at home, began to recede. Instantly he felt empty. Out of boredom he opened the pages of *The Records of the Ten Continents of the World,*[7] which he had brought with him, and mechanically set the book on his knees. Even though his eyes fell on the book, he failed to catch the words; the conversations in the car very naturally entered his ears. Slowly, he looked up. The train was going at full speed alongside sugarcane fields.

"Liu, where are you going?"

"Taipei."

"Hey! What made a thrifty fellow like you want to go to Taipei!"

"Well, partly because I can't help it."

"You yourself wanted to go. What do you mean by 'I can't help it'?"

"The police in our village forced me to go."

"Well, is that right? Anyway, Liu, don't feel put out. They say the exhibit is the greatest fun there ever was in Taiwan; see it once and you can afford to depart from this world in peace!"

"See it once and you can afford to depart from this world in peace!" Master Tou-wen repeated after him like a parrot. His trip north would be worthwhile if Taipei was the Taipei that people looked forward to, he thought. He seemed to have forgotten all the changes in Taipei. Fu-Front Street,[8] Fu-Center Street, Fu-Back Street—former city streets appeared one after another in his mind. The faster the train went, the deeper he indulged in the fantasy.

"Mang-ka![9] Mang-ka!"

Upon hearing the cry, he came back to himself from the reverie.

"Ah, Mang-ka! The Mang-ka of 'First, Fu; second, Lu; third, Mang-ka'!"[10] His heart beat fast, as if he had met a long-separated old friend.

The train went past the Wan-hua station. After it went past two intersections, its windows reflected the imposing Sugar Industry Building, Exhibit Hall No. 1. As the exhibit hall was announced, the passengers in the car all scrambled to the windows to take a look. Master Tou-wen also stood on his toes to look. Ah! Right on the former site of the city walls of

Taipei was the Exhibit Hall. His heart was pounding like a jackhammer as he fell weakly into his seat.

The train arrived at the Taipei station at three o'clock. The passengers, exhausted from the long hours of sitting in the train, fought their way to get off, pushing and jostling one another. Master Tou-wen followed the human wave through the exit gate. In the confusion of the milling crowd, as he hobbled along, his toes could not help touching other people's heels at each step. Finally he found himself pushed by the human wave into a corner on the left side. He looked up at the streets. Lots of cars were weaving their way in the streets. At an intersection towered an arch, on which he caught the words: "In Celebration of the Fortieth Anniversary of New Government." Instantly he recovered from his trepidation. The imposing structure towering before him seemed to grin at him maliciously. He shook his head, recalling the lines, "Recently erected are the mansions of the new nobility; changed in style is the court dress from that of the *ancien régime*."[11] He was filled with a sense of nostalgia and loss.

Master Tou-wen was a smart student in his younger days. He became a hsiu-ts'ai at the age of nineteen. He then worked for the provincial administration of Taiwan under the Ch'ing dynasty.[12] At age twenty-seven, when he was about to take the provincial-level examination, Taiwan was ceded to Japan.[13] Consequently, his journey to success was cut short. He gave up the hope of bureaucratic advancement. He settled down in K Village and, acquiring a few acres of good land, decided to spend the remainder of his life as a farmer. At his home he had a detailed atlas of Taiwan. In the early days of the new government under Japan, which was quite uninformed about the affairs of Taiwan, he was prevailed upon several times to come out and offer his help. With stubbornness, he declined. In fact, he refused to have anything to do with politicians.

In all appearances Master Tou-wen was leading the life of a hermit. But in his heart he was not. His blood frequently boiled on behalf of his compatriots. Even though he did not participate in the practical activities when the Social Movement was reaching its heyday, he did contribute a lot to an affiliated activity of the movement, the cultural movement.[14] As more Taiwanese learned to speak Japanese, fewer of them were able to understand Chinese. He understood that Japanese was for the Taiwanese people a necessary tool for making a living. But it was also necessary for them to know Chinese, since the very identity of the Taiwanese people was involved with the Chinese language. As he decided to revive Chinese, he gathered some comrades and formed a poetry club, promoting the writing of classical Chinese poetry. The promotion had quite an impact on society: poetry clubs cropped up everywhere; poetry writing became a fad all over the island; the number of practicing poets at the

time almost equalled that in the golden days of the T'ang dynasty. However, while he tried to make use of poetry to salvage the moribund
Chinese language, shameless poets used it as a tool to socialize, to curry
favor from those in power—they even composed poems in memorial of
deceased Japanese politicians, with whom they were utterly unrelated.

As Master Tou-wen witnessed such a perverted phenomenon, he became remorseful about ever setting up a poetry club in the first place.

"Classical verse isn't poetry; only the mountain songs from the mouths
of the common people are poetry," he often remarked with a sigh. He
came to regard himself as a sinner in the Taiwanese literary circle because
he was the first to establish a poetry club. In the spring of 19—[15] when all
of the poetry clubs of the island gathered in Taipei to compose verses, he
believed it was an opportunity to reform the ills of writing classical verse.
Thus for the first time in his life he took a train. Maybe because he was
not quite well, maybe because he was totally unprepared—anyway, just
as the train's steam whistle sounded, Master Tou-wen was so frightened
that he passed out.

Today, fifteen years later, he had come to Taipei.

On the street before the Taipei station, the crowd swarmed toward the
museum like a wave. Master Tou-wen was like a rudderless boat without a
sense of direction: the geography of Taipei was no longer what he had
remembered. Somehow, while he was at a loss, he was pushed right to
the entrance of Exhibit Hall No. 2. Without thinking, he followed the
crowd into the first section for cultural displays. He glanced at a model of
Chih-shan Cliff,[16] and then walked to the left. On a door were the characters: "Room No. 1: Education." As a learned man, he could not resist
taking an interest in matters of education. He scrutinized a map of school
distribution, but was very disappointed by the fact that since he did not
know Japanese he could not fully understand it. He shook his head sul-
lenly. He then stood before a picture in which there were three students
standing in a row in a school yard, the two on the right each carrying a
spade, the one on the left carrying an abacus—all of them swaggering.
Master Tou-wen was puzzled, and when he looked at its caption, he was
unable to read it. In his helplessness, he stopped someone and asked,
"Please, what does the caption say?"

"'The Great Leap Forward of Taiwan's Productivity is initiated by us,'"
the man explained to him, looking him over, and broke into a guffaw.

"Ha, ha! . . ."

"Ha, ha! . . ."

Another two explosions of laughter suddenly started at his back. He
hastened to turn around, and met contemptuous looks from two Japanese
students, standing with arms akimbo, muttering you didn't know what.

He felt a crushing sadness at the insult. He thought, If I knew Japanese I
would certainly debate with them to the bitter end.

"Runts! Bandits![17] Japanese barbarians!" He could not help but let it go,
regardless of whether they could understand or not. "Even though the
rise and fall of a nation is fated, and the Ch'ing dynasty has already ended,
yet it doesn't necessarily mean that the Chinese people . . . All this fuss
about the Exhibit—it's just meant to brag about . . . Forget it. . . . 'The
Great Leap Forward of Taiwan's Productivity' indeed! Only you Japanese
devils are able to have a 'great leap forward.' I'm afraid Taiwan's youth
don't even have the chance to inch forward. All this talk about education,
indeed!"

He lost all interest, and left in a huff. He felt a pang of regret: he
considered his trip a big waste! Instead of seeing the exhibit it would be a
better idea to visit the Taiwan Provincial Yamen![18] Upon the thought of
the Taiwan Provincial Yamen he felt like going back to his former self of
forty years ago, and all his pent-up frustration vanished in an instant.

"Sir, where are you going? Need a ride?" A rickshaw puller who had
been squatting outside the exhibit hall noticed that Master Tou-wen was
hesitating; he stood up to accost him.

"I don't need a ride. I'm going to take a look at the Taiwan Provincial
Yamen."

"Taiwan Provincial Yamen? Huh! Do you know where it is, sir?"

"On Fu-Center Street."

"Oh, no! Not there."

"No? Not there? Then . . . ?"

"I don't think you're a local person, sir. No wonder you don't know they
have built the Taipei Municipal Hall on the former site of the Taiwan
Provincial Yamen."

"What? Municipal Hall . . . ? Then it . . . ?"

"Take it easy, sir. Now I can say I had a good reason to accost you. I've
been sitting here all day long without making a penny. Please let me take
you to the Taiwan Provincial Yamen for twenty cents."

Fifteen minutes later Master Tou-wen got off the rickshaw in front of
the Taiwan Provincial Yamen in the Botanical Garden. After the rickshaw
puller had left, the old man sat under a coconut palm and, facing the
yamen, lost himself in meditation. Why is it so deserted when it used to
bustle with life? Ah! The facade of the yamen retains its old look, but
where did all the remembered things of the past go? Overwhelmed with a
sense of the capricious turns of history, he slowly stood up and leaned
against the coconut palm. He groped in his breast pocket for the letter he
had received the other day. He took the letter from the envelope. His
glance fell on the letter, but all he saw was the colophon at the margin of
the letter paper: *Image of the Isle of the Immortals.*

It was late autumn. The garden was deserted as nightfall descended. Fallen leaves rustled in the breeze. He relaxed his grip, and the letter was wafted away in the wind, only to settle down on the paulownia leaves that strewed the ground.

NOTES

1. *Hsien-sheng,* here rendered as "Master," is a title of honor, which, when used in conjunction with a person's given name, suggests that the one referred to is a professional or someone with intellectual qualifications. It is not to be confused with the standard usage of "Master" to address a boy too young to be called "Mister."

2. Wen T'ien-hsiang (1236–82), the last prime minister of the Sung dynasty, was executed by the Mongols after a three-year imprisonment. When in prison, he wrote "The Song of Righteousness," which expressed his patriotic sentiment and his reconciliation to the thought of death.

3. An imaginative account of a pastoral utopia by T'ao Ch'ien (365?–427), one of China's greatest poets.

4. Also variously known as *ch'ung-yang mu* and *ch'iu-feng,* its botanical name is *Bischofia javenica.*

5. *Hsiu-ts'ai:* A successful candidate of the county or prefectural level in the feudal civil service examination system.

6. *Tang-chü-che,* in the Chinese original.

7. *Hai-wai shih-chou chi,* as in the Chinese original, most likely ought to be *Hai-nei shih-chou chi,* whose authorship has traditionally been attributed to Tung-fang Shuo (154–93 B.C.), even though it may have been composed after the third century A.D.

8. A *fu* in the Ch'ing dynasty was the approximate equivalent of a prefecture. "Fu-Front Street" obviously indicates the location of the street relative to the administrative building.

9. Mang-ka, here transcribed to approximate its Taiwanese pronunciation, is the old name for Taipei. In Mandarin, it is Meng-chia.

10. A Taiwanese proverbial saying with reference to the three most prosperous cities in the earlier days of Taiwan, namely, Tainan (seat of Taiwan *Fu*), Lu-kang, and Mang-ka—in that order.

11. From "Autumn Meditations: Eight Poems" by Tu Fu (712–770).

12. In 1887 Taiwan became a province of the Ch'ing Empire and had its own *hsün-fu* (governor).

13. In Chinese, *huan le chu.*

14. Under the Japanese rule, Taiwanese frequently tried to work within the system to demand their rights and raise their ethnic consciousness. The Taiwanese Cultural Association, established in 1921 by Chiang Wei-shui, was the most notable example of such an effort.

15. Ellipses in the original.

16. A small hill on the outskirts of Taipei.

17. A pejorative reference to the Japanese, stressing that they are short.

18. A government office.

YANG K'UEI

(1905–)

While Yang K'uei (pen name for Yang Kuei) can be broadly identified as a patriot in the tradition of Lai Ho, his antipathy for the Japanese has less to do with politics than with class. This is evident in his first work of fiction, "Newspaper Boy" (Sung-pao fu, 1932), an autobiographical story about his experience in Japan. At the end of the story, a Mr. Yorifuji confronts the narrator with this question: "I've lived in Taiwan for some time. Do you like the Japanese?" After some deliberation, the newspaper boy confesses that he likes his colleague Mr. Tanaka more than his own brother. The reason is that whereas Mr. Tanaka, an exploited newspaper boy like our autobiographical hero, has treated him with all the respect and assistance due a comrade, his own brother is a policeman serving the Japanese overlords in Taiwan. It is in this light that "Mother Goose Gets Married" in our anthology should be read.

One of the highlights in Yang's life is his founding of New Taiwan Literature (T'ai-wan hsin wen-hsüeh) in 1935, which was suppressed by the Japanese authorities two years later. After serving jail sentences more than ten times, he aborted his literary career and took up farming. The story in "Mother Goose Gets Married" is based on this period of experience. He resumed his literary activities after the war and served as editor of two newspaper literary columns until he was jailed by the Nationalist Government in 1950, presumably because of his leftist sympathy. In 1982 he was invited by the International Writing Program of the University of Iowa to visit the United States for three months. His works are included in Taiwan Literature under the Japanese Occupation (Kuang-fu-ch'ien T'ai-wan wen-hsüeh ch'uan-chi).

Mother Goose Gets Married

Translated by Jane Parish Yang

I.

Flower gardeners, like parents the world over, all hope that the plants they raise blossom into hearty, beautiful flowers.

But during late spring and early summer, weeds also flourish and keep me especially busy. I root them out, but they grow right back and the process repeats itself. If I neglect to weed for several days, the whole garden becomes choked with wild grass.

I had to leave home to pay my last respects to the young Mr. Lin Wen-

33

ch'ien, who had passed away, and, at the same time, to undertake some unfinished business on his behalf. Though I was away from home for less than ten days, the whole garden had very nearly turned into a thick lawn. The flower shoots, hidden by the weeds, could be seen only by parting the wild growth. These flowers, robbed of their sunlight and mineral nutrients by the weeds, had become thin, yellowed, frail, and, just like the pallid young intellectuals of our day, devoid of any vitality. Most of them withered and died.

After I returned home, I was kept busy weeding the garden for many days. Before I had finished weeding half of it, the stubborn weeds would grow back thick and tall where I had first weeded.

A mixed feeling of weariness, sadness, anger, and impatience occupied my mind as I weeded, recalling the early death of Lin Wen-ch'ien and his ruptured home. I was unable to calm myself.

A weed called cattle crest grew in the yard. Its roots were long and dense. Cowhands made rope from this weed to tie up their cows. Like a man ready to fight to the death, I would stand with my feet planted firmly apart, grabbing the cattle crest with both hands and pulling with all my might. I would pull until I was red in the face and sweat rolled down my back, but the weed wouldn't budge. I would have to call my son over to help. The two of us would yank this way and that until it finally came out with a "pop" and we fell backwards along with it. We often lacked the strength to get back up again. Because the roots were so numerous, every time we pulled up a bunch of the cattle crest, several small flower shoots would be pulled up with the weeds. One had to use all one's strength and sacrifice many flowers in order to pull them out.

"These damn weeds!"

I would hold the cattle crest in my hand, amazed at its roots, which were as bushy as the hair of the Furies. Then I would angrily throw it to the ground and trample on it. The children would fight over who would get to jump on the weeds and imitate my tone of voice: "These damn weeds!" Then they would grin at each other, laughing lightheartedly the way one does after trying with all one's strength and wits to get rid of a vicious power that bullies the good.

II.

I met Lin Wen-ch'ien in the special reading room in the Ueno Public Library. I don't remember the date; I can recall only that it was a sweltering afternoon and I was soaked with perspiration. But the rest of what had happened is clear in my mind.

At that time I was studying at Nippon University. I often fell asleep during my aesthetics course from two to three o'clock in the afternoon, so I had to go to the Ueno Public Library right after class to make up for what I had missed in the lectures. This was perhaps due to my laziness. The professor lectured with enthusiasm—his voice was like a silvery bell tinkling in the breeze—but I was never able to concentrate. My notebook was full of question marks, not like the notebooks of the bright scholars who were able to record everything the professor said, including, I think, how many times he coughed. I thus didn't have any free time to wander around the Ginza, but was a constant visitor to the library.

One day I was in the library looking for information on primitive art, which I hoped would answer some of the questions the professor had raised in class. I was carefully going through the card catalog when someone patted me on the back. I looked around and saw it was my classmate in the economics department. He looked at my notebook, so different from the others, and laughed. Though we had often run into each other at school, we hadn't established a personal friendship. But we knew we were both Taiwanese, and it was a rare pleasure to exchange talk on our homeland in this faraway place of Tokyo. We became fast friends.

At the time, I was studying primitive art in order to gain a deeper understanding of the very nature of art. His wealth of knowledge about the economics of primitive society helped me resolve many questions. We often discussed this in the shade in the park. Sometimes we would continue the discussion in my three-tatami sized room, finally moving to his eight-tatami sized room. His room had chairs, tea and snacks, and quite a few reference works. It was a more convenient place for long talks. Our discussions were enthusiastic and frank, and during each we both were passionate debaters. What set us apart was that he led a comfortable life, with no economic cares, and I had to go to the night market every evening to work as a hawker to pay for my tuition and living expenses. By dusk the face of this passionate debater would change into that of a petty-minded and most ingratiating businessman.

My life went on like this for three months, until he discovered that this double life I was leading was affecting my studies. Then he volunteered to pay my expenses. This allowed me to devote all my energy to research as he did, and I became his constant companion in his studies.

I returned to Taiwan five years earlier than he did, but as soon as he got back he came to see me. He quietly walked up behind me as I was squatting down in the flower garden, and tapped me on the shoulder, just as he had done before when we first met in Ueno Public Library. But this time he did it listlessly.

We both had changed much in those five years. I was shocked by the changes in him, and perhaps he felt the same way when he saw me. Anyway, it was he who had changed most. Before, he had the bearing of a gallant young master, steady and energetic. But now? Could it be that he had forgotten and left that part of him back in Tokyo? It was a long time before I recognized it was Lin Wen-ch'ien by his eyes and lips.

He clumsily repeated over and over how he envied me.

"What a joke . . . what is there to envy?"

I tugged at my scraggly inch-long beard, and chuckled to myself. If the kind of life I had been leading these past five years was worthy of envy, then what in the world wasn't? For those who had majored in art in college, it was simply impossible to find a suitable job. Except for dressing and painting oneself up like a "sandwich man"—wearing two billboards for advertisements and pounding the drum on the street all day— nothing became of our studies. I wasn't willing to sell my soul that way, so I took on a number of odd jobs that demanded physical labor. As a result, my health deteriorated. On the advice of and with financial assistance from some friends, I took up flower gardening. This was vastly different from being a laborer; I could control my own schedule without being pushed around by others. And it was a much more enjoyable job.

III.

As soon as I saw Lin Wen-ch'ien, I realized how tired he was. But the fatigue that showed on his face was probably not from the long journey. More probably it was the result of some radical change in his life.

Though he didn't have a scraggly beard like mine, his face seemed withered and pale. His former intense, energetic air had completely vanished. His face seemed that of someone disillusioned and lost.

I went to the stream at the back of the garden to wash my hands and feet, then led him into my small hut. It was about the size of eight tatami mats laid down in one piece, much larger than the minuscule three-mat room of mine in Tokyo where we had held our heated debates. But book shelves, trunks of clothes, quilts, and miscellaneous items were strewn all over the mats. The children had pulled everything out again to play, so there wasn't room for anyone to sit down. I hurriedly put some things away and made room in the corner of a torn mat.

He was very exhausted. I hadn't even invited him to sit down before he plunked himself down, closed his eyes, and stretched out his legs. He leaned against the mud wall, his clothes becoming smudged with dirt. I became alarmed and brushed them off, then stuck a page of newspaper between his back and the wall. But he said, "Never mind, there's no need to . . ."

He, who used to be so fastidious about his clothes, now paid no attention when they were dirty like this.

"I've changed completely."

I was staring at him, thinking how strange his reaction had been, when he slowly opened his eyes and sighed.

"You don't look well. Are you sick?" I was still worried.

"No, no," he said, and then he began slowly to relate what had happened to him during the five years we had been apart. I listened as he told his story, and both of us fell into a painful, depressing state of mind.

IV.

He said that for about three years after I returned to Taiwan, he had continued his research much as before. But from the fourth year on, his father kept telling him to come home, and he didn't send him money as often as before. Lin Wen-ch'ien knew right away that the family was having financial problems. Unable to give up his research, he chose to move into the three-tatami sized room I had once rented and to copy my lifestyle, going to the night market and working as a hawker to pay for his living expenses, anxious to put into practice what he had learned about economics.

At that time, Marxist economic thought was at the peak of its popularity. It seemed as if all his hotheaded classmates had been altered by its appeal, calling for class struggle and taking part in the movement to put their theory into practice. But he kept to his own principles, believing that through compromise, not struggle, the same goals could be reached. Of course, he also believed that the economic system that emphasized the acquisition of individual wealth was already outmoded. Being a young man with a spirit of righteousness, he actually looked forward to the end of such an anachronistic system. For this reason, he worked hard to formulate an economic theory that would benefit the masses without resorting to the principles of class struggle. After intensive study of the economic life of primitive men, he was convinced that if the capitalists were to operate on the basics of fairness and benevolence, his "co-prosperity" economic plan could be carried out without struggle and bloodshed.

He was heir to the temper and way of thinking of his father, who was a prominent sinologist in his hometown, and as a young child he had been greatly influenced by Confucian ideas:

> What I have heard is that the head of a state or a noble family worries not about underpopulation but about uneven distribution, not about poverty but about instability. For where there is even distribution there is no such thing as poverty, where there is harmony there is no such thing as underpopulation, and where there is stability there is no such thing as overturning.[1]

These are the words of Confucius which Wen-ch'ien had heard from his father since childhood. But it was because of his family's practice of egalitarianism that their own financial resources were totally exhausted. In an age of greed and selfishness, their Confucian persuasions brought them only bankruptcy, not peace of mind. Ironically, they thought this was due to their lack of consideration for the public interest. If they had acted truly unselfishly, they would not have been troubled by their financial losses.

Although Wen-ch'ien's father inherited more than a thousand acres of ancestral land, the family had all led a frugal life. Naturally, they didn't squander their money on wine and women, gambling or opium. But when it came to helping others, their generosity and charitable ways had no limits. Just as Lin Wen-ch'ien had underwritten my tuition and living expenses, his father had paid for the tuition of even more children from destitute families. Whenever someone became ill and had no money, or if a family couldn't afford to bury its dead, Wen-ch'ien's father would pay for all the expenses. When the anti-Japanese movement arose, it generated a mass movement of national culture and a demand for democracy and freedom. The elder Mr. Lin contributed most generously to the people working for such causes. He never pressed for the rents from the lands he rented out, which were his only source of income, or for rents in arrears. As a result, all his property, including his own house, was mortgaged—and all fell into the hands of one company.

One Mr. Wang, a senior executive in that company, had the power to save the Lins from bankruptcy. To be fair, it must be said that this Mr. Wang was not a man without feelings. Indeed, he often praised the elder Lin's character, saying Mr. Lin was the person he respected most. He had also personally advised Mr. Lin not to worry about his financial crisis. However, he mentioned one condition which Mr. Lin, though open-minded as always, found difficult to accept. This increased Mr. Lin's worry and anxiety and it was this condition which drove the old man, who could have been able to die content, to a miserable end.

Wang's single condition was a request that Mr. Lin give his daughter, Lin Wen-ch'ien's only sister, in marriage to Wang as a concubine. If old Mr. Lin agreed to this proposition, not only would the bankruptcy notice be canceled, but other advantages would follow. For example, he would leave old Mr. Lin a little property for his livelihood. In addition, Wang could place Lin Wen-ch'ien in an important position, allowing him to use what he had learned in Japan and eventually restore the prosperity of the Lin family.

This condition really wasn't unreasonable. Indeed, at a time when some people were forced to sell a child in order to live, the condition which Mr. Wang attached to his proposal was, at least in the eyes of some people, most attractive. Besides having a wealthy and powerful son-in-law in Mr. Wang, old Mr. Lin could not only keep part of his property but

also help his own son find a good job. He stood to gain three things by just
giving up a daughter. Convinced that his offer was irresistible, Mr. Wang
gave a banquet for friends as an advance celebration.

But that was not the way old Mr. Lin looked at things. When he was
informed of Mr. Wang's intention, he nearly had a fit. However, after he
had soothed his injured feelings, he was forced to take stock of his situation. After all, he was at a dead end. For one moment he told himself not
to yield an inch, since he was an old man whose days were numbered. But
then he considered his son, who was about to enter society, and his
daughter, Hsiao-mei, and he had second thoughts. He knew that once
bankruptcy was declared, the future of his children would be bleak. He
thought back and forth on it and finally, tears streaming down his face, he
agreed to Mr. Wang's offer. And he fell ill immediately.

Though the brother and sister understood the old man's difficulty, they
couldn't accept what he had done. Hsiao-mei resolutely said that she
would die rather than marry a dissolute man with no sense of national
pride. As for Wen-ch'ien, he had more reason to object to the arrangement, if only because the whole idea ran counter to what he stood for. He
could not for any reason sacrifice the happiness of his sister to solve his
own financial problems. Thus old Mr. Lin died without solace. Not only
did his utopian plans remain unrealized, but even during the last hours of
his life he was denied the peace of mind he deserved.

Lin Wen-ch'ien came to my flower garden to look for me just after he
had buried his father. Bankruptcy would befall him, his elderly mother,
and his frail younger sister at any moment. It was then that I realized the
true meaning of his "envy" of me. Though my father, who raised me and
my brothers in poverty, did not leave us with any land or a straw hut, he
didn't leave us in debt, either. Thus we could muddle along and live a
relatively quiet life. This was quite a blessing!

I kept staring at this good man, Lin Wen-chien, and thought of his
family, the one who had died and the ones still living. Feeling sorry for
them, I wept uncontrollably.

After he came to see me, Lin Wen-chien and his sister received three
warnings and threats from Mr. Wang. But since his father was no longer a
cause of concern, and after seeing that the kind of life I led was not
altogether unbearable, Wen-ch'ien resolutely rejected Mr. Wang's request. And in no time, the bankruptcy announcement arrived.

Somewhat to his surprise, Wen-ch'ien felt completely relieved after the
auction. Immediately, he sold off all the unnecessary articles, rented a
tiny plot of land, and built a small house. There he planted sweet potatoes
and vegetables to maintain a simple life.

V.

Time passed quickly. Another five years went by. Because I got an abundant amount of sunshine, fresh air, and appropriate exercise during this time, I conquered my tuberculosis and regained my health. Because of the experience gained over these past few years, our life became a bit more comfortable. I often thought of my old friend, and just as I was hoping to help him out in some way, the sudden announcement of his death came.

I hurried over to his place.

During these five years, both of us were busy making a living and couldn't meet often as we had in Tokyo. Even so, we still sent word to each other at times, and whenever we had the opportunity we sought each other out for a long talk. His family had never done manual labor before. Income from sweet potatoes and vegetables was also less than that from raising flowers. Naturally they were much worse off than we were.

Perhaps it is really true that snobbery is a part of human nature. When his father was alive, and signs of their financial trouble had not yet appeared, guests would flock to their door. Yet now, even local people whom Mr. Lin had helped substantially and who were now well off had completely forgotten the existence of this family. Lin Wen-ch'ien's death did not in any way attract their attention. When I entered his house, I found only his mother and sister crying and a few neighbors helping out. Those who came to pay their respects were very few, and it was all quite desolate.

After hurrying all the way, I rushed into his bedroom, which also served as a study. I was panting and trying to catch my breath when I saw his corpse, covered with a blanket. I couldn't help feeling shocked. I went over and lifted the blanket. How pitiful he looked, thin as a shadow. The sun had tanned his face a dark brown, and his beard had grown long. Although he was just over thirty, he looked like an old man of fifty or sixty who had died a natural death. I gripped his hand, thin as a bamboo rod, and noticed a trace of blood on his lips. His hands were frigid. My breath came hot and rapid in my chest. I did not usually cry in public, but my eyes clouded over and tears streamed down my face.

A long time passed before I raised my head. It was then that I discovered a thick pile of a draft manuscript on the table by his feet. The title was "Vision of a Co-Prosperity Economic Plan." It looked as if he had been working here right up to the day before, since there were no specks of dust on the tabletop.

In order to hide my tears, I bent down to take a look at it. His sincerity was apparent in every word, every sentence, stirring up memories from the past. If it weren't for his corpse lying there before me, I wouldn't have been able to believe he was dead.

Hsiao-mei said that on his last day he was still digging up sweet potatoes in the garden! This kind of labor was too strenuous for a man with his physique. Moreover, it was apparent from the hastiness of his writing that he knew he was dying. Racing with the shadow of death, he tried frantically to complete the manuscript. Though the front part of this work, which approached two hundred thousand words, was yellowed, the ink of the last twenty some pages was fresh. Traces of blood were evident, another example of how he had forced himself to finish it even as he was coughing up blood. I again gripped his hand, this thin bamboo rod, and wept.

VI.

This was the second year of the war in East Asia. Many young men had been drafted by the Japanese military government to serve as soldiers, laborers, and medics. The industrial buildup destroyed many people's livelihoods and the rationing of necessities made it mandatory for the people to tighten their belts and wear ragged clothing. Except for those who used their power and influence to become wealthy from the war, everyone else endured the hardship in silence. Whoever dared speak out would be accused of "rumormongering" and of "spy activity." Japanese agents, relying on the special network they had constructed, thus captured many persons.

At a time when guns and bombs were sounding all around, Lin Wench'ien had put all his energies into finishing that "Vision of a Co-Prosperity Economic Plan," still hoping that mankind could find its conscience and regain primitive man's simplicity and purity. Nothing could have been more naïve than this. As a friend, he surely was worthy of respect. But, unfortunately, a man of his convictions could not find a place in the world we lived in, and what he held to be his "vision" would benefit no one, much less himself.

Thinking while I worked, I had pulled out a lot of weeds. Weeds which in the past could only be put into the compost pile could now be used as feed for the geese. I used the manure basket to collect them, and as I took them over to the goose pen, the children were just gathering around it, yelling and jumping. Even the baby, not yet two years old, copied his brothers and sisters in laughing and clapping his hands. I thought they were happy about something, but it turned out the flock of ducks had stretched out their necks and were leaping and pecking at the miniature seed rice hanging out from the eaves.

"Papa, the ducks are really shameless!" said my second son, who had just begun kindergarten in April, as he insistently tugged on my hand.

Since the implementation of rationing, we had to reduce our rice consumption by eating millet gruel twice a day; rice was served only at dinner. The children were constantly hungry and searched for sweet potatoes to bake in the stove. This led their mother to call them "shameless." For this reason, they were happy to see the ducks gobble up the food the way they themselves did, as if they had found moral support in the ducks' actions.

Two or three ducks were leaping up, then fighting over what they had pecked off the millet stalks. After finishing those kernels off, they stretched their necks up again even higher. In this way the lower sheaves were pecked clean, but the ducks couldn't leap up high enough for the rest. They just stood underneath, shaking their tails and staring up at the millet stalks. Then from behind them a duck ran up, stepped on the back of the one in front of him, and leaped mightily. Perhaps the bound stalks had become loose, for with this assault, the grains came tumbling down and the brave duck flipped over in a somersault. The other ducks who had been waiting at the side, their necks outstretched, rushed forward in a pack and trampled the one who had just flipped over as they each latched onto a stalk and dragged it off. The duck who had flipped over quacked as he was stepped on. By the time he scrambled to his feet, the spoils had all been carried off and he was left there in a daze.

This little scene was quite amusing and I laughed along with the children but I couldn't help feeling sorry for the duck that had been stepped on. But the children, who had gathered around to watch the ducks' performance, happily clapped and stamped their feet, even happier than when watching a circus.

"Hey, hey, you'd better hang them up higher. If the ducks eat all these seeds, what will we do next year?" I said to my wife, who was laughing gleefully along with the children.

The millet grains were easier to store than sweet potatoes and were the best way to make up for the shortage of rice, especially since they could be raised between the flowers in the plot. In addition, spreading fertilizer and watering could be done at the same time, not to mention that space could be saved. The other gardeners all said my way of planting was like killing two birds with one stone.

My wife laughed as she gathered the remaining stalks into a bundle, bound it tightly, and hung it up high. The ducks pecked the ground clean, then stretched out their necks toward the stalks hanging high above them. Only after failing to reach the grain did they go elsewhere in search of food. A duck's capacity for food is very large. They eat both sweet potatoes and grain. At a time when people were going hungry, I didn't

want to raise them at all, but someone had given them to us and my wife
brought them home. As a result, I could only watch them go hungry. It
was really hard to bear.

Raising geese, though, was much easier. Geese only need to feed on
grass. Grass from the garden was plentiful. When the children got out of
school they could herd the geese down to the grassy area to feed. They
did this every day and had already become fast friends with the geese,
whose white feathers looked most lovely. When the children held the
geese up to play with them, the geese would honk contentedly in their
laps.

"How heavy!" My second son, who had just entered kindergarten,
imitated his brother in picking up a goose, but because he couldn't carry
it, he almost dropped it. Frightened, the goose spread its wings and
squawked.

"Come on!"

Putting the geese down, the brothers raced to the grassy plot. The
geese frolicked in the pond for a while, then spread their wings and, as if
flying, raced over.

"Faster, faster! The black one's faster!"

Both geese had white feathers, but one's bill was black, the other
yellow. The older child rooted for the black bill, the younger one for the
yellow bill.

"Faster, faster! Go, yellow one!"

The two brothers acted like cheerleaders, chasing behind to spur the
geese on. By the time they got to the grassy area, the two geese had
already arrived and were feeding on the tender green grass. Which one
had won, the black or the yellow? They didn't know, and couldn't have an
answer from the geese even if they had asked, so the two boys started to
quarrel over it. Finding their argument to be futile, they finally lay in the
grass and watched the geese feed, reconciled.

When the gander took a step in the grass, the female goose closely
followed. Sometimes they went forward together, their rumps bumping
against each other, like a pair of newlyweds very much in love.

Wife follows when husband goes ahead a bit,
Geese don't make chicken shit.

The children gleefully changed the local folk tune this way to poke fun
at them. The white geese strolling in the brilliant sunlight were a beautiful sight to see. They ignored the children's mockery and reveled in the
unobstructed expanse of grass. They cuddled up as they waddled along
eating the green grass.

Squatting all day pulling weeds had made my back sore, and I walked
down to the grassy plot, too.

"Papa, when will our geese give birth to a baby?"

"They don't give birth. Geese lay eggs like a chicken."

"Oh! Eggs give birth to babies?"

"Right. After they sit on the eggs, the little goslings will come out."

"What a bother. Why don't they give birth all at once like rabbits?"

It was really beyond me. The children often asked strange questions like this and I had a hard time dealing with them. For example, my second daughter, who always liked to be first, couldn't accept the fact that she would always be the younger sister.

As for the question why geese don't give birth to babies, I had to think a long time before coming up with the answer. "Rabbits have milk but geese don't." In this way I was able to give the children a passable answer.

"That's right. Geese don't have milk. But then how do mother geese feed their babies once they are born?"

"That's why they lay eggs to raise them!"

"Oh, I see."

"I want a little gosling. Chin-hua's goose raised five goslings. They're a lot of fun!"

"Really? Our geese are big now. I think they'll be laying eggs pretty soon. Let's prepare a nest for them."

The brothers, their expectations raised, addressed the geese saying: "Hurry up and lay eggs so you can raise some babies!"

VII.

The director of the hospital brought the section chief of the General Affairs Department over to the flower garden because they were planning to plant two hundred giant cedar trees around the hospital.

I had flowers for cutting and potted plants here. Decorative trees, shrubs, and fruit trees had to be ordered first before another gardener would send them over. Gardeners all had their own specialties and when ordering from each other would offer twenty to thirty percent discounts.

"Do you have any samples here?" the director asked, after looking around the garden plot.

"Yes, I do. The trees are all planted in the seedbed on the mountain-side."

This was a lie. I had rented a plot on the mountain, but what I had planted were sweet potatoes and cassava to supplement our diet of rice. Because of the capital investment, it was impossible for me to deal directly with this kind of plant, which had to grow for many years before it could be sold. However, claiming the cedar trees to be mine would make a better impression on the customer. I had learned how to tell this kind of little falsehood early on.

"Then when can you deliver them?"

"In about two or three days." Thus the transaction was completed, two hundred four-foot tall trees, sold for seventy cents apiece, were to be delivered to the hospital within three days.

Ordinarily, earning two to three dollars a day was considered pretty good. I didn't expect a transaction worth more than a hundred dollars to be completed this simply. Each tree cost me fifty cents, so that for two hundred trees I could earn forty dollars. Subtracting the cost of delivery and planting, I could still clear more than twenty dollars profit. I was elated.

At this time, the children herded the geese home.

"Oh, these two geese are really beautiful! Did you raise them?" asked the director, patting the children's heads. The children responded to this praise by giggling and bragging: "This is the male and that one is the female. They're going to lay eggs soon and raise little goslings!"

"That's wonderful, just wonderful . . . Someone sent me a gander. I'm thinking of raising it but can't do it without a female . . ."

Before the director could finish, his companion broke in. "That's right. He's growing up and you'd better find him a mate. Ha, ha, ha!"

"Ha, ha, ha! That's right," the director said to me. "It wouldn't be right not to get him a bride. This female goose of yours is all right. Would it be possible for you to let me . . ."

The children, who had become worried when they heard the director wanted our female goose, tugged at my clothes and secretly said, "Don't give her away." Of course I didn't mean to let someone else have this "perfectly matched" couple. But, on the other hand, seeing how important a customer he was to us, I couldn't give him a flat no. I could only say, "We only have this one pair. If you want one, please wait awhile and I will find you one."

When they heard what I said, the children were no longer worried. But they still seemed to fear the director would take the geese by force, so they herded them into their pen immediately.

The director was, in fact, quite open-minded and didn't insist on taking this female goose. He just said, "Do what you can for me," and began looking around for flowers.

"This speckled bamboo is nice, how much is it?" the director asked, turning to his companion. "It would look good planted in that hexagonal flower pot at home."

"That's right. It would look really nice."

Because of the female goose incident, I was afraid he was unhappy, so I said: "If you like this one, then I'll give it to you." I began to dig it up.

"Well, then thank you. Dig up three of them, then."

Sensing that he didn't want the female goose anymore, I generously dug up three speckled bamboo, wrapped them in a newspaper and gave them to him.

"What is this?"

"Bulbous root lily."

"Please wrap up twenty," the director said.

I began wrapping them up, but without waiting for me to finish, he asked again: "What's that?"

"Hydrangea."

"Dig up two of them . . . And this?"

"Grotto flower."

"And over there?"

"Garden dahlia."

His wanting this and that made it hard for me to keep up.

Though I was a little concerned, I thought to myself that no matter how shameless a person might be, he couldn't want so many things just given to him. But I was also embarrassed to say the price right then. I thought I'd wait until he asked the price, then explain which I could give to him for free and tell him the prices of the others. But he ordered the children to call two rickshaws for him and didn't mention prices again. With only a "thank you," he left with a full load of flowers.

I became anxious and said, "I'll give you the rest of the flowers, but I bought this potted banyan tree in order to rent it out. The original price was six dollars. I'll let you have it for the original price."

Sitting in the rickshaw, he looked at the potted plant in his lap, then at me and said: "Six dollars? That's cheap, but it's too heavy and hard to carry. I'll pick it up next time." He then returned that old potted plant to me. But what he had already taken alone canceled out the twenty dollar profit I could have made.

This transaction had been in vain.

VIII.

Early the next day I went to four or five gardeners to find the giant cedar trees. Because they were scarce, no one was willing to sell them for under sixty cents apiece. I then went to several flower gardeners in the countryside and was finally able to buy them at fifty-five cents apiece. But since the price had already been settled, there was nothing I could do about it. All I could do was deliver the goods to the hospital as promised and hire two workers to plant them.

When the trees were ready to be planted, the director and the section chief supervised. The three of us took a whole day to plant those two hundred trees. By the time we had watered them, it was already quite

late. I ordered two bowls of noodles for the workers and sent them home
when they finished. After finishing a task, one always relaxes a bit. I
didn't even care about the loss anymore.

The next day I delivered the bill to the hospital. Because the director
was not there, I gave it to the section chief and asked him to pay as soon as
possible. He looked the bill over, said they would notify me when they
would pay, and turned to go. I hurriedly stopped him and asked, "When
will that be? "

"Maybe the end of the month." He knitted his brows as he spoke.

Why not say straighforwardly "the end of the month"? Why add a
"maybe"? This really puzzled me. This was the first time I had been
involved in such a large transaction. Part of the capital was borrowed. I
still owed the gardeners more than twenty dollars. If the date of payment
couldn't be settled on, what was I to do?

I have always hated to run into my creditors. I remember once I owed
twenty dollars to a rice shop and the owner took me to court over it.
Having to stand up in front of the judge was as uncomfortable as standing
before the court of hell. Thus, having waited until the end of the month
without any word from the hospital on when they would pay, I went over
early one morning to inquire about it. I had to wait a long time until the
section chief came to work. I hurried over to him.

"What is it?" He looked straight at me but without giving me his full
attention.

I almost blurted out, "What else?" but I restrained myself, comforting
myself with the thought that a man in his position was bound to have
many things to attend to. So I took a deep breath and politely explained to
him the purpose of my visit.

He finally seemed to remember and said, "Oh, you're the gardener.
Too bad. The director said the giant cedars you sent over weren't like your
samples. They're too slender."

"Samples? What samples?"

"Weren't there several trees in your garden? The ones you brought
over aren't the same at all."

"Who said those were samples? Those were yard trees over six feet tall,
two to three dollars each. You ordered four-foot tall saplings. How could
they be the same?"

"But that's what the director said. Well, then, come back and talk to
him yourself."

It was already the end of the month and all he said was "talk to him
yourself"! He was clearly making it difficult for me. When the trees were
sent over to be planted, they were present to supervise. If there had been
a problem, why didn't they say so then? Why did they wait so long before
they found fault? What was I to do? If it were my own money, then

waiting a few more days wouldn't have mattered, but I needed the money to pay back the other gardeners.

"Could you please speak to him right away about this?"

"All right. You wait here."

At least his manner of speaking was quite pleasant. But if the director used the same excuse as the section chief, I would be in trouble. I had to pay the cedar growers tomorrow.

But the section chief, who said he would be back soon, failed to show up. More and more patients arrived. The sound of straw sandals on the floor was irritating.

I sat on a bench in the waiting room and kept an eye on the door to the director's office. The worried looks and low moans from the patients, some of whose heads were bound in gauze, added to my depressed feeling.

The nurse came back and asked for my registration card. I shook my head. She looked at me strangely and walked away.

After a long time, the section chief finally came out.

"You'll have to wait to speak to him. He's busy right now," he said when he saw me.

I didn't feel like talking any more. Though I was distraught, I didn't want anybody to attend to my business if it meant a longer wait for those suffering people to see their doctor. So I simply said, "Well, then, please help me out because I have to use this money to pay back other people." After that, I took my leave.

I didn't feel like doing anything when I got home. I just lay on the bed and waited until noon, then went back to the hospital to see the section chief. This time his attitude was a little different. He repeated again and again that the cedars I brought over weren't the same as the samples. he suggested that I go to see the director and talk it over with him, for it was the director who had ordered them and who came out personally to receive them when they were delivered.

The hospital at noon was different from in the morning, deserted as if after an ebb tide. I opened the door to the director's office but found only the nurse on duty inside taking a nap.

"Excuse me, is the director in?"

"He went to inspect the hospital rooms," she said, yawning.

All I could do was retreat to the bench in the waiting room to wait. A person anxiously listening for footsteps in this silent corridor would certainly be mistaken for a mentally ill patient by others. The nurse, peeking out to see if I was still waiting there, asked about my illness in that tone of voice, saying I should come back earlier some other day. I didn't know whether I should laugh or cry about it. I said I wasn't looking for him because I was sick but for other business. She then smiled and left.

I waited until two-thirty, when the door creaked open and I saw a man in a white physician's coat come in. It must be him, I thought to myself, and immediately stood up and cocked my head to look. But it was his assistant, not the director. I slowly returned to the bench to wait. I had never felt such boredom in my life. After waiting about another half an hour, I finally met up with the director.

In order to resolve the situation smoothly, I controlled my temper and first mentioned the business of his asking me to find a new bride for his gander. I said the children had asked all around and finally found a plump and beautiful goose. The beautiful bird weighed eight and a half catties and sold for a dollar a catty. I thought that finding him a new bride for less than ten dollars would please him and that he wouldn't cause me any more trouble. Thinking this way, I spoke in a very casual manner. I tried to please him by speaking of the goose as a new bride, and hoped he would laugh. I was prepared to accompany him in a chuckle. But he showed no reaction and the pat little speech I had prepared fell apart. He acted in such a haughty manner, not saying whether he wanted it or not, that I never saw the smiling face I had hoped for. Was it that he also had to personally look over the goose before he'd be satisfied?

I could do nothing but ask him directly for the money.

"You should blame yourself," he said "Businessmen should take care to keep their word. If the cedars you sent had only been a little smaller than the samples in your yard, that would have still been all right. Besides, you charged a high price."

His face was very severe and his tone unusually harsh, like a judge's. He was talking to me as if I were a swindler.

"The ones you ordered were four feet," I said, no longer able to conceal my discontent. "Which ones weren't four feet tall? All those two hundred saplings were over four feet tall. Some were even closer to five. You mentioned they weren't the same as the samples. We never talked about any samples. The ones at my house are yard trees that were planted for many years. They're not saplings. Adult trees and saplings are not the same—that's perfectly natural. Besides, when we delivered them you personally came out to look them over. If there was anything wrong, you should have said so then. How can you mention this now after they have been planted for so long?"

"You! How dare you blame me! If I had said they weren't right when you delivered the trees and made you take them back, wouldn't that have been a lot of trouble for you? I felt sorry for you and here you go blaming me. And I thought you were a sensible person."

Sensible? I didn't understand at all what he meant.

Though I was very unhappy, at this point I only wanted him to pay up as soon as possible. I didn't really care if I had to take a little more loss. I had already breached my contract with the seedbed gardener many times, how could I face him again? So I controlled my hatred and spoke conciliatorily: "How about settling it this way? We'll go together to any seedbed garden you consider the cheapest. If you find any cedars sold at a lower price than mine, I will take it."

I thought this was the fairest and the only way out, but my suggestion was received only with mockery:

"You're really foolish! You think I have that much time to spare? You really don't have any business sense."

"I don't have any business sense?" I said in amazement. What did he mean by this? I was puzzled. Aren't many large transactions conducted by bidding? Then why was my suggestion met with ridicule? It seemed that I had underestimated the director, who was a doctor of medicine as well as a man with business sense.

I had been running the flower garden for many years already and did business every day. When customers came to buy flowers and we had settled on a price, then the deal was made: cash on delivery. There were some who owed me money for some time if they hadn't brought money with then, but they had never lagged so long. Moreover, these were transactions of five and ten cents; they never exceeded three to five dollars. Could it be that large transactions are special? No matter what, all I hoped for now was for him to pay me as soon as possible and get it over with. From now on, I wouldn't dare accept another transaction that promised a large profit, if I had to go through similar troubles—not to mention a bad deal like this one in which I lost a great deal of money.

"You're right. I have no experience doing such large transactions like this one, so please help me out." I almost begged him now: "For if I say they're not expensive and you say they are, if I asked you to check with other seedbeds to compare and you say you haven't time, then I really don't know what to do next. My garden work is busy and I've spent all this time trying to collect payment on this. This really makes it difficult for me. Please help me out. Let's be a little more precise, all right? If only you agree to pay me now, pay me whatever price you want to pay."

"All right. I'll go talk it over."

"Who do you still have to go talk it over with? Sir, can't you decide right now?"

"No."

He yawned and stood up. I still hadn't collected what I came for. I had come again in vain.

IX.

The end of the month had already passed. The next month I went to the hospital five times. Sometimes I couldn't find the director, other times when I found him I didn't receive a definite answer. I was so angry that I almost went mad, but because I wouldn't be able to pay back the other gardeners' bills if I didn't get the money, I could only put up with it. In the end he lowered the price to fifty cents a tree and I accepted, though it meant losing more than twenty dollars. But even though the price was agreed upon, he still didn't specify when payment would be made. He kept on delaying.

Another month passed. The giant cedars planted around the hospital all began budding and were unusually green and beautiful. But I was a complete wreck. The gardeners from the countryside kept writing me letters urging me to pay. Repayment of their bills depended wholly on when the director paid me. If he didn't say when he would pay, I couldn't write them back. I thus passed every day anxious and depressed.

The weeds in the garden had already grown tall, but I didn't have the peace of mind to weed them out. After another ten days or so, the owner of the seedbed garden personally made a visit to my home. He walked in with an angry look on his face as I sat blankly in front of the table. I invited him to sit down and made tea for him. I apologized to him and explained why my payment was late. I felt so bad about the whole thing that even my ears became hot.

"Ha, ha, ha!" The seedbed owner's hearty laughter surprised me. I looked at him curiously as he continued. "I'll collect the money for you."

He seemed so confident that it was hard for me to believe it.

"You're going to collect for me? You think you can collect the money for me? You mean it?"

"Of course I mean it. Schools or other organizations delay payment occasionally for one reason or another, but the public hospital's accounts are independent. If the director doesn't want to give you a hard time, he can pay you any time."

"Is that so? Then why has he caused me so much trouble on purpose? That I really can't understand."

"The reason is very simple, and you'll know in time. But that female goose of yours, can you let me take it along? That's the price you have to pay."

"Uh, humph . . ."

"You're not willing? Then I have no way to collect the payment for you."

"She's already laid eggs and hatched eight little goslings. And the children really like her the best. If you take her away, I'm afraid . . ."

"She's not the children's lover or your daughter-in-law. Geese are all the same. Just buy another one, and I'm sure the children will love her all the same. And, after some time, she will care for the goslings just the same."

As he spoke he went over to the goose pen, put his hand in to grasp the female goose's neck and pulled her out. After tying up her feet, he took her away. The goose flapped her wings and squawked and, as if imploring me to rescue her, looked at me. I felt bad, but in front of my creditor, I couldn't save her.

Thus he took command of me, and with goose in hand, he led me first to the director's dormitory, then to the hospital to find him.

"Mr. Director," the seedbed owner intoned, "the goose which you liked so much has already been sent over to your house. The new bride and groom get along very well and seem quite happy."

Actually the female goose, having been placed in that strange place, squawked for quite a while and squatted forlornly in the corner. This smooth-talking seedbed owner, however, made up a story and described the scene vividly, as if the new couple did get along well. Perhaps this was the secret of doing business.

When the director heard this, his attitude changed completely. That overbearing man changed in an instant into a nice man with a smiling face.

"Really? Then I really can't thank you enough."

It was hard for me to believe a person could change this quickly. But the evidence was right before my eyes. The director continued:

"Please wait right here." He stepped out and quickly returned, informing me that I could go to the accountant's office to get my money any time now. In the short time that we had to wait, he had also ordered the nurse to pour tea and offer us cigarettes.

As we left, the director accompanied us to the door, repeating his thanks over and over.

When I went to get the money from the accountant, I was surprised to learn that the bill had been calculated according to the original price of seventy cents a tree.

As we walked home, the seedbed owner looked back and smiled at me.

"Well, how about it? Whatever he wants, you give it to him. That way, even if you say each tree is a dollar, or even a dollar and a half, he will never argue with you. The reason? Simple enough. This is a public hospital, and why should he care if something he orders is expensive. But whether you give him something or not is another matter. Some people in his position would openly demand a commission, to be invited to dinner, or a flat payoff. Since he didn't ask for any of this, you can't say he doesn't have some self-respect."

"So that's what it was."

If it was a "truth" I had just discovered, it was also a fact of life that deepened my anger and depression.

"This is 'co-prosperity,'" the seedbed owner added.

The Japanese had used "Co-Prosperity" as their slogan to promote their war in East Asia. Its effect was now evident even in a rural farmer.

"'Co-prosperity'? How does it apply to me?" I looked at him, puzzled.

"Your business will go smoothly and the other party also benefits from your prosperity. If this is not co-prosperity, what is?"

Business will go very smoothly and everyone involved will benefit. It sounded attractive, but behind it there must have been many who had to pay for it.

"Vision of a Co-Prosperity Economic Plan"—I thought again of Lin Wen-ch'ien's work.

Lin had once blamed the English merchants for bribing Ch'ing dynasty officials in order to run their opium trade on mainland China. In some businessmen's eyes, this was truly "co-prosperity." What a hateful term! And today I played a part in it as well. I shook in disgust. I immediately paid the seedbed owner what I still owed him and walked off, as if trying to escape from him. Walking home, I held the rest of the money in my fist and felt uncomfortable. These forty dollars couldn't be called a profit. All I could say is that the deal came off even—if I didn't consider marrying off Mother Goose as a loss.

Lin Wen-ch'ien died young because he had labored on his "Vision of a Co-Prosperity Economic Plan." And I played a "co-prosperity" role to make a living.

My conscience was hard on me.

When I got home, the children had already returned from school. They had taken the geese down to the grassy plot to feed as usual, but their former innocent liveliness was missing. The gander, having lost his mate, and the goslings, having lost their mother, seemed lonely and sad. They scratched left and right and moaned lowly. "Old mate, where have you gone?" It seemed as if he were really calling out to her as he looked for her. The goslings wandered about in confusion and ate nothing.

I decided to work on Lin Wen-ch'ien's unfinished thesis and fill in his incomplete sentences. It was something I had to do to make up for my own wrongdoings. This probably wouldn't be easy for me because I had no training in economics. But unless I finished it, there was no hope for a beautiful tomorrow.

"Unless co-prosperity can be achieved without sacrificing the interest of any one person, it is not true co-prosperity . . ."

As I wiped my tears with a handkerchief, I suddenly felt that these last words written by Lin Wen-ch'ien had firmly taken hold of my heart.

NOTE

1. From *Analects,* XVI:1, tr. D.C. Lau, *Confucius: The Analects* (harmondsworth: Penguin Books, 1979), pp. 138–139. D.C. Lau says that the "text [in the original] is corrupt here. In the light of what follows, this passage should, probably, read: '. . . worries not about poverty but about uneven distribution, not about underpopulation but about disharmony, not about overturning but about instability" (*ibid.,* p. 138).

Part Two

Taiwan Fiction since 1945

CHUNG LI-HO   (1915–1960)

It is commonly agreed that Chung Li-ho's fiction represents the first flowering of first-generation writers after Taiwan was restored to China in 1945. Born to a farming family in Pingtung, he had, since primary school, been keenly interested in literature, particularly traditional Chinese popular novels. Failing to enter high school, he helped his father manage a lumbering business and spent the rest of his time reading the major writers of the May Fourth period. In 1934, he fell in love with Chung P'ing-mei, a farm girl several years his senior. Since marriage between members of the same surname (Chung) was regarded at that time as incest, Chung Li-ho eloped with P'ing-mei to China in 1940. They stayed in Peking throughout the war. In 1946 the couple returned to Pingtung, where Li-ho worked for some time as a substitute junior high school teacher. Soon he was attacked by tuberculosis and had to be confined in a hospital from 1947 to 1951, exhausting all their financial means. He remained virtually a cripple until his death in 1960, relying on his wife to support the whole family. The anguish of atrophied manhood and the burden of guilt as a failed husband are movingly captured in the present selection, "Together Through Thick and Thin." The author of one novel, six novellettes, and twenty-six stories, Chung Li-ho provides a vital link in Taiwan fiction between two political eras. Whether autobiographical or impressionistic, his narratives bear intimate witness to the trials and hardship of rural Taiwan in a period of transition. In 1966 Taipei's Yuan-hsing Press published Chung Li-ho ch'uan-chi, *his complete works in eight volumes.*

Together through Thick and Thin

Translated by Shiao-ling Yü

I

After getting off the Sugar Company's mini-train, I searched all around but did not see a trace of P'ing-mei. I felt slightly surprised. Maybe she did not receive my letter, I thought to myself, otherwise there was no reason for her not coming to meet me. She is my wife; I understand her perfectly. Another thought crossed my mind: maybe she could not make it on time. Then I would certainly meet her on the way. With this thought, I picked up my bundle and slowly made my way home.

Home was in the foothills of the mountains to the east. Not having walked for several years, and weakened by long illness, I found this walk home quite an exertion.

It had been fully three years since I had left home to be hospitalized. Other than the time when P'ing-mei visited me in the hospital during the second year of my stay there, I did not see her again. Three years, and I spent every day of these three years thinking of her and longing for her. I did not know how they managed at home during these three years. Did they live well? Or not well? Even though my medical expenses during this long period had almost depleted our family fortune, I still tried to think about the better of the two possibilities. Perhaps I was not thinking, I was merely wishing—wishing they had lived well. It had to be so, otherwise I could have no peace of mind.

This was admittedly because I loved P'ing-mei so, but besides love, there were other reasons. Our union met with violent opposition from my family and from the old society. It was after much hard struggle and at the cost of breaking relations with our families that we finally became husband and wife. We paid a high price for our life. Because of this, we shared good fortune and hardship, and loved each other without holding anything back during the more than a decade of our life together. We did not desire high position and good pay, or huge land property; we only wished to have a thatched hut surrounded by a bamboo fence, where we could live out our lives in peace and tranquility, and in loving companionship. This was all we wanted.

We spent the first five years of our married life away from home. Since my return to Taiwan in the second year after the Japanese surrender, we were rarely separated from each other even for a very brief period. Little did I expect that this illness would keep me in the hospital for three years. I could well imagine how P'ing-mei must have missed and worried about me during all this time, just as I had done about her.

A broad road stretched from the village to the east. After I went past the school and down a little slope, the road forked. The small path that led to the northeast was the shortest route to my home. As I walked down the slope, I noticed a grove of trees by the roadside, and under the shade of the trees a woman who had a child with her looked in my direction from time to time.

It was P'ing-mei! I walked over to her; she came up and took the baggage from me.

"P'ing-mei!" I could hardly suppress my agitation.

P'ing-mei lowered her head, tears rolling down her face. The child pressed tightly against his mother. He looked at me, then looked at his mother. Li-erh, who was only a baby when I left, must be four years old now, I reckoned.

As I gazed at P'ing-mei and our child, my heart was filled with mixed sadness and happiness, and a host of other emotions. P'ing-mei wiped her tears with her sleeves. I let her cry for a while. In three years, she had become much thinner.

"P'ing-mei," I asked her after she had quieted down a little, "didn't you receive my letter?"

She quietly looked up. There were no more tears in her eyes, they still glistened with dampness.

"I got your letter," she said.

"Then why didn't you come to the station to meet me?"

"I didn't want to," she muttered. "There are too many people in the station."

"You're afraid of those people?"

This reminded me of the time when I left home on a two-week trip. P'ing-mei could not help crying when she came to the station to see me off. She cried as if I were going on a long journey and we were to be separated for many years. Her crying had made me quite depressed.

"You don't want people to see you cry, right?"

P'ing-mei said nothing, lowering her head even more.

I was silent for a long while, then asked her, "Now that I am back, do you still feel sad?"

"Oh, I am so happy!" She raised her head. Holding the child's chin, she said to him, "Here is Daddy, why don't you call Daddy? You promised me at home that you would!"

Our agitation had by now gradually subsided, and there were traces of happiness on her face.

I asked her, "Did you live well at home?"

She gave me a sad smile, "I lived very well!"

I looked at her in bewilderment, and suddenly felt guilty. I took her hands and caressed them again and again. Her hands were very thick and were covered with bruises old and new; the palms were full of thick calluses. The more I looked at them, the worse I felt.

"Looks like you've been very hard on yourself." I said.

P'ing-mei pulled her hands away from me. "This is nothing," she said. After a slight pause, she added, "As long as you're getting well, it doesn't matter that I have to work hard."

II.

In our home, everything looked neat and tidy. The house, inside and out, and all household articles, big and small, were sparkling clean. The house was filled with a serene, peaceful, comforting atmosphere that could only come from a woman's thoughtful, solicitous concern. The moment I stepped inside I was enveloped by a feeling of affection, warmth, and coziness, the kind of feeling that only a person returning home after a long absence can feel, the kind of feeling that makes a wandering soul settle down.

On the other hand, I discovered what a difficult and impoverished condition we were in. I saw clearly how much of our family property had been washed away by my illness; I had almost deprived P'ing-mei and our two children of their means of livelihood. This thought greatly pained me.

"Maybe I should have saved the property for you and the children," I said as we were going to bed that night. "With the property, you and the children will not have to worry about your living expenses in the future."

"What are you talking about?" P'ing-mei was quite upset. "I couldn't wait for you to get well and leave the hospital. Now that you're home, I'm very happy. Don't talk nonsense, you'll only make me angry."

Deeply moved, I drew her to me. She gave in to my pull and came to lean on my shoulder.

"They all said that you were not going to get well, and told me not to sell the land but to save it for the children and me to live on. But I didn't believe that you would die." After a little while she added quietly, "We've suffered so much, Heaven will have mercy on us. I want you to live to be a hundred so you can watch our children grow up and watch me die peacefully in front of your eyes. The lucky wives die before their husbands. I don't want it to happen that when I die you're no longer around; that would make me sad."

The only property we had left was about a half acre of not very fertile land to the east of our house. During these years, P'ing-mei had mastered all the skills of a farmhand: plowing, hoeing, planting, and harvesting. When she finished working on our own land, she would work for the wealthy families nearby or for the Department of Forestry on its afforestation project. At the time I came home, she was working for a monastery—opening up mountain land for cultivation. She would finish all the household chores, then take her sickle and go to work. At noon and in the evening she would rush home to start the meals. Although she worked herself so hard, she always did everything with a smile.

One day it was already dark when she got back from the temple. Without sitting down to catch her breath, she picked up the cooking pot and went into the kitchen. Watching her bustling about, I could hardly contain myself. I asked myself: Why can't I cook the meals?

The next day, I set to work. Fortunately, it was not too difficult to cook for a family of four. When P'ing-mei came home at noon, lunch was ready. She was at first surprised, then became worried.

"This will not tire me out." I put on a most convincing smile and assured her that her worries were unfounded. "I want to help out a little so you don't have to rush back and forth."

From then on, I gradually learned the domestic duties of a housewife: cooking, washing dishes, sweeping, feeding the pigs, sewing, and looking after the children. The only thing that I did not quite master was washing clothes. Thus, without our knowing it, we had exchanged our respective roles and duties: she worked outside the home, I worked inside, as if she were a good husband, and I a good wife.

On the days when P'ing-mei worked on our own land, I would take a pot of hot tea to the field for her every morning so she could rest a little while drinking the tea. I thought she would welcome this refreshment after having perspired from working. As I watched her happy and contented expression when she drank the tea, I also felt happy. Since I had no choice but to let her work like a man, I could only hope that she would have beautiful smiles for me. As long as she was happy, so was I.

III

Though material comfort was not part of our lot, our devotion to each other enabled us, to a certain extent, to lead a fairly happy and satisfactory life. Our difficulties were mainly financial. Our little patch of land could hardly support a family of four and P'ing-mei could not always find other work. As a result, we always lived with uncertainties.

One evening as we were sitting in our courtyard, a dozen people carrying lumber passed by the road in front of our house; there were even a few women among the group. They were the illegal loggers often reported in the newspapers. They would steal into some remote places in the Central Mountain ranges in the morning to cut down the teak trees belonging to the Department of Forestry, and carry the wood out after sunset to sell to the merchants.

Silently we watched the people pass. Suddenly, P'ing-mei said to me that she wanted to go with these people to haul lumber the next day.

I was taken aback. "You? You haul lumber?"

With this exchange, the pitiable image of a logger came to my mind. He was dripping with sweat from head to toe, panting like a workhorse, and his face was flushed red. I felt a sharp pain in my heart, as if pricked by a needle. That was a dreadful prospect.

"P'ing-mei," I said sternly—but I could tell that I was pleading—"there is no need for us to come to that. We can manage by watering down the gruel."

Despite my brave words, I knew perfectly well how hard our days were. What was worse, there was no prospect of improvement. Besides, it was not always possible to stick it out by "watering down the gruel."

The seven essentials of every household—firewood, rice, cooking oil, salt, soy sauce, vinegar, and tea—were a source of enjoyment for other people; for us every item was a burden. People could not possibly imagine how a poor family felt about such things; even I had just come to understand them myself. Problems that were hardly a matter of concern to people under normal circumstances were, for the poor, difficulties that took all their energies to solve.

From the time our children started school, their educational expenses became another problem that we had to contend with. In addition, there were medical expenses, even though I no longer had to take medicine every day. Pressures came from all sides.

Finally, the day came when P'ing-mei went to haul lumber!

Silently I watched her join those people and start toward the mountains. I felt an indescribable pain in my heart, as though I were watching my beloved being led away by jailers. I never hated myself so much for my weakness and inadequacy as I did at that particular moment. I clearly sensed an irresistible force in our midst, which cruelly controlled our actions and lives. Our will to resist had been crushed.

Shortly after sunset, P'ing-mei came home safely, shouldering a piece of wood through the back door. There was not a dry spot on her shirt, and a big patch of her pants was also soaked through. Her face was covered with sweat. Her hair, drenched in sweat, was very disheveled; some of it stuck to her face, making her look fierce. When she saw me, she parted her lips and tried to smile. But that was not a smile at all; it was twisted into a grimace by the weight of the log on her shoulders. I suddenly felt something in me, forcing me to cry out, but I turned my head away without saying a word. I could not bear to look at her. I did not dare ask her questions either.

She carried the log into the house and leaned it against the wall. It was a piece of teak wood with the bark on, about three and a half inches thick and thirteen feet long; it could fetch twenty dollars in the market. As soon as P'ing-mei came out of the room, I shut the door and did not mention anything about it all evening—I was afraid to mention the word "lumber."

"You don't like me hauling lumber?" P'ing-mei finally asked me. My silence seemed to have hurt her deeply.

"It is not that I like to haul lumber," she explained, her voice choking with emotion. "We have to make a living. There is no other way!"

I could not describe my feelings in that moment. They were just too confused to be identified. There was hatred, there was sorrow, there was also fear. I hated myself for not being able to support my wife, for having to depend on her for support. I was sad because my wife had to be a lumberjack. On the other end of the lumber I saw a bottomless pit, and we were drawing closer to it with every step. And this made me frightened.

IV.

The following day, P'ing-mei went to haul lumber again. For her lunch, I prepared two rice balls wrapped in bamboo leaves, tied with her kerchief. This way she could just discard the wrappings after she'd finished eating without the additional burden of a lunch box. The less she had to carry the better.

From around noon that day, I kept looking toward the mountain slopes in the east. On the one hand, I was anxious for P'ing-mei to come home; on the other hand, I wanted to see if there were any suspicious people lurking around. This precaution was very important, for on it depended the safety of the loggers.

Although our local station was frequently patrolled by the police from the Department of Forestry, if no one from the office came to inspect, these policemen rarely ventured out. Even when they did, they made only routine checks. Days like this were usually safe. If their superior came to inspect, then it was another story. For the sake of safety, the lumberjacks hired a special messenger who checked on the news every day. As soon as he heard something, he would immediately go into the mountains to warn them. His intelligence was highly reliable. He often got the word even before the inspector left his office. The regrettable thing about him was that he was very fond of drinking and gambling. Once he started to drink or gamble, he would forget everything. This worried the loggers the most.

Shortly after noon, three or four people in white suddenly appeared from the south. I leaned against the window frame and watched intently for several minutes. Alas! These must be people from the Department of Forestry!

After this discovery, I paced in and out, unable to keep myself still for a moment. From time to time I would walk to the yard and look toward the mountains in the east. There were two parallel roads that turned in different directions just beyond the temple, one going east, one bearing slightly to the northeast. The eastern route passed in front of the patrol station, so the lumberjacks all preferred the other route. If the news was bad and they could take neither road, they had to climb over the mountain ridge to escape. If that happened, it would only mean trouble. I prayed that it would not be so.

I thought about the messenger—I did not know what that drunkard was doing! Still not a trace of him, that confounded scoundrel!

The sun was slanting toward the west and it was almost evening. Everything was quiet. There was no trace of the messenger, either. I was getting even more worried and nervous. The sun was now touching the top of the mountains, evening's dark shadows were slowly spreading out, becoming deeper and darker. It was time to start the fire to cook supper again.

Suddenly I heard heavy footsteps hastily walking past the courtyard. When I looked, it was none other than that cursed drunkard. He was walking very fast, almost running.

"Is P'ing-mei gone, Ah-ho?" he shouted to me as he walked past.

"Left a long time ago. Where are they?" I asked.

"At Fang-liao."

"You . . ."

But that drunkard was already gone.

As I attended to my household chores, I paid close attention to the mountain pass to the east. This was a crucial moment—the moment when the forest patrols set out to arrest the offenders, and the loggers tried to slip through the line of surveillance. If they bumped into the police, the fortunate ones could escape capture but had to lose their precious lumber; the unfortunante ones would be caught with their loot. Then there would be fines and a three-month prison term. Who their families would depend on for support during this period, only Heaven knew.

It was getting dark. All was quiet. Obviously something ominous was going to happen. Where were the loggers? Had the forest patrols been dispatched? Did the messenger arrive in time to give the warning? Why did he come so late? That drunkard!

It was now completely dark. A new moon appeared in the sky. I served the children supper and told the older boy to take his brother to bed. Then I rushed toward the eastern mountain pass, although I knew my action would probably be in vain.

After I walked past the temple I turned into a valley, then down a creek and up a slope until I reached a stretch of field along the creek. Just as I got to the end of the path in the rice paddies, a din of shouting suddenly erupted in front of me. Someone was hollering in a loud voice, "Don't run away! Don't run away!" There was another uproar made of many cries of "Wa-ya . . ." that sounded like a stampede of frightened cattle.

I ran forward with all my strength. I had gone only a few steps when I met a group of people running toward me, carrying logs on their shoulders. I dodged quickly into the shadow of the trees. I saw five or six men run past, panting heavily, with two patrolmen in hot pursuit. When they were about thirty feet from the loggers, the patrolmen yelled angrily, "Don't run away! Don't run away!" This was followed by a series of "pong! pong! pong!" sounds. The men must have thrown away their lumber.

I came out of the shadows and continued to run toward the interior of the mountain. Discarded logs lay by the roadside. Farther up the mountain came a series of cries, "Over there! Over there!" I saw countless

shadowy figures running confusedly in the vacant field by the creek on
the other side of the road. Three persons in the back were pursuing, two
of them in plain clothes. Those in front did not have logs on their shoulders any more.

"Stop! Don't run away, damn you!" a voice shouted in Mandarin with a
heavy southern accent.

Another voice came from the little creek close by. The creek was about
forty feet away, just below the road. Two figures dashed out of the
shadows and into the hazy moonlight, followed by another and yet
another. The third one, I noticed, was a woman, and she was less than
twenty feet away from the forestry patrolman behind her. The little creek
was full of craggy boulders, and the four shadowy figures staggered and
tottered on the boulders with a bobbing motion. Then the woman
stumbled and fell. In that instant, the shadow behind her leapt forward
and dashed at her.

"Ai-ya!"

I let out a cry. At the same time I was seized by a dizzy spell and almost
lost my balance. By the time I steadied myself, all had returned to quiet
around me in the silvery moonlight. The struggles of a moment ago, the
chasing and commotion, all seemed like a bad dream. But it was no
dream. Close by my feet there were logs scattered all over the ground. I
realized with intense pain that P'ing-mei had been captured!

V.

Feeling utterly helpless, I dragged myself home with two wobbly legs
and an aching heart. On the little creek, I met two forest patrolmen and
three plainclothesmen; they stared at me with surprise and suspicion.

After walking for I did not know how long, I finally got home. When I
saw the dim yellow light that filtered out through the window I felt
indescribably lonely and sad. But when I stepped into the house I
thought I was dreaming again and for a moment remained frozen by the
door. Ah, there was P'ing-mei sitting squarely on the chair! She had not
been captured by the forestry patrolman, my beloved wife!

"P'ing-mei! P'ing-mei!"

I rushed forward and grabbed her hands, and began to caress them
with abandon. I felt as if something very hot were burning in my breasts.

"Where have you been?" she asked me.

But I did not hear what she said; I only heard myself talking: "I saw you
caught by the patrolman."

"Me?" She looked at me with raised head. "No, it wasn't me," she
continued slowly, "I was in the back. When I saw the patrol chasing

people in front of me, I hid in the woods. But when I was climbing over the mountain, I slipped and fell. Right now my left shoulder and one of my ankles are hurting a little. You can rub me with some ginger later."

I looked at her again and I discovered the bruise on her left cheek, the mud on her whole body, especially on her left shoulder, and the grass in her hair.

I took a piece of ginger, cut it open, and placed it in hot ash to warm it. Then I poured a half cup of wine and asked P'ing-mei to lie down in bed. When I unbuttoned her clothes I was greatly shocked by what I saw: the left side of her body, from shoulder to ankle, was covered with big and small bruises and cuts, some light, some quite serious. There was a bruise the size of a palm on her pelvis. A piece of skin was rubbed off her shoulder, the bloodstain still fresh. I could tell these were all new wounds. I applied penicillin to the cuts; the bruised places I rubbed back and forth with ginger dipped in wine. When I got to her pelvis, P'ing-mei groaned from time to time.

"P'ing-mei, tell me," I said to her, "it was you who fell down in the creek, right?"

She said nothing. It was only after I questioned her repeatedly that she admitted it.

"Why did you try to hide it from me?" I said disapprovingly. "Your wounds are quite serious."

"I was afraid you might feel bad," she said.

That tense and frightening chase of a while ago reappeared in my mind, and the tears I had held back until now rolled down my cheeks in a steady stream.

As I rubbed her body, I reviewed in my mind our life together—from courtship, marriage, until now. The hard, bitter life that we shared for more than a decade was a record of the struggles of our two souls. Now one had fallen, and the other was trying desperately to carry on the struggle. The road ahead was full of obstacles; how could a woman do it all alone? Poor P'ing-mei!

The sadder I became the more my tears fell.

P'ing-mei sat up suddenly and asked me gently, "What's bothering you?"

I clasped her to my bosom, letting my hot tears wet her hair.

"Please don't feel so bad." P'ing-mei stroked my head and said even more gently, "It doesn't matter that I have to work hard. As soon as you get well, everything will be all right."

Beside us our two children lay sleeping, breathing evenly and peacefully, oblivious to what was going on.

The following day I would not let P'ing-mei go to haul lumber again. I promised her that we would find another alternative.

Later I found appropriate employment in town—writing advertisements for a movie theater. The work was light. I could finish it in two hours, and still have plenty of time left; it wouldn't interfere with my convalescence. Although the pay was low, with our thrifty lifestyle it was enough to make up the deficiencies in our income so that we could meet our living expenses. And P'ing-mei did not have to go out to work any more.

With this arrangement, I solved only half of the problem. The other half remained: my illness. I had to overcome it as soon as possible. Only then would I be able to face P'ing-mei, my beloved wife, without feeling apologetic!

LIN HAI-YIN (1919–)

Though a native of Taiwan, Lin Hai-yin was raised and educated in Peking, returning to her birthplace only when the Communists were about to take over mainland China. For this reason, as she notes in the biographical sketch for her Self Selections *(Lin Hai-yin tzu-hsüan-chi, Taipei, 1975), she is considered "more Pekingnese than the Pekingnese," both for her speech and for her manners. And perhaps it is for the same reason that her stories, when compared with her contemporary, Chung Li-ho, are less concerned with the vicissitudes of an island beset by social changes, if only because Taiwan in the early fifties was to her no less familiar a place than it was to the mainland refugees.*

However, the ironic perspective through which her "Lunar New Year's Feast" (included in this volume) is told can only be maintained by a native Taiwanese. Almost to a man, the emigré writers from the mainland were sincerely convinced that they would one day be able to end their exile in Taiwan and return to China. They were too involved to tell the difference between fond hopes and pipe dreams, which are the stuff Lin's present story is made of. An accomplished writer, Lin is also a noted editor, responsible for discovering such talents as Chung Li-ho, Huang Ch'un-ming, and other young writers to appear in the latter portions of this anthology. She has seven volumes of stories to her credit. Remembering South of the City *(Ch'eng-nan chiu-shih, Taipei, 1960) has just been made into a movie in mainland China.*

Lunar New Year's Feast

Translated by Hsin-sheng C. Kao

Going to Third Uncle Hsü's home to offer my New Year's greetings was a spiritual burden. But a rewarding duty of this sort indeed could not be passed on to anyone else. As my father-in-law on the Mainland constantly reminded us: we should pay frequent visits to Third Uncle Hsü's house, for after all, our two families have known each other for generations.

Arriving at the front gate and staring at the newly painted vermilion doorway, I could not help but feel a certain uneasiness: coming once a year like this to offer my businesslike New Year's greetings—what obvious hypocrisy! Worst of all, however, was my stubborn husband, putting

68

on airs of importance greater than those of an ex-governmental department head such as Hsü Yü-ju, whom we fondly called Third Uncle Hsü.
So, for the past two years I had had to go all by myself, and each time I
had no choice but to tell lies. Last year my excuse was this:

"Lao-liu[1] has had to go to the south on a business trip for a few days.
When he gets back, he'll call on you to offer his belated New Year's
greetings."

"No need for such a bother—you're too polite. Making a few more
business trips means making a few more extra dollars. Nowadays public
servants are really having a hard time. How are things? Everyone well?
Any letter from your father-in-law?"

Just listen to him, how solicitous he is about our family! Did he ever
treat us shabbily? Why was my husband always so unappreciative? In an
instant another year had gone by, and once again the same task fell upon
me. What kind of excuse could I possibly make up to make my story
sound convincing?

While I stood there, still hesitating, the vermilion door slowly opened
and a boisterous noise came from within, made by a group of New Year's
visitors taking their leave. From some distance I saw Third Uncle and
Aunt Hsü standing at the entryway, nodding and waving to the guests
outside. Then, just at that moment, a new group of visitors swarmed in
from behind me, and I merged in among them as they moved inside, took
off their shoes, proceeded to the living room, and made bows. I had
managed to squeeze myself in beside Third Aunt Hsü when she recognized me.

"Oh, it's you! Just you alone?" Having said so, she looked for my
husband among the guests, and I was forced to tell a lie again. Knitting
my brows, I said: "Two of our three children ate themselves sick, and Lao-
liu stayed home to take care of them, so I alone. . . ." I regretted the
words as soon as I said them. I could curse heaven and earth, but I should
never have told a lie at the expense of my three darling children! They are
as robust as cows.

"Really? Did you call a doctor? Why don't you take them to the Central
Clinic for an examination? The public hospitals aren't reliable. The few
extra dollars you'd spend would be worth it."

Hearing this, I felt uncomfortable, yet had to say yes. Today Third Aunt
Hsü was all done up quite prettily. The expression "yesterday better than
today, this year older than last" cannot be applied to her. For all appearances Third Aunt Hsü actually looked younger than last year—the nails
on her dainty fingers polished scarlet, holding a tall glass of tea under the
tip of her nose, her white face aglow from the piping hot steam—the very
picture of a lady of leisure sipping tea, as one would see in a traditional

Chinese painting! Who would be more fortunate than Third Aunt Hsü? Yet she complained all the time.

"Aiya! To tell you the truth, nothing here can compare to the Mainland! This atrocious weather, this Japanese house that makes you take off and put on your shoes time after time, and I come near to a fit every time the kids jump around on the tatami.[2] Say, why hasn't Miss Chang come to give me my injection today?"

"There, there, we still have hope of recovering the Mainland. I know you've suffered all these years here in Taiwan." Third Uncle Hsü came over to comfort his wife, and I hurriedly stood up, preparing to deal with the questions he was certain to ask. I really had no reason to feel annoyed by these people; everyone in the Hsü household treated us with such politeness and concern, even though there seemed to be a touch of pity in their politeness, a tinge of charity in their concern!

Third Aunt Hsü dragged me into her bedroom to join a group of women guests. At the same time, out in the living room there came another large group of visitors expressing salutations with folded hands. I heard a guest declaring:

"Congratulations, Chief! Congratulations!"

This caught me off guard. Was Third Uncle Hsü made some sort of a departmental head? He should have known that as a housewife I was very uninformed about almost everything. Why didn't he tell me about it beforehand? Now I had lost my opportunity to offer him my timely congratulations, and it made me feel so stupid. However, in that same instant of puzzlement, Third Uncle Hsü announced:

"Congratulations one and all! Now that Taiwan is no longer bound by neutrality,[3] a counterattack against the Mainland can be expected any day now!"

It was only then that I felt relieved. All they were offering their congratulations for was Taiwan's de-neutralization. And Third Uncle Hsü's former title as "Department Head" might be restored at any moment following the imminent counterattack against the Mainland. Although today Third Uncle Hsü still appeared to be living in comfortable retirement without an official position, the situation this year was certain to be totally different from before.

As evening lights went on, the Hsü household was packed with visitors. I wanted to get up and take my leave, but could not find the hostess. Coming and going should be done openly, I should not just sneak out. So I positioned myself among the guests quietly, and waited for Third Aunt Hsü to reappear. Yet somehow, without knowing it, I had followed the other guests and soon found myself seated at the banquet table. I sat there like a complete idiot, because I could not figure out why this New Year's at the Hsü household should be different from past years.

"A toast, Chief! Next year we won't be offering you our New Year's greetings in Taipei!"

"San-yeh,[4] our fellow countrymen on the Mainland are all depending on your comeback to free them from their misery! Here's to you!"

"Yü-lao,[5] on behalf of all the hometown boys now in Taiwan, here is a toast to you!"

And so, offering and receiving toasts, playing the finger-guessing game,[6] and urging his guests to have more food—such rounds of activities finally had Third Uncle Hsü reeling in drunkenness. Third Aunt Hsü's cheeks, too, became flushed. During the course of conversation, it became clear that Third Uncle Hsü was really readying himself to rise to the challenge of recovering the Mainland. One of the measures taken seemed to be the setting up of an organization of fellow citizens of his hometown. Even some kind of provincial government had been formed, and its "governor" appointed.[7] It was also mentioned that this time it would not be like what had happened in Chungking, when, not moving fast enough, they were a step behind and every piece of fat was snatched away by their light-footed colleagues.[8]

I overheard the lady sitting next to me saying:

"These years in Taiwan, I have had enough of housemaids' tantrums. After returning to Peking, the very first thing I'll do is to look for our old Mammy Chang from San-ho County!"

"When I return to Shanghai, I'll most certainly bring along our family tutor, Miss Liu, as well. How could our children manage without her?" So cut in a lady from Shanghai.

She then went on to say how she could leave six children at home while staying out all night to play mahjong without any worry, all because of Miss Liu, who acted as baby-sitter, housekeeper, and tutor, and recently even did the hepatine injections.

Someone asked about Miss Liu's monthly salary, and she held up two fingers, waving them: "This much."

"A good bargain indeed!" A matron stuck her tongue out: "Even our Ah-chiao asks for two hundred and forty!"

"That's why I'm certain to bring her back with us when we return to the Mainland. Really, she doesn't even have a temper."

Ah, everyone was waiting for the fight back to the Mainland. But who was going to fight? And they had all sorts of plans—such plans, indeed! I felt I was in a dream, as if I too was affected by this euphoria, my spirit drifting across the Taiwan Strait . . . to my younger sister left behind on the Mainland, my aged mother- and father-in-law, countless relatives, . . . I didn't even know whether it was joy or sorrow. Suddenly, in my dreamy state, those delicate ruby-ringed fingers that held a glass of amber-colored wine were claiming my attention again:

"You should drink up, too, young lady. After our successful counterattack against the Mainland, we'll all have lots of clout. Your husband, Lao-liu, will at least get a position as the head of the tax office! You won't be as hard up as now. The few people here in Taiwan won't even be enough to fill all the fat positions on the Mainland!"

I raised my glass and suddenly found myself thinking of what had passed through my ears a while ago: governorship by volitive Mammy Chang from San-ho County . . . the family tutor brought straight home. And now, Third Aunt Hsü was talking of an assignment for my husband as tax office head! Anyway, I was grateful for Third Aunt Hsü's good intentions. I lifted my head and gulped down the wine at once. I felt suffocated inside.

Taking my leave, I walked down dark deserted lanes, my rainshoes splish-splashing on the soft mud. The sound was not pleasing, yet it was quite rhythmic. I was in a hurry to get home, but I had lost the way. My mind was given over now to Mammy Chang, now to the tax office head appointment, now to the Hsü household. Heaven and earth seemed topsy-turvy. I couldn't tell east from west.

It was drizzling. I touched my hair and found it was wet. I sneezed. My chest felt all stopped up, as if all sorts of grievances wanted to burst out from my throat.

I hurried on, until I was beneath a dark yellowish street light to the end of the short lane. I leaned on the lamp pole and used all my strength to press down upon my stomach. Unable to hold it any longer, I bent over toward the stinking gutter and started throwing up. The filth in my chest was finally washed away with the water of the stinking gutter. My thanks to Taipei's open sewers that function so marvelously! It was when I straightened my back up and breathed in some cool air that I understood the true meaning of "the pleasure of getting something off one's chest."

Then, completely sobered, I was able to see my way home. Third Uncle Hsü's Lunar New Year's feast had almost put me in a state of total confusion.

NOTES

1. "Lao-liu" is literally "Old Sixth." It is an informal way of referring to either the sixth son or daughter in the family. Here it is used as a proper name in reference to the narrator's husband, who is apparently number six of the siblings.

2. Straw matting used as a floor covering in a Japanese-style house.

3. Immediately after the outbreak of the Korean War, President Truman neutralized the Taiwan Strait (June 27, 1950) in order to prevent a takeover by Communist China while at the same time restraining the Nationalist Government on Taiwan from taking military action against the Mainland.

4. Literally, "Third Master." Here it is used as a respectful form of address.

5. Literally, "Venerable Yü." Here it is used as a proper name.

6. A popular game among drinkers at a dinner table. Penalty for the loser: yet another cup of wine.

7. It was not uncommon for refugees from the Mainland during the fifties to set up their regional political organizations in anticipation of the "eventual recovery of the Mainland." Thus, if a group of "hometown boys" from Kwangtung Province got together, they would select their "governor" and other positions from among their cronies as if the whole Kwangtung Province would fall under their control as soon as the counterattack was launched.

8. Chungking was the provisional capital of China during the Second World War (1937–1945). It was reported that as soon as the war was over, there had been rapacious Kuomintang high-ranking officials who raced each other to former Japanese-occupied areas and appropriated for themselves whatever properties and valuables they could lay their hands on.

CHENG CH'ING-WEN (1932–)

Cheng Ch'ing-wen received his degree in business administration from National Taiwan University in 1958. In the same year his first story, "Lonely Heart" (Chi-mo ti hsin), was accepted by Lin Hai-yin for publication in United Daily *(Lien-ho Pao). Since then he has led a remarkable dual career as writer and administrator at Taipei's Hua Nan Commercial Bank. He was educated in the Japanese system until after the war, when he, like his contemporaries, was reoriented in Chinese education. His study of Japanese has enabled him to render valuable service in translation. Thanks to his efforts, a number of early Taiwan writers who wrote in Japanese are now available in Chinese. A conscientious writer who makes it an article of faith not to employ uncommon diction in his narrative, Cheng Ch'ing-wen reveals, through stylistic simplicity, his abhorence for pomp and artificiality. In this respect, "Betel Palm Village" can at once be read as a "period piece" demonstrating the tremendous changes that have occurred in rural Taiwan since Chung Li-ho's days, and an affirmation of rustic virtues over urban values resulting from industrialization. His stories are collected in* The Coconut Trees on Campus *(Hsiao-yüan li ti yeh-tzu-shu, Taipei, 1970), in* Modern Heroes *(Hsien-tai ying-hsiung, Taipei, 1976), and in* Self Selections *(Cheng Ch'ing-wen tzu-hsüan-chi, Taipei, 1976). The present selection was published in* United Daily, *July 31, 1979.*

Betel Palm Village

Translated by Charles Hartman

Some students had left for home on afternoon and evening trains after the commencement yesterday morning. Others were getting ready to leave this morning. Only a few were still in Taichung.

Hung Yüeh-hua went into the business district of the city to buy some souvenirs for her parents before leaving for home. She had spent four years studying in Taichung, and now, as she walked through the streets, she saw many familiar spots—the park, the library, the cinemas, the small restaurants—and suddenly realized that she would probably not often have a chance to see them again in the days ahead. So when she passed a

74

place she knew well, she could not resist the impulse to take a longer look.

She thought of her classmates, how she had often passed by these places with them before. Mostly they had been girls, but sometimes a few boys had come along too. But there was one boy, and only one, who had never gone out with his classmates. He was Ch'en Hsi-lin.

He had not come to commencement yesterday, nor had he come to sign yearbooks or to say good-byes.

Why had he not come? What was more important than yesterday, the end of four years of student life? No one had seen him since his last examination. Could he be sick? But then she remembered his strong, dark body and couldn't put it together with his being sick.

At school he was different and almost never socialized with the other students. But he worked hard, and his grades were very good. She had only spoken with him once, last year when they were together in the same farm intern group. They talked a lot then, but after that one time he became a stranger again. She really could not understand him—but then she never thought she would want to understand him, either.

So why did she suddenly think of him again today? Was it because he did not attend commencement?

She reached the train station and looked at the times for the trains back to Taipei and then looked at the southbound schedule. Perhaps she should go see him. She bought a ticket on the southbound local, then suddenly asked herself why and hesitated a moment, but the ticket was already bought.

The train was about half an hour late, and after an hour's ride, when she arrived at the small station it was already past one in the afternoon. Few passengers were there, to get on or off the train. The sun was blinding.

Although she had never been here before, the name of this small station had remained in her mind for over two years. She and her classmates had been returning from a trip south during the winter vacation of their sophomore year. She was sitting by the window and looking out to the west, where she saw a large red ball sinking below the horizon.

"How gorgeous!" she and her friends exclaimed in unison.

The train was passing through a large field, and she had seen a square farmstead, ringed by tall betel palms and crowned by the beautiful setting sun. "Betel Palm Village"—a beautiful name—flashed into her mind and was linked together with the beautiful sunset.

But Betel Palm Village was quickly left behind, and the sun dropped below the horizon. The sky had been fire red, and she had looked at her watch: 5:35.

She closed her eyes, recalling that beautiful scene. Then the train began to slow to a stop. The conductress announced the name of the stop over the intercom and said there would be a slight wait to allow another train to pass by. She opened her eyes and fixed the name of the stop in her mind.

· As she was leaving the station, the ticket collector raised his head and glanced at her. Nothing like this would ever happen in cities like Taipei and Taichung. She felt that everyone was looking at her, especially the girls. Was her skirt too short? Her heels too high? She suddenly felt herself blushing.

Betel Palm Village—how to get to the place she had seen two years ago from the train window? She knew Ch'en Hsi-lin lived there. He had told her so last year during their farm internship when he had talked to her about the problems of growing betel nuts.

"'Betel Palm Village'," he mused. "What a gorgeous name! Just like a rural watercolor scene. But actually . . . Well, I hope you have a chance to come and see for yourself."

"Is it really all right for me to come?"

"Why not?"

But he never actually invited her, and, after that time, he had never even spoken to her again.

During second semester she had time for more electives and took easy courses. But he still took a heavy load, so they seldom had a chance to meet. When they did by chance run into each other, he seemed to avoid her intentionally. Soon final exams were over, and everybody graduated. But he did not even come to commencement. Was it possible he had already forgotten he had invited her to have a look at his Betel Palm Village?

But she had not forgotten. Now her problem was how to get there. The direction she knew. Just follow the train tracks south. But judging from the speed of the train that day, the distance must be at least two or three miles. And she had not asked Ch'en Hsi-lin how to get there or what bus to take.

She left the station. Out front were two rows of grocery stands, with fruit, fish, and meat, and six or seven snack vendors. The narrow streets and walls all seemed covered with the black ash color distinctive of the region.

Even though it was well over lunch time, there were still a few customers at the small eateries, and she could hear the sounds of cooking and see the woks still steaming. She also saw a stand with sweet things like peanut soup, red bean soup, and rice cakes. A narrow-lipped teapot whistled unceasingly. She saw some cakes and fritters in a small glass case and two or three customers eating with lowered heads.

Then she remembered she had had nothing for lunch. Boarding the train on the spur of the moment, she had forgotten to eat. She saw a jar of mien-tsa[1] and remembered how as a child she would eat it at the small stand in front of the temple when she visited her grandmother in the countryside. But after her grandmother passed away, she did not often visit her mother's family, and even less often did she see mien-tsa.

She ordered a bowl, surprised that she had found mien-tsa in a place like this.

The proprietess of the stand, a short, squat woman in her fifties, scooped some mien-tsa powder into a bowl, skillfully scraping the back of the soup spoon on the lip and pouring in hot water from the kettle. The powder bubbled, and she stirred it with the soup spoon.

"Excuse me," Hung Yüeh-hua said. "Along the railroad tracks there is a family that raises betel nut. Could you tell me how to get there?"

"Which family?"

"They have a boy who went to college in Taichung."

"You mean Ch'en Hsi-lin?" a man sitting down across from her asked. He was eating peanut soup and fritters.

"You know him?"

"He's our agricultural expert around here. If there's a question about seeds or fertilizer or anything, we ask him."

"How can I get there?"

"I'll take you there on the motorcycle, if you want to go."

"But isn't there a bus or a taxi?"

"Sure, but they're inconvenient. The buses don't run very often, and when you get off, you've still got to walk quite a way, and you might get lost. It's better I take you."

"But I couldn't!"

"Why not? You know, whenever I meet city folks, I get the feeling they don't trust people."

"But I. . . ." She felt a bit embarrassed.

"Are you a classmate of his?"

"Yes."

"I have to go next door to pick up a few things I bought. Wait here a moment."

The man was also named Ch'en. They rode the motorcycle along a small path through the fields. On both sides of the path the fields consisted of black soil, now mostly turned over in preparation for planting the second crop.

The scorching sun was directly overhead. In about ten minutes they were at Ch'en Hsi-lin's house, and indeed it was the Betel Palm Village she had seen from the train. But it seemed a little smaller than she had imagined.

She stood in the entrance and, looking east, could see the train bed stretching far away into the distance.

The man who had brought her turned out to be a distant cousin of Ch'en Hsi-lin. The house was red brick and looked already very old. In front was a cement courtyard for drying grain, where chickens and ducks were running back and forth, shitting at random. The house was surrounded on all four sides by two rows of betel palms. Most were as tall as the house, but a few were shorter and looked as though they had been planted later. Some of the trees were in bloom; others were already bearing fruit. Ch'en Hsi-lin had told her that betel palms, in addition to being able to replace bamboo as fences, also had a greater economic value than bamboo.

Ch'en Hsi-lin was not at home. His mother came out, said he was working in the fields, and told his cousin to go call him back. But Hung Yüeh-hua wanted to go see him in the field, which was behind the house and faced the railroad tracks, probably west.

The sun shone fiercely. She went behind the house, and all she saw was a paddy field. Some areas were already filled with water and, reflecting the sky, looked like a vast mirror. Far away she could see several shadows moving back and forth in the muddy field. They seemed to be chasing something with steps now large, now small. The scene seemed almost comical. There were several women wearing bamboo hats with colorful pieces of cloth attached to protect their faces from the sun. But judging from their figures—their faces were hard to see—one of them was rather young. "Who could she be?" Hung Yüeh-hua asked herself. But almost immediately she checked herself and blushed. Why was she thinking about something like that? It was none of her business.

The path through the field was only a foot wide, and, when she walked, her heel would sometimes sink down into the ground so that she had to be careful not to fall down.

As she approached the workers, she saw Ch'en Hsi-lin. He wasn't sick at all. She saw him stop and turn his head to look at her. He looked surprised for a moment, then taking the nearest path he walked toward her. He wore a short-sleeved shirt, but she could still see his broad shoulders and large biceps. He looked much darker than he had in school. His legs looked like he was wearing boots, the mud almost up to his knees. His body also showed traces of mud.

"I never expected . . .," he said, taking off his bamboo hat.

"What are you doing?"

"Stomping in the stalks."

"Stomping in the stalks?"

"Haven't you ever seen it done? You stomp the rice stalks into the mud so they will decay faster. Since the time between the first and second crop is so short, we have to stomp the old stalks into the ground."

"I never knew anything about it."

"That's not surprising. They don't tell you about such things in the classroom or during the farm intern period."

"Why didn't you come to graduation yesterday?"

"We're too busy here. Right now everybody is hurrying to transplant the rice seedlings."

"Am I interrupting you then?"

"Of course not."

"Can I try?"

"It's hard work."

"But I just want to give it a try."

"Aren't you afraid of getting your clothes dirty?"

"That's all right," she said in a mild tone of embarrassment.

"You should wear a straw hat; the sun is very strong," he said, giving her his own hat.

"What about you?"

"I've got this one," he said pulling a cap from his pants pocket. "I'll get you a bamboo pole for a staff."

"But you're not using them."

"We're farmers."

"But I studied agriculture too, and even though I graduated yesterday, I'll just consider this as a little make-up work," she joked.

It is true: she had studied agriculture. But she and Ch'en Hsi-lin were completely different. She had been assigned to the agriculture department as a result of the college entrance exams—she did not score high enough to enter the college of her first choice—while Ch'en Hsi-lin had come to the department eagerly and on his own, hoping to learn something that would help him improve his crop yields.

Hung Yüeh-hua took off her shoes and socks. Even though her skirt didn't reach her knees, she carefully lifted it up a little and cautiously stepped into the paddy.

Ch'en Hsi-lin introduced her to the others working there. The young girl was his sister, Yü-lan, a student at a teachers college in central Taiwan. The other woman was his sister-in-law.

When she stepped into the paddy, she felt as though her whole body was sinking in. She felt insecure. The muddy ground seemed to be pulling her down, and she rapidly sunk in up to her knees. She quickly pulled her skirt up, revealing her white thighs. She blushed again.

She watched the others stomp. Ch'en Hsi-lin was beside her. He and the girls were stomping quickly and accurately. He wanted to give her a bamboo pole but she said no. She saw a clump of stalks in front of her and was about to stomp them down, but her feet seemed embedded in the mud and she could not pull them out. She pulled with all her strength. Her foot came out, but she almost fell down. Ch'en Hsi-lin gave her the pole and insisted she use it.

She stomped slowly. It was her first time in a rice paddy. As she was putting her foot down, her body was unsteady. When she was stable again, she was in mud up to her calves and felt as though she had suddenly become shorter.

The freshly ploughed mud was strewn with clumps of old rice stalks. Some were pointing straight up, others were at an angle, and others were under the water. Since the rice had just been harvested, the ends of the cut stems were still sharp. She smelled an odor, which, although she had never smelled it before and had no way to describe it, she knew was the smell of the soil.

She tried to stomp the stalks down properly, but sometimes she stepped off to the side, and half a clump would remain, so she would have to pull her leg out and stomp again. Sometimes if the stems pointed upward or were buried unseen under the mud, they pierced the soles of her feet when she stepped down. At times the pain was too much and caused her to wince and bend forward slightly. Sometimes the mud was sticky, which made it impossible for her to pull her feet easily. At other times it was slimy, as if there were mud fish slithering around. And sometimes it spit out from around her calves and soiled her skirt and her thighs. She stomped very carefully, afraid of falling down.

The area that Ch'en Hsi-lin did was much wider than hers, which was only a narrow strip, and crooked at that.

Every time she stomped down, the mud oozed up and separated her toes. She noticed that Ch'en Hsi-lin's toes were also spread apart, and that his arches looked wide and thick. She suddenly thought it strange that he could fit such feet into his boots.

A little after three o'clock they stopped for a snack of sweet potatoes in gruel, with fermented black beans and minced pickled turnips. They rinsed off their hands and feet and ate standing on the path. Ch'en Hsi-lin's sister Yü-lan asked Hung Yüeh-hua a few questions about the city and kept admiring her skin. Hung Yüeh-hua had never eaten such food before, but decided it tasted better than anything else, especially the yellow sweet potatoes in the gruel.

The rest was very short—just the time they took to eat. Hung Yüeh-hua looked down at her feet, which were still covered with a little mud that had dried in some places and felt congealed and caked. Most of the polish on her toenails was gone, and dirt was stuffed under the nails in a round curve like a crescent moon. Her arms were red and felt burned.

When the meal was finished, they began to work again. Ch'en Hsi-lin wanted her to take a rest, but she insisted on joining them.

The sun was still very hot, and the sweat poured unceasingly from her forehead and stung her eyes. She was thirsty; her throat was dry. Her back was wet with perspiration. Her steps became slower, and she had trouble straightening her back. She felt like she had never perspired so much in her life.

Her stomping gradually got slower and the steps smaller, so that Ch'en Hsi-lin had to do even more to allow them to maintain the even progress of the work. Sometimes she missed a clump or did not stomp it completely under, so Ch'en Hsi-lin came back to stomp it again.

"I'm glad you came to see me," he said.

"Eh . . ." she replied, her face blushing again as the sweat seemed to pour forth even faster.

"Actually, I wish our other classmates had come along too."

"They all went home."

"What are your plans from here on? Travel? Marriage? Work?"

"My father has already found me a job."

"Doing what?"

"A trading company."

"Trading company?"

"Exporting handicrafts. It's only temporary. I just can't find anything that suits me better right now."

"It sounds all right to me. But, you know, I've often thought recently that many people who want to study things like agriculture can't get the chance, while others who don't want to or don't have to study such things crowd in and take up the limited number of places in the universities," he said.

"I've had the same thought sometimes, especially recently, just before graduation, when I had so much trouble finding a job. I understand what you mean. In fact, sometimes I think I made a mistake."

"But it's certainly not your fault. Of course, anybody can study anything he likes. It's just that there are some who really want to study something and never get the chance. Take me, for instance. I took the college entrance exams three times before I got in, while you others were assigned to the agricultural department because you didn't do well enough to be admitted to the department of your choice. You didn't really want to study agriculture. You remember the first time we went to school farm? You all thought you were going on a picnic, breaking up into little groups to chat—some even brought cassette players along so they could listen to music while they watched the hired hands work," he said.

"But we had farmers in our department too—like you. And some of them did very well and want to go on to the experimental station or to grad school."

"Very few. Very few. The vast majority will do something else after graduation. It's not only a loss for them, it's a loss for society as a whole."

"But what can be done about it? I studied hard back then. Everybody wants to do as well as he can on the entrance exams. Everybody feels it's better to study something than not to study at all."

Ch'en Hsi-lin listened and then was silent. After a while he said: "I'm sorry. I shouldn't have mentioned those things to you."

Hung Yüeh-hua was about to speak, but she swallowed her words. She felt bad and blushed once again. Her head dropped down, her steps became heavier, her waist became sorer and weaker. She seemed stuck fast in the mud, with no way to pull herself out. She tried hard to straighten her back, looking at a clump of stalks a few feet away. With all her strength she pulled on her foot. It came out, but her body swayed. She tried to regain her balance, but her body tottered even further and she fell over backwards into the mud.

She fought to get up, but the ground was too soft, and she sank in deeper. She tried to push herself up with her hand, but it only sank down into the mud. Her other hand clutched the bamboo pole, which now only flailed back and forth in the empty air.

"Are you all right?"

Ch'en Hsi-lin raced toward her in big steps and pulled her up. Her arms and skirt were solid mud.

"I really shouldn't have said those things," he said, helping her to the path. "I'll have Yü-lan take you back so you can change clothes."

"I'm sorry. I've held up your work."

Yü-lan heated some water for Hung Yüeh-hua to bathe with. The house had no bathroom. The washing-up place was in a corner of the kitchen, and there was no curtain. It was still broad daylight, and she hesitated a moment.

"It's all right. We all wash up like this. I'll watch out for you," Yü-lan said, sitting down by the door.

The kitchen had only one small window, from which she could see several green shadows swaying back and forth outside. They were probably the leaves of the betel palms.

Yü-lan gave her some of her own clothes to put on and washed the dirty ones. Yü-lan was not as tall as Hung Yüeh-hua was but was a little heavier, so Hung Yüeh-hua was able to fit into her clothes. The clothes had a yellowish tint and an alkaline odor, but she didn't know whether it was the nature of the cloth or the water the clothes were washed in that was the cause. When she put them on, she had a strange feeling, as though something was crawling on her, especially on her neck, shoulders, and arms. Perhaps she had caught too much sun; indeed, these areas were all red.

She washed the mud off her lower legs, revealing white skin once again, but she still could not wash the mud from under her toenails. She discovered many red lines where the rice stems had scratched her legs. They itched.

"I like you a lot," Yü-lan suddenly said.

"Please excuse me. My coming here has just caused you trouble."

"Not at all. You're the first of my brother's classmates to visit us. He's certainly very happy. We all hope you can come again."

"I'll be going back to Taipei today. I really don't know when I'll be able to come again. But I'll never forget what's happened today."

Yü-lan showed Hung Yüeh-hua around the house and told her that ten years ago when Yü-lan's brother had just started agricultural high school he had urged their father to replant the betel palms as a replacement for the original bamboo fence around the house. The father had strongly opposed the idea, but her brother had so many good reasons that her father was finally convinced.

An hour or so later, Ch'en Hsi-lin and the others returned. They had finished stomping the rice stalks into the ground.

Hung Yüeh-hua wanted to hurry back to Taipei at once, but Ch'en Hsi-lin, Yü-lan, and the others pressed her to stay for dinner. His mother had already killed a chicken she had raised herself and cut off an entire leg for her. It was a country custom to keep the legs for the children to eat, so Hung Yüeh-hua felt herself blushing once again.

She was too embarrassed to eat, but then it would be rude not to eat. She looked at the chicken leg in her bowl and picked at the rice around it with her chopsticks. But Ch'en Hsi-lin's mother insisted she eat, talking unceasingly about how country chickens were certainly better tasting than city chickens. She then took the chicken leg, dipped it in soy sauce, and returned it to Hung Yüeh-hua's bowl, threatening to force-feed it to her if she did not eat.

Ch'en Hsi-lin's mother was about sixty. She was short, but her movements were still energetic, and she was still strong. Hung Yüeh-hua had seen her lift a large wooden bucket of slop for the pigs with one hand.

Hung Yüeh-hua picked lightly at the chicken leg with her chopsticks, then pulled off the skin with her fingers and placed it on the table. She had never eaten chicken skin. When Ch'en Hsi-lin saw this, he reached over with his chopsticks, grabbed up the skin, and nonchalantly plopped it into his own mouth. She blushed again.

After dinner, Ch'en Hsi-lin asked her to come out by the railroad tracks for a look at the sunset.

"That's all right."

"But since you're here, you might as well have another look."

"I'd like to go back," she replied.

"Then I'll take you to the station on the motorcycle."

The sun had just set, and the western sky was a single patch of fire red. Countryside sunsets were gorgeous.

The motorcycle sped quickly between the fields where the water reflected the color of the sky. Hung Yüeh-hua held tight with both hands to the strap on the seat. Her head was against Ch'en Hsi-lin's back. The cycle was going very fast, and the wind was strong. Should she inch closer? She blushed again at the thought.

The wind rushed past, and her hair was flying about when suddenly something blew into her eye. She blinked repeatedly, but it was still embedded in her eye, which began to water in a steady stream. She didn't dare release her grip on the strap and could only lower her head and rub it against her shoulder. But the more she rubbed it, the more her eye hurt. She thought of asking him to stop, but knew they would reach the station in a few minutes. Perhaps she could hold out for a while.

By the time they reached the station, she could not open her eye, and her face was covered with tears.

"What's the matter?" he asked.

"I think I've got something in my eye," she answered in a nasal tone, the tears having already gotten into her nose.

"Let me have a look," he said and opened her eyelid with his fingers.

"It's a mosquito."

"Very big?"

"No, just a small one. Hold still," he said, moving his lips in close and blowing hard, then opening the eyelid with his fingers again.

"Better now?"

"A little," she replied, blinking her eyes and wiping her cheeks with the back of her hand. "I've really caused you a lot of trouble today."

"Why do you keep saying that? I'm glad. I really never expected. . . . I'm really glad I saw you again."

"I'll think of you when I pass by here on the train again."

"And when I see the train passing by, I'll think perhaps you're on it, expecially if the sun is just about to set behind the mountains."

NOTE

1. Spicy roasted flour served in hot water with sugar.

LI CH'IAO

(1934–   )

Li Ch'iao (pen name of Li Ch'i) has been in poor health since childhood. In the autobiographical sketch provided for his Self Selections *(Li Ch'iao tzu-hsüan-chi, Taipei, 1974), he mentioned that when he was seven he was attacked by malaria for a period of one year. This narrow brush with death convinced him of the precariousness of human existence, paving the way for his immersion in Buddhism later. "After I have studied Buddhism for some years," he writes in the short preface to* Self Selections: *"I have found that many phenomena of life, be it social, natural, or scientific, can be explained, within the limit of my understanding, in terms of Buddhism." "The Spheric Man," though strikingly similar to Kafka's "Metamorphosis" in its evocation of unintelligible horror, is an effort to explain the absurdities of life in the Buddhist scheme of existence. Summing up his life at forty in 1974, Li Ch'iao confides to us that he will spend the rest of his days in "teaching, writing, and cultivating mountain orchids. [Of course] I will continue to read the Buddhist scriptures and retain my habits as a vegetarian." A prolific writer since 1962, he recently crowned his achievement with a trilogy of epic proportions chronicling the fortunes of the island from the early Chinese settlement up to near the end of the Second World War. This trilogy consists of three novels totaling about one million words:* Cold Nights *(Han-yeh),* The Deserted Village *(Huang-ts'un), and* Lone Light *(Ku-teng), all published by Taipei's Yüan-ching Press from 1979 to 1980.*

The Spheric Man

Translated by Marston Anderson

Chin Chih-sheng had stayed in bed for two days. No one had ever seen or heard of a strange illness like his. Even that learned authority on internal medicine, Dr. Liu, just knitted his brow.

Two days ago the weather had suddenly turned cold. As the dim morning sky lightened, Chin Chih-sheng's bladder burned unbearably with the night's accumulation of urine, but he couldn't shake off his drowsiness. Reluctant to open his eyes, he fumbled his way to the toilet. This was a happy, beautiful moment. He quickly undid his buttons—

85

Suddenly a hot, wet sensation passed down his leg. He opened his eyes. His mouth gaped. He was still snug in his blanket! To think that a full-grown man could wet his bed! But with his shame was mixed a secret pleasure, the kind of satisfaction a child feels after playing pranks or raising hell.

As he came out of the toilet, the clock on the wall read half past six. His four children and wife were already up. Seeing that his wife hadn't noticed him, he slipped quickly into the bedroom and thrust himself under the covers.

"About one hour left, you hear? Slouch!" His wife's voice was penetrating, even at a distance, but once he determined that at least she wasn't standing at the head of the bed grinding her teeth with her arms akimbo, he could afford to ignore her. He decided to sleep another thirty minutes—no, fifty minutes; if he rose at 7:20 or a little later, he could still make it. What's a few more minutes anyway, he thought.

He carefully tried to nurse what was left of his drowsiness, but his pants leg was icy cold, raising goosebumps all up his calf and thigh, even as far as his waist. He couldn't sleep, but he really wasn't willing to get up. He let his thoughts wander idly; that was always more pleasant than climbing out of bed.

His wife was grumbling again, this time close to his ear. This was still nothing to get anxious about, since he had long ago cultivated a special skill: to his wife's prattle, his colleague's stares, his boss's roars, he could "listen" attentively for a long time without letting his nerve centers impart any meaning to the sound waves they received. To use psychiatric jargon, he had a sensory but not a cognitive recognition of them: he merely heard a roaring sound, what might be called "cacophony."

Evidently his wife was letting loose with her ineffectual tongue as usual. Now he heard the sound of cloth rubbing against cloth. It was his wife taking off her ragged pajamas and dressing for work. Suddenly a disturbing image appeared, as if projected on a screen: the skimpy bra, the swollen breasts, the plump round buttocks, which had not been affected by the poor quality of the food the family ate.

"Mei-chi, I've failed you in every way!" This familiar, repulsive phrase bored its way out from his heart's core. "Good-for-nothing!" He borrowed his wife's expression to chastise himself.

After scolding himself coldly this way, he immediately offered himself some sympathetic consolation. "Chin Chih-sheng, you're a good man, a sincere good man. You've been wronged! You deserve to see better days. Don't worry, though, with any luck they're coming soon. But you're too weak. Height, 170 centimeters; weight, 50 kilograms; blood pressure, 99 over 60, too low; you're anemic." Brooding, he fondly stroked his own lean cheeks, then smiled dejectedly.

His body was curled up in a ball under the covers. He now arched his back even further and drew in his neck, burying his head in his breast. He hugged his folded legs tightly and let his palms touch his rump, making an almost perfect sphere. This was a habit he had formed long ago—he didn't remember when. This position, or rather the stimulation this position gave to his joints and muscles, produced in him an indescribable joy.

There was, of course, another secret known to no one: he felt most protected and secure when he chose to sleep in this position. It gave his partner in bed no point of attack from any direction.

The room was quiet and lonely now; his wife and four children had left. The clock had long ago struck 7:30. He knew the moment had arrived. He drew a deep breath, and pushed himself out of the blanket.

But for some reason his whole body maintained its position, and to his surprise his limbs were heavy and intractable. This was a very uncomfortable sensation.

"Is it my anemia that made my arms and legs numb?" he thought, feeling a wave of pity for them.

Finally he managed to get out of bed, but his limbs were still stiff, and if he did not stay fully alert, they seemed to contract. If he didn't get on his way soon, he would have to ask for the day off, which was a frightening thing, since the procedure demanded close contact with the boss. He would have to drag his immovable frame in to pay homage to the boss's oily pink mug.

At 8:01, after signing in, he sat in his place and arranged the official documents on his desk. Then he went to the lavatory. This was another habit of long standing. Every morning, as he looked over the documents with their dense web of numerals, he felt a sinking in his bowels and his rectum dilated. It didn't matter if he'd already relieved himself, or skipped breakfast, like today.

He liked to squat on the toilet and let his mind wander. This was especially true when he was squatting on the tiny old-fashioned toilet at home. With the door shut, it was so dark he couldn't see his own hands. He could make faces or quietly curse his enemies, with no chance of being found out. But the ten dollars it cost to have the sewage dredged each month was really too exorbitant, and if his wife were to clean it out he'd have to help out too. His pleasure was dampened by this thought.

The company lavatory, though it was bright and spacious, was vaguely oppressive. He felt alone and vulnerable, but so long as the doors and windows were locked up tight, he would be secure and fearless again.

"I am the greatest man in the world!" He said in a voice loud enough for himself to hear. And with the index finger of his right hand he wrote it out carefully on the white tiles, again and again.

This singular habit—that whenever he entered the lavatory he would unconsciously recite this sentence several times in a whisper—had originated in high school. He had been a rather prominent student, exceptional in class and a marvel on the exercise field. He was a member of the school's volleyball and table tennis teams and, from his junior year, captain in charge of raising and lowering the flag.

Then an unfortunate incident occurred during the first term of his senior year. It was the day of the twentieth anniversary of the school's founding, to be celebrated with a martial review and various drills. As captain, after reporting the number of students to the principal, he called out, "Let the review commence!" Just as he drew his breath to yell out the command, something gave at his waist, and a chill ran down his legs—his belt had burst and his trousers slid down, revealing his white thighs!

He froze, as ripples of uncontrolled laughter arose. He yanked up his trousers furiously and fled through a gap in the ranks. Suddenly the sharp burning sound of laughter exploded. He hid in the lavatory, his whole body trembling and soaked in a cold sweat. Then his tears poured out.

"No, no, it isn't true! It must be a ghastly nightmare!" This pleading cry rose from his heart.

"I'm a good student, a remarkable athlete!" He comforted himself. "Someday I'll be the greatest man in the world!"

This was a crippling assault on his psyche. Since that time, he had become quiet and reserved, and he walked with his head down, not daring to look others straight in the eye. Painfully shy, like a young girl, he would blush bright red if anyone looked at him.

From that time on, he would repeat this sentence every time he entered the toilet: "I am the greatest man in the world." Since the day he noticed this inexplicable habit, he had resolved many times to break it. But after several attempts to suppress it, he found the habit had a force of its own, pressuring him harder and harder until he was no longer able to contain it, and he had to blurt the sentence out. Later he realized this sentence was like a sedative or a wonder drug to relieve his heart of its nameless anxiety. He had only to say it softly in the restroom, and both body and mind would relax, refreshed. It was a wonderful feeling, like that of a badly constipated man after a good shit.

Because of his family's poverty, he couldn't continue his education. One after another, his hopes had been dashed. By the time he had married and become a father, he had also withdrawn from his idealism, and gradually grown old. The only two treasured means of relaxation for him were to drink a cup or two of wine behind his wife's back, and to hide in the toilet and repeat this sentence.

Today he felt very uneasy. Random thoughts flickered uncontrollably in his mind, making him miscopy three numbers in succession. He longed to chat with someone, or idly hum a few notes. But his supervisor was sitting right behind him, and to his right was the self-important section chief Wang, whose mouth seemed to be permanently sealed by adhesive cement. On his right was Miss Yang: whenever you lifted your head by accident and caught her glance, she would purse her lips, wrinkle her nose, and roll her eyes, as though you were making a pass for her tender young flesh! That youngster opposite him was the most hateful of all. When they had first met during summer break this year, he had grabbed Chih-sheng's palm and nearly broken his hand off shaking it: "I'm a graduate of the Foreign Language Department of National X and Y University. How about you, Venerable One?"[1] Pshaw! Damn the smartass! A Venerable One at 42? I'm a graduate of a private high school, how's that? He ground his teeth and swallowed hard.

"It's a lonely world! A desert!" He cried out to himself, and miscopied a "7" as a "9" again.

Work let out at 5:30. He left the office as quickly as possible, but didn't rush home. After work he usually paged through books at the stalls by the post office, then pored over the advertisements and preview posters at a couple of movie theaters. If he went home too early, he would be the one to cook dinner.

The clocks in the watchmaker's shop already pointed to past six before he decided on a direction, lowered his head, and directed his steps homeward. Walking with his head down was also a kind of pleasure: for one thing, as long as you avoided the busier thoroughfares, cars would yield to you if you walked slowly, head lowered; for another, it meant you didn't have to bow and scrape publicly before Foreman Puss and Chairman Cur; third, you saw no one and could pursue your own thoughts at will, as in the toilet.

This was a broad, smooth asphalt road. The vehicles in the fast lanes tangled chaotically, like ants running from a destroyed anthill. Motorbikes brushed past him, letting out a string of farts. Several times the streamers on the handlebars of these hell-on-wheels brushed against his earlobes. He lost his temper and yelled out at the top of his voice, "Hey! Damn you!"

Annoyed, he kicked an egg-sized stone with his right foot. The stone egg rolled a considerable distance before stopping, only to be kicked again by his left foot. As he conveyed this amusing stone egg along the road with him, a rare smile broke through at the corner of his mouth. This stone made him think of his boss, whom they all called "Rotten Egg" behind his back. He remembered "Rotten Egg" chewing out that youngster opposite him this afternoon:

"Idiot! To think you went to college! I'm warning you: make that mistake again, and you're finished! Now out of my sight! Get rolling!"

"Yes sir, Mr. President. Please forgive me this time . . ." The youngster stifled a sob in his throat.

"Out of my sight! Get rolling! The farther from my sight the better!" Rotten Egg slammed his fist on the desk.

Everyone in the office held their breath as this "sound effect" emerged from inside the boss's room. When the youngster came out like a whipped puppy, Chin Chih-sheng kept his head lowered as though hypnotized, not daring to look at him. But in his heart he was screaming, "Serves you right!"

Rotten Egg liked to point at the noses of his subordinates and scream, "Out of my sight!" Then after three seconds or so he would add the words, "Get rolling!"

Of course Chih-sheng had had his share of this kind of scolding. At first he had been really upset and considered quitting in a huff, but when he thought of the uncertain future ahead, and envisioned his wife's expression and his children's faces, he had to close his eyes tight and swallow it. Later, as he grew accustomed to the scoldings, he became insensitive to them, and even a bit amused by them. He had once gone as far as to make a record of the scoldings he had received on a calendar he kept under the glass on his office desk—each time he was reprimanded, he would make a mark. A half year later he had accumulated more than fifty marks.

Now he kicked the stone egg so that it went rolling to a distance; the rock was still controlled by his feet. As he kicked it, he imagined the pleasure of rolling. Rolling was truly a marvelous manner of traveling! Fleet as a deer dashing through the forest at night, to roll forward and back, from quiescence to movement, and again from movement to quiescence, was to move without leaving a trace.

Suddenly he thought—no, one should say that the brooding of months and years suddenly materialized as a concrete, integral idea: he felt that if one were to abandon the human standpoint, that is, to give up the human aesthetic prejudice, then one would find that the human form was certainly loathsome and comical to look at: an elliptical lump of flesh which, for no reason, put out four thin strips of flesh, all about equal in length, two from each end. To this another small lump of flesh covered with black thread was attached by a short stump of flesh. The appendages gave the whole a threatening bearing, combative and full of animosity.

Thus, what was basically wrong with the human form was probably the unfortunate four strips of flesh. If you cut them off, or if they disappeared, man would be a most amiable, lovable creature—a ball of flesh. You had only to say once to this soft, compliant ball of flesh, "Roll!" and it would roll out of sight, quite naturally, without any argument . . .

As he walked he brooded over these profound questions, and once home, he sprawled stupidly on a ragged rattan chair and continued his ruminations.

His two boys were playing table tennis; the white ball was pitched playfully and nimbly from side to side by their paddles. His two girls were juggling, each with four small beanbags. Their little hands moved rapidly, rotating the beanbags in turn, one in the hand, three in the air, eight between the two, up, down, up, down. How marvelous it looked!

Before he knew it, he was transfixed by these beanbags. He borrowed two from his daughters and imitated their juggling game. The soft round beanbags felt comfortable in his palms.

"If only I were still an eight- or nine-year-old child!" He felt a deep envy for his children.

But an eight- or nine-year-old child must go to school. There was no freedom at school. Better six or seven. But three or four was better yet, or two or three years old, resting on his mother's breast, without a care or worry. How fine! he thought. Brooding to abstraction, he wrapped his two arms about his chest, and clutched his arms with his fingers, as if sunk in the faded dreams of childhood.

"Hey! You still sitting there?" His wife's hoarse cry came suddenly from behind him.

"Huh . . . what is it?" He looked about anxiously. The children were no longer there, and the lights were still off.

"Everyone's waiting for you," his wife grunted, and stamped into the kitchen, from where her cold remark emerged, "Good-for-nothing!"

"Daddy, dinner's ready!" his oldest daughter called in a sharp voice.

He quickly dismissed his wife's abusive words, but when he caught sight of what little food they had on the table, the echo of his wife's lament became audible again: "Good-for-nothing!"

After dinner, his children finished their homework and went to bed at a little past eight. This was the time his children used to go to a neighbor's house to watch television, but a month ago he had suddenly received an unsigned note: "Mr. Chin Chih-sheng: Please restrain your children from crowding around our windows and peering in. It's not that I would deny others a view of my television, but dark shapes outside the windows constitute a psychological threat to the people inside. . . ." From then on he and his wife had laid down the law: it was no longer permitted to "take a peek" at other people's televisions.

After his wife had tidied up the kitchen, she took out her cashmere yarn and began knitting. This provided a side income, bringing in three or four dollars every evening. On Sunday, when Chih-sheng took over the cooking, she could knit an entire sweater and earn eighteen dollars.[2] During the week, his wife worked ten hours a day in a textile mill (eight hours according to the original contract, but everyone "willingly" worked two hours overtime), yet in the evening she still labored at this exhausting, eye-damaging handwork. It made him uneasy, and he had once tried to learn the knitting himself, but he was too clumsy and ended wasting the yarn.

"Chin-sheng? . . ." his wife asked him as she knitted.

"Yes? What is it?" Half-conscious, he was on the verge of dozing off.

"You should find a job on the side to supplement our income," his wife said, yawning.

"I . . . I've tried, but . . ."

"The rent is due in three days. To renew the lease, they're sure to want three months' rent in advance."

"You think they can drive us out if we don't pay?" he flared up.

"They have our contract in their hands. If we don't honor it, they might go to our guarantor to make trouble!" his wife reminded him rather coldly, staring at him with her nose wrinkled.

"But we don't have the money! Don't you remember, we have just paid our oldest child's tuition."

"What's more, your brother sends word he wants three thousand dollars from you by the end of the month to build a grave for your parents!"

He closed his eyes. He had to find a way not to listen.

"You don't care?" His wife struck the table with her knitting needle and glared at him.

"How can . . ." He stood up, shook his head, blinked, and bit his lips. He turned about and glanced down at the ground, hoping to bore in somewhere and hide, but there was no crevice anywhere. He felt an irritating twinge in his nostrils as he said, "But I've given you every cent of the money I've earned!"

His wife followed his words with her favorite phrase, and he couldn't help but intone in unison with her in his mind: "Good-for-nothing!"

That night he dreamed he had somehow returned to his childhood days when he had just learned to walk. This was a welcome, friendly setting for a dream: the balmy spring breeze, the lazy spring sunshine, his mother's benevolent smile, her loving caresses, her kisses . . .

He was startled awake the next morning by the slam of the door as his wife left for work.

His wife and children had all left. He heard only the ticking of the old clock. Still curled up deep in the covers, he slowly and greedily savored the aftertaste of his dream. Or rather, he pretended to forget that it was time to rise, hoping by some chance to continue his dreaming.

"I'm still a child who's just learned to walk! On my mother's breast . . ." he told himself.

"No, I still can't walk. I'm an infant . . ." He practiced sucking under his blanket.

How could everything be so familiar? It was as though he had seen and felt these things only yesterday! This was an extraordinary sensation: everything partly true, partly false. Everything seemed on the point of vanishing, and yet also slowly coming into being. He felt agitated, exhilarated. But with his excitement was mixed an inexplicable tragic isolation. Something was about to be born, something about to expire. Amidst this growth and destruction, he felt clear headed one moment, muddled the next. His heart beat madly. He heard the weeping of an owl, or an infant.

Suddenly, for an instant, a bright white light flashed in his eyes. The white light gradually turned pink, then bright red. He discovered himself wrapped in some soft, crimson membrane.

"That's it! I'm back in my mother's womb! I'm hiding in the placenta!"

Yes, this time he clearly saw, or rather, he clearly perceived his environment: his back was arched, his neck was coiled tightly, his four limbs were curled about his chest. From his navel radiated blood vessels and the placental membrane. This was the tranquil, solitary space of the womb. The amnion and placenta nursed him well. How snug he felt! He found himself lying feet up, head down, as though cradled, gently rocking. A round ball of flesh. . . .

He discovered that he had indeed become a round ball of flesh.

He recalled that there were many times he had felt this way, but today things were different: no matter what effort he exerted, he couldn't extend his tightly coiled arms and legs. He laughed to think of the bad joke he had brought on himself, but he had to admit it was true. He started to worry.

"It seems I've contracted a strange illness—I'm just fantasizing."

The realization that his condition was indeed serious had the strange effect of calming him: in cases of illness, it was expected that one take the day off work. He began to consider the tangible problems:

"When my wife sees I'm not just loafing idly in bed, but have become a large ball of flesh, deposited here, unable to rise, she will naturally not be so savage. Who knows, when Rotten Egg hears the news, he might even come see me. Haven't I labored ardently as his clerk for over ten years? Maybe this sudden disease which has bent my back and coiled my limbs is the result of exhaustion after all that time bent over my desk! Maybe Rotten Egg will turn benevolent, and send me to a first-rate hospital for treatment. Maybe he will find my family a spacious room—and pay the rent himself, of course." At this point, his body coiled up more tightly. Without thinking he rocked lightly—with about a thirty degree roll.

"Yes, I can't walk, but I can roll! With one roll I could roll out of sight!"

As his heart expanded, unfortunately his bladder also swelled to the utmost. He fretted a while, then painfully pushed the blanket to the foot of the bed with his shoulders. Rocking his body in ever larger arcs, he finally perfected a complete 360-degree roll. He checked out the angle, then rolled just to where his feet and palms extended over the edge of the bed.

He struggled to press his shoulder and collarbone towards his spine, and stretched his arms out as far as possible. Then straining at the waist, he shifted his body forward so that his chin rested on the edge of the bed. The next step was to support his body's weight on his elbows and, using his hands and feet, slowly lower himself from the bed with a crawling, rowing, rolling movement. He crouched there in a ball; then with his two hands assisting his calves, he employed the power in the soles of his feet to "convey" his body to the toilet.

After relieving himself, he "conveyed" himself to the kitchen. A ferocious hunger attacked him. Fortunately a chair stood in front of the kitchen cabinet. With effort he climbed onto it, opened the cabinet, and ate the cold steamed bun his wife had left him.

The strange thing was that after he had accomplished these things the strength in his hands and feet gradually diminished and they started coiling. In a few minutes he clearly noticed that his fingers and the tips of his toes began to grow stiff and numb. Now his hands, feet, and arms were all incapable of independent movement; his body's energy was spread generally throughout, rather than distributed to each individual part according to its special function.

"Since you've contracted into a ball of flesh, then be happy as a ball of flesh! You are a living ball of flesh now, a fetus, so you can only think the things a fetus would think." He mildly cautioned, then reassured himself: "Chin Chih-sheng, accept your fate! What's called for now is resignation."

He was sunk in random, confused brooding.

"Can a fetus think?" He began to wonder. "Probably not, but why not give it a try?" What does a fetus think? Of its peaceful environment, of warm feelings, and tasty nourishment? No, a fetus takes in nourishment through the umbilical cord. His head was buried in his breast, and in his unconscious he seemed to see a stream of yellow liquid nourishment entering his belly.

Can a fetus make sounds? He felt his mouth was stuck fast by something. He made a sobbing sound, "woo-oo," but feeling that somehow wrong, changed it to "ee-ee . . . ao-aow . . ."

A fetus needs exercise. He strained to stretch out his hands and kick his legs, but the range of his movements was small. In the placenta inside the womb, the fetus has little room to move.

"Now no one can bully me . . .

"Now no one can harm me . . .

"Now I am truly safe . . ."

His thoughts soared. He rocked his body again slightly, then with the help of his elbows and palms, he slowly rolled from kitchen to den.

"Haha! I am really rolling! What a wonderful way to move!" He heard his own laughter, but the words did not pass from his lips.

Once in the room he contentedly rolled about, pushing and crawling, then climbed onto an old rattan chair and "deposited" himself there, panting. In various parts of his body—his neck, the top of his head, his elbows, wrists, ankles, knees, and the top of his feet—he felt a dull pain amidst the numbness, but in his heart he felt incomparably cheerful.

He was "deposited" with his head down and feet up. This was the most comfortable position. Through a corner where the glass was broken he gazed out the window at a patch of sky. The spring sky was a pale blue color, with light white clouds.

"Ah! How lovely the world is! How wonderful!" He sighed happily.

Late that afternoon, just as Chin Chih-sheng was considering relying on his own power to return to bed, he suddenly heard his wife cry: "The kids? Where are they? Not even one of them home? Where have the four of them gone today? . . . Aiya! You! . . . What's happened?" his wife was yelling and shouting, just as he imagined she would.

What could he say? A fetus can't speak.

"Chih-sheng! You . . . what in the world are you doing? What the . . ."

He couldn't see his wife's face, but just hearing her trembling voice was oppressive enough. Answer her? A fetus not only can't speak, but probably can't even fully comprehend the language of these full-grown humans. The important thing now was to use his own power to climb into bed.

His wife was still chattering away, making strange noises. The children had returned. Little Ah-hui seemed to be crying with fright. But shortly after, the children were gone again; these things didn't really matter to them.

Movement was increasingly difficult, except, of course, rolling. Just at the most difficult moment, his body suddenly felt lighter, and he "rose" onto the bed. It was his wife who had reached out to help him at the right moment. She was, after all, his wife.

His wife sat at the head of the bed, crying and asking a lot of foolish questions. Probably frustrated when he didn't answer, she pushed him fiercely with both hands. As a result, his body, originally lying back-down on the bed, effortlessly rolled over 180 degrees, until he lay with his back arched up. He suddenly envisioned a tortoise with its hard shell facing heaven: so now he too had taken on a turtle's ridiculous appearance!

"Ma, what's Daddy doing?" Ah Fang's voice, Ah Fang, daddy's gentlest child.

"Go call Chi-hsiang, buy two buns each—here, three dollars, take it!"

"And Daddy?"

"We'll find something else for Daddy to eat!" His wife suddenly stood up; could she be losing her temper again?

"Where's Mother going?" It was Chi-hsiang's deep voice; he was growing up!

"To call the doctor!"

His four children had been noisily coaxed away with three dollars. The room was suddenly quiet. His wife was really in a state this time, it seemed. But what was he to do? This was a disease, an unusual disease.

Oh, to lie this way was too unsightly; he'd have to return to the head-down position. Hm, that's right! Years ago, when he had practiced yoga, he used to assume a similar position.

He heard a racket outside. He could imagine his children walking along dejectedly, chewing on their buns. How pathetic! He felt like going out to embrace them! But no, a fetus couldn't walk on its feet, and there was never any hope of doing so.

The children were hailing Mommy. His wife was back.

"Chih-sheng, are you better?" his wife said gently. Was his wife gentle after all?

Was he better? Better how? His wife told him the doctor would be arriving soon.

Now, here was a difficult question he ought to resolve: Is this after all some strange disease? Or the normal appearance of the fetus?

At first he had lumped the two together; but if he was a fetus, what need was there for a doctor?

Perhaps he was neither a fetus nor a sick man and this was only a dream.

No, such a preposterous dream was impossible. Besides, a dream would not be this clear.

This was no light matter. Surely it was a serious mistake to treat the fetus as an illness, or view an illness as a fetus?—even though it is true that people do turn things topsy-turvy often enough.

Ah! It was better not to think of these things. It was simpler to just be a fetus. A fetus rests in its mother's womb—but here he was "deposited" on a hard wood-frame bed. A fetus is joined flesh-and-blood to its mother—but this woman in front of his eyes was not his mother; this was a woman called his "wife," with whom he shared a very deep relationship.

The light came on. His wife was complaining bitterly that the doctor had not arrived.

Now, looking up at her from below, he could see his wife's features clearly in the lamplight. A strange, foreign object! His wife had a very sharp chin, jutting down to a point. Beyond her chin were two tightly curled lips, curving down at the sides. Beyond this was a hilly region, with two tall peaks facing each other; in between were black tunnels like the steep precipices of a dead volcano's crater. Beyond the mountain peaks were valleys overgrown with weeds; in the valleys, a flash of lamplight was reflected, probably from a couple of ponds. Further on things were less clear: above a lofty bulge were many deep ridges, like a terraced field or the grooves made by an ax. And finally came a black mistlike covering, quite frightening to look at. This then was a human face? This was his wife?

"Ma, the doctor's here!"

His heart beat madly on the doctor's arrival. Doctors were generally merciless, moneygrubbing demons. That his wife had managed to fetch him was very strange. Maybe the doctor would take the fetus and soak it in formaldehyde for a specimen, or dissect it for an experiment. Then what would he do?

"Dr. Liu, look at him! He won't say a word; he just lies there like a boiled shrimp!" His wife was sobbing.

"Hm, hm, I see, I see . . ."

Dr. Liu was as fat as a sacrificial pig offered at the Chung-yüan Festival.[3] His palms were as soft as a woman's breast, all thanks to the nourishment provided by the blood and sweat of his hapless patients. Chin Chih-sheng had never imagined his emaciated body would be examined by him—by the famous local internist Dr. Liu!

Dr. Liu encountered a difficult problem as he tried to open Chih-sheng's clothes at the chest. "This won't do, this hand . . ." he murmured. He nearly broke Chih-sheng's neck trying to pry his head off his chest for the routine examination—the eyelids, pupils, the larynx, behind the ears. Since it was impossible to get to Chih-sheng's chest with the stethoscope, the doctor opened Chih-sheng's shirt as far as possible and listened to his back instead.

"Strange . . ."

"Except for being a bit weak, he is rarely ill," his wife said.

"Has he been injured in his back or elsewhere?"

His wife didn't make a sound; perhaps she was shaking her head. Actually, his back had probably been injured more than three months ago when she had pushed him off the bed one night.

"His chest . . . has he had surgery on his chest?"

No doubt his wife was still shaking her head.

"Has he taken any toxic substances lately? For example, alcohol—does he often indulge in liquor?"

"Not a drop."

Ha! Ha! Little did she realize he often drank wine, though he seldom bought more than two dollars' worth at a time, enough for one small glass and a plate of peanuts, but surely not enough to hurt anyone.

"Does he have any special habits or hobbies?"

"No. He's a bit lazy, likes to sleep, and daydreams a lot."

"Well . . ." Dr. Liu hesitated.

"What's wrong with him, then? Will you please save him!" From the tone of his wife's voice, she was almost begging him on her knees. Really, why the fuss!

"I think . . ."

"Yes? What's wrong with him?"

"First we'll give him a tranquilizer and see how he reacts."

No sooner said than Chih-sheng felt a sharp prick in the buttocks. This sudden prick made him break into a cold sweat. He almost cried out. Very well! Suddenly his limbs jerked violently, and his body curled again, perhaps even tighter.

"Dr. Liu, what shall we do next?"

"Let him sleep a bit. If his body stretches out a little in his sleep, and his taut nervous condition relaxes, that will prove the source of the illness is not organic but functional. If that's the case, it is not within the scope of the internal medicine I practice."

"What do you mean?"

"If after he has fallen asleep, he is still like that, first thing we will do tomorrow is to take x-rays of his bones, then send them to Taipei and have several specialists examine his bone structure."

"But . . ." His wife said just one word, unable to go on. It was enough.

"Please don't worry. This is a unique case, and for purposes of research, we will finance everything except the price of drugs."

His wife still had a lot of questions, and one by one Dr. Liu explained to her eagerly, as though he were expounding on a valuable antique. What a bore, what insufferable nonsense! Anyway, the tranquilizer was taking effect and Chih-sheng was gradually losing consciousness.

Unaware of how much time had passed, he opened his eyes. His wife lay dressed beside him, looking troubled even in her sleep. As for himself, he was still lying on his side holding his knees in both hands.

"So, it's not a dream!" The various events of the day suddenly returned to him.

Once again, his belly was unbearably full. He rushed to the toilet at top speed to relieve himself, and then returned to the bedroom. Just as he was lying down to sleep again, he discovered two buns resting on the dresser. Why not eat them?

"Oh, so I *can* walk?" He didn't really know if this was a blessing or a curse.

Turning his head, he saw his wife sleeping soundly like a dead pig. Instinctively, he slipped quietly out of bed again.

But another strange thing happened at this very instant: the area about his shins and knees suddenly weakened unbearably. All at once his body contracted and he crouched down . . .

"Ah . . ." He felt like crying out, but something obstructed his throat and he couldn't catch his breath.

The same feelings, the same sequence: his heart seemed to be floating, half drunk; his limbs began to grow numb, beginning with the fingers and the toes. His body, at first half crouching, half prostrate on the ground, slowly coiled into a ball. Within perhaps five minutes he had returned to his spherical form.

Dong! Dong! The old wall clock rang out twice.

"Go out and look about! It is so quiet this time of night," he told himself.

He very much wanted to get up and take a look at his sleeping wife again, but he didn't have the strength. He could only roll along gently and slowly. He rolled to the sitting room. The front door was open: his wife had been too tired, and his children didn't understand the importance of locking up doors yet—both were pardonable.

Outside, how fresh it was! A spring evening. The sky was full of sparkling stars, like a silver fantasy. No fear now of encountering any dogs or cats; having gnawed up their rats and pig bones, they'd be fast asleep.

There was a long alley, at the end of which was a dirt road. If you followed the road uphill, it connected with an asphalt street leading downtown; downhill, the road led to rice paddies.

The asphalt street would be hard to roll on. The dirt road was far better. As he rolled along, inch by inch, the soil against his hands, feet, and neck felt fine, cool, and soft as a mother's hand.

"This then is the ideal environment for a fetus!"

Fine. Stop here for a while. A little farther on are the rice paddies. "Rivet! Rivet!" The crisp croaking of a frog sounded intermittently. Ah, how fine that croaking, a thousand times better than that little frog of a singer he once saw on the Chang's television, shaking its head and wagging its arms, yelling, "I am a jazz drummer." How beautiful the stars far up in the sky, so still, so timid! A thousand times better than the feeble light emitted by the dark, square lamps along the asphalt street. Some say each star is an ancient silent world. If he could only shake off this raucous, cruel world, if he could be reincarnated in one of those worlds, rolling several inches deep in its soft, fine dirt, he wouldn't mind at all! And what was to fear in that? Who wrote those two famous lines?

Ch'ang-o should regret having stolen the elixir:
The green sea—the blue sky—her heart every night![4]

Ah! Either the poet was too earthbound, or did Ch'ang-o really crave the world? But there was no doubt about one thing: those who sing in praise of these two lines had either not yet tasted all the bitterness of human life or they were simply too unprepared for Buddhist enlightenment.

Ah, indeed, it is for no one to tell. All these things were so distant, so abstract, and so insignificant, at least for the moment. What mattered now was to continue his carefree rolling, to keep hold of this moment, which belonged to him, which no one could disturb.

Well, what should he do now?

"Why not take advantage of your position and sing a song!"

Impossible! He hadn't sung in years!

Anyone can sing, everyone likes to sing; it's just that in days past, you couldn't do things as you wished.

That was right. He should sing. This was his chance. How about: "I Want To Be a Good Boy"?

> I want to be a good boy,
> Pure of body, true of mind,
> Wherever I go,
> I shall be admired, I shall be admired.

"Beautiful, beautiful! Who would have thought you could sing so well?"

Huh? Strange! Since you can sing, surely you can talk as well?

He looked around; if there was no one to disturb him, he could speak out loud; he could say what he wanted to say, curse what he wanted to curse—

Oh, someone's coming: You won't be able to sing or speak!

"Run! Run!" But where?

Listen! It was his wife, squawking like a mother goose or a giant gander, and the sound of scattered footsteps . . .

They're coming, all coming! They're getting nearer. You can see them. Terrifying! All those long, black shapes, relentlessly approaching.

What could he do? It was his unavoidable fate to be seized and dragged back. To roll again now was no use. It was hopeless.

But there was one way: to shut his eyes and not look. Really it was best to shut one's eyes and not see these people, these doings of the world.

Let come what may! Just shut your eyes and—

NOTES

1. "Lao hsien-sheng," a respectful form of address to an old man. Here it is used with mocking overtones.

2. The exchange rate is about forty Taiwan dollars to a U.S. dollar.

3. A Taoist festival falling on the fifteenth day of the seventh month under the lunar calendar.

4. These two lines are by Li Shang-yin (813?–858). In James J. Y. Liu's translation, the complete poem, entitled "Ch'ang-o," reads:

> Against the screen of "mother-of-clouds" the candle deep shadow;
> The Long River gradually sinks, the morning star sets.
> Ch'ang-o should regret having stolen the elixir:
> The green sea—the blue sky— her heart every night!

See *The Poetry of Li Shang-yin: Ninth-Century Baroque Chinese Poet* (Chicago: University of Chicago Press, 1969), p. 99.

CH'EN YING-CHEN (1936–)

In a 1973 essay I assessed Ch'en Ying-chen's (pen name of Ch'en Yung-shan) position in Taiwan literature as follows: "In as much as he has spoken the truth as he knew it, in as much as he dares to challenge even himself when he had suspicion about his former conviction, Ch'en Ying-chen is . . . an unique writer as well as an honest man" ("How Much Truth Can a Blade of Grass Carry?" Journal of Asian Studies, *Vol. 32, No. 4, 1973, p. 638).*

The validity of this statement is borne out by a recent interview in which he told Lind Jaivin: "Fifteen years ago I was quite a radical; I saw mainland China as the answer to all questions. But now I know that is nonsense as well. For example, with regard to foreign investment, I thought mainland China was handling the situation very well. But now look at how they so desperately cling to the trouser legs of the foreigners" ("On Power, People and Priorities," Asiaweek, *5 Feb. 1982, p. 43).*

Charged with alleged "subversive activities," Ch'en was given a ten-year prison sentence in 1968. However, the death of Chiang Kai-shek in 1975 brought about an amnesty and he was released in September of that year. Though the nature of his "subversion" has never been made public, it is easy to see from his writing why he has been treated like an outcast by the Kuomintang. His works can be roughly divided into three periods. His fiction in the early sixties is dominated by narcissism and nihilism. The second period, culminating in such tendentious pieces as "My First Case" (Ti-i-chien ch'a-shih, 1967; included in Chinese Stories from Taiwan), *bears testimony to the author's loss of faith in the capitalist order. His third period began in 1977. Disenchanted with communism and suspicious of capitalism as represented by the multinational corporations in Taiwan, he would be moving in a spiritual void if not for his strong conviction in the values of traditional Chinese culture. "Night Freight" and the ongoing series of stories clustering under the general title "Washington Building"* (Hua-sheng-tun ta lou) *are the patent works of the post-incarceration period. As can be seen in the present selection, Ch'en at this stage seems to be less concerned with dialectics than with the question of Chinese selfhood being sapped by the forces of modernization. Ch'en graduated from Tamkang College in 1960 with a B.A. in English. He now runs a printing shop in Taipei. A discussion and a bibliography of his works can be found in* Chinese Fiction from Taiwan: Critical Perspec-

102

tives. *Under the auspices of the University of Iowa's International Writing Program, he was invited to the United States for three months in the fall of 1983.*

Night Freight

Translated by James C. T. Shu

I. The Stuffed Long-tailed Pheasant

Mr. Morgenthau went past Lin Jung-p'ing's office with big strides. "*See you, J.P.*"[1]

"*See you,*" Lin Jung-p'ing answered.

He saw the hulking shadow of Mr. Morgenthau move out of the empty main office toward the garage shrouded in twilight. A maroon Lincoln Continental slowly backed out and gracefully skirted the garden and the flag stand. The guard already had the gate open. Lin Jung-p'ing watched through his window as the car drove noiselessly out of the Taiwan Malamud Electronic Company. Noiselessly the young guard bowed, and noiselessly he closed the gate.

Lin Jung-p'ing lit his pipe again. "*See you, J.P.*" Mr. Morgenthau's deep, vigorous voice seemed to be still reverberating in the big, empty office. It was long past office hours. Just before the office was about to close for the day, Mr. Morgenthau had invited Lin Jung-p'ing to his room to discuss a few fiscal matters. Because the director of finance of the Malamud Company–Pacific Area was coming next week, the usually unruffled Mr. Morgenthau had recently been bustling from day to night trying to get several reports ready. Consequently, Lin Jung-p'ing, who was in charge of the financial department, had been working overtime every day. However, even in the midst of stress Mr. Morgenthau had not lost his knack for pranks, pranks which suggested an animallike vitality: impromptu teasing of the female workers; dirty jokes; loud-mouthed cursing, followed by a pat with his large hand on the shoulder of the Chinese manager who happened to be the object of the curse, and an "*OK, Frank, don't let our discussion affect your appetite for lunch,*" and then a guffaw.

At the end of office hours they had been anxiously discussing how to account for a fairly sizable "public relations expense."

"The office in Tokyo, J.P., can never understand that public relations expense is a rational expense in China." Mr. Morgenthau shook his head while exhaling lingering, bluish smoke. "Any expense that brings efficiency and profits counts as rational management, as—"

Lin Jung-p'ing smiled helplessly. He was a sturdy fellow from a farming family in southern Taiwan. Under his balding crown, his brow was often touched with slight melancholy.

"Let's play politics with Tokyo. You see, this year we've made good grades in three quarters, enough to please them." Lin Jung-p'ing spoke in fluent English. "As soon as they're pleased, the accounts can be easily dealt with."

"You're right, J.P." Mr. Morgenthau's voice was surprisingly low and slow.

Lin Jung-p'ing looked up from the documents, to find Mr. Morgenthau gazing out the window in glee, his good-looking, pale blue eyes glittering dispassionately.

"You're right, J.P." Mr. Morgenthau said tenderly. *"Let's play Tokyo politics*—but look at her, J.P., the little filly."

Lin Jung-p'ing looked out the window. He saw Liu Hsiao-ling with some other girls of the company, their day's work done, walking toward the edge of the flower garden. Her thick, long, lushly dark hair made her bare arms appear extremely alluring. Her build was gorgeous, all right, but if it were not for her svelte, sturdy legs, she would not have that special charm, since her face was not that beautiful. Mr. Morgenthau called her a "little filly" exactly because of those legs.

Without any expression on his face, Lin Jung-p'ing watched Liu Hsiao-ling and the other staff members get on the bus. Mr. Morgenthau opened a new pack of Winstons. Lin Jung-p'ing filled his pipe. Silently, the two of them puffed away. The bus finally left. The big office suddenly appeared empty, vast, and profoundly quiet.

"J.P., the loan of the Owen bank—" Mr. Morgenthau started. They returned to business. But it was obvious that Lin Jung-p'ing had suddenly begun to feel uncontrollably dejected. When the discussion came to an end, Mr. Morgenthau's big, pale blue eyes looked at him with concern. "You look tired, J.P." he said. "Since I'm going to play a little golf tomorrow, you don't have to come so early. Take a good rest, J.P." This made Lin Jung-p'ing ashamed of his unexplainable depression. He smiled, arranged the papers spread out over half the desk, and got up to leave.

"Take a good rest, J.P., old boy," remarked Mr. Morgenthau behind him, cheerfully.

Lin Jung-p'ing entered his own office and put every document in place. On top of the low cabinet sat a family photograph in which he was standing behind his wife and two daughters, who were smiling with open mouths.

It was getting dark outside the window. He cleaned his pipe by tapping it on the ashtray. He was surprised by the dull, unpleasant sound of the pipe striking the marble ashtray. He stood up. His sense of loss was gradually changing into a dull sadness. He turned the light off, pulled the door shut, and left his office in haste.

He drove his Escort, which his company had just got for him as a replacement, into the thickening twilight. As he stared quietly at the road before him, his sense of depression calmly and relentlessly surged from his heart to permeate his four limbs. His thoughts wandered: "Even if they're both new, you can tell the difference between driving a Ford and driving a Yülung."[2] He tried to find topics to talk to himself about; he tried to remember what it felt like when he first drove a Yülung car; he tried to find a suitable topic for his scheduled speech at a Jaycee luncheon; he tried to choose a piano instructor for his eldest daughter from between the two music major coeds someone had recommended to him. But hard as he tried to avoid it, Mr. Morgenthau's impudent, puckish, leering expression forced its way into his thoughts and hovered in his vision.

"Is it true that Linda hasn't said anything to you?" Mr. Morgenthau asked, his pale blue eyes, decorated with golden eyelashes, looking Lin Jung-p'ing directly in the face. Jung-p'ing suddenly thought of the vacant gray eyes of the cougar in an American T.V. commercial promoting automobiles.

"Said what to me?" he answered. He could almost envisage his own impeccably calm expression.

Mr. Morgenthau looked at him cunningly, curiously. "Linda hasn't said anything, J.P.? Really? Very interesting, J.P.," said Mr. Morgenthau impudently, prankishly.

"Said what to me?" he said. He was indeed surprised, but he was well aware that his innocent expression was completely perfect. "What did she want to tell me? Tell me that you're to raise my salary?" he said.

They both burst into roars of laughter, in good American style.

"You deserve a raise, J.P., believe me," Mr. Morgenthau said, "You've got a head like a computer, J.P."

It was getting much darker now, as Lin Jung-p'ing turned his car onto a road that led to the spa district. It was a mountain road noted for shade trees. After the car made two turns on the slightly sloping road an almost perfectly full moon unexpectedly appeared, hanging in the part of the sky close to the downtown area and emitting a gentle, feeble, off-white light. "What did she want to tell me?" He thought of his innocent expression. He began to feel ashamed.

Some time before eleven in the morning, Liu Hsiao-ling, who was Lin Jung-p'ing's secretary, entered his office. Unlike her usual self—a composed, dexterous secretary—she banged around a lot in the steel office filing cabinet. He looked up and saw her shoving in a big stack of papers with unusual impatience.

"Linda," he broke the silence by calling her English name.

She seemed surprised, then looked down quietly. Lightly biting her thick, rouged lips, she switched her eyes rapidly from the papers in her hands to the wall. Lin Jung-p'ing noticed the gleam of tears in her eyes. He took out his pipe, and asked in English, "Anything the matter, Linda?"

Liu Hsiao-ling's lips quivered slightly. She looked down quickly, strings of tears dropping onto her hands, clasped in front of her waist.

"Sit down," he said. "Tell me what's the matter—slowly."

She finally sat down opposite him. Silently taking the handkerchief he offered, she carefully wiped off her tears and the moist spot on the tip of her nose. Her eyes were small, especially on a face that was a little too wide. Her nose was long, thin, and firm, but her thick, soft lips gave her face an indisputable sensuous charm.

She was now looking at a piece of carved Philippine mahogany hanging on the wall behind him. Before low thatch houses, a farmer, apparently on his way to work, was leading a water buffalo; Lin Jung-p'ing once told her that it was an almost perfect replica of a scene from the Taiwan countryside—if only the farmer were wearing a coolie hat.

"I've typed your letter, the one you wanted sent to Tokyo to be transferred to New York. When I went to give a duplicate to the boss," she spoke with composure, "he said, 'Linda, you're a pretty girl.'" She paused a while, then continued, "That's the way he talks to every girl. I said, 'Thank you.' He said, 'Linda, someone told me you like the way I wear my moustache.'" She looked at Lin Jung-p'ing in scorn. "It's got to be you who told him that. All the men in this company have a slave mentality."

This past summer Mr. Morgenthau had left Taiwan for his annual one-month vacation. He sent Lin Jung-p'ing postcards from Hong Kong, Singapore, Iran, West Germany, and Denmark, one after the other. Lin Jung-p'ing was the only one of the five managers in the company to receive these scenic postcards. Then Mr. Morgenthau wrote him from his old home in the state of Maryland, U.S.A., saying that he had grown a moustache and asking that Jung-p'ing keep it a secret in order to give the people in the company a "sexy surprise" when he came back to Taiwan. When Mr. Morgenthau returned, none of the girls in the office were interested in their boss's moustache.

Once, in a small Japanese-style inn in the spa district,[3] Lin Jung-p'ing had brought up the boss's moustache to Liu Hsiao-ling. He suggested, "Chinese girls associate beards with aging and sloppiness."

"I don't think so. The girls in our company are all just too young," she said, intently making up before the mirror. "Actually, I'm quite attracted to his moustache. So thick, above such a naughty, youthful mouth." She then burst into laughter in front of the mirror, exuding a charm tinged with abandon. He was lying naked in bed, leafing through *Time* magazine. He laughed wordlessly, feeling a kind of jealousy which he could nevertheless live with.

"No wonder he kept smirking at me so," she said with indignation. Lin Jung-p'ing smoked his pipe in silence. She continued: "'I'm leaving, Linda,' he said. He stood up casually. Suddenly, he embraced me . . .'" She looked Jung-p'ing straight in the face, her eyes suddenly turning moist. "Fuck him, the pig!" she went on vehemently, her face reddening. "'Let me go, or I'll scream,' I said. He suddenly let go of me, saying, 'Linda, don't let me frighten you. I didn't mean anything bad, Linda.'" Her voice was calming down. "Fuck him," she said woefully. "Pig."

Lin Jung-p'ing looked angry. He felt an ambiguous kind of anger which caused the hand holding the pipe to shake slightly. It was not the kind of imperious, all-out, self-indulgent anger that he would direct toward his wife and children at home. An American boss who took him as his buddy and referred to him with intimacy as "*old boy*"; his own sky-rocketing future; the millions of U.S. dollars he was handling; his devising of two financial report forms strongly recommended by the Pacific headquarters and in use by all the branch Malamud companies in the Pacific-Asian area; the new Western-style house which sat on 2,304 square feet of land in a high-class suburb—what a rose-colored universe it was. And sitting before him now was Liu Hsiao-ling, his secret mistress for the past two years, who had just been insulted. Despite his sense of shame and menace to his injured male ego, however, his anger was rapidly evaporating on its own, like a trickle in the desert which vanished helplessly in the unrelenting sands. Nevertheless, he began to feel real resentment, the kind of resentment brought about by shame.

"I see," he knitted his thin brows.

She noticed that his face was twisted—by anger, cowardice, and forced arrogance. I've never seen another man who looks so ugly when he's angry, she thought to herself, feeling sorry for him. Still, she said, "See? You don't even mean to argue with him! Women are so easy to push around."

"Hsiao Liu,"[4] he said, pleading with her in Chinese.

She stared at him. His face was all apology. A look of tormented tenderness spread over his thirty-eight-year-old face. She suddenly felt like crying, though not because of sadness.

"Hsiao Liu, can you go wait for me in Little Atami[5] when you get off work?"

She shook her head violently, warm tears trickling down her cheeks.

"I've got something to tell you," he said gently.

She remained silent.

"Actually, I've known all this month that something is on your mind," he said. "Is it—Chan I-hung?"

She looked at him, surprised. So he knew? But she never expected his reaction to be so calm, even though there was a touch of melancholy to the calm. Indeed, a moment ago she had gone straight to Chan I-hung's office, as soon as she left the office of the insulting Mr. Morgenthau. But Chan I-hung had gone to the Taxation Bureau and was not back yet. Now, in the face of this man with whom she had formed a surreptitious, intimate tie for two years, she was aware that a story was drawing to an end.

He laughed a lonely laugh.

We need to talk about it, she thought, sighing. She folded his handkerchief into a neat square and put it back on his desk. "Try to come early," she remarked, and walked lightly out of his office. He made a phone call home: "I'm going with the boss on an unexpected trip to the south." There were no complaints from his wife. He hung up.

He was sweating a little. The mountain road in the district was narrow and zigzagging. It occurred to him that every time he took Liu Hsiao-ling to Little Atami she would praise his good driving skill when they were on this very circuitous stretch of mountain road. Inside the car, she would giggle while being thrown to the left and the right. He would be intent on his driving, biting onto his pipe and remaining perfectly silent. Tonight, lights swayed between shadowy pines in the hilly spa district; occasionally there flowed into his car some Japanese tunes, crudely sung by jolly Japanese tourists.

Liu Hsiao-ling watched his car entering the parking lot from the balcony of Little Atami. The dog belonging to Little Atami was barking, not in an unfriendly way, though. A middle-aged obasan[6] shouted to quiet the dog. "Toshi, hey, Toshi," she chided her darling dog in a way very Japanese, then went on to express her welcome. "I haven't seen you for a long time," the obasan said. Liu Hsiao-ling heard Lin Jung-p'ing ask for a room, and watched him walk toward the balcony steps. She turned around to add some more beer to her glass, then looked up quietly at the lights of Taipei in the distance.

He sat down beside her. She pushed a glass of beer toward him. He held the glass, quietly watching the bubbles collapse. The moon was high now. She stuck a Dunhill in her mouth that perhaps had been in her bag three days. He lighted it for her. The flame from the gas lighter shone on her tender, fleshy lips. He began to drink his beer slowly.

"Maybe I can find another job for you," he finally began. "Next week when I go to the Jaycee meeting, I'll ask if there's some suitable job."

The obasan brought along a plate of fried peanuts, a bottle of chilled beer, and another glass. Liu Hsiao-ling said hello to her in a friendly way, then suddenly added, "Oh, yes, obasan, we're not going to need a room for tonight." She laughed, looking cheerful, and remarked to Lin Jung-p'ing, "We've got to attend to some other things still, don't we, J.P.?"

He hesitated a little, then said, "Please prepare the supper for us, something simple and not greasy." He smiled wearily, "We're leaving right after supper."

A taxi hurtled in from the side gate of Little Atami and came to a screeching stop right in front of the balcony. Two Japanese, obviously drunk, came out of the car with two prostitutes, who were as much pushing them as holding them up. The obasan scurried down from the balcony, all smiles. The dog was barking. "Toshi," the obasan scolded.

Both of them looked quietly at the Japanese below the balcony.

"As soon as a man leaves his hometown, he becomes as if perfectly free," he commented. The year he was promoted to financial manager and went to Tokyo for the training at the Malamud-Pacific Division had certainly been the best time of his life.

"Actually, you don't have to trouble yourself trying to find a job for me," she said.

"What?"

"Actually, you don't need to find a job for me," she said, adding beer for herself and for Lin Jung-p'ing. She poured the beer slowly, making sure the bubbles did not overflow. "I'm going abroad soon," she said.

He knew that one of her aunts lived in America. She used to say, "She's the only one in this world who really loves me." Last winter when he was promoted to financial manager, he told her that it was out of the question for him to get a divorce. She raised hell day after day. Then, finally, she gave up. It was then that she talked about going to live with her aunt.

He was speechless.

She looked at the distant lights of Taipei district that were glowing even more prominently in the thickening darkness of the night. The bridge that connected this area with the city was transformed into a straight line linked by equidistant lights.

His thoughts were in tumult. He took his pipe out of his jacket pocket and put tobacco in it carefully. He could hear the rowdy songs of the Japanese engaged in drinking downstairs. He lighted his pipe, until it looked like a tiny lake of fire. In no time, the fragrance of the tobacco began to permeate the dark room.

"J.P.," she asked cheerfully, "You've changed the brand of your tobacco?"

He was surprised at her cheerfulness. In the past, every time she mentioned going abroad she would shed tears, tears that made him feel guilty and impatient.

"Given to me by a friend," he said with a smile. A maid brought in the supper, some Taiwanese-style food.

Liu Hsiao-ling finished a bowl of congee in no time. He had somehow lost his appetite.

"J.P.," she said, "You've never really loved me."

She attacked a dish of picked cucumber with gusto.

"But you're not to blame," she continued. "I myself never believed that I couldn't do without you."

"Hsiao Liu, please," he implored.

"You should eat a little," she said. She ladled congee into a bowl for him. "Recently I've often cried and thrown tantrums," she laughed, with a lonely echo in her voice. "It was nice of you to be so patient."

"Hsiao Liu," he said. "We've been together so long now. You know my feelings very well. Besides, I'm the one to blame."

She just laughed calmly. Suddenly the sound of water was heard, dripping from a height down onto the ground. As they looked downward into the darkness beneath the balcony, they saw a Japanese urinating in the flickering light from a Japanese-style stone lantern in a small garden. She quickly turned her face away. He smoked his pipe, remarking with a smile, "Japanese—you know, 'politeness, yes; propriety, no.'"

She looked at him, uninterested, but asked nevertheless, "'Politeness, yes; propriety, no'?"

"Polite talk, bowing, and bending the body. But also pissing everywhere, and making a racket when they drink. 'Propriety,' I think, means 'a system of proper conduct.'"

"J.P., when it comes to love," she said seriously, "it's not a matter of who owes it to whom, or who is to blame or not to blame. At least that was what Chan I-hung told me."

"Chan I-hung?"

It occurred to her immediately that she had made a slip of the tongue. She held her beer glass with both hands, turning the glass in her hands.

"In the past you said that society, your children, your relatives—but one thing you never mentioned: your new position in the company—" she laughed with a sarcasm that she believed wouldn't hurt, "you said all these made it impossible to divorce your wife in order to marry me. Actually you knew very well they weren't the reasons."

"I don't mean to deny it," he said in agony. "But the matters of feelings aren't simple. You know very well."

"J.P., I'm not arguing with you," She looked at his sad face. "Maybe we can put it this way: You love me in your own way—to the extent that it doesn't break up your family or force you to marry me—and you find in me a receiver of your feelings, but you do not monopolize me. But what about me? What am I supposed to do? Well, it is true that you have said that any time I find someone I can go to, you won't stand in my way."

Silent, he stared at the looming shadows of the trees and, beyond them, hundreds of thousands of lights in the distance. The traffic of cars on the bridge had noticeably decreased. The equidistant lights that signaled the bridge suddenly appeared lonely.

"So you're leaving." Finally he sighed. "Is it Chan I-hung?"

She fell silent this time.

Chan was a young man who had scarcely been in the company one year. He was said to be very capable. He became the head of the newly formed subdepartment of capital accounting in no time. He had a shock of long hair, which was usually unkempt. His shoulders were extraordinarily broad. A man of few words, he chain-smoked when working. Gradually, Liu Hsiao-ling came to recognize that he was uncouth, arrogant, and full of cynicism and rebellion for no good reason. Once, after typing a long letter, she suddenly turned her head and caught him lifting his head to loosen his necktie and smoking a cigarette that he had just lit. He was attending to business papers with his chin propped up in one hand, as if lost in deep, troubled thought. His ungroomed, angry face touched with savagery, his extraordinarily broad shoulders, his open collar and loosened necktie—all contributed to an ineffable appeal that immediately and unaccountably made her blush in the fraction of the second when she looked around. At that time she was having daily quarrels with J.P. She was feeling so bad that she was on the brink of being destructive, or self-destructive. To alleviate the intense feeling of the pain of disappointment with a new kind of intense feeling, she debased herself by enhancing the alluring charm that a mature young woman has and seduced Chan easily. Since she had never anticipated it, it was more or less to her own surprise that she found herself desperately in love with this unruly and moody young man.

"None can judge love," she said. "In every unhappy love, there is always one party who insists that he has been cheated and made a plaything of by another party."

"James is a good young man," he sounded heavyhearted. "Why are you taking the trouble to become an exile in America then?"

"Anyone who is in love—me included—expects the other party to return an equal amount of love," she remarked. "It never occurred to me it could be so unfair."

He recalled those days. During the day he was the boss and she was his secretary. As soon as office hours were over, she would get him to some secret place and quarrels, tears, shouting matches, and threats would begin. Finally the day arrived when she said, "J.P., I've come to terms with myself, but let me take time leaving." "Nobody wants you to leave, Hsiao Liu. Only I've no right to ask you to stick with me," he said. Since then they might as well have been separated, even though they were still together.

She's really leaving now, he thought, puffing on his pipe. Looking straight at her face, which appeared a little weary in the moonlight, he suddenly had an impulse to say, "In matters of love, women are by far more honest and courageous than men." But he refrained from uttering it. Instead, he stammered, "James is very capable—has promise. You—well, I can recommend you for a better job. It would be easier for you to get on with him."

She said nothing, combing her hair nervously with her hand. She would like to thank him for his consideration, but it would be too much like standing on ceremony. She looked at the congee that he had not touched—it must be cold by now—and remarked from reflex, "You should eat a bit, J.P."

She should not have said that, she realized. She heard her own quivery voice, which made the tears that she had tried so hard to suppress flow unchecked over her face.

"What's the matter, Hsiao Liu?" He was disconcerted.

She began to sob.

Just last night Chan I-hung roared to her, "Don't you cling to me. I'm not a trash can, getting what other people throw away!"

"James . . ."

"I'm not any fucking 'James.' I'm Chan I-hung!"

"I never dared expect you to marry me. You just go ahead and treat me as a bad woman. I'll give birth to the child on my own and raise it by myself. I'll go far away from you."

She cried. She was past being a dreamy girl, and she felt pathos when she discovered herself to be incurably in love with Chan. Why was it that she could love, wanted to love, but could only expect another helpless separation?

"What's the matter? What's the matter?" Lin Jung-p'ing asked sadly. He took her into his arms, patted her softly, wiped away her tears with his handkerchief, and kissed her flowing hair time and again. "What's the matter? What's the matter?" he asked.

He embraced her. He genuinely felt how much he was in love with this woman. His status, his career, his selfishness had made him hypocritical and turned him into a weakling. The moon was leaning westward. The entire spa district fell into a deep sleep following exhausting sensual indulgence.

She stopped crying, and returned the handkerchief to him.

"I'm sorry," she said softly. "We should leave now."

"What's the matter with you?" he sounded lonely.

"Nothing. Just felt like crying." She smiled apologetically.

As they stepped down from the balcony they saw Little Atami's famous display at the counter: a stuffed Japanese pheasant perched on a delicate, sinuous branch, its beautiful tail almost six meters long emitting a magnificent glitter, even under the fluorescent light.

The clerk at the counter looked sleepy. While Lin Jung-p'ing was paying the bill, Liu Hsiao-ling stood beside the tiny Japanese-style garden and watched the cloudy evening sky.

"Come back soon please," the clerk spoke in his stiff Japanese, watching their car glide away into the darkness.

II. THE WARM, SUPPLE BREASTS

Liu Hsiao-ling put the beer back in the refrigerator. It was a sultry evening. The chilled beer would cheer him up, she thought. The food on the table was getting cold. She took a look at the tiny electric clock on the wall. He was a half hour late. She was a little worried, but not angry. She turned on the television and sat down on the couch, whose cover had just been replaced. It seemed he was always careless about being on time for their dates, she thought, and once he even forgot about the date altogether. Alone, she laughed soundlessly to herself.

The TV program she randomly tuned to was showing a story about a young girl enamored with her married, middle-aged boss. A middle-aged man greedily lit a cigarette in a manager's office, took a deep drag, reclined in a chair, and slowly exhaled the white smoke. Beyond the executive office door some clerks were deep in work; but a female clerk was gazing at the man in the executive office. A sudden close-up showed the face of a dreamy, wide-eyed girl. Some soft music flowed in from afar. The girl's voice was heard in an aside:

If only I could rest my hand on his melancholy, weary brow to let him know that there is a woman in this world who loves him so much, so much . . .

Liu Hsiao-ling burst into cackling laughter. She lit a cigarette, and thought that Chan I-hung no doubt would say, "Those stupid soap operas." The executive on the television seemed somewhat cultured and indecisive. Where would you find a man like him in the real world of business? J.P. wasn't one, she thought.

Late that night when she was with him in his car on the way back to Taipei from Little Atami, J.P. remarked, "I realize now. Actually you should have told me earlier."

She did not say anything. The car turned onto the bridge that they had looked at from afar some time ago. It's just as well that he knows it, she thought. Everything seems to have been planned on an intangible time-table: when the time arrives, things just happen.

"Actually you should have told me earlier," he said. "Now I realize Chan I-hung should not know about our affair."

She was not sure whether his last sentence was a query or a judgment. She looked at the way he was intent on driving. His face was not without a touch of sadness, but not the kind of sadness that sought other people's pity. She leaned against his right shoulder softly.

"Things can always be arranged," he said. Mechanically, he brought the car to a stop at a red light. He patted her head tenderly, saying, "Maybe I'll have a talk with him at some right time . . ."

"No!" Liu Hsiao-ling abruptly straightened up. "I've made up my mind to go to the United States," she said. "Besides, it's my business, it's not a business decision for you to have the last say."

Then she laughed, casually, but as if at a loss.

Actually she should have felt offended then, she thought, now sitting in her living room—offended that he treated her as an object to be "arranged." But she could not take offense at the seriousness with which he gave her away to Chan I-hung. It had been two years now, and she knew how selfish in matters of love a man of more passionate nature than he could be. So when he said "Things can always be arranged," what she felt was mostly despondence, a mixture of appreciation and sympathy of sorts.

The telephone on the table beside her rang. She picked up the phone as a robber would seize his loot. It was Chan I-hung.

"Hello, what happened to you?" he asked.

She was gasping rapidly. She ground out the remainder of her cigarette in the ashtray.

"Your call startled—startled me so much," she giggled.

"I don't think your heart is quite right. You should go see a doctor."

She could hear the street noise behind him.

"Where are you? If you don't come soon," she said, "the food will get cold."

He was laughing on the other end. He said that after leaving the office, he had gone back to the place he rented and was so tired that he fell asleep. "I've just taken a bath. I'm hungry," he said.

She hung up the phone and took two dishes to the kitchen to warm up. She felt an incurable rippling sweetness in her heart. She felt like singing something, but a teardrop imperceptibly glided down her cheek. "Oh, James, you rascal," she muttered to herself, lighting the stove and turning on the vent, "why do you keep me waiting and waiting?"

She thought of her father, a one-time politician who was active in Northern China in the thirties. After he came to Taiwan he suddenly became indifferent to politics—he was even indifferent to all the matters of his own family. The year Hsiao-ling was born he had used up all the money he had brought with him from the old country. After waiting out the month's confinement following childbirth, Liu Hsiao-ling's mother had had her hair permed, and went forth to be the breadwinner. As the fourth wife to a man thirty years her senior, she soon showed extraordinary ability in public relations and business. Taking advantage of her link to former Bureau Director Liu, she opened a fashion store, a trading company, and a restaurant. As her businesses became more and more prosperous, she—scarcely over thirty years of age—became more and more glamorous. According to Amah Chou, who came with her from the old country, Liu Hsiao-ling's step-brothers and -sisters came to have reasonably good food and clothing only after that. As Liu Hsiao-ling was her mother's only child, it went without saying that she was well taken care of.

But the father kept to mandarin gowns all year round—a quilted one for winter and spring and an unquilted one for summer and autumn. He could not be bothered by anything. Sometimes he read Taoist works, such as Lao Tzu and Chuang Tzu. Sometimes he did some calligraphy, and sometimes he practiced shadowboxing, or wrote on the relationship between *The Book of Changes* and acupuncture to be published in the t'ung-hsiang-hui[7] newsletter. At first her mother would plead with him to dress better, and to socialize on some occasions. "Ai, Pao-lien," he would laugh. "Since I returned from studying military science in Japan in my twenties, what things haven't I had a hand in, and what things haven't I seen!" So he kept to his two gowns and remained unconcerned about anything.

When Liu Hsiao-ling was old enough to understand things, her mother's businesses had become more prosperous, and her father appeared more and more like a shabby, hanger-on member of the family. Her mother started referring to him as a "dirty old codger," and bossing him around, even before her daughter's eyes. Her mother stayed out overnight more and more, frequently socializing or playing mahjong. The rumor that she had another man finally reached the family after having gone full circuit outside. As her step-brothers and -sisters moved out one by one, either boarding in or commuting to school, Liu Hsiao-ling began to revolt against her mother, the potent authority in the family.

In Liu Hsiao-ling's sophomore year in high school, her father fell ill. Her mother sent him to one of the best hospitals, and once every two weeks would go to the hospital to settle the bills for medical treatment and a special nurse, without, however, bothering to stick her nose into the sickroom. Liu Hsiao-ling was a quiet young girl then. Every day she would keep her father company, although he spent more time sleeping than being awake. One night when she went home, she saw in their living room a gorgeously decorated Christmas tree, with a big pile of gifts under it.

"Set up for you by your mother," Amah Chou said, beaming.

She stood in the living room without saying a word. Then, still without saying a word, she took down all the decorations from the tree and moved them, and the gifts under the tree, to the middle of the yard. She struck a match and lit up all the colorful boxes. The amah stood by, sobbing quietly. The light of the fire made her face all red. It was a cold winter night. Liu Hsiao-ling suddenly felt exhausted. She did not return to the hospital to keep her father company that night. And it was during that night that he passed away.

She dished out the food she had just heated onto a big plate, wiping its edges clean. She had never seen her father as a young and ferocious man, who, in the words of Amah Chou, "once executed a dozen people without blinking an eye." The father she knew was a sloppy, timid old man, who allowed himself to be ridiculed, cursed, and betrayed by his wife.

The bell was ringing. She turned off the stove and rushed to the door. As soon as the door was opened, she was overwhelmed by the odor of liquor. She noticed Chan I-hung's face, which was purplish from drinking. She backed away silently to let him in.

He stared at her with sodden eyes, smirking all the while.

"Didn't you say you had been sleeping?" she asked, vexed.

He plumped himself down on a sofa. He was wearing blue jeans of quality material; his dark yellow shirt was a little dirty. He seized the cigarette case on the tea table with one hand, drew a cigarette out with his fleshy lips, lit it, and puffed nonstop. The cigarette bobbed up and down between his lips.

"Didn't you say you were coming over to have dinner?" Her back was leaning against the living room door. She sounded hurt.

"I just drank. I haven't eaten yet," he seemed to be consoling her. "I invited Old Chang to have a drink."

"Old Chang?"

"Yes, Old Chang, the security guard." He stood up and made for the dining table, casually picking up a slice of meat and stuffing it into his mouth.

"Oh, I see," she said. "I'm going to heat up a couple of dishes."

She turned cheerful. Her place was an apartment of seven hundred and twenty square feet: a bedroom, a small living room adjacent to a small dining room, a kitchen, a bathroom, one next to the other, compact and complete. While she was heating the food, she asked, "Old Chang—what about Old Chang?"

"Damn," he cursed, smoking slowly while taking off his shoes and socks.

Old Chang was the gate guard for their company. Yesterday morning the personnel office posted an announcement saying that Old Chang had been fired because he used the company's security room to indulge in drinking and whoring late at night.

"Damn, Old Chang just had bad luck," Chan I-hung said. "Otherwise, how come the foreign devils happened to catch something done late at night?"

He went to the dining room, opened the refrigerator door, and poured himself a glass of ice water. He insisted that the firing wouldn't have happened if Manager Ko of the personnel office had put in a word.

"Besides, the woman wasn't a whore at all. She's Old Chang's girl friend. She works in a Japanese factory in the export processing zone in T'ao-yüan," he said. "As for drinking, everybody knows he drinks."

"*You know what I mean, eh?*" While he was drinking water, he talked to the television, mocking Manager Ko's way of speaking. Manager Ko was fond of speaking in English, and he spoke well. Only he interrupted a sentence with "*You know what I mean, eh?*" several times; it got on one's nerves. "*You know what I mean, don't you, eh?*" Chan I-hung waved his left hand, continuing, "*You know—know* shit. Son of a bitch . . ." Liu Hsiao-ling, heating the food, could not keep from tittering.

The door bell rang again. "*You know what . . .*" Chan I-hung was still mocking Manager Ko as he went to answer the door. A thin little boy was delivering a cake.

"A birthday cake?" He was puzzled.

Liu Hsiao-ling came rushing in from the kitchen, thanked the thin little boy, and gave him ten dollars extra for a tip. The little boy left happily. Chan I-hung closed the door, looking at her, still unable to figure it out.

"It's your birthday. Today," she said, turning aside her head.

"Oh," he said. "Oh—oh."

His usual mocking expression was instantly replaced by a deeply thoughtful one.

"Oh—oh," he said again.

Her eyes turned slightly moist. Never saw such an individual so negligent about himself, she thought.

"I knew you invited me over to have dinner, but I had no idea it was my birthday dinner."

She laughed. "I'm hungry," she said. She glowed in the light. She wiped the sweat from her face with a napkin. She wore snow-white pants, and her body was uncommonly seductive. She clasped his waist with both hands and, pushing him along, walked toward the dining table. He had a firm, smooth waist. Of all parts of his body, his waist spoke best of his youth. J. P.'s waist had long ago softened and sagged.

They began to eat. The table was covered with Taiwanese dishes he didn't know how she had learned to cook: a small plate of salted oysters, a small pot of pork hock noodles, a plate of fried pork chunks, half a steamed chicken, and others. "Are they like the real thing?" she asked in the midst of eating. None of the dishes were authentic Taiwanese cuisine except for the chicken. All the same, he kept saying, "H'm, h'm, not bad," and kept at the beer. The balcony had become completely dark. Two potted pomegranate trees stood motionlessly in the light filtering out from the room.

This was his twenty-eighth birthday. And for the first time, quite to his surprise, someone had taken the trouble to remember it, and thoughtfully prepared a birthday dinner for him as well. His apparent arrogance and cynicism were dissolving. He remarked suddenly, "Hey, this is the first time anyone ever celebrated my birthday."

She put down her chopsticks in the process of picking up some food, and looked at him. He started to talk.

Thanks to a comfortable family background, his father was able to have a complete high school education under the Japanese rule. The third year after his father graduated from high school, Taiwan was returned to China. Chan I-hung's grandfather died the same year. "The property Grandpa left was not much at that time—a pharmacy and a fabric store on the main street, and less than one hectare of land in the country," he confided leisurely. In the political upheaval the next year, his father was wrongfully implicated and almost lost his life. After that, his father, that strong young man, suddenly turned to alcohol and sensual indulgence. "Grandma was very worried, and she presently married him off," he smiled. After his marriage his father managed to pull himself together again, but he soon went bankrupt because of the unstable financial situation. "Sometime after that, I was born, and then my brother and my sister," he remarked thoughtfully. "Father managed to get a job as an art teacher in a grade school by asking favors from friends." Life was hard, understandably. "When it came to celebrating a kid's birthday, we just didn't have the extra money for it. Besides, it just wasn't the thing to do in the country," he said.

She was listening attentively, not because there was anything extraordinary in his story, but because he was describing a childhood so unfamiliar to her. Through his reminiscences, she entered into memories caught in the mildewed yellow tint of old photographs. She poured him a glass of beer, thinking of that cold Christmas night. She thought of the colorful boxes of gifts going up in flame, of her father, who had died a lonely death.

He drank the beer silently. He was thinking of the letter from his father which he had received today after work. As usual, his father talked in the letter about having received the money Chan I-hung had sent, and about how he often used "the older brother in charge of big responsibilities in an American company" as an example to inspire the other children. What was unusual was that for the first time his father wrote: "I have been a loser all my life . . . I hope you will work in order to stand out."

"When one gets old and comes to the conclusion that he is a failure, it must be a painful feeling." He thought of his father at home, who was thin, though quite healthy, whose eyes were as deep-set as his own, and who was extraordinarily fast in his talk. Since his childhood he had been used to hearing his father complain in his rapid manner about the school principal, the dean of students, the financial instability that caused his bankruptcy about thirty years ago, politics, weather, "those mainlanders," and so on.

"Over the years I grew up quietly in the midst of poverty and discontent," he went on, his small, fully fleshed-out face turning increasingly pale from too much drink. "The poverty of my family and the failure of my father were almost like a rope or a whip that compelled me to 'study hard to move up.' So, considering the situation of my family and the failure of my father, I shouldn't have had the chance to study at all, but I did manage to get an education, from one level up to another. I finished college, and then got a master's degree." His face showed anger. "But nobody ever asked me what I wanted for myself, what I really wanted to do . . ." He pounded his breast.

"You've drunk a lot," she said with tenderness.

"'Son, you see, we've sacrificed ourselves so you can get ahead. You see, you're to move ahead of people,'" he mimicked his father. "'It's all right to sacrifice ourselves, son, but you must go where we've tried to go but failed to reach in our lifetime.' That's them for you," he added in agitation, first waving his hands, then raising his eyebrows. Then he burst into laughter.

"You've drunk a lot," she said. "You must have already had a lot to drink with Old Chang."

She dragged him into the living room, and made him sit in the rocking chair next to the television set.

"O.K. I worked my head off studying," he said excitedly, "worked my head off, damn it. I couldn't tell my old man: 'Why do you want to enslave me with your own failure? Why?'" He shook his fist in the air, which caused the rocker to swing slightly. "Because I saw clearly that the taste of failure was hard to stomach, damn it! Life in my family was grim and stifling. Mother went about her work like a machine—a shoddy, inefficient machine: housekeeping for others, doing laundry, baby-sitting. Father complained and cursed all day long."

She fetched an iced towel and wiped away the beads of sweat on his brow and neck. When she unbuttoned his shirt and put the towel on his thin, broad breast, he started giggling.

"Icy cold," he said, pushing her away. "Well, since there was no way out, it was just as well that I worked my head off studying." His high-strung voice suddenly relaxed. He covered his brow with both hands, lightly rubbing the corners of his eyes close to the bridge of his nose. "Just imagine, I used to sleep only three or four hours a day in those years. A teenager, with poor nutrition—I wonder why studying like that for several years didn't kill me."

He began to rock the chair slightly. She stayed there, quietly paring a chilled pear for him. She stared at him. This was the first time she had ever seen a man reveal his bruises. Not until now had she seen the inner mind of a man who was ordinarily rude, arrogant, and unruly. Her heart was aching.

"Have a pear," she said, giving him the pared, juicy pear. "It'll help you sober up."

He bit into the pear woodenly, the juice trickling down from the corner of his mouth. She went over to wipe his mouth. Her aching heart felt a surge of intense warmth as she wiped his face. Under the lamplight in front of the television, which was still tuned to some program, a woman was attending to—sadly attending to—the bruises of a man, soothing the hurt, dividing it up to be shared by both. This was the very happiness Liu Hsiao-ling had yearned for! She fell into a reverie. She thought of her broken marriage. Just to hurt her mother, upon graduation from college she had married a bachelor ten years her senior who worked in a shipping company. The break-up of the marriage was due less to his physical impotence than to the eccentricities resulting from that impotence. After the divorce she had come to Malamud, and had led a lonely life since, wandering from one man to another.

He was still woodenly eating his pear, when suddenly he asked, "Hey, is there wine? I don't want beer."

"No," she said. "Besides, you shouldn't drink any more." She walked to the television set to change the channel. "Watch some TV," she said.

But he staggered out to get a bottle of Twin-Deer and a wine glass from the cupboard, and then staggered back to the rocking chair.

"Chan I-hung!" She was worried and went over to wrest the bottle away. As he raised his elbows to protect the bottle in his hands, his left arm touched her braless breast, soft, yet extravagantly ample. His senses, even though somewhat dulled by the alcohol, experienced a profound shock in that fraction of a second. He looked her straight in the face, silently, with the stare of a drunk.

"You've drunk too much," she complained, "too much."

He just stared at her, without a word, though there was no eagerness of desire in the stare.

"Give me the bottle, like a good boy," she said. "Go take a bath. Let's go to bed early," she coaxed him with provocative affection.

He silently drank down the glass of wine in his hand. He thought of her extravagantly ample breasts. Slowly and carefully he poured another glass of wine, and stammered, "Hey, you said you're pregnant. Is that true?"

"Give me the bottle!" she said.

"Is that true?" he asked.

"Whether I'm pregnant or not—what does it have to do with you?" she said with a smile. She knew it was simply out of the question to try to take the bottle away from him. She turned around to watch the television. The screen was showing a Taiwanese-language soap opera with all its ruckus.

Chan I-hung was tittering all to himself.

She got up to clear the table, humming a popular song.

"Don't go away," he turned to fetch the cigarettes from the tea table, and struck a match with his slightly trembling hands.

"I'm just clearing the table," she explained as she did this. "I might just as well put off doing the dishes until tomorrow."

He watched the television silently, puffing on his cigarette. The alcohol began to make him lose heart.

"Whether you're pregnant or not—what does it have to do with me, erh?" he seemed to be saying to himself.

"What?" she asked from the kitchen. The dishes made a screeching sound as she placed them in the sink. He said nothing, watching the television blankly.

She came out of the kitchen, drying her hands, and sat down beside him.

"What?" she repeated her question, looking at his pale, purplish, suddenly tired face. "Let me turn on the water for you to take a bath."

Silently, slowly, he drank the wine, watching the television.

"Hey," he said, "what do you think of Taiwanese men?"

The kind of question a drunk man asks, she thought. Still, she answered in all earnest, "There's one Taiwanese man in my heart." She looked at his profile, which always seemed a little lonesome, a little vexed. "He's most manly, a real man. I love him." She felt unaccountably sad. "But he doesn't love me. No, he doesn't," she repeated, "No, he doesn't, he doesn't."

"Look at those Taiwanese," he stared at the screen. "Look at those Taiwanese. Either crazy or stupid, every one of them."

Absently, she looked at the Taiwanese-language slapstick series, which was a fracas and in bad taste.

"If a mainlander—" he said, "a mainlander has learned to know the Taiwanese from this kind of drama series since childhood—what image of the Taiwanese will he have?"

She listened attentively, almost forgetting that it was a drunk's gibberish.

"Of course," he said, "people who write this kind of series are themselves Taiwanese." He laughed sadly.

"Do you want a bath?" she said. "Let me go turn on the water."

He remained silent a while, then suddenly said, "Did you say it's none of my business whether you're pregnant or not?"

She cackled. "What's the matter?" She was beaming.

"Of course it's none of my business whether you're pregnant or not," he said.

"Let me go turn on the water for you," she said tenderly.

His voice was high and quivery. She saw an ugly, horrible face, distorted by rage and excessive drink. Her heart was sinking rapidly.

"Might just as well have it out," he shouted. "Do you—do you think I don't know what's going on between you and J. P.? Ha!"

Her arms and legs began to feel cold. The storm came up with unprecedented abruptness. He was a jealous man, violently jealous. Time and again they had engaged in vehement arguments over things from her past which had come to his knowledge. She was surprised, however, that he had found out about her relation with J. P.

"Of course it's none of my business whether you're pregnant or not." His face was as ashen as a piece of old paper. He shouted madly, "Can't you tighten up the belt of your pants a little?"

His words were like a sharp knife suddenly piercing her breast. Her face blushed from shame and fury. Her tears fell like a torrent.

"You deceive me so," he said.

Suddenly he turned around, and slapped her squarely in the face. As he swung his hand at her for the second time, she sprang up by reflex, holding the sharp fruit knife in her hand.

He also stood up from the rocking chair. He saw the woman who used to take his scolding, even his beatings, without a murmur now standing before him grimly with a sharp knife in her hand. His addled head could not make out the meaning of the scene at the moment. He gasped, "You take—me—to be—the kind of—crazy—stupid guy—on television?"

His voice had obviously lost its edge. He noticed that the woman's left cheek was swollen and showed the clear imprint of his hand. She backed down a couple of steps, holding the fruit knife tightly, saying, "Don't be rough on me anymore. I'm with child." Her voice was as dignified as her expression.

"Chan I-hung, listen well: Whether you believe it or not, I'm carrying your child. But you don't have to worry," she swallowed, and continued clearly, "I—Liu Hsiao-ling—will never force myself on you or ask you to marry me. As I said, I'll give birth to the child on my own and bring it up by myself. Both the child and I will go far away from you."

He stood woodenly. His drunkenness was for the most part gone. "I'm carrying you child"—her words reverberated in a spot in his brain that had just sobered up. He had witnessed the most primitive courage of a mother. Gradually, tears were drying on her cheeks, cheeks swollen from his slap. Still, she was holding tight to her sharp knife.

"I would never casually allow just any blood and flesh to grow in me," she said, unconsciously combing her hair with her hand. "I'm carrying this one because—" her voice was a little quivery, "because—I love you."

Instantly her eyes went moist. But she suppressed her emotion as if out of alarm, blinking her eyes hard, holding the knife tightly. She struggled silently with her feelings. A long while later, she said, "Go. Take a bath."

He remained standing a while, deep in thought. Then, he put on his clothes and picked up his overcoat from the sofa.

"What are you doing?" she said.

"I'm leaving," he said.

She lowered her head, without a word, and put down the fruit knife on the tea table. He happened to see her little finger bleeding, obviously injured from holding the cutting edge of the knife so tightly.

"Go then." She slouched down on the sofa. Blood dripped down on the cuffs of her snow-white pants, making dark red spots.

He hesitated, but the little bit of fragile male pride that was still left compelled him to make for the door. Suddenly she grasped his leather belt.

"What are you doing?" he said.

"Don't go," she said pitiably. Her tears came down like rain water. She began to sob, "I won't tie you down." She went on, still sobbing, "If you have to go, go tomorrow morning. You're—drunk—so drunk. Too danger-ous—to ride a motorcycle . . ."

She finally let herself go; her cry was so pitiful.

He turned around, embracing her tightly.

"Hsiao Liu!" he said under his breath. "You injured your hand. You—do you know that?"

She cried so much her body shook. He felt her braless breasts, soft, and conspicuously more ample than usual, heaving rapidly in his embrace. Her solemn announcement "I'm carrying your child" occupied all his thoughts.

"Don't cry." He patted the back of her neck lightly. "You've injured your hand."

Two lines of warm tears had been running down his purplish, sodden face, unnoticed.

III. THE DESERT MUSEUM

After one week's delay, Mr. Solon O. Bowdell, Director of Finance of the Pacific Division of the Malamud International Company, finally arrived at the Taiwan Malamud Electronic Company with two other people. The entire financial department, from Morgenthau and Lin Jung-p'ing on down, was kept nervous and busy for four days. Early in the morning of the fifth day, S.O.B. (Mr. Solon O. Bowdell) took the flight for Tokyo, leaving Mr. Dasman in Taiwan to continue with the financial situation of the Taiwan Malamud. Once again Lin Jung-p'ing's competence had received very high praise. His Chinese way of avoiding taking the full credit—his knack for appropriately attributing part of the credit to Mr. Morgenthau—pleased the latter tremendously.

The four hectic days were over. Mr. Dasman, the financial auditor left behind, was young, smart, and easygoing. He was very friendly with everyone at Taiwan Malamud. Since Mr. Dasman's audit started on the fifth day, the financial department decided to get all the staff together to give him a banquet after work that day. It would double as a farewell party for Liu Hsiao-ling, who had decided to resign and leave for America early next month.

After work, Chan I-hung went back to his small apartment, changed into a new indigo-blue suit, and arrived at the restaurant where the banquet was to be. In the elevator to the third floor, he looked at himself in the big mirror and found himself to have thinned down a lot. In front of the elevator two lovers were nestling up to each other. It seemed to him that the depression he had had no time to deal with in the past few days was like this elevator: heavy, but as nimble in its ups and downs as a cat.

He entered the reserved banquet room on the third floor.

"Hi, Chan!" Morgenthau said jubilantly.

"Hi!" Chan I-hung said.

A waiter brought him a glass of juice mixed with a little mild liquor. He found the card on the table with "James Chan" on it, and sat down.

"James, you look tired," Mr. Morgenthau said from the other side of the table, gesturing to him with the glass of juice in his hand. "J.P. said you did a good job the past few days."

Chan I-hung gestured to Mr. Morgenthau with the glass in his hand. "Thank you. But it's really nothing . . ." he said.

Just then, Lin Jung-p'ing and Mr. Dasman came in, escorting Liu Hsiao-ling and starting a reverberation of "Hi's." Lin Jung-p'ing's light brown suit was obviously of top material and tailoring, but the print and color of his tie were insufferably vulgar. Mr. Dasman, who had not changed the heavy, checked Scottish tweed jacket he had been wearing all day long, looked casual, as usual. His beard had a golden sheen in the soft light.

Liu Hsiao-ling was wearing a wine-red evening gown that trailed to the floor. Her dense hair fell naturally in delicate billows onto her shoulders. The loose, silk dress by no means hid her svelte, firm body. Without a word, she smiled and nodded to everyone who greeted her.

Chan I-hung lowered his head, sipping the juice mixed with mild liquor. Since Liu Hsiao-ling had entered the dining room she had not once looked straight at him. But exactly because of this he knew that she had already spotted him. He should not keep to himself in front of such a crowd, he thought, but it was hard for him to casually engage someone in chitchat. Unconsciously he got out a cigarette, and was surprised when a struck lighter was put before his nose.

"Thanks," he said, suddenly conscious of the lighter. "Thank you very much."

"I've never seen you so affluently dressed," J. P. said in English.

Chan I-hung laughed, thinking of J. P.'s English: it was the first time he had heard "affluent" being used to describe one's dress.

"Over the past few days," J.P. said, "if it weren't for you . . ."

"Really nothing," he said, deciding to let himself go and look his superior straight in the eye. There was no trace of mockery on J. P.'s face, and none of the hypocrisy or arrogance of a high-ranking employee. He set to detailing for J. P. the problems that had come up when he had gone over the audit with Mr. Dasman that day. Lin Jung-p'ing listened carefully, asking one or two expert questions from time to time.

A waiter popped in to ask what kind of drink they wanted. It cut short Chan I-hung's account.

"Whisky!" J.P. said.

Chan I-hung raised the glass of juice he was drinking and told the waiter, "I don't want anything else. Just refill this for me later. Thank you." J.P. stared at him incredulously. The atmosphere in the dining room had long since been quite lively. He noticed that a waiter had started to serve the first course of appetizers to Liu Hsiao-ling's group. Mr. Morgenthau and Mr. Dasman were sitting on either side of Liu Hsiao-ling, talking quite exuberantly, as if vying with each other in saying something to her. She just smiled, calmly and decorously. She was wearing an enameled bronze necklace that matched her belt. Chan I-hung saw on the bronze plate large, deep green lotus leaves overlapping each other in a delicately tasteful fashion. Beneath the lotus leaves were a pair of quails painted in blue and dotted with tiny white flowers.

On the night when they had celebrated his birthday in her apartment, they had decided to get married as soon as possible. The next evening he had accompanied her to buy the wine-red silk gown she wore this evening. They had also bought some jewelry at a jeweler's: the enameled bronze necklace etched with archaic patterns, the bronze belt, and the bronze ring. Each had the same pattern of dark-green lotus leaves and quails. She then accompanied him to order his custom-made, indigo-blue suit.

But only a few days later they had gotten into a violent quarrel again. His jealousy over her past amounted to a kind of madness, a sickness. Their quarrels increased in intensity with each passing day. They exchanged the most vicious and obscene curses. Once, in his apartment, he had lost his mind in extreme fury, striking her and kicking her like a madman. She seized a cushion to protect her belly and curled herself into a ball. By the time he had come to himself, she had already staggered out. She did not cry, curse, or even moan.

She was gone. All that was left in the room was his regret and guilt. He smoked a cigarette. He paced around. He turned on the television and stared blankly at it. When he could no longer tolerate it and had gone out to take a taxi to her apartment, it was almost midnight. Finding her windows shut and the lights all out, he got out the key and opened the door. Not a soul was inside. As never before, he was seized by an uneasy feeling. At this moment she came back. The left part of her forehead had a bluish swelling. He strode toward her, but she nimbly succeeded in avoiding his embrace. The odor of medicine told him that she was just back from a hospital. In the kitchen she opened the refrigerator and poured herself a big glass of ice water. She leaned on the doorway, looking at him while sipping the water a little at a time. In her eyes there was no hatred, and undoubtedly also no love.

"Fortunately the child was all right, the doctor said." She spoke as if to herself.

"Hsiao-ling," he said.

Calmly, she divided up the water and gave half to him. He held her hand with the glass of water. "Sorry," he stammered. She walked away, and sat down on the sofa.

"Please don't say that," she finally said.

They fell into silence. The sound of someone hawking stuffed dumplings wafted in from some distance away. She took out a thick envelope from a pocket, saying, "It's come."

He took it and looked it over. It was a stack of immigration forms sent by the American embassy.

"I'm leaving next month."

He did not say anything, returning the forms to her immediately. He wanted to smoke but he did not have his cigarettes with him. Plunk! She threw the stack of forms onto the television set and sighed. "I'm with child, but you've got nothing . . ."

He turned and left. As he was about to go down the stairway he had a glimpse of her calmly closing the drapes over the French window; she didn't bother to look at him. Vexed, he rushed all the way down the stairway and stepped out into the street. He walked rapidly down the red-brick pavement lined by maple trees. "Go, go away. The farther away the better!" he shouted inside himself. He did not notice that it was raining lightly until he was stopped at a railroad crossing by a long line of freight cars rumbling by.

"Sir, how would you like your steak done?" a waiter in a dark brown uniform asked.

"Medium well." Chan I-hung grinned at the waiter. He noticed that the waiter's collar was slightly yellowed from grimy sweat.

"Actually," Lin Jung-p'ing, who was sitting beside him, said, "you can go abroad to get a master's degree."

"Forget it," Chan I-hung smiled, shaking his head.

"The financial department is going to be expanding next year," J.P. said.

"Forget it," Chan I-hung said. This time he did not smile. He turned his head and toasted his colleague, Alice, on his left with a sip of wine.

"They have a new singer in The Wooden Gate Restaurant," Alice said. "A skinny little thing, still a bit countrified. But when she sings Joan Baez's songs, it sounds like the real thing."

"Oh?" Chan I-hung said.

J.P. saw through Chan I-hung's hostility clearly. So he knows! he thought. He had gone with Dasman to bring Liu Hsiao-ling here, but now he had to sit one table away from her. This was no more than a signal to indicate to Morganthau that "I have nothing going on with Linda." He saw Morgenthau and Dasman sitting on each side of Liu Hsiao-ling, engaged in lively conversation. He was resentful of the two foreigners. No, he thought, shaking his head slightly, the most hateful one ought to be myself.

After the woman who used to be his mistress was insulted by his foreign boss, Lin Jung-p'ing had to pretend to his boss, almost by instinct, that he knew nothing of it, had to pretend that there was absolutely nothing between the woman and himself. A person like me . . . he thought.

"Manager Lin," Davis Hsü said, "let me offer you a toast."

Lin Jung-p'ing displayed a broad smile, raising his wine glass. Davis was a self-made young man. Ten years ago when he had graduated from commercial school he had gone to work for a U.S. military unit. The cutback in American servicemen had cost him his job. He was recommended to Lin Jung-p'ing by a Jaycee friend. Lin Jung-p'ing was immediately certain that even though Davis lacked impressive educational qualifications, he was able and could endure hard work. Without hesitation, he gave him important responsibilities, which had made him very grateful, and now Davis held his wine glass with both hands respectfully and said, "Let me offer you a toast." His pale complexion was blushing from awe and shyness.

"What do you do to pass the time?" J.P. said, trying to be as amicable as possible.

"Ah, ah," Davis stammered, "study English a little."

Lin Jung-p'ing complimented his English out of politeness. At that moment there was some gleeful uproar at Liu Hsiao-ling's end. Lin Jung-p'ing squinted his eyes, noticing that Mr. Morganthau's face was flushed with drink.

"J.P., have you ever heard of anyone who likes deserts?" Mr. Morgenthau shouted from across a table. "Linda said she loved deserts—what a peculiar interest."

Lin Jung-p'ing looked at Mr. Morgenthau without expression. Mr. Morgenthau's moustache looked particularly striking against his complexion reddened from alcohol. "You sonovabitch!" he cursed inside himself, "You're no more than an idiot." He knew that in two years the headquarters in New York was going to adopt a new policy to turn the administration of all branch companies over to natives as much as possible—"insofar as necessary and feasible." He had already started preparation, first to put loyal ones in the financial department, then to tell Morganthau to get out.

"You should go get a master's degree," Lin Jung-p'ing turned to say to Chan I-hung. "I can consider sending you abroad at company expense."

"Forget it," Chan I-hung said.

"You should visit the Sonora Desert in Arizona, then," Mr. Dasman told Liu Hsiao-ling. "They have a very good desert museum there."

While pretending to be talking enthusiastically about a new movie with his neighbor Alice, a hard-working girl who worked on form-filling, Chan I-hung perked up his ears, trying to hear across the noise the talk on the desert at Liu Hsiao-ling's end. Mr. Dasman, who called himself an amateur ecologist, was describing the desert museum—how modern scientific instruments had been installed to give a vivid explanation of the process of evolution; how special optical equipment made visitors able to

see the amazing way that desert animals lived, most of which were noc-
turnal animals.

"Oh, I've never heard of that before, not at all," Liu Hsiao-ling sighed.

"Deserts are full of life and activity," Mr. Dasman said, "only people
don't quite understand them."

"But Mr. Dasman . . ." Liu Hsiao-ling said.

Chan I-hung listened intently. He lighted a cigarette. Alice's English
was not very good, but she seemed also to be listening carefully.

"How pretty Liu Hsiao-ling looks tonight!" Alice said.

This time Chan I-hung turned his face to one side, and drank the juice
mixed with mild liquor in unison with J.P. "You should have a little wine.
You can drink," J.P. said. "No, no," Chan I-hung said. He could detect
J.P.'s very ambiguous sadness. He began to think of the night he had
rushed in a huff out of Liu Hsiao-ling's house into the street. Since then,
they had not been seeing each other, even though every day, after he
returned to his untidy room after work, he would helplessly think of her,
and of the line of freight cars stopping him at the crossing—a long line of
immense, black freight cars rumbling before him, moving toward the
south. Oh, toward the south, his hometown: his hometown, with only two
small streets; beyond the streets, an expanse of plain, neither big nor
small.

Not long after he had gotten to know Liu Hsiao-ling, Chan I-hung once
went with her by night train to his home in the rural south. In the train,
the light was soft and the seats were comfortable. She allowed him to hold
her hand, while her right hand fidgeted with the gauze window curtain. It
was then that she talked calmly about a scene that had appeared and
reappeared in her night dreams for the past dozen years: a vast expanse of
white desert.

"Every time I see sand on a construction site, I can't keep from going
over to touch it," she said.

He listened absentmindedly. He was wondering about his father's reaction when he found out that he had brought home one of those "mainlander women." He smiled in silence.

"But it's altogether different from the sand in my dream," she said.

He sat up a little, stretching out his hand for the glass of tea on the tray.
He saw her head, with long, billowing hair, leaning to one side, reflected
on the glass pane of the window. Outside was the infinite dark night. The
lights in the distance spun around slowly, moving backward. The profile
of her face, as she chewed gum mechanically, appeared calm, contented,
but lonesome.

She said the sand in her dreams was white.

"Not pure white," she said, "but the kind of white like egg shells."

He burst into laughter, remembering the time when he was stupid enough to make a practice of eating two raw eggs in liquor each morning. An acquaintance in the days when he was serving in the army said that it would enhance virility.

She turned and looked at him in wonder.

"Even egg shells," he said, "are not of one kind."

She held his hand close to her, but not for her life would she allow his hand to touch intentionally, mischievously, her ample breasts. Again, she leaned her head to one side on the glass of the window, gazing at the dark night outside.

"It's that kind of white. White and absolutely clean sand, immense and without bounds wherever you look," she said.

"Got to have some cactus or something," he teased.

She shook her head.

"Or a few skulls of cattle."

Once again she shook her head solemnly.

She said that the first time she had had such a dream was when she was in high school. The silent, white, boundless world of sand frightened her. Every time she woke up from the dream of the desert, she would cry helplessly. Sometimes she had to stuff the hem of the blanket into her mouth to stifle the sound of her cry.

"Then, as I got older, I probably became used to it," she said. "Gradually I was able to gaze at the vast expanse of sand in the dream."

She thus became interested in real deserts.

Chan I-hung gave up on the small steak and let the waiter remove the plate. He wiped his mouth carefully with a napkin. Not having had a good appetite in the first place, he now felt stuffed, sated with the flavor of ketchup. Mr. Morgenthau suggested that everyone take turns toasting the evening's two guests of honor. Chan I-hung saw Liu Hsiao-ling spring up. In that instant, standing upright, she was the very image of gracefulness.

"No," she said, "let me thank everyone."

The two foreigners also stood up. After some confusion, everyone at the table finally stood up. Chan I-hung looked at the floor, holding his long-stemmed glass firmly.

"You can't forget us, Miss Liu," Alice broke out.

He raised his head, and met Liu Hsiao-ling's sad, somewhat tipsy eyes on him. He saw her describe a half circle in the air with the wine glass in her hand in invitation to everyone to drink.

She was wearing nothing on her plump fingers. Silently, he drank up the little juice remaining at the bottom of his glass. As everyone sat down again, he thought of the ring in the pocket of his jacket. He groped with his hand and found it still there. It was the bronze ring that matched the necklace and belt she was wearing; on it was etched the pattern of dark green lotus. The ring was with him because he had intended to put it on her finger at their civil marriage that they had planned to take place soon.

Mr. Morgenthau seemed to have started talking about politics.

"*S.O.B. said that we multinational companies here will never let Taiwan be wiped off the map . . .*" Obviously drunk, Mr. Morgenthau pressed his face close to Liu Hsiao-ling. "Strange," he said. "We American businessmen think Taipei is hundreds of thousands times better than New York, and you fucking Chinese think the United States is a fucking paradise."

Chan I-hung saw Liu Hsiao-ling's face withdraw stiffly. "I don't think the United States is a paradise," she said with a polite smile. Appropriately, she deleted the expletive from before "paradise." She was neither embarrassed nor angry; in fact she was a little contemptuous of Mr. Morgenthau's loss of self-control. Quickly, Chan I-hung moved his eyes toward the wall. He felt a chill in his stomach, a gradual blankness in his brain. After all she's the kind of woman who has seen the world, he thought. "*And you fucking Chinese think the United States is a fucking paradise,*" Mr. Morgenthau repeated himself. "Isn't it strange, Mr. Dasman?" Mr. Dasman broke into a guffaw. Alice could not understand the English dirty word, and she laughed with him in innocence. Chan I-hung took a deep breath. His brain was churning. Mr. Morgenthau was still going on with some gibberish, but all that Chan I-hung felt was "*fucking Chinese*" spinning in the vast emptiness of his brain. He felt a slight, involuntary tremor in his hands.

He broke out, "Gentlemen, watch your language . . ."

He spoke in English. His voice was peculiarly weak. Except for Lin Jung-p'ing no one heard what he said. Lin Jung-p'ing looked at him in surprise. Chan I-hung was hurt by the weakness of his own voice, and became furious. He jumped up.

"Gentlemen, you better watch what you say," he said. His face was pale and he was breathing fast. Instantly the dining room quieted down. It seemed that no one knew exactly what had happened.

"I am resigning to express my protest, Mr. Morgenthau," Chan I-hung said, his face contorted in agony. "But, Mr. Morgenthau, you owe me a serious apology."

"James . . ." Lin Jung-p'ing said under his breath.

"An apology such as one would expect from the citizen of a great democratic republic," Chan I-hung said.

Abruptly, Chan I-hung turned to Lin Jung-p'ing, a sad, anguished smile on his face. "J.P.," he changed into Taiwanese, "let's not quarrel in front of the barbarians." He forced a smile, making an effort to maintain a calm tone. "I don't know about you. As for me, I can't take this kind of rotten life anymore!"

He strode from the dining room, without bothering to look back.

"Chan I-hung." Liu Hsiao-ling jumped up. "Chan I-hung!" she called out. Gathering up her long gown that trailed to the floor, she ran out of the dining room, with its cozy, gorgeous chandelier, after Chan I-hung.

IV. THE ENAMELED BRONZE RING

Somewhere not far from the restaurant, Liu Hsiao-ling caught up with Chan I-hung. She grasped his arm. Quietly, they walked down a small slope that led to a thoroughfare. Several times she stole anxious glances at his profile as he was staring straight ahead. The contortion of fury, sorrow, shame, and agony on his face when he left the banquet had disappeared. He looked tired, yet relieved and peaceful—a new look, even to her.

A taxi drove slowly alongside them as if to invite them in. Chan I-hung shook his head amiably at the driver, and the car sped off. As Liu Hsiao-ling silently looked at the vanishing lights of the car, Chan I-hung took her right hand and put the enameled bronze ring on it.

She began to cry.

"Don't go abroad," he said quietly. "Go with me to the country."

Trying hard to keep herself from crying out, she nodded her head incessantly.

"Don't cry," he said tenderly.

Suddenly he remembered the long line of freight cars passing the crossing, the long, immense black freight cars, cars that rumbled toward the south, where his hometown was.

NOTES

1. These words, as well as a number of expressions in the later part of the story, are originally in English. They will be represented by italics throughout.
2. The Yülung Automobile Company is a Chinese automobile manufacturer in Taiwan.
3. Presumably Pei-t'ou, a resort town in the neighborhood of Taipei, which is famous for its spa facilities. The town sports a Japanese-influenced subculture; it also attracts numerous Japanese tourists.
4. "Hsiao" literally is "little," usually preceding the surname as an informal (sometimes intimate) way of address.
5. Atami ("Hot Sea," as the characters read in Chinese) is a famous resort town in the Izu Peninsula of Japan.
6. A Japanese expression used in addressing or referring to an older woman.
7. Literally, "The Association of the People from the Same Region." Chinese away from their home "regions"—mainlanders exiled in Taiwan, or native Taiwanese students leaving home to study abroad—tend to join their regional *t'ung-hsiang-hui.* The "region" can be a town, county, province, or several provinces (for example, Manchuria).

HUANG CH'UN-MING (1939–)

Among the writers represented in this anthology, Huang Ch'un-ming should be a more familiar name. His The Drowning of an Old Cat and Other Stories *(1980) was published by Indiana University Press. A peripatetic writer celebrated for his sympathetic portrayal of little people in small towns, Huang was relatively uninterested in topical subjects until a series of international events affecting Taiwan's political entity forced him to change direction. First it was the State Department's decision to return the Tiao Yü T'ai islands to Japanese jurisdiction in 1971. In the same year, the Nationalist Government was expelled from the United Nations. Then came the "Nixon* shokku"*—President Nixon's visit to Peking in 1972. Though no Kuomintang loyalist, Huang nevertheless felt the snub as a Chinese national. But to read "I Love Mary" as an anti-American story would miss the point, for the butt of the author's ridicule and contempt is reserved for the "imitation American," the* chia Mei-kuo jen. *Like "Night Freight," Huang's story is a "cautionary tale" about the corrosion of Chinese identity in the teeth of a superior materialistic culture. Huang graduated from Pingtung Normal College but finds himself temperamentally more suited to be a writer. He supports himself by odd jobs, seldom staying in the same position for more than a year. By common consent, Huang's* tour de force *is "A Flower in the Rainy Night" (*K'an-hai ti jih-tzu, *1967, included in* Chinese Stories from Taiwan). *His works are listed and discussed in* Chinese Fiction from Taiwan: Critical Perspectives.

I Love Mary

Translated by Howard Goldblatt

A RECTIFICATION OF NAMES

Ta-wei Chen's legal Chinese name was Chen Shun-te.[1] He had found it necessary to adopt the name Ta-wei Chen because he worked in one of Taipei's foreign establishments. The foreign name was intended as a convenience for his foreign employers, but unexpectedly his friends and acquaintances, even his wife, also took to calling him Ta-wei. When foreigners or English-speaking Chinese friends addressed him, Ta-wei easily became *David*[2] in standard English pronunciation. All his other friends

pronounced the name in true Chinese fashion, with two distinct tonal
syllables—Ta-wei. But it really made no difference, for whenever he was
addressed as Ta-wei, either in standard English or in transliterated Chinese, it evoked the same quick response. However, on those infrequent
occasions when someone called him by his formal Chinese name, Mr.
Chen Shun-te, or, more intimately, by his given name alone—Shun-te—
his reaction was considerably blunted. He would first pretend that he
hadn't heard; when the name was repeated he would contemplate it
momentarily; but on the third mention, he would once again pretend that
he hadn't heard, even though by then he would be somewhat dis-
gruntled. If the person hadn't the patience or the confidence to call out a
fourth time, that person could get our hero to turn around and acknowl-
edge his presence only by a slap on the shoulder. In short, whenever
someone addressed him by his true Chinese name, his reaction, far from
being natural and spontaneous, was carefully measured. Still, it would be
inaccurate to say that he was repelled by his Chinese name; often, for
example, when someone used it he would eventually turn around and
respond with evident embarrassment:

"Oh, pardon me, I'm sorry. Were you addressing me? You must have
called me several times. Ai, I'm just about deaf in my left ear. When I was
a child, one of my teachers hit me on the ear and damaged it permanently. Foreigners don't believe in corporal punishment with their students, you know."

On other occasions he might react with displeasure:

"How was I to know you were addressing me? There are so many
people named Chen Shun-te it's enough to drive a person nuts! No one's
called me Chen Shun-te for a long time—call me Ta-wei." Naturally his
displeasure at being called by his Chinese name was linked to the identity
of the person addressing him and the class to which that person was
supposed to belong.

The clear difference in responses between being called by his foreign
name on the one hand and his Chinese name on the other was solid
evidence of how he had thrown himself into his work at the foreign
company over the past four years; Ta-wei Chen had disembodied himself
from Chen Shun-te and had immersed himself totally in his work environment. He was just the kind of person his foreign employer liked to
have around. This preference had nothing to do with personal affection,
but was a potential source of inestimable benefits in virtually every aspect
of promoting his company's position locally. But Ta-wei Chen never
wavered in the belief that his relationship with his foreign employer was
nothing less than true friendship, a belief that had long since become the
rock-bottom support for his psychological well-being.

As far as his outward appearance was concerned, Ta-wei Chen had become a sort of stooge. He slept well and had a good appetite, which gave him a look of affluence that belied his youthful age. Stooges like him have a unique personality trait: they are totally servile toward the cruel taskmasters above them and can stoically accept any adversity forced upon them. Otherwise how could he, for instance, have functioned in this foreign establishment—especially under the supervision of a swaggering boss like Raymond—without getting the axe or calling it quits? On the other hand, for those who were socially below him, no matter how servilely or stoically they took what he dished out, it did them no good at all.

In a nutshell, it was no easy task to work for a man like Raymond for all these years and even manage to develop a paunch. Moreover, Ta-wei's affectations gave him the appearance of a tendril coiled around the branches of a great tree, bathing in the spring sunlight and blossoming forth. He was unabashedly content with his present circumstances. During leisure hours away from the office, his favorite pastime was stretching out on the sofa, raising his legs slightly, and spreading his delicate fingers atop his slightly protuding belly, which rose and fell with the rhythm of his hurried breathing. Once in a while he would observe his reclining image in the bay windows of the coffee shop across the way, and at such times he felt he could almost see in this reflection a view of his own promising future.

Somewhere along the way, Ta-wei's friends had begun using a sound-alike word for the second half of his name, for which an appropriate translation might be "Potbelly." This he discovered through some notes his friends had left for him in which they had unabashedly called him Potbelly. Even those friends who customarily called him David began using Ta-wei—Potbelly. Fortunately for him, in Chinese this term sounded exactly the same as the Ta-wei meaning David. There had been a time when the distortion of his name had bothered him, but, to his amazement, before long even his employer, Mr. Raymond, had begun addressing him by the name Ta-wei. He thought about this for a while and wound up delighted with the turn of events, seeing it as a blessing in disguise. For some time after that, he laughingly said to nearly everyone he met:

"Shit, even my American boss calls me Ta-wei—Potbelly. Hey! Shit!" He would be grinning so broadly his eyes would be narrow slits, for he interpreted this development as an indication that the relationship between him and his employer had undergone a change, that they were now closer than ever. And so, when he learned that his boss was being transferred back to the States, he pestered Mr. and Mrs. Raymond until he was blue in the face, begging them to leave Mary with him. For the first few days he got on their nerves, and he knew it. But secure in the knowledge that Mr. Raymond called him Potbelly, what was there to fear? He knew they'd let him have Mary if he kept it up long enough, and this realization served to embolden him. He could not have felt more deserving.

AN AMERICAN LIFESTYLE

Ta-wei spent NT$4,000[3] to buy a copy of a painting of a faded lotus by the renowned artist Ch'i Pai-shih, and with great difficulty drove from the frame shop in Taipei to the foreign residential community of T'ien-mu. As he sped down Taipei's major artery, each time he approached an intersection he prayed to himself, mumbling softly, "Green light, please, a green light . . ." But every single traffic light evoked an outburst of cursing, for it was one red light after another. He breathed a sigh of relief as he drove up to the lane where the Raymonds lived, for a glance at his watch showed that he was twelve minutes early for his four o'clock appointment to bid them farewell.

Ta-wei instinctively considered very carefully what he would do with these twelve minutes. During his employment with this establishment, experience had taught him the value of time from a foreigner's point of view. A man like Raymond was obsessed with the scheduling, utilization, and demands of time, and Chinese who worked for him understood that they had to always be on the alert. As far as Raymond was concerned, punctuality meant being neither early nor late, and this concept of time was clearly understood by Ta-wei and a few of the others. Raymond demanded that every job be carried out precisely on schedule, like the smooth flow of a river. To him it was more than a simple matter of efficiency—it was a sort of work ethic; more than that, it was the epitome of the laborer's art. Time and again he emphasized the concept that any job carried out with this principle firmly in grasp produced its own enjoyment, that labor itself was a form of pleasure. He was content in the belief that he was the founder of a school of philosophy.

Throughout his experience, whenever Ta-wei or one of the others fell short of being punctual or failed to complete a job on time, no matter how insignificant it might be, Raymond never missed an opportunity to preach his philosophy. And he didn't stop with singling out the individual in his rebuke:

"I won't deny that China has a 5,000-year history, that she's got 5,000 years behind her. But if this is the way things have always been done, then those precious 5,000 years have been wasted. If you're time conscious, you don't need 5,000 years, or even 500—200 is more than enough. I'm afraid I'll be dragged into the mire by you people if you don't mend your time-wasting ways."

They had been subjected to more of this type of officious prattle than they cared to remember. It had all come to a head when several of Ta-wei's Chinese co-workers had banded together to demand an apology from Raymond for one of his insulting outbursts against their country. Ta-wei had prudently kept himself above the fray. His noninvolvement led to the resignation of his co-workers, which in turn resulted in added pressures on him at the office. He was fearful that Raymond would repeat his public tirades and that his new co-workers would again unite in defiance. As a result, he was more heedful of punctuality than ever before.

As his car approached the Raymonds' lane, with twelve minutes still to go, he chose not to bring the car to a stop, but stepped down on the gas pedal instead and shot past, casting a quick glance at the Raymonds' home as he did so. Looking straight ahead again, he was relieved by the assurance that the Raymonds were not out in front. He had not yet forgotten his harrowing experience at the frame shop: when the shopkeeper had told him that the job wouldn't be ready for another two hours, he had jumped to his feet and started screaming at the man. By now it all seemed so amusing. As he drove past one Western style residence after another, he was conscious of how fresh and clear the air was. In another year or so, he figured, one of the homes in this neighborhood ought to be his. He drove around the block, lost in thought. When he arrived back at the entrance to the lane, he quickly brought the car to a stop and looked at his watch—it was four minutes to four.

He knew there wasn't enough time to make another turn around the block, so he decided to play it safe by staying where he was and smoking a cigarette. He lazily put a cigarette into his mouth but quickly took it out again, for he realized how embarrassed he would be if the Raymonds spotted him waiting there before the appointed hour. He got out of the car, raised the hood, and stuck his head and upper body into the engine space. He tinkered around for a moment until he was nearly overcome by the steam from the engine. He was painfully aware of why he was having to make such a show of being busy.

While Ta-wei was feeling miserable about himself, his hands were fumbling around inside the engine space. He came perilously close to removing the radiator cap and scalding himself, saved only by the fact that he brushed his hand against the radiator and burned it. This made him angry, but then amused him. About all he could do was mock himself by cursing: "The Chinese are lowdown scum! We're a lot stricter about time when we work in foreign companies than when we work for our fellow countrymen. And that's the shits!"

The four minutes were nearly up. It would take about two minutes to finish his tinkering and negotiate the distance to Raymond's gate. That was just right. Arriving two minutes late would give him a chance to make some proper apologies. He had learned his lessons well after working so long under Raymond: whatever the job, it was always best to be less than perfect. By intentionally letting some tiny defect remain, he gave Raymond the opportunity to do some nit-picking, after which Ta-wei would deferentially promise to improve in the future. This always pleased his employer, sometimes to the point that he would bestow some comforting balm:

"Actually, Ta-wei, you've done just fine. I've made my demands so strict for your own good, to help you do even better work. Do you understand?"

Of course he understood. This little speech of Raymond's was invariably orchestrated by Ta-wei himself, so whenever he heard it he nodded and said "I understand, I do."

The effect on Raymond was an assurance that his astuteness had not been misconstrued as nit-picking, that the other man had understood him and was grateful. For this he would reward Ta-wei with extra attention and affection.

As for Ta-wei, he was content in having mastered the psychology of his boss. Their relationship was indeed a fragile one: while it was necessary for Ta-wei to avoid damaging his superior's self-respect and sense of authority, it was equally important to keep the man's haughtiness in check. All this was above and beyond the call of duty, but because Ta-wei had played the game so well, his employer was forced to admit that he was satisfied with the performance of his employee. What did it matter to Ta-wei that he had to endure all that officious prattle, as long as he could achieve these results, especially since he himself had orchestrated the whole affair? Whose business was it anyway if what happened to him was precisely what he had asked for? This had always been the guiding principle in his thoughts and deeds.

Everything was going according to plan. As he stood at the Raymonds' gate, his hand raised to ring the bell, he was greeted by the barking of a German shepherd inside. He was given a fright, and began shouting: "It's me, it's me, Ta-wei!"

But the dog kept it up unrelentingly until Ta-wei heard Mrs. Raymond shout: "It's okay, Mary, it's okay. Stop barking now, stop barking. Ta-wei is your new master," she said as she unlocked the gate. Mary's nose was the first to appear as the gate opened just a crack, then the dog pushed the gate open enough to squeeze through. Ta-wei was nearly frightened out of his skin by the menacing sight of the approaching dog. "Mrs. Raymond . . . ," he yelled. She followed the dog out the gate and laughed as she saw Ta-wei backing up hastily, his arms thrust upward, and looking as though he were about to be launched into the air.

"It's all right, she won't hurt you. Come here, Mary!"

The dog obeyed at first but quickly turned and bounded back over to

Ta-wei, where she sniffed him up one side and down the other. She paused in the area of the groin, sniffing long and hard, so frightening Ta-wei that he was reduced to protesting weakly: "Ma . . . Mary . . . Mary." The more he tried to back off, the higher his rear end arched, and he was barely able to stand on his shaky legs. As for the cherished area being so carefully scrutinized, it grew so numb it might as well have been frozen.

"Mary, come here," Mrs. Raymond shouted.

"Please, please hold onto her, all right?" Ta-wei pleaded fearfully.

"It's all right, she won't bite you. Come over here and pet her. Just do it gently and everything'll be fine. She just wants to get to know you. Isn't that right, Mary? Good girl." Mrs. Raymond knelt down to hug the dog and give her a kiss.

It was obvious to Ta-wei that he was expected to follow her lead, so he walked slowly over, patted the dog gently, and very gingerly called her name. He seemed ready to spring to his feet and scream in terror. But Mary wagged her tail and refrained from barking, so that Ta-wei's soul, which had beat a hasty retreat from his body, began cautiously to make its return.

"You see, isn't everything just fine now? You don't have to be afraid of her." Mrs. Raymond got to her feet. "Come inside and sit down. Jim's taking a shower, but he'll be right out."

"Oh, I'm sorry, I've come at a bad time."

"No, we were expecting you at four o'clock. Have a seat. Can I get you something to drink?"

"No, thanks, don't go to any trouble."

"Please have a seat." Once he was settled, Mrs. Raymond asked: "Would you like some tea? Or would you prefer coffee or cola?"

Now everyone knows that these are the most common, most natural of all civilities, but they made Ta-wei squirm uncomfortably. Feeling terribly ill at ease, he didn't quite know how to handle the situation. He felt that Mrs. Raymond's politeness was more than he deserved, that she was treating him too well. Having just managed to sit down, he sprang back to his feet and objected: "Nothing for me, please, there's no need."

"But I am going to get you something, so what'll it be?" By now Mrs. Raymond was beginning to feel uncomfortable, too, but she forced a smile to let him know that it wasn't such a big deal, and softened her tone of voice.

"Then I'll . . . I'll have a cup of coffee."

"Coffee's more expensive than the others."

Ta-wei's obvious discomfort had by now tickled Mrs. Raymond's fancy, so she decided to tease him a little.

"Oh, then tea will be fine."

She laughed out loud. "President Carter has urged us to drink more tea, but since you're a guest in our home, we won't let that stop us. Coffee it is, then. Sugar?"

"No, no sugar. Thank you, thank you very much." Ta-wei politely refused Mrs. Raymond's offer, unable to shake the feeling that she had no need to be so polite to him, that he was putting her to too much trouble. The truth was, not only did he take sugar in his coffee, he used more than most people, and this sweet tooth was the cause of all the cavities in his teeth.

"You look like you're putting on weight, so you're better off cutting down on sweets. You sit where you are and play with Mary awhile. You'll be fast friends before you know it." With that she turned and started off to the kitchen, rolling her eyes upward and letting out a deep sigh as she walked past the screen, as though a great load had been lifted from her.

Mary followed her mistress into the kitchen, then turned and walked back into the living room. As Ta-wei softly called her name, she walked briskly over to him and meekly allowed him to stroke her back. She buried her nose between his legs, forcing him to sit like a young lady, his legs pressed closely together off to one side. Before long, he and Mary were getting along beautifully. Ta-wei steadied her head with one hand, pointed to her nose with the other, and said, not forgetting that he had to speak softly and in English: "That's some snout you've got there, some snout." He laughed at his own joke.

In the kitchen, after filling up the kettle and setting it on the stove, Mrs. Raymond went over to the bathroom and spoke to her husband, softly enough that Ta-wei couldn't hear: "Hurry up, will you? I really can't stand that man."

Raymond laughed heartily: "He's a good fellow," he said.

"I don't care what he is, I still don't like him. Now, hurry up." She walked back to the kitchen, adding along the way: "Jim . . . please!"

"Okay, okay," he answered, turning off the shower.

Meanwhile, in the living room, Ta-wei was playing with Mary, thinking to himself that from now on she belonged to him. The thought that after today he could take her out in the car on days off brought him a sense of self-satisfaction. He rubbed and rubbed her head, and was soon not only completely at ease with the dog, but was even developing a fondness for her. Meanwhile, she lay down and stretched out lazily, letting Ta-wei do whatever he wanted to her.

Raymond strode into the living room, saying as he entered, "A hot day today. Sorry to keep you waiting while I cooled off."

Ta-wei quickly stood up. "Oh, I just arrived." Mary jumped to her feet and ran over to lick Raymond.

Ta-wei was wondering whether he should give Raymond the painting right away, but he decided to wait for Mrs. Raymond, since the gift was actually for her. He drew back his hand that had reached out for the package, beginning to feel strangely ill at ease.

"Will you be taking Mary with you today?"

"It's all the same to me," he said with an embarrassed smile.

"Go ahead. My wife's resigned to it." Raymond patted Mary. "Mary, Ta-wei's your new master. Understand?"

"Mary, come here," Ta-wei said softly. To his surprise, Mary bounded over to him.

"Hey, she really listens to you."

Taking advantage of Ta-wei's distraction, as soon as she reached him Mary stuck her nose in between his legs, just as Mrs. Raymond walked in with the coffee. Ta-wei quickly pushed the dog away and slammed his legs shut, accidentally giving Mary's head a solid rap with his knees. "Oh, I'm sorry. I'm sorry. I'm terribly sorry!" He rushed forward to apologize to the rapidly retreating Mary. The excessive concern over how this was being taken by his hosts caused him considerable nervousness, which in turn was an embarrassment to them. Mrs. Raymond scowled at her husband, but he merely shrugged his shoulders and smiled.

"Don't worry," said Raymond, "dogs have hard heads." Seeing his wife put the coffee onto the table, he said: "Come on, drink your coffee."

"Oh, thank you very much." By now, Ta-wei was in a state of near panic. He had just finished apologizing, and now he was being given coffee, for which he had to express his thanks, and then it was back to apologizing. "Oh, excuse me, I'm so sorry . . ."

"You ought to take a look at your knees and see if they're hurt. If they are, we're the ones who should be apologizing." This little joke by Raymond eased the tension and put them all in a lighter mood.

Ta-wei's thoughts returned to the gift; the time had come to make the presentation, so before the laughter had died out, he picked up the package and said to Mrs. Raymond: "This is for you. I hope you like it."

"Oh, another gift for me! What is it? May I open it now?" This was the first time since Ta-wei's arrival that Mrs. Raymond seemed to be truly pleased.

"You're always giving my wife things, but never anything for me," Raymond said with a smile.

Fortunately, Mrs. Raymond spoke up before Ta-wei was again thrown into a state of nervous embarrassment.

"That's enough of that talk. You tease people too much."

"You see how smart you were to give her a gift—she's taking your side now."

"Just ignore him," she said to Ta-wei. "Shall I open it?"

"By all means, but . . ." Mrs. Raymond cut him off before he had finished.

"Don't tell me, let me guess."

"Ta-wei, you'll have to learn that women love surprises. They appreciate something more if they have to guess what it is."

Mrs. Raymond paid them no attention, turning the long package over and over and shaking it to guess its contents. Actually, she knew right away that it was a Chinese scroll. Ever since she began making preparations to return to the States, she had been looking forward to taking several good scrolls back with her, and now her wish was about to be partially fulfilled by what she was holding in her hand. Whether this particular painting was good or bad didn't really matter; her happiness was already halfway complete, so she said spiritedly: "I'll bet it's a Chinese scroll, right?"

"That's exactly what it is," Ta-wei said with a nod of his head, sharing her happiness.

"You see, I was right," she said to her husband.

"Mrs. Raymond, how about guessing the name of the artist and the theme of the painting," Ta-wei said.

"I'll bet she can. All the foreigners in Taipei consider her to be a real China hand."

Ta-wei's comment had filled her heart with joy, and her husband's praises made her even happier. "Do you really think I could guess it?"

"Unless my memory fails me, I'm sure you'll be able to guess this particular artist," Ta-wei responded, intending to boost her confidence.

"Really? Do I like his work?" She was so happy her eyes were nearly popping out. She thought hard, then asked: "Is he one of my favorite Chinese artists?"

"Ta-wei, you're really something. Even I don't know which artists my wife likes," Raymond teases.

"Jim, keep quiet and let me think!"

"Okay, I'll keep quiet, but let me first register one complaint with Ta-wei," he said with a smile. "Ta-wei, you shouldn't have told her a moment ago that she would know, because now if her guess is wrong, she'll blame me. Okay, that's all, I'm gonna get a beer."

"Hold on a second," Mrs. Raymond said, "don't leave till I've guessed. Otherwise, if I do get the right answer, you'll say that Ta-wei told me while you were out."

"Whoops, now if she doesn't guess it, I won't get my beer."

"I was just joking. You go ahead, and get me one while you're at it." Then she asked Ta-wei eagerly: "How can you be sure I know this particular artist? Are you positive?"

"I'm positive."

"That's strange," she said as she racked her brains. "How come I can't be sure I know?"

"I'm just sure, that's all. Here, I'll give you a hint," he said ingratiat-
ingly. "Do you remember that time I took you and several other American wives to visit the orphanage? Well, in the cafeteria you mentioned to
Mrs. Smith and some of the others that you were fond of this particular
artist, and that . . ."

"All right, that's enough. In the orphanage cafeteria, you say?" Having
drawn a blank, she wasn't sure she believed him. She began to suspect
that he was making fun of her when he said that she had been discussing
famous artists during her tour of the orphanage. But when she sized him
up again, she doubted that he was that sharp-witted. So she recom-
menced trying to figure out Ta-wei's hint. Her recollection was hazy, but
she thought she knew the answer. "I think I've got it," she said excitedly,
"I think I've got it. Jim, I've got the answer," she yelled to her husband.

Jim was just then entering the room with the beers. "Who is it?"

"It's . . ." Mrs. Raymond said very deliberately, "Ch'i . . . Pai-shih."

"Right—" This did not catch Ta-wei unprepared; without a thought for
the tens of thousands of cells that would suffer under the onslaught, he
began clapping his hands loud and hard the moment she said the name.

"Is it really one of Ch'i Pai-shih's paintings?" Mrs. Raymond asked, her
mouth cracked in a broad grin, her hand outstretched as she reached for
the proffered can of beer.

"It sure is!" Ta-wei seemed the happiest of all, as he too reached out to
take the beer Raymond was handing him.

"Come on, let's drink to Lucy, our China hand," Raymond said with a
chuckle, snapping open his can of beer.

"Oh! This is wonderful!" Lucy opened her can of beer. "Ta-wei, thank
you very, very much."

Seeing Mrs. Raymond nearly beside herself with delight, Ta-wei suddenly grew uneasy, and although he too started to open the can of beer,
owing to a rush of sudden anxieties, he was unable to snap it open as they
had done; instead of the popping sound that should have emerged, it just
sort of fizzled.

"I really do like Ch'i Pai-shih!" Mrs. Raymond said emphatically.

Ta-wei's spirits plummeted even further. How was he going to break
the news that this was only a copy? If he was going to say it, he should
have done so at the very beginning: she was sure to be disappointed if he
told her now. Seeing that she was about to open the package, he cleared
his throat a couple of times and said, "Uh, Mrs. Raymond."

"Call her Lucy, she'd like that." Raymond turned to Lucy. "Wouldn't
you?"

"Lucy, uh, Mrs. Raymond, there's something I have to tell you." Accustomed as he was to addressing her in formal fashion, in his nervousness he called her by both her familiar and formal names, and all that

kept the Raymonds from laughing out loud was the seriousness with which he said there was something he had to tell her. They stood there speechless, listening to his explanation. "With all the Ch'i Pai-shih paintings around, there are bound to be a lot of forgeries. I can't guarantee that this particular one is an original." He was by now quite flustered.

"Tsk-tsk!" Lucy's disappointment showed as she untied the silk ribbon.

"Open it and take a look," Raymond said.

For a moment the only sound to be heard was the unrolling of the scroll. Lucy spread it out on the rug and they all looked at it in silence, no one willing to express an opinion. Actually, they could tell at first glance that it wasn't bad. Raymond broke the silence with an involuntary "umh." Lucy and Ta-wei, thinking he was going to say something, looked over at him. With their eyes on him, Raymond voiced his impression of the painting: "It looks pretty good to me."

"To me, too," Lucy commented as her smile began to reappear. Ta-wei was pleased with their reaction.

"It is pretty good, isn't it," he said. "My friend is an expert."

"It looks pretty old."

"The older it is, the greater the possibility that it's the genuine article," Lucy said. "Who knows, maybe our luck's held out and we've got the real thing here."

"Mrs. Raymond's got a point there. Buying antiques depends a lot on luck, even when experts are involved. My luck's been pretty good so far, so this is probably the real thing."

Raymond and his wife turned simultaneously to look at Ta-wei, causing him to shrink back considerably.

"Thanks ever so much." The politeness of Lucy's response was evident by the change in her tone of voice. "How did you find this painting?"

"I had a friend buy it from an aristocratic mainlander who had fallen on hard times."

"You bought it?" Lucy nearly shouted. "That must have cost a pretty penny. Now I feel bad!"

"No, no, it's nothing, nothing at all. How could this possibly compensate for all Mr. Raymond's done for me over the years? This little thing doesn't begin to express my regard for you." He rubbed his hands as he spoke, all the while looking strangely apologetic.

"You're much too polite." Raymond was embarrassed by the earnestness of Ta-wei's expression of gratitude.

"I mean it, I really do. I'm truly grateful."

Mr. and Mrs. Raymond wondered what they had done for Ta-wei to make him feel that way, for whenever they discussed him at home, they generally concluded that he was a pig or a dog, until by and by, any reference to him came out "that pig did this or that," or "that dog did thus and so." It was not something they did unconsciously. Now here he was, standing in front of them expressing with genuine sincerity his boundless gratitude, causing them considerable discomfort. Lucy's distress stemmed in part from the fact that in the brief period of time before returning to the States, Ta-wei had already given her a pair of bracelets, two custom-made Chinese gowns, and now an antique scroll. Whether the scroll was authentic or not, she was moved by its power as an artistic creation, and this feeling served to increase its value in her mind. She felt that she had no right to accept so many gifts from Ta-wei, and was eager to calm her troubled heart.

"Hey, where's Mary?" she said, looking around. Mary, who had been resting in a corner of the living room, bounded over to her. Mrs. Raymond hurriedly straddled the scroll, which was still on the rug, knelt down, and wrapped her arms around Mary. "Jim, roll up the scroll before Mary ruins it."

"I'll get it!" Ta-wei stepped in to pick the scroll up off the floor.

"Ta-wei, are you going to take Mary with you when you leave?" She continued hugging the dog intimately.

"I don't have to. I can wait a few more days till you leave, if you'd prefer. I'm in no hurry."

"Lucy, we have so many things to take care of that we won't have time to look after the dog."

"I know, I was just asking," she said as she petted the dog.

"I'm in no hurry. I can imagine what Mrs. Raymond must be feeling now."

Raymond had been restraining the smoldering anger inside him: he had to be very, very careful, since lately Lucy had been arguing with him at the drop of a hat. He was afraid that during a real flare-up she might fall to pieces and he'd be unable to save the situation. This was one of the reasons he had asked to be transferred back to the States. That way he could get Lucy to a doctor—the only apparent alternative was divorce. The situation with Mary, simply stated was: they had paid NT $600 for this part-German shepherd in a pet shop on Hsin-yi Road shortly after their arrival in Taipei, and it was he, not Lucy, who took care of the animal. But as time went on, if he so much as called the dog's name once too often, Lucy would get angry and start an argument. Even if Ta-wei hadn't asked them to leave Mary with him, they would not have spent the several hundreds of dollars it would have cost to take the dog back home with them. And Lucy knew it. As for her husband, he was nauseated by the disgusting sight of his wife kissing Mary in the presence of Ta-wei.

Lucy was also a very cautious person, and she knew Raymond's thoughts on the matter. So she let the dog go. "Is the doghouse finished?"

"It was finished several days ago. It cost me NT $2,000. I even bought a book on dog care, which I've read carefully the last three nights."

"You take him with you today." She was looking directly at her husband, for whom this statement was intended. She knew he was angry. Then she added: "Mary's been in heat the past few days, so make sure you don't let her mate with any strays. She must mate only with a pedigreed German shepherd."

"Absolutely!" Then Ta-wei laughed: "Really, you must be joking. How could she ever mate with a stray!"

Raymond was obviously growing impatient, but at this stage only Lucy was aware of it. "I've already let the dog go," she was thinking, "so what are you getting so huffy about?" She forced herself to control her temper, saying to Ta-wei instead: "There's one thing that still troubles me. I know there's nothing to worry about with you, but I'm afraid that someone might steal Mary and cook her. No other people in the world except you Chinese eat dog meat—you even call it 'fragrant flesh'!"

"I know, it's really barbaric," Ta-wei responded apologetically. "But I'm different from the rest of them—I don't do things like that."

"I know you don't, but don't you let anyone else mistreat her. I plan to ask Mr. and Mrs. Brown to look in on her, not because we don't trust you, but because of our concern over Mary."

"I know, I know. I'll take good care of her."

Raymond could no longer hold back the anger that was welling up inside him, so he decided to leave the room as a sign to his wife not to go overboard. Naturally, he was protesting not for Ta-wei's sake, but for his own. Lucy saw what was happening and decided to stand up to him.

"Mary, come here." Lucy called Mary over to her, where the dog stood up with her paws on Mrs. Raymond's legs and gave her a wet kiss on the mouth. This threw a fright into Raymond, for he knew that if he walked out now, there'd be a real knock-down, drag-out fight afterwards. So he decided to stick it out and stay where he was. Lucy hugged the dog, sneaking a look at her husband as she said to Ta-wei: "Mary's a very intelligent dog, smarter than some people I know. Dogs are like people: if you love 'em, they'll love you back. She understands me when I say 'I love Mary.'" As though that were a signal, Mary reached up and licked her mistress. "You see, I wasn't fooling. You call her and see what she does."

"Mary, come here." Sure enough, Mary bounded over to Ta-wei, who quickly snapped his legs shut.

"See what happens when you say you love her."

Ta-wei was more than a little hesitant, for he didn't dare say the word "love," even to a woman. How could he possibly say it to a dog? He didn't think he could bring himself to say it, but Lucy wouldn't let him off the hook: "Hurry up, tell her you love her. I'm sure she'll understand, and she'll like you for it."

Suddenly, for reasons he could not fathom, he grew light-headed, then blurted out: "I love Mary, I love Mary, I love Mary." He wasn't even aware of what he was doing until the words were out. Mary friskily put her paws up on his legs, stretched toward him, and began licking his face all over with the slobbering tongue of a dog in heat. He was startled nearly out of his wits.

"You see, she understood you!"

Seeing the funny expression on Ta-wei's face, Raymond could no longer remain silent:

"Ta-wei's English has always been very good," he observed teasingly, "but when he said 'I love Mary' just now, it sounded almost musical."

This comment made everyone laugh, and the sight of Lucy laughing so happily came as a big relief to Raymond. They exchanged a quick glance, and the concession of defeat in his eyes made her laugh ever more spiritedly. Looking first to her master then to her mistress, for some mysterious reason Mary joined the merriment by barking enthusiastically.

Ta-wei was completely oblivious to the fact that during their conversation a violent cold war had occurred between the Raymonds. He was much too happy about being allowed to take Mary home with him today to take notice.

Having settled Mary into the back seat, he saw things differently now than when he complained nervously about the children's getting the seat dirty. Seeing Mary jump willingly into the back seat of the car blinded him to the muddy footprints she made on the seat cushions as she hopped around nervously. He was extremely attentive to whether or not he was being noticed by people on the street: each time he stopped at a traffic light, he glanced to the right and left and into the rear view mirror to see if anyone was watching him, after which he turned back to play briefly with Mary. She was fussing and fretting in the back seat, scratching at the side and rear windows and leaving abstract masterpieces in slobber on the windows with her wet tongue. All of this naturally captured the attention of bystanders and drivers of cars behind him. Not that any special significance could be attached to their reaction to all this activity, but there was no mistaking that Ta-wei pictured himself as having taken a giant step up the social ladder, and that his lifestyle was more and more in the American mold.

Never before in his life had he experienced the euphoria that accompanied him on the trip from the American residential district through the streets of Taipei, with Mary seated behind him.

"LAI" IS *COME*, "CH'Ü" IS *GO*

The Raymonds returned to the States.

On every conceivable opportunity at the office, Ta-wei deftly turned the conversation to a discussion of Mary's daily activities, thereby hinting at the closeness of his relationship with the former manager. Naturally, he limited his comments to Mary's presence in his home, and how he and his family had to wait upon her. There was never a word about all the distress Mary caused his wife, Yü-yün—Jade Cloud.

According to Ta-wei, this foreign dog was highly intelligent, not your usual brainless mutt. As for poor Mrs. Chen, who had never learned English—one of her husband's great disappointments—no matter how many times she called the dog with her Taiwanese accent—"Mei-li"— Mary never once wagged her tail to express the liberally used American greeting "hello," and no wonder.

Mrs. Chen had opposed the idea of bringing Mary home from the very beginning, basing her opposition solely on a fear of dogs she had carried with her since being bitten once. All this proved to Ta-wei was that she was not only a shallow woman, but a selfish one as well.

"What a woman you are! I'm perfectly willing to talk this out in a civilized fashion, but have you asked yourself whether you're being rea- sonable or not?" He raised his voice and said self-confidently: "You're afraid of dogs, so you don't want anyone else to have one. Someday, if you choked on some food, you'd be so skittish you'd force everyone else to stop eating. That's called 'Better unfed than dead.' You're a high school graduate, so you should at least understand the logic of what I'm saying."

"But, but the children are afraid too, and you know it."

"Of course I know. With a scaredy-cat mother like you, how could they be anything else?"

"Don't talk like a tyrant, okay?"

"Just let me handle my own affairs. My mind's made up!"

Yü-yün knew that the case was closed as soon as Ta-wei said "my own affairs."

Ever since their marriage had been arranged by Assemblyman Lin from their hometown, she had observed this Chen Shun-te, how he had worked his way up from an English teacher at a rural middle school to a position with a Taipei trading company. Within two years he had risen to the position of manager. Then as soon as the opportunity presented itself, he took a job with this foreign concern. He climbed and clawed his way up the ladder, and on his personnel file a minor promotion appeared every year or so. All of the major and minor incidents that comprised this personal history, all of the decisions, had been Chen Shun-te's alone—his wife had played no role at all. In fact, there was no need for her to get involved in any of this. They had food to eat, clothes to wear, and a place to live, so the question was no longer one of need or practicalities; it was time to talk of creature comforts and status. Yü-yün intuitively felt that this sort of lifestyle precluded her from questioning anything her husband did. Although she often suffered considerable emotional distress over the despotic arrogance that was fostered in her husband by his accomplishments at the office, there were still some bright spots in her cloistered life, thanks also to her husband's career achievements. Virtually all of their friends, relatives, or old schoolmates at reunions congratulated her on having married someone who had done so well in a foreign company. Then when these people considered the increased possibility of Ta-wei and Yü-yün's going overseas, they were downright envious. This phenomenon of securing others' envy and praise for something that caused her so much emotional distress made it tough for Yü-yün to diagnose her problem. Hearing the flattering comments of friends and relatives strengthened her resolve to put up with her overbearing husband.

On this occasion, Yü-yün would not have even considered opposing her husband's plan to keep the pet if it hadn't been for her uncontrollable fear of dogs. The whole affair ceased to be a simple matter the moment Ta-wei said truculently: "Just let me handle my own affairs. My mind's made up!" Yü-yün viewed it with the same fatalism as she felt toward Ta-wei's achievements at the office; she knew for certain that the raising of a dog in their home was now a foregone conclusion. Nonetheless, she continued to be bothered by what Ta-wei had told her: it was to be a big German shepherd. She even had nightmares over this. She briefly considered telling Ta-wei about her dreams, but past experience told her that he would react by screaming or laughing at her. Finally, after suffering through several more nights of bad dreams, she decided to speak up:

"The coffee's ready. Drink it while it's hot." Seeing that Ta-wei was in a good mood, she continued: "Why don't we get a small dog? Something like a Pekingese or a Pomeranian. They don't get too big and they're awfully cute. The children would really like one of them."

All of this talk greatly displeased Ta-wei, but, detecting the pleading tone of her voice, he took pity on her. Following a swallow of coffee to settle his nerves, he said: "You're wrong if you think I want to raise just any old dog. I'm only interested in raising the Raymonds' dog." A thoughtful pause, then he continued: "Our relationship with Raymond hasn't ended just because he's returned to the States. Who knows, he may return someday." It occurred to him that this analytical explanation showed that deep down he was nothing but a schemer, and even though it was only his wife he was talking to, he was embarrassed nonetheless, so he let the matter drop right there. Actually there was yet another reason behind his decision to take the dog into his home, and that was his complete intoxication with the American lifestyle. Even though he didn't elaborate on this, Yü-yün was still able to grasp the essence of the matter. There was no mistaking what he meant by "my business." It did not occur to her that he had said it for the simple reason that he did not want her to annoy him any more. This happy misinterpretation of "my business" resulted in her feeling that she had wronged him, which caused her deep remorse. And so she abandoned her opposition to adopting Mary and began making mental preparations for the dog's arrival.

On the afternoon that Ta-wei brought Mary home, he was so pleased with himself that he began honking his horn before the car had even pulled up to the house. This sort of thing rarely occurred in Ta-wei's life. That's not to say that he seldom honked his horn. Quite the contrary, he was famous for doing so whenever he came to a pedestrian crossing, and especially during the period just following his purchase of an older European car from one of his foreign colleagues last year. On those occasions when he took his whole family out for a ride, he would go out and start up the engine, then lay on his horn to get the others moving, usually causing poor Yü-yün to scurry around the house in such a flustered state that she would forget to bring something, or she would leave the children's shoes untied and shirt buttons undone until everyone was seated in the car. They were by now quite accustomed to Papa's fondness for honking the horn, although they seldom heard him doing it in such obviously high spirits upon his return home.

"Hey, Daddy's home," the children called out, quickly falling under the spell of the horn's infectious gaiety.

"Mommy, Daddy's home," the youngest chimed in.

Naturally, Yü-yün had heard the horn too, and she was reminded of the joyous scene on the familiar TV commerical for mortgage insurance, where the head of the household returns home to his beloved family. Each day as he drives up to his home he toots his horn once to announce happily to one and all: "I'm home!" And there are the wife and kiddies lined up at the doorway joyously awaiting Father's return. Today, since this sort of emotional blaring of the horn was uncharacteristic of Ta-wei, Yü-yün unconsciously related it to her experience in front of the TV and had the feeling that she was tasting the sweetness of model family life.

By the time Yü-yün and the three children had rushed to the front door and opened it, Ta-wei had already parked the car and was standing outside holding the leash with both hands, a broad grin on his face as he prepared to lead Mary across the street. The sight that greeted Yü-yün as she swung the door open was of Mary, a rotund canine the size of a brown bear, and she was so stunned she nearly slammed the door shut immediately. Instead she huddled the children close to her. She was riveted to the spot. Her innate fear of dogs was not going to go away just because she willed it to, especially when confronted with a brutish, lively animal like Mary.

Ta-wei had no preconceived notion of what sort of welcome would be awaiting him, but he was something less than pleased by the sight of his

wife standing there looking frightened to death. Fortunately for her, the
flow of cars, which kept Ta-wei from crossing the street, afforded her the
opportunity to spot the look of displeasure on his face; realizing how tense
she must appear, she struggled to compose herself and look as relaxed as
possible. The most noticeable effect of this inner struggle was a frozen
smile on her face. As for her hands, she maintained a tight grip on her two
children, the one on her right by the collar, the one on her left by his
shoulder, hugging them both close to her.

By now, although several breaks in the flow of traffic had appeared, Ta-
wei remained where he was, unable to drag Mary, who was agitated over
being taken from her master and mistress, across the street. In reality,
rather than say Ta-wei was dragging Mary, it would be more accurate to
say that Mary was dragging *him*. Now Mary was turning back constantly
and pawing the car door, trying to get in, or tugging on the leash in an
attempt to dash up one end of the street or the other. And there was Ta-
wei, looking like a man engaged in a wrestling match: grappling with all
his might, his round, perspiration-streaked face so flushed it looked like a
watermelon stripped of its rind. All the while he was shouting incessantly:
"Mary! Mary!" Poor Yü-yün! The frightening sight of the struggle across
the street erased even the weak smile she had managed for her husband's
welcome.

For Mary it was a series of trial-and-error experiments: since there was
no going back, and the left and right avenues of escape were closed to her,
there was nothing left but to bolt across the street. Much to everyone's
surprise, in a flash she had crossed the street, dragging Ta-wei along with
her. This sight so frightened the three children, who watched her rush
headlong toward them, that they spun around, held onto their mother's
thighs and waist for dear life, and cried out in terror. Their mother
meanwhile shut her eyes tightly as though facing an impending calamity
that she was powerless to ward off. She bent over deeply to protect her
children in an act of ultimate maternal love, but when what she feared did
not materialize, she opened her eyes to discover that Ta-wei and Mary
were nowhere to be seen.

"Where's Daddy?" she asked.

Her oldest son, Tsu-wei, timidly stuck out his arm, prepared at any
moment to pull it back, and pointed into the house.

Yü-yün finally straightened up, but the two smaller children held onto
her as tightly as ever. She thought for a moment, then decided she'd
better go inside before Ta-wei blew his stack.

"Come on, let's go inside."

When they heard their mama say this, Chin-wen and Han-k'e⁴ grasped
her even more tightly to keep from having to enter the house.

"Foolish children," she said, bending down, "don't be afraid. Didn't

Daddy tell us not to be afraid? Daddy would be angry if he saw you like this. Be good boys and come inside with me, all right?"

Han-k'e started to sob. Yü-yün didn't know what to do now. Just then Ta-wei came noiselessly up behind her. He didn't say a word, which left her in a quandary, not knowing what to say. She could see at a glance that he was really steamed up.

Ta-wei was angered by his family's reaction, but he was angriest at Mary for her lack of obedience. To top it all off, he was embarrassed at not having any control over the dog, for he was sure his wife had noticed the fear in his eyes, and this loss of face had put him in a foul mood. But in fact Yü-yün had been in such a state of fright herself that she had no idea her husband was afraid of Mary. If that weren't enough, his pudgy body had been strained to its limit by the struggle with Mary.

Nonetheless, his mood and his exhaustion were momentarily eclipsed by pangs of pity for his wife and children as he stepped outside and heard what Yü-yün was saying, and when he saw how petrified they were of the dog and of him. He kept his sullen thoughts to himself. Without saying a word, he bent down to pick up Han-k'e and carry him into the house, but he was shocked by the boy's reaction of wailing hysterically and lurching backwards to keep from having to go inside.

"Okay, okay, we won't go inside! Daddy'll take you all out for ice cream." With that he headed toward the car parked across the street.

"Do you have your keys?" Yü-yün asked him.

"Come on!" he said impatiently.

Yü-yün closed the front door and crossed the street, where she joined the rest of the family in the car. Ta-wei then drove them all to an ice cream parlor. They negotiated the entire trip without exchanging a word. In fact, Ta-wei did not lift the veil of silence until the ice cream was on the table and the children were attacking it with gusto.

"Don't be afraid of Mary," he finally said. "She's a nice doggie, and in a couple of days she'll be your very best friend." Yü-yün was struck by how gentle, how fatherly he sounded, and was comforted by his tone. "Han-k'e, are you still frightened?" Ta-wei asked.

Han-k'e smiled and looked into the others' faces, then, with a notice-able trace of apprehension, said what he knew his father wanted to hear: "No."

"Good boy, that's the way to be." Ta-wei patted his son on the head, then turned to the next youngest: "Chin-wen, are you afraid of her?" Chin-wen was too busy eating to say anything, so he merely shook his head and smiled.

"Daddy's not sure if that means you're not afraid, or what," Ta-wei said.

"I'm not," he snapped back in a soft voice, like he was fibbing, which embarrassed him.

"Tsu-wei, how about you?"

"Not me!"

"Right, there's nothing to be afraid of. Mary's gonna be our watchdog and keep the thieves away. We don't have to be afraid of her—only thieves have to. You kids certainly aren't thieves."

By now everyone was in high spirits, so Yü-yün spoke up: "Where'd you put the dog?"

"I tied her up in the patio and opened a can of dog food for her."

"I never imagined she'd be so big," Yü-yün commented, still experiencing a few trembles.

Ta-wei quickly gave her a warning with his eyes. "Sure! We want her to be big. No thief would ever dare come to our house after seeing her." Yü-yün quickly comprehended the look he had given her: he didn't want her to say anything that might give the children cause for fear.

"Daddy, our big doggie is an American dog, isn't she?" Han-k'e asked in the proud manner of someone who could boast of American ties.

"That's right! Mary's an American dog. Mary is an American name. From now on, call her Mary as often as you can, and she'll be real happy."

Seeing that the children were no longer frightened by the mention of the dog, and that they were chatting about her happily, Yü-yün turned to look at Ta-wei, willing to concede defeat.

When they arrived home, it was clear that the children weren't nearly as frightened as they had been, and although none had the courage to go straight to the patio to take a look, they did go into the kitchen to watch her though the window. They immediately cried out excitedly, all at the same time:

"Daddy . . . the big doggie's in trouble—she smashed all your orchids!" Since they were all shouting at once, their parents couldn't understand what they were saying, although they knew that something was wrong. Ta-wei was already walking over toward the patio, and when he heard the children shouting, he burst through the door and discovered that some thirty potted orchids had been knocked to the floor, ten of them lying there smashed. He was livid with rage. Yü-yün and the children held their breath, waiting to see how Ta-wei was going to punish Mary. Oh, how well they knew what these orchids meant to Daddy! For accidentally knocking over a single pot one day, Tsu-wei had received a spanking, and all the children were forbidden to play in the patio after that.

Mary began wagging her tail when she saw Ta-wei enter the patio; she strained at the leash, trying to jump at him, happy sounds of welcome emerging from her throat. He raised his hands to get her to calm down, but she stood up on her hind legs, pawing the air in front of her as she tried to reach him with her forelegs. Ta-wei kept his distance and tried to quiet her down with hand motions and a steady stream of commands in

English. Neither would give in, especially Mary, whose struggle didn't seem to tire her in the least. Ta-wei moved a little closer, holding on to one of her front paws with one hand and patting her head with the other, saying over and over, "*Nice dog.*" All of this finally won Mary's confidence and she eased back down, putting all four feet on the floor, allowing Ta-wei to pat her head to demonstrate how obedient she was.

Ta-wei's attention was caught by four pairs of disbelieving eyes looking at him through the kitchen window; he turned back and barked out angrily to Yü-yün: "Get a broom and clean this mess up—what are you staring at?"

"The dog," she stammered fearfully.

"She hasn't gobbled me up yet, has she?"

Yü-yün walked into the patio with a broom and dustpan, her nerves so taut that the slightest scare would have been sufficient to give her a nervous breakdown. Hardly daring to breathe, she begged Ta-wei: "Don't . . . don't you let her go! I'd die of fright!"

She bent over to pick up some broken flower pots, in such a jittery manner that she looked like someone clearing a mine field with her bare hands. The children also got jittery as they watched her through the window. The only thing that kept her moving was the constant stream of English mutterings directed at Mary by Ta-wei. She hoped that he would keep it up at least until she finished tidying up.

As Ta-wei worked at calming Mary down, he managed to find the time to direct Yü-yün in her work, telling her where to put the flowers and accusing her of being stupid when she didn't do things the way he wanted. As soon as the reclining Mary, who was used to being pampered, heard Ta-wei switch from English and adopt a harsh tone of voice, she quickly got to her feet and struck a menacing, restless pose. Ta-wei immediately switched back to English and changed his tone of voice: "*No! No! Not you, not you . . .*" He grasped the leash firmly with one hand and patted her gently on the head with the other, stroking her all the way down her back. Before long she was stretched out comfortably on the floor again. As she was tidying up, Yü-yün never took her eyes off the dog, while her every move was in turn scrutinized by Ta-wei, as he watched to see if she damaged any of the orchids.

Yü-yün held an unearthed orchid in her hand, the root of which was just hanging by a thread, causing her considerable uneasiness. After a moment's reflection, she concluded that she had better not make the decision, so she raised it up and asked: "Look at the root on this one. It's about to snap off. Shall I remove it?"

"What's that? You want to break off the root?" Ta-wei had heard only the last few words without seeing clearly what Yü-yün was holding, and he blew his stack. Again the greatest impact was on Mary; not understanding a word of Chinese and recognizing the anger in his voice, she assumed that the hostility was directed toward her. She sprang to her feet. Ta-wei reacted quickly: "Not you. Nice dog," he said in a comforting voice, "nice dog." Yü-yün was angered by the realization that in Ta-wei's eyes she was lower than a dog. What surprised her most of all was that she felt far less threatened by Mary this time when the dog stood up. Why was that?

"Put the flower down and get the floor swept. And hurry up!" This time he spoke to her in a soft, intimate tone of voice to prevent any misunderstanding on Mary's part. Finishing what he had to say in Chinese, he switched to English and said to Mary, who was already looking at him suspiciously: "Nice dog. Nice dog." His hands were busily petting her.

After a few moments, when Yü-yün was nearly finished cleaning up, Ta-wei said confidently: "See, what's to fear from her? If you're nice to her, she'll obey you. Nice dog." While instructing Yü-yün, he was constantly watchful of Mary's mood, so he spoke in a mixture of Chinese and English. Not for a moment did he let up with his petting of the dog, even introducing some style to his movements: "You'll get along just fine if you pat her on the head or move your hand down her back like you were brushing her coat. Oh, and you can gently scratch her in the hollows of her legs too." He gave her a demonstration of the latter. This was so soothing to Mary that she stretched out on the floor invitingly and let herself be rubbed and rubbed. "You see what I mean? She likes this best of all." Ta-wei watched Mary, stretched out comfortably on her back, her hind legs pawing the air as he rubbed her, and he was so intrigued that he began to scratch her hard in the hollows of her legs. Mary cocked her head, opened her mouth, letting her bright red tongue loll lazily to the side as she stared at the magic fingers that were bringing such pleasure to her. From time to time she gazed up at Ta-wei. "There, you see how she understands me. From now on, if you'll just rub and pet her regularly, she'll do what you want her to."

Yü-yün had picked up all the shards of broken pottery and had walked out with her dustpan. Ta-wei was completely oblivious to her feelings; he was too busy petting and making friends with Mary. By now, disappointment was written on the faces of the children as they watched the activity through the kitchen window. They had assumed from the beginning that Daddy was going to give Mary a sound whipping, and, considering all those orchids, which Daddy loved as much as life itself, strewn all over the floor, he might even beat her to death. They were astonished to see him direct his anger at Mommy, saving his soothing gestures for the very dog that had ruined his orchids. What was happening in front of their eyes was unique in their experience. Finally, Han-k'e could hold back no longer:

"Daddy," he asked, "when are you going to beat Doggie to death?"

His two elder brothers' eyes lit up at this question. But for some reason, Ta-wei didn't catch his son's drift, so he asked Han-k'e with a puzzled look: "Did you say beat Mary?" Seeing his son nod his head, he continued: "Why would I want to do that?"

"Since Doggie knocked over all Daddy's flowers, won't you beat her to death?" Han-k'e's brothers, feeling that he had said exactly what was in their hearts, gleefully turned to watch first him then their daddy.

"Oh!" Ta-wei finally understood what his son was driving at. He knew he had to give an answer that would satisfy them all. "That's right, Daddy'll really give Mary a whipping. This time, uh, this is her first day here and she didn't know. But the next time she knocks over the flowers, Daddy'll beat her within an inch of her life."

Since Ta-wei hadn't been expecting this question from his son, he had momentarily been stumped for an answer, and while trying to come up with an answer, he had unconsciously stopped rubbing Mary; this plus the speech that was so strange to her ears caused her to rise with a start, and in order to get Ta-wei's attention, she bounded over toward him. He had been crouching down, and there wasn't enough time to straighten up before Mary leaped onto him, sending him sprawling to the floor and crashing into the flower pots that had been spared the first time around. Down they came, stands and all. Poor Ta-wei was lying there pinned to the floor by Mary's forelegs and before he even managed to extricate himself he was already shouting: *"No! No! I love Mary! I love Mary . . ."* Mary nuzzled up to him and planted several wet kisses on his face with her tongue. He climbed to his feet unsteadily, picking up the leash with one hand, and, not daring to be remiss, quickly patted Mary lightly, all the while spewing out a torrent of English phrases calculated to get into the dog's good graces.

Mary quickly calmed down, but the children just stood there wide-eyed, not knowing what to make of Daddy's actions.

"Daddy, what're you sayin' to Doggie?" Han-k'e asked.

"I'm bawling her out—can't you tell?" He was angry as hell, but dared not raise his voice.

His children knew no English, so they accepted his explanation as an act of faith.

Fortunately for all of them, Mary had come to their house on a Saturday afternoon, and since the next day was Sunday, that meant that Ta-wei would be around to attend to her needs. Yü-yün congratulated herself over this, but her relief was short-lived, for from then on, it was she who would have to spend the most time with Mary. This added a great many unnecessary difficulties to her life; over the coming days she would suffer countless indignities and hardships because of that dog.

As for Mary, she soon began to feel penned in. Granted that on this vast earth the ten kilometers or so that separated the foreign residential community of T'ien-mu from Taipei was an insignificant distance, nevertheless Mary, who had left the Raymonds' home and had come to Ta-wei's house, where the people, language, and surroundings were different, not to mention other less obvious factors, experienced the disquietude of a timid person traveling alone in a foreign country. At every opportunity she tried to escape from these unfamiliar surroundings; sometimes, reminded of Lucy, her former mistress, even if the leash was securely fastened, Mary would strain against it until she tired from the exertion or forgot what it was she was struggling for.

Following Mary's first day at Ta-wei's house, when she had wreaked such havoc in the patio, the flower pots were all suspended from the ceiling by wires. But when they were hung too low, Mary could knock them down, since she was as tall as a man when she stood on her hind legs. When they were raised out of her reach, then the line was too high for Yü-yün to use as a clothesline. What really angered Yü-yün was that whenever she accidentally bumped one of the pots while hanging out the laundry, one would think that she had touched an open sore on Ta-wei's body: the slightest touch evoked screams and curses, until Yü-yün began breaking into a cold sweat whenever she had to go out into the patio for any reason. Her fears stemmed partly from her wariness of the dog and partly from all the precautions she had to take to avoid bumping the flower pots while standing on a stool to hang out the laundry.

In the end, in the peculiar manner of human beings, she reacted as though Ta-wei had taken a lover, directing her anger at the usurping slut; in this case, the object of her scorn and anger was, needless to say, Mary. She grew to hate Mary, but because she was afraid of dogs and afraid of Ta-wei, who was Mary's biggest supporter, she could muster no true resistance whatsoever.

Several days later, as Yü-yün was sweeping the patio, in a careless moment she loosened the dog's leash, freeing Mary's wild spirit in the process, and the dog leaped and bounded throughout the apartment, looking for a way to the outside. Mary grew more and more restless as she fantasized that she could hear Lucy's voice, until she grew almost frenzied. She dashed wildly around the apartment for more than an hour, until the place looked like it had been struck by a private minityphoon: the kitchen pantry was lying on its side, its contents of jars and bottles strewn all over the floor; in the living room every lamp and vase had crashed to the floor; the lampshades and two embroidered cushions were ripped; the carpet was stained black from the soot in the fireplace; and even the children's room was a disaster area, owing to Yü-yün's tardiness in closing the door. Finally, every curtain and drape in the house, most notably in the living room, had been ripped from its curtainrod and was lying in a heap at the base of the window. Yü-yün had tried her best to stop the destruction, running back and forth behind Mary, broom in hand, and yelling for all she was worth, but it was all in vain.

She had placed an urgent phone call to Ta-wei, asking him to come home right away and take care of the dog, but the timing could not have been worse: after having just regaled his co-workers about how wonderful Mary was working out at his home, it would have been a loss of face to admit to problems; besides, he was trying hard to impress his new employer. So there was Yü-yün, reporting the gruesome details of the catastrophe that had befallen her, and not only did it elicit no reaction from Ta-wei, but, to Yü-yün's great bewilderment, he answered as though he hadn't heard a word she was saying. As she described the scene with growing urgency, he responded in a voice dripping with congeniality: "Um, um, uh-huh, uh-huh, fine, fine," over and over. Then he interrupted her before she had finished, taking pains to sound as pleasant as possible: "That sounds fine to me, go ahead and do it that way. Bye-bye!" Then he added a few comments in English, obviously not intended for Yü-yün's consumption. For some moments after he had hung up on her, Yü-yün stood there staring at the receiver in her hand and wondering if perhaps she had dialed a wrong number.

Mary finally grew tired of her frenzied activity and let herself be led back to the patio, where Yü-yün tied her up. The entire apartment was a shambles. In terms of activity, Mary's had now come to an end, while Yü-yün's was just beginning. Her ability to put up with painstaking work, with which she had always been blessed, dissolved as she surveyed the scene of destruction before her. The thought occurred to her that if she left everything just as it was until Ta-wei got home that night, he might begin to question the wisdom of raising a dog. But this thought brought tears to her eyes. Who would have dreamed that the very family that had given her such security could have been thrown into such utter turmoil by the addition of one female dog? She sighed bitterly. She lay on the sofa as though in a trance, and although her heart was severely troubled, there was at least some rest for her weary body; just then her gaze fell upon a pile of excrement on the wool rug that had gone unnoticed up till now. She looked more closely, then jumped to her feet. It had taken Ta-wei a full year to obtain this red rug, whose precious nap he treasured as much as the hair on his own body. Many of his rules around the house had been formulated to protect this rug. This was forbidden, that was out, the children were not allowed to eat anything on the rug. The sight threw Yü-yün into a panic; she had to think of some way to remove the offending stain. The children would soon return from school, so there was little time to get the place cleaned up—once they got home, she'd be busier than ever. Putting her mind to it, she somehow managed to straighten the apartment up. It was, after all, the right thing to do, she thought, because if Ta-wei saw it like it had been, he might let the dog off the hook and vent his anger on her instead.

The disastrous episode with Mary occupied Yü-yün for the better part of the day. As she figured it, reason was on her side, but she knew that it would be futile to point out the physical toll it had taken on her; on the other hand, Ta-wei would be visibly saddened by the damage inflicted on the apartment and its contents. Having thought it all out carefully, she calmly sat and waited for Ta-wei to return home, when she could lay before him her case against Mary.

Ta-wei was home—it was all of five minutes earlier than usual, which meant he must have rushed home. He entered the apartment with a scowl on his face. Without saying a word, he followed Yü-yün from one end of the apartment to the other, surveying the damage. Yü-yün kept up a running commentary until she came to the rug. Ta-wei could hold back no longer: "Just what the hell do you do around the house anyway?" he bellowed.

"Wh—at? Are you blaming me for this?" Yü-yün had taken courage from a conviction that she was blameless in the whole episode, and now here she was, getting yelled at. The accumulated anger gave her voice an uncharacteristic shrillness.

"Then you tell me, how did Mary get loose in the apartment in the first place?"

"I was sweeping up the patio, and she, she just ran in." Yü-yün wasn't feeling so confident any longer.

"What a stupid, useless woman . . ."

"If you'd listened to me when I said not to take the dog, none of this would've happened."

"Rubbish! You're too stupid to know what's goin' on."

"Aha! Now I understand. Anyone who touches your precious orchids, or your rug, or your car, or your dog is in for trouble." She was releasing all her pent-up resentment.

"Shut your bitching mouth!"

"Oh?" Yü-yün's anger evaporated and she laughed cynically as she said dispassionately: "I've got the mouth of a bitch, eh? Well that's an improvement, 'cause in your eyes I'm lower than a dog."

Whenever Yü-yün could no longer appeal to Ta-wei's reason, she resorted to complaints of her destiny, the lot of women, and the unkindness of fate. She didn't want to go that route this time, since the source of the problem was a dog, but what else could she do? Feeling very sorry for herself, she reverted to a fatalistic view, as she went over in her mind all that had happened to her. This was, she thought to herself, about what she could expect for the rest of her life, and this train of thought gave her renewed courage. Within a remarkably short period of time, she had changed from a person who feared dogs to one who had the nerve to deal with a huge German shepherd like Mary. To be perfectly fair, "having the nerve" is a little wide of the mark; "putting up a bold front" would be more like it.

Every morning after Ta-wei left for work and the children were off to school, Mary made a fuss to go outside and relieve herself. Of all the duties Yü-yün had to perform, this one of letting the dog out caused her the greatest tension, while it was the happiest time of the day for Mary. The tenseness of the confrontation between the two of them was obvious to anyone who saw Yü-yün leading Mary outside on any given morning. The one would be hopping around gaily, the other holding on to the leash for dear life. The tauter the leash, the greater Yü-yün's apprehension. Then when Mary, with all her bulk, planted her feet on the ground, there was no way in the world Yü-yün was going to budge her. Sometimes, Yü-yün would tug in one direction, but the dog would pull in the other. When Mary had a mind to go, there was no stopping her. She would strain forward on the leash until the best that Yü-yün could hope for was to slow her down a little, as she watched her hand turn purple in the tightening handle of the leash. For the first few days, she thought her poor right hand was going to drop off. But none of this really mattered so long as she was able to drag Mary home after the dog had relieved herself and had gotten a little exercise.

One morning, as Yü-yün took Mary out for her daily walk, they were met at the gate by a pack of male dogs Yü-yün had never seen before. A panicky feeling gripped her. She quickly wrapped the handle of the leash around her wrist. (Up until recently, this is how she had always held onto the leash, but two days earlier, Mary had pulled so hard in an attempt to break free that the leash had torn the skin on Yü-yün's wrist. That's why she was holding it in her hand today.)

One of the dogs sidled over and sniffed at Mary's tail, then without any warning quickly mounted her. Yü-yün, in the midst of extreme embarrassment, bent down to pick up a rock to drive the mongrel off, but in the process she also frightened Mary, who bolted forward, causing the leash to pull hard against the still unhealed wound. Crying out in pain, Yü-yün let the leash drop, and off Mary ran, dragging the leash behind her. This development so shocked Yü-yün that she forgot all about the pain in her hand and ran after the dog, shouting for all she was worth: "Mei-li, Mei-li!" Her voice was so shrill it didn't sound anything like her. Just then she lost her footing and crashed to the ground, hard, the sound of her latest "Mei-li" dying on her lips. This was all Mary's fault, and Yü-yün hated her for it. But she knew she'd have to answer to Ta-wei if Mary were lost while she was supposed to be watching over her. So even though she took a really bad fall, she still had her wits about her, and before she even had time to climb to her feet, her head was raised as she watched to see where Mary was heading. Realizing that at any moment she would lose the dog among the pedestrians on the street, she sprang to her feet and bounded off after the dog without even stopping to look for her sandals.

"Mei-li—Mei-li!" she shouted and ran, and ran and shouted, pointing ahead of her as she went along: "Kind . . . kindly . . . up ahead . . . dog . . . the dog . . ." She was so flustered and winded she couldn't manage a complete sentence. Meanwhile, blood from her skinned knees oozed down her legs until she appeared to be wearing red stockings. Some of the passersby pointed this out to her, but there was no time to worry about herself. In that instant when she had let go of the leash that was holding the dog, it was as though she herself had acquired an imaginary leash, which was pulling her after the fleeing dog. She hoped with all her heart that someone would head the dog off for her, but she was so winded she could hardly breathe, let alone say anything. She took a gulp of air and shouted laboriously: "P . . . please, help me! Grab that Dog!"

She had slowed down a great deal and was falling farther and farther behind—she could barely see the dog. Her shouts were now nothing more than whispers, and she felt herself starting to black out. Like a piece of worn out machinery, she was exhausted and slowing down, but she put all her effort into each and every step. No hint of her earlier mood was evident in her plodding steps, and she was running on instinct alone now, sensing that she was drifting away, little by little. Even her heart was numbed to the point that she felt no more urgency in retrieving the dog, nor any concern over the possibility of having to face Ta-wei with the bad news. So why was she still running? She couldn't have told you. She ran like this, injuries and all, for some three or four blocks, until eventually the people who saw her could not have guessed that she was chasing after a dog. Some of the more softhearted ones attributed her look of despondency to the probability that she was suffering a nervous breakdown.

Just as Yü-yün was on the verge of giving in to despair, a young man, towing Mary behind him, came walking up to her. She could scarcely believe her eyes! Gathering her wits about her, she was once again gripped by the fear she had experienced at the moment Mary broke loose. Now it was all over, and Yü-yün could not hold back her tears. She thanked the young man through her sobs and bowed her head in gratitude, causing him great embarrassment. She held her hand out weakly to take the leash from him, but when he saw how she was trembling, he held back.

"Would you like me to handle the dog for you till you get home?"

"Thank you, thank you so much. I hate to trouble you." To her surprise, another gush of warm tears coursed down her cheeks in response to his offer. She was ashamed to see the state she had been put into because of a dog. But neither the young man nor any of the people who had been watching the incident could have imagined how selfless and herioc she considered the young man to be in returning her dog to her.

Once the dog was penned up in the patio, Yü-yün found herself getting angrier and angrier. She picked up the broom and turned to give Mary a good beating because of what had happened. She paused momentarily, raised the broom over her head, then hit the dog a couple of times, shouting: "Damned dog! Damned dog!" Mary leapt to her feet and strained at the leash, giving Yü-yün a scare that she might somehow snap the leash in two, the consequences of which Yü-yün preferred not to even consider. She threw the broom to the floor, like a prisoner of war abandoning her weapon to save her own skin. Mary sized the broom, then walked over and began chewing on the bamboo handle, eventually with such force that she tore it to pieces.

Yü-yün's completely natural impulse to exact punishment from Mary for the trouble she had caused had backfired—the dog's subsequent actions had been a very effective threat. Yü-yün sat on the sofa rubbing her wounds and resolving to once again oppose—forcefully this time—Ta-wei's desire to keep Mary. She surveyed her injuries: both knees and both elbows were badly skinned, and the pain she was feeling in her heart was far greater than if it were being pricked by needles. Her unhappiness was mounting. As she daubed iodine onto her wounds, she muttered to herself: "Damned dog! I mean it, someday I'll slaughter that damned dog!"

By afternoon, scabs had begun to form on the injuries Yü-yün had sustained that morning. Since they were all located on joints—elbows and knees—they made any movement difficult and painful. When it was nearly time for Ta-wei to get off work, Yü-yün sat down in the living room, hoping that as soon as he entered the apartment, he would see her iodine-covered knees and ask what happened, giving her an opening to voice her opposition. But no such luck: when he walked in the door, even though he was standing directly opposite his wife, he didn't so much as notice her knees, even though they stuck out in all their redness like Japanese flags. He held his suitcoat with one hand, using the other to loosen his tie as he walked directly into the bedroom. This took even the children by surprise. Yü-yün signaled them with her eyes not to say anything, but Han-k'e couldn't hold back:

"Daddy, come and look at Mommy's red legs!"

Ta-wei was just then waving hello to Mary through the window, to which she responded with a few frisky barks.

"Did you feed Mary this afternoon?" Ta-wei yelled from the bedroom.

Yü-yün was so enraged she didn't know what to say. So she didn't say anything.

"Daddy," Han-k'e said as he entered his father's room, "the big doggie bit Mommy here and here and . . ."

Before Han-k'e had finished, Ta-wei rushed into the living room. "What about Mary?"

"Are you blind?" She lifted up her skirt even higher so he couldn't miss it.

But Ta-wei characteristically mistook her action as suggestive, and he grew impatient with her. Once he noticed that her knees had been skinned, he reacted like a man deceived.

"What do you mean, Mary bit you?" he asked angrily.

"I never said that Mei-li bit me!" But then, after a moment's reflection, she lost her temper completely: "So, you'll only be happy when the dog bites me, huh? From tomorrow on, you'll not find me taking care of that dog of yours!"

Ta-wei wasn't very happy to begin with, and when she referred to Mary as "that dog of yours," his mood turned even worse. But then, Yü-yün's injuries were serious enough that he had the common sense to be less harsh with her. The only way he knew to keep his anger in check was to button his lip and say nothing.

"And look," Yü-yün said as she raised her arms in the air, "my elbows too."

Ta-wei took a good look and cooled down considerably, asking her as tenderly as he could, "How in the world did that happen?"

Ta-wei's question and his tone of voice came as a godsend to Yü-yün, and the sudden change of heart produced an effect on her narration of the morning's events, which she related to him in detail: the basic facts remained, but the attendant circumstances underwent considerable modification. First, she introduced a lightheartedness that was lacking during the incident itself, then she passed over some of the more grue-some details. If she were going to gain his sympathy or present a reasoned opposition to the raising of a dog, common sense dictated that even if she didn't want to overdo the darker aspects, she should at least not hold anything back. But then a few nice words from Ta-wei, plus a show of emotion and pain as he looked at her damaged joints, won her over completely. When she had finished recounting the morning's activities, she had to laugh at herself over what seemed even to her to be a comical incident: in fact, her narration was regularly punctuated by her own laughter.

Ta-wei had calmed down completely, but not because of Yü-yün's as-sumption that he had been touched by her story; actually, this calmness had followed the entertaining spectacle of Yü-yün describing the events of the day.

"Ai!" Ta-wei sighed with a laugh, "I wonder how the Raymonds managed to handle Mary?"

"What makes me maddest of all . . ." Yü-yün so seldom found Ta-wei willing to listen to her on any subject and was so happy to find him that way now that she got carried away with what she was saying and paid no attention to anyone else. "She won't come to me when I call her. You're the only one she listens to."

"Who told you to be so stupid? I don't know how many times I've tried to teach you a few basic English words, but you still can't say them. Now I've told you that her name is Mary, with the accent on the first syllable, not like you always say it—Mei-li—with no accent at all. Your English stinks."

"You know good and well that I studied rural home economics, and English wasn't part of the curriculum. You're always laughin' at me 'cause my English is no good."

"Take, for instance, simple words like lai for *come* and ch'ü for *go*; find anyone who's never even been to school and in no time at all they'll have 'em down pat." Then he added with a laugh: "You call Mary 'Mei-li.' Maybe Mei-li is a dog who belongs to someone else—some Chinese. Of course Mary doesn't listen to you, since you call her Mei-li. Oh, yes, you, you're the one who's stupid, but you blame it all on Mary."

"Okay, I'm stupid. I'm only good for taking care of three kids, so you go find someone who speaks English to take care of that dog of yours."

But she really didn't mean it, for from then on, whenever she had a free moment, she practiced the words in the "Ninety-nine English Sentences" booklet that Ta-wei had bought her so that she could communicate with Mary: "lai" is *come*, "ch'ü" is *go, nice doggie* is "ha gou-gou . . ."

WHOM DO YOU LOVE, ME OR THE DOG?

Mary gradually began to respond to Yü-yün, though one should not assume that Yü-yün's English showed any real improvement; it was merely evidence of mutual compromise. When she called the dog's name, there was still a trace of the "Mei-li" sound, but Yü-yün did the best she could. As long as the dog knew she was being called, Yü-yün had passed the test, if barely.

Yü-yün's injuries had healed, leading to a disappearance of Ta-wei's remorse; the latter diminished at about the same pace as the scabs on Yü-yün's knees and elbows. Moreover, Yü-yün's mastery of a few English words fell somewhat short of bringing the Chen's troubles with Mary to an end. Without even trying, Mary brought all sorts of grief to Yü-yün just by being in heat.

This time it was the real thing, and the news was out: on this particular morning as Yü-yün was making breakfast for Ta-wei and the children before they left the house, there was a knock at the door. She walked over, opened the door, and was greeted by an astonishing sight: the knock had been made not by a person but by a nondescript mongrel. Yü-yün's terrified screech startled the dog into stepping back a few paces, though he kept his eyes fixed in her direction. Yü-yün looked around, spotting, much to her horror, a pack of about ten dogs of all shapes and sizes, all of them staring fixedly at her.

"Ta-wei, come here, quick! My God, what a shock!" She stepped back and closed the door enough that the dogs could not get in.

"What's all the excitement?" Ta-wei asked as he walked up to her.

Yü-yün threw the door open. "See for yourself! Just look at all the dogs we've got here!"

This took Ta-wei completely by surprise. He stepped out onto the porch, waved his arms and shouted "scat!" Then he made as if to drive the animals away. He took three steps forward—so did the dogs. He stopped—so did they. He went back inside the house—the dogs surged forward again.

"Mary's in heat, and they're all males. We've got to be careful that she doesn't mate with any of these mongrels."

"But how did they know? And where are they the rest of the time?" Yü-yün was puzzled.

"You couldn't get this sort of punctuality if you sent out invitations—it's their incredible sense of smell," Ta-wei said with a chuckle.

"But that one even knocked on the door!" She pointed to the big black dog that was standing ten to twelve meters away. "That black one's the one that did it."

"Close the door. I'll be damned if I'm gonna let Mary mate with dogs like that. Lucy made it perfectly clear that Mary was to be mated only with a pedigreed dog. Besides, Lucy said that since this is Mary's first time in heat they'd decided not to let her mate. So we've got to be extra careful."

"Who's Lucy?"

"Mrs. Raymond—that's who!"

"Oh!" Yü-yün thought for a moment, then asked: "What're we gonna do about all those dogs outside? Do you think anything will happen when I take her out for a walk?"

"That's right! You'll have to keep her inside from now on. Let her relieve herself in the patio. You go and get a bucket of sand."

"Now, where am I gonna get a bucket of sand?"

"You can find it at any building site."

Mary changed a great deal while she was in heat: she lost her appetite, and on those few occasions when she felt like eating something, it was always a spur-of-the-moment desire. If the food was even a little late in coming, she started a real row. What sorts of food would she eat? Only two: stewed beef and canned dogfood from the American PX. Once the desire and the supply were taken care of, Yü-yün had to worry about feeding her, and the whole procedure took on the appearance of the children's game "paper, scissors, rock," a game Yü-yün invariably lost. Mary was not an easy dog to please.

The first two or three days were unbelievably tense for Ta-wei, and it took little to make him fly off the handle. Yü-yün took so much verbal abuse from him over the dog's feeding schedule that she felt more resentment than usual—her days were long and difficult.

On the third day of the pack's vigil, one of the dogs was run over by a passing car. One would think that this sort of tragic warning would diminish their number, but quite the contrary—the pack grew larger by several dogs. All different types were represented, although they were nearly all the long-haired foreign import variety. These animals, with their long coats, were highly susceptible to skin diseases in the tropics, particularly here in the Taipei basin, with its hot, humid climate. No matter what the pedigree, whenever a dog suffered from this kind of malady it looked like any other mangy cur and was dumped unceremoniously out on the streets. Some of them were in such bad shape that their fur was gone and their skin rotting away, while others were crippled in one way or another. In fact, with the exception of two or three shorthairs, they were all sick or injured. They arranged themselves around the front of the Chen house in a sort of arc, their eyes glued on the front door. When the door was closed, as it was most of the time, they just lay there lazily conserving their energy. But at the slightest stirring in the vicinity of the door, they were on their feet, bright-eyed and bushy-tailed. If it turned out to be a member of the Chen family, and not Mary, the dogs watched warily to see what the people had on their minds before making any moves of their own.

By afternoon it was apparent to Yü-yün that Mary was hungry, so she looked in the pot to see if there was enough meat to feed her. There wasn't. She'd been so busy that morning that she'd been unable to go to market. There was no time like the present, since the children were in school, so she ran to the market, bought some vegetables and meat, and rushed home. But when she went through her purchases in the kitchen, she discovered that the beef was missing. She remembered distinctly that she had bought more than NT$100 worth of beef and had put it with everything else. She checked the bottom of her grocery cart—nothing. How could it simply disappear? She hadn't a clue. Mary, who was now getting quite hungry, started raising a ruckus in the patio, but Yü-yün, who had just lost over NT$100 worth of beef, had too much on her mind to give Mary much thought; she turned and retraced her steps to the market, where she checked with all the tradespeople she had dealt with, but to no avail. She had no choice but to buy some more.

Yü-yün made her way back home, a package of beef in her hand and a belly full of anger. When she turned the corner near her house, she suddenly gasped, "Oh, my God!" She blinked and looked again, but there was no denying what she was seeing. Somehow, Mary had gotten loose and was unmistakably coupled to a dog much smaller than she in the shadow of the door. Yü-yün nearly flew into the house and phoned Ta-wei at the office. After waiting for him to come to the phone and pick it up, she quickly dissolved into tears.

"Oh, what'll we do? Come home, hurry!" She was crying out of desperation.

"What is it?" Her unchecked sobbing made Ta-wei feel that he had never known her to be so feminine, so weak. He knew instinctively that something was seriously wrong. "I'll be right home."

Yü-yün hung up the phone, flung herself down onto the sofa, and cried her heart out fearfully. About ten minutes later, Ta-wei drove into the driveway, and the moment he stepped out of the car, he no longer had to ask what the problem was. On the way home he had been concerned about Yü-yün, wondering what could have happened to reduce her to such pitiful sobs. He also found himself concentrating on his wife's many good points. But he was shocked out of his reveries by a totally unexpected sight: instead of seeing Yü-yün in distress, he was a witness to the mating of his beloved Mary to a street dog.

He burst into the living room. There was Yü-yün, cowering before him.

"Ta-wei, I'm sorry," she said, "I'm so sorry. I don't know how it happened, I'm sorry, I'm sorry . . ." She was crying pitiably.

Ta-wei was fuming as he walked over, jerked her to her feet, and slapped her twice across the face, screaming as he did so: "What did I tell you before all this happened? You drop dead, woman, you just drop dead!"

"I'm sorry, I'm sorry . . ." Holding her face, she resembled a child begging forgiveness from an adult, as she repeated "I'm sorry" over and over.

But Ta-wei knocked her hands away and slapped her time and again.

"You horrid, selfish woman! You're afraid of the dog. You hate it, so you've been wanting to get back at me. You probably think I don't know what you're doing. Well, you can just drop dead!"

All of a sudden, the cowering Yü-yün dropped her hands, stood up straight, and faced him dry-eyed. He froze on the spot; the hand with which he was about to slap her stopped in mid swing. Yü-yün casually straightened her mussed hair and said: "Ta-wei, do you know how despicable you are?"

"Despicable?" he shouted in the puffed up manner of a bully.

"I've taken all I'm going to take from Uncle Sam's lackey! You can go and . . ."

"Uncle's Sam lackey!" He raised his hand in a threatening gesture.

"Go ahead, hit me if you want to. I'll neither cry nor beg for mercy, and I won't even try to protect myself."

"Then why did you let Mary mate with that mongrel? Why?"

Yü-yün's sudden and virtually complete metamorphosis was in fact nothing more than an awakening to a single reality. This awakening was born in the midst of a highly contradictory frame of mind and took shape as she realized that although personally blameless, she had been experiencing the raw terror of someone facing a calamity, until Ta-wei's vicious slaps snapped her out of it. Everything was suddenly clear as a bell, and she knew exactly what she had to do.

"I owe you my thanks," she said calmly. "A moment ago I was in a daze, fearfully begging for your forgiveness, but your coldhearted slaps opened my eyes. I've always blamed Mary, hated her, in fact, but now I see the light: I had an unreasonable fear of you, and because of that I feared your orchids, your wool rug, your car, and your dog. But now I see how foolish I was. What's there to be afraid of?"

Ta-wei stood there staring at her, his hands resting on his hips.

She continued: "We'll forget about the past. What I want to know is . . ." She paused briefly. "Whom do you love, me or the dog?"

"I love the dog!" Ta-wei screamed hysterically. He turned on his heel and ran into the house, where he grabbed a stick and rushed back outside.

There in full view beyond the doorway were Mary and the nondescript cur, locked together, appearing for all the world to have fused into one. Their performance was being scrutinized by an admiring audience of horny male dogs, whose emotions ranged from envy to hatred. Ta-wei burst forward in a fit of uncontrollable rage, grabbed hold of Mary's leash with one hand and flailed out with the stick, striking with full force the mongrel that had been blessed by fate. By the second or third blow, the animal began to wail loudly: it broke free and ran for its life.

The beating with Ta-wei's stick and the pitiful wails of the victim were all the lesson the other dogs needed; with nothing to envy, hate, or admire, they all slinked out of harm's way, their tails between their legs.

Ta-wei quickly and anxiously put Mary into the patio, tied her up, then got into his car and drove back to the office.

Yü-yün sat on the sofa during all of this, the very picture of calmness. As she reflected on how the scales had fallen from her eyes, how she had suddenly felt herself to be a woman of substance and power, she experienced wonder, but not without a trace of inexplicable fear.

Silently she gathered up the clothes she would need. When she went out onto the patio to fetch the clothes that had been put out to dry, she wasn't at all intimidated by the flower pots hanging over her head. Not only was she unafraid of Mary, she even pitied her. Returning to the living room, for the first time in her life she trod on the rug free of the feeling that she was walking on thin ice, added proof of how clearly she now saw things.

When the three children returned home from school, Yü-yün said to them: "Mommy's going over to Uncle's house for a few days. Do you want to come along?"

"Sure," Han-k'e responded, with a clap of his hands.

"What about school?" Tsu-wei asked.

"Mommy can take you."

"Can you drive?" asked Chin-wen.

"Who says we have to have a car? What's wrong with buses?"

"Mommy, let's not let Daddy come, okay?" Han-k'e said with a heavy heart.

"Why not?"

"Because he'll bring the big doggie with him."

This brief exchange with her children, in which she saw how happy they were to be leaving home, showed her how she and her husband had failed in the education of their children.

Ta-wei arrived home about a half hour later than usual that day. When he opened the door and discovered that the house was empty, his thoughts from the drive home of how he should go about smoothing things out with Yü-yün after this afternoon's blowup were driven out by a surge of anger.

His carefully planned move of adopting Mary had been one of the concrete steps in an overall design to climb the promotional ladder in the foreign company where he worked—one of the most critical steps. But where had this critical importance led? In the end, he was left with only a fleeting image of his importance, which had little or no relevance to the realities that faced him. As a result, in his mind this importance loomed larger and larger until it was stretched so far out of proportion that it assumed an almost sacred, inviolate nature. This was the pedestal upon which he had placed Mary. To ruin Mary was, in his eyes, to throw away his own future, at least insofar as his social mobility was concerned, making all of his past labors go for naught. Consequently, he was unable to put himself in Yü-yün's shoes—he was convinced that she was ruining his career. With this semi-intuitive conclusion preying on his mind, he found additional faults with her for taking the children from him. Actually, he could just as easily have found fault with her if she had left them behind. He hated her—she disgusted him. And so, not only did Yü-yün's departure cause Ta-wei no disquiet whatsoever, it served to strengthen the heretofore vaguely formed belief that she had betrayed him. But even now there was one tiny bit of evidence that Ta-wei still had some affection for Yü-yün, and that was the incredulity her forceful opposition had evoked in him, especially after so many years of accepting everything that he had dished out.

If this were not enough to trouble his heart, there was always Mary's adventure in copulation this afternoon—a dog that anyone could see was rather remarkable locked together with a street mutt. His complex feelings of remorse and frustration were superseded by the simple emotion of anger. To top it all off, the thought of the end product of today's fiasco, in terms of Mary's belly, made him fidget unbearably.

He took a look around the room, letting his gaze fall on the dog. Returning to the living room, he picked up the phone book, located a veterinarian, and anxiously dialed the number.

"Hello, is this the Humane Veterinary Hospital?"

"Yes."

"I have a question concerning a dog."

"Yes, what is it?"

"What are the chances of a dog's getting pregnant from a single mating?"

"Pretty good, but of course it depends on the breeds."

"A German shepherd and a mongrel."

"Oh! I'd say about one hundred percent. Hee-hee-hee."

"Can a dog have an abortion?"

"Wah—ha-ha-ha. An abortion for a dog? Forget it. Just let her go ahead and have her litter in three months or so. Hee-hee-hee, an abortion for a dog, really." The vet seemed to be talking to someone next to him.

"You see, what happened was a purely accidental mating."

"Well, what harm can it do to the shepherd? As for the mongrel, to hell with her—just let her have her puppies. Hee-hee-hee."

"If that's how it was, everything'd be easy. Unfortunately, you've got it backwards: the shepherd is the female, and she was given to me by an American. The male is a little mutt with God knows what kind of blood. It's not fair! What should I do?"

"What should you do? Hee-hee-hee." He turned and said to someone next to him: "An American dog was knocked up by a mutt, hee-hee-hee."

"Well, can she have an abortion or not?"

"Sure, it's possible, but I've never heard of anyone doing it."

"Then what do other people do in cases like this?"

"They let 'em have their puppies. You can still sell 'em if they look anything like a shepherd. And if they don't, just dump 'em. Hee-hee-hee, hee-hee-hee."

"I want an abortion."

"You? Or the dog? Oh, ha-ha-ha, ha-ha-ha. He said he wants an abortion." The phone picked up the other person's comment: "Is that a man or a woman on the phone?"

"Is an operation necessary?"

"When did the happy event occur?"

"About 2:30 this afternoon."

"Then a shot'll take care of it. I'll tell you what, I'm busy now, so call back in half an hour."

"Okay, fine. Thanks."

"Think nothin' of it, hee-hee-hee."

Ta-wei's mood had lightened because of the infectious laughter over the phone, but in the final analysis the happiness belonged to someone else, not to him. By the time he had hung up the receiver, the oppressive atmosphere of the room again hemmed him in. Just then Mary began to bark a rather coquettish welcome to him, a sound that rang in his ears until it seemed to fill the room and blot out everything else. His anger at Yü-yün increased.

Meanwhile, at the Humane Veterinary Hospital, the first order of business was to contact the pharmaceutical supply.

"Hello, this is the Humane Veterinary Hospital. Is Pharmacist Hsü in? . . . . Hey, it's been a long time. . . . Yeah. . . . Right. Say, do you have any womb-contracting medicine? Either that or some 'aphrodisiac hormones'? . . . . Oh-oh, no, no, no, nothin' like that; I wouldn't dare. . . . You're joking, ha-ha-ha, hee-hee-hee. You see, there's a guy who wants an abortion for his dog! . . . . Yeah, hee-hee-hee. . . . So what do you think I should use? . . . . Um, um, right, um, uh-huh. The dog's safety is paramount. A lot depends on the owner; we don't want him to get us for malpractice. . . . No, that's no good. I won't do it. . . . Um-hm, that's what I think. Look here, I wouldn't feel right having you make a special trip just for this, so why don't you send over a couple of boxes of insect repellent as well, plus two dozen insecticides, and, uh, oh, yes, and some multiple vitamin shots—a dozen should do it. . . . I sure appreciate this. . . . Uh-huh, about twenty minutes? Fine, thanks a lot."

Meanwhile, Ta-wei was contemplating a thirty-minute vacuum; he sat there in the living room not knowing what to do with himself and seeing nothing that needed his attention. He tried his damndest to clear his mind of all thoughts of Yü-yün, for he was riled up enough as it was. Forcing himself to think of his job, he naturally thought of his Chinese co-workers: he was disdainful of those who treated him well and was disdained by those whose companionship he sought. These thoughts of his interpersonal dealings in that small circle revealed his loneliness.

There was, he reflected, a good chance of his making a trip to the States each year, though it was more or less dependent upon his accomplishments at the office, and this all led back to Yü-yün and her influence on his work. And so he was right back to thoughts of her, despite all his efforts to the contrary. Mary's barking drew him out of his musing and right back into a blaze of temper. Thus, with zero productivity he passed a half hour.

The thirty minutes were up, so he immediately placed a phone call to the Humane Veterinary Hospital, then walked out the door with Mary in tow.

To his astonishment, Mary climbed into the car and very calmly sat on the rear seat, showing no trace of the high-strung temperament that had characterized the past few days when she was in heat. She seemed to have grown wisely obedient, sitting there awaiting the future with complete resignation. But all Ta-wei had on his mind was the letter—his second to date—in which he would have to report to the Raymonds on Mary's life in his home.

He located the Humane Veterinary Hospital. One glance was all Dr. Liu needed to realize that Mary was anything but a thoroughbred shepherd: large head, a large, puffy body, a little on the stupid side—it was immediately obvious that this was a dog totally lacking in training, physical or disciplinary. Forgetting any concerns for the feelings of its owner, as far as Dr. Liu was concerned Mary was a common, worthless dog. He had always been a straightforward, outspoken man, but fortunately he had his share of discretion, which now dictated a momentary pause. He stopped himself from divulging the truth that would have crushed Ta-wei. Noticing how indulgent Ta-wei was of Mary, Dr. Liu thought back to how Ta-wei had told him over and over during the phone conversation how valuable a dog she was, how she had been given to him by an American, and how, in a careless moment, she had been allowed to mate with a mongrel. The dog's owner had even okayed an abortion. The aggregate effect on Dr. Liu was that he treated Mary as a pedigreed dog, mainly because that was the best way to justify a steep medical bill.

During what appeared to be a very complicated set of procedures, Mary was aborted and given a shot of multiple vitamins. The doctor praised the dog to the skies in the tone of an expert, not neglecting to recommend a set of dog brushes and some dog shampoo. He closed with some advice on dog care.

"Thanks, thanks a lot," Ta-wei said with sincere gratitude.

"Just call if there are any problems."

Mary was once again secured in the patio, so Ta-wei went into the kitchen to scare up something to eat. Without warning, Mary suddenly began to bark and jump around wildly, straining against her leash with such force that the sound reverberated throughout the house. Ta-wei hurried over to the patio and found that Mary was no longer the calm, obedient dog she had been earlier in the car. She had grown wild again and was struggling bitterly against her restraints.

"*Mary, what happened?*" Ta-wei called out anxiously, although he kept his distance as he watched her gnaw viciously at the wood and moan pitifully. He noticed that she was excreting great quantities of bloody vaginal fluid, and that the rear half of her body was trembling uncontrollably.

Ta-wei placed an urgent phone call to Dr. Liu.

"What's happening to her? Why didn't you warn me?"

"There's nothing to worry about, this is a normal reaction. Don't think for a moment that an abortion is a simple procedure."

"Are you sure there's nothing to worry about?"

"See what happens during the next half hour, then call me back."

As soon as Ta-wei hung up, Dr. Liu quickly called Pharmacist Hsü as he intensely scrutinized the medicine bottle, which he had retrieved from the trash can.

"Hello," he said, "didn't you send me 'aphrodisiac hormones'?"

"That's right."

"Shit, I trusted you completely, so I administered it without even looking at the bottle. It looks like I've screwed up."

"What was it I sent you?"

"Womb-contracting medicine."

"It really shouldn't make any difference. How much did you administer?"

"All of it. I figured that a dog's constitution was stronger than a human's."

"You're the expert, so you should know what you're doing."

"Shit! You sent the wrong medicine, so quit tryin' to pass the buck. Well, it looks like we'll be eating dogmeat stew for a while, eh? Hee-hee-hee, hee-hee-hee. The guy says the dog's suffering a lot."

"You know damned well the dog won't die, and might even be better off because of it."

"Shit. Ha-ha-ha, hee-hee-hee . . ."

Ta-wei kept his vigil beside Mary. The worst had passed, it seemed, and she was now lying down while Ta-wei rubbed her and watched the rhythmic spasms of her belly. Mary rewarded him by licking his hand softly.

Ta-wei was reminded of Yü-yün's question:

"Whom do you love, me or the dog?"

NOTES

1. The usual order for Chinese names is surname first, here Chen Shun-te.
2. Italicized words are in English in the original.
3. The current rate of exchange is slightly under NT $40 for one U.S. dollar.
4. A transliteration for Hank.

LIU TA-JEN (1939–)

*Until he became embroiled in the Protect Tiao Yü T'ai movement in late
1970, Liu Ta-jen was a frequent contributor to Taiwan's literary journals.
His political activities interrupted his graduate studies. But more unfortunately, as a result of his participation in the movement he became a non-
person in the eyes of the Nationalist Government, which initially
discouraged students demonstrating against Japan for fear of souring its
relationship with its neighbor. Debarred from reentry to Taiwan and
financially unable to continue his study in the United States, he took a job
as a translator at the United Nations, a position he still holds. The tribula-
tions and final disillusionment of one such patriot as Liu Ta-jen are
reenacted in Chang Hsi-kuo's "Red Boy," included in this volume. In this
sense, "Chrysalis," published shortly before the student movement, is a
premonitory tale about the misery of expatriation tormented by misgiv-
ings of one's worth and purpose. It foreshadows the author's subsequent
participation in active politics as a means to offset the burden of guilt and
spiritual sterility. Liu Ta-jen has a B.A. in philosophy from National
Taiwan University, and an M.A. in political science from the University of
California at Berkeley. After not writing for almost ten years, he broke his
silence with the publication in serial form of a projected trilogy of three
novels in* The Seventies (Ch'i-shih nien-tai), *a Hong Kong monthly. The
first installment of the first work,* The Plankton Community (Fou-yu
ch'ün-lo), *appeared in the October issue of 1981, and is now available in
book form (Hong Kong, 1983). His pre-1970 writings are collected in*
Impressions of the Red Soil (Hung-t'u yin-hsiang, *Taipei, 1970).*

Chrysalis

Translated by Cordell D. K. Yee

I.

The view from the side of the house facing the sea was extremely vast.
Except for a few old pine trees which squatted between sea and sky, bent
into hunchbacks over the years by the strong ocean wind, all you could
see from the long Japanese-style hallway was a blue expanse, especially
on a clear day. Of course, depending on whether it was windy or rainy,
clear or overcast, sunrise or sunset, this tiresome blue could change ten

thousand times in the blink of an eye. Yet there were always white thread-like ripples emerging from folds in this boundless blue silk, unfolding imperceptibly, like flower buds, extending like hand pulling hand, rushing toward your eyes. Open the window—and behind the odor of rotting aquatic grasses and dead marine animals, the wind followed, scraping the glassy blue sea like a trillion knife blades. It seemed that the deafening, ever-present sound of motion had extended a shapeless hand from the ocean floor and—pushing, pushing—was piling up the white waves into the form of a giant. Later, once the hand relaxed, the waves crashed at the feet of the old pines and receded soundlessly into the blue expanse.

Mo Lao,[1] looking like a statue, had struck his habitual pose. He sat on his beloved old copper-brown sofa, holding a cup of amber T'ieh Kuan-yin tea with both hands and covering both legs with a plaid woolen blanket.

"This year the butterflies have come really late," he said.

The next morning, however, the weather was perfect, as usual. It was almost the end of October, and yet the weather was perfect here on the mid-California coast, as if specially granted by heaven. Mo Lao, holding a cup of steaming T'ieh Kuan-yin tea with both hands, sat facing the window. Looking out at that incredibly tiresome pane of blue glass, he said:

"This year the butterflies have come really late."

But perhaps because of my younger eyes, I, standing behind Mo Lao's chair, had already seen butterflies float by from time to time, like withered leaves driven by the wind. They flitted past the edge of the scene composed of the old pines, and then, as if straining to climb the last hill, mounted the air currents that flowed over land. Soaring upward, they passed by our room and vanished into the grove of trees in the front yard.

II.

Getting to know Mo Lao has been one of my great harvests of the past several years. I say this not because I am now Mo Lao's youngest son-in-law. To think about it carefully, there is another reason why I feel a little grateful. I cannot say clearly what this reason basically is—perhaps it is Mo Lao's imperturbability.

It was brought unconsciously into our lives by Hsi-hu. Hsi-hu, ah, my Hsi-hu. I was deeply infatuated with her boundless femininity. Three years ago, when we moved from the east to the west coast, crossing the American continent for the first time, I first met Mo Lao, who had secluded himself here in retirement. It was not until then that I truly understood the changes I had undergone the past few years, that I truly understood Hsi-hu—my wife—and the source of her boundless femininity.

Mo Lao has already been retired for more than ten years. Up till now those who visit him frequently have mostly been celebrities and political figures who were popular at one time. Although these people have already set down roots and started new lives in this alien land, they tacitly regard Mo Lao's place as another kind of social activity center. The strange thing is that during these gatherings Mo Lao has never been at the center of conversation. He is usually like an observer or an understanding audience: only occasionally, during short breaks in the conversation, does he interject a few sentences. Perhaps it is this unobtrusive manner that attracts visitors to his place in groups of three or five. Until now I have never chanced upon Mo Lao meeting a lone visitor.

After we moved in with Mo Lao, the crowds of visitors gradually thinned out. Each member of our small household of three generations gradually grew accustomed to one another's ways, and then it seemed as if we had always been living together. Behind the house the waves pounded with an unvarying rhythm. The laughter and chatter of five-year-old Hsüan-hsüan and three-year-old P'ing-p'ing livened up our days, which flew by like a succession of hydrogen balloons.

It was on peaceful, happy days like these that I took stock of myself, a thirty-six-year-old historian who had published two books, who taught at a reputable institution of higher learning and who regularly presented remarkably solid papers at the conferences of the Association of East Asian Studies. I was deeply afraid. Yes, I was deeply afraid. Mo Lao's tranquil profile, Hsi-hu's happy smiling face, and Hsüan-hsüan's and P'ing-p'ing's laughter and chatter all made me deeply afraid. Yes, on days when I faced the sea while keeping Mo Lao company, I saw myself, stripped layer by layer, more and more clearly on the window in the long hallway. It was almost like the bamboo shoots that I remember helping to peel during my boyhood whenever I squeezed into my mother's kitchen: even the slender, inner fibers of the meat could be seen clearly, becoming whiter and whiter. I was deeply afraid.

Although I had been studying history for half a lifetime, I was no good at analyzing myself. Nevertheless, because of this addiction to history, for many years I had kept a set of "historical materials" about myself. While living in the country with Mo Lao, I began to trace my own development. My fear certainly had its historical origins. How did it come about? How did it slip into my inner life? What was its process of development like? What did it portend? How would it change me? And what about my relationships with Hsi-hu, Hsüan-hsüan, P'ing-p'ing, and even Mo Lao? On those days when I faced the sea with Mo Lao, I slowly wrapped myself in this troublesome problem. On the one hand I felt anxious and helpless, as if gripped by a powerful hand. On the other hand I was secretly excited, since I felt that through rational means I would finally discover the hidden meaning of the problem. In the end this contradictory search summoned forth experiences that were already close to being forgotten. I remembered much of the sad and joyful past: being lost in a big stack of materials, reconstructing a historical event, finishing the manuscript of my first book, and—ha! ha!—not being able to sleep after seeing Hsi-hu for the first time. I finally found this passage in the diary I had kept ten years ago:

> Talked with Chang about revolution. Couldn't sleep the whole night; I was feeling really low. Chang cited the life of Aleksandr Herzen[2] as an example to show that intellectuals had a habit of projecting their own utopian visions on the dissatisfied masses: that is their nature, their pathetic attitude. Illogical, illogical, very illogical. True, Herzen did project his visions on the masses. He also wandered his whole life through England and Continental Europe, and never returned home. But, all the same, idealistic revolutionaries must analyze the situation, judge the situation, as the basis of their choice of action. Herzen did not return home because his time had not come.

Ha! Ha! Now I'm afraid I don't even know for sure who Herzen is. He was probably just another exiled anarchist who lived during the nineteenth century. At the time the diary was written our hearts were all for those exiled anarchists. For someone who was already twenty-six years old and still so fervent about anarchism, surely this must be a sign of stunted intellectual growth. It must be that countries that develop late also produce youth who develop late.

Nothing can be more tedious than reading a diary like this now. My twenty-sixth year thus shamelessly and brazenly stood before me. At that time there were probably about a hundred Chinese foreign students on campus, but probably no more than six or seven I thought much of. As a result, these six or seven people and I would often gather together to do what we considered to be relevant and important. For example, the informal seminars held once every month. I came to know Hsi-hu on one of those occasions. Now when I think about it, I feel ashamed. But Hsi-hu was the kind of girl who kept you company to the end, always interested and never interrupting, no matter how ashamed the things you did in front of her made you feel later. The subject of discussion that day was "China's land problem," which I cannot think back on without turning red in the face. But then she was there with her usual tranquility, and her presence made everyone feel at ease and sure of himself. Yes, what we discussed was definitely "China's land problem." It is recorded clearly in my diary. And it was my turn to report that day. But the entry in the diary had only this:

> Met at Ch'en's house. Eight people came. I reported on "The Crux of China's Land Problem and the Road toward Its Solution." She? Who was she?

And that's exactly what I wrote.

After we were married, these small gatherings continued, most of the time in our small studio apartment. The problems we discussed never failed to be of the kind that makes me feel embarrassed. Now when I casually leaf through the "historical materials" of that time, I see eye-catching titles like these: "The Population Explosion and Economic Development"! "Intellectuals and Their Sense of Mission"! "Types of Fascism"! This could not but make me remember how, at the start of every meeting when we were getting set to argue, our faces and ears flushed, Hsi-hu took advantage of the moment to bring in a tray of fresh, ice-cold gelatin. Ha! Ha! The musical rest notes of my twenty-sixth year were these trays of pure white gelatin inlaid with purplish-red cherries.

The year I turned twenty-seven I submitted a synopsis of my doctoral dissertation. Its title was "Economic Oppression of the Industrial West and the Reform of the Light Shipping System of the Late Ch'ing."

During these peaceful and carefree days, looking closely at the cheeks of my spirit slowly wasting away was not necessarily frightening. This I knew. But Hsi-hu growing plumper day by day, the children swiftly growing up, and my father-in-law never aging in a state of inertia often affected my nerves, making me more and more uneasy. It was a moonlit night more than three months ago. After putting the children to bed, Hsi-hu quietly found a soft cushion and leaned against my knees. Like a paper-cut on the wall of the playroom at a nursery school, the big yellow moon hung motionless, high above the horizon. Suddenly she broke the silence, saying:

"I haven't had one for more than two months."

We just sat there until the slowly rising snoring of Mo Lao in the next room startled us from our thoughts.

III.

This year the butterflies actually came nearly a month late. Could it be that in the north the winter was late too? Yet these delicate little creatures, beating their silky wings of alternating black and red, finally made their way over here. And they came by the millions. It is said that some of them fly three thousand miles. What force drives them to make this journey once each year? Entomologists cannot explain why they come, but one scientist is silly enough to venture this theory: the reason why they do not mind flying a thousand miles to come here is that they get special sap from the trees in a nearby garden of about six square miles. Whenever I imagine these living things, these monarch butterflies, holding on to tree trunks and breathing wildly as if drunk, I feel an intense pain in my heart.

This year Hsüan-hsüan made a fuss about participating in the children's costume parade at the butterfly festival. Hsi-hu made her a lined coat out of a silk hanging left over from our wedding, dressed her up to look like a girl of the late Ch'ing or early Republican period, and then cheerfully led her into the crowd while P'ing-p'ing sat on my shoulders.

This year tourists came in great numbers. The afternoon sun, even in November, was still warm. In the park the fir and eucalyptus trees were completely covered with tired monarch butterflies. Most of the latecomers were still in the air, darting about, searching for a suitable landing place. Mo Lao walked beside us. Occasionally he used his cane to draw our attention to where the mass of butterfles had gathered.

"They are really strange things," Mo Lao said.

I put P'ing-p'ing down and let her grandfather take her by the hand. I mounted a telephoto lens onto my camera and began taking close-ups of the butterflies. Over the past three years I have taken at least four to five hundred photographs with butterflies as the subject. Through these few photographs, their living habits have become all too familiar to me. But up till now not a single photograph has satisfied me. It's not that they are technically flawed. Even if they were, I wouldn't have minded. After all, I am not a professional photographer and I don't intend to become one. But somehow, I have always felt that something is missing in my photographs of monarch butterflies—something they should have.

I pointed my camera toward a spot where there were few tourists and began to work, selecting a willow whose withered branches and twigs were drooping. Viewed through the lens, the scene was extremely frightening. The willow's branches and twigs looked very much like a disheveled old woman with at least a thousand monarch butterflies silently hanging to her body. I felt as if my blood had frozen. I took more than ten shots rapidly until I felt as if I were about to throw up. Then I took my camera and went back. By that time it was already dusk, and most of the tourists had left. I crossed the park lawn and hurried toward the spot where Mo Lao and my family were to wait for me. In the distance I could already see the two children playing with their mother on the grass. Off to the side Mo Lao sat alone on a stone on an artificial hill, resting himself on his cane, supported by both hands. The sun's rays leaked through the gaps between the sparse leaves of the cypress tree behind him, splashing him with gold glitter. My hand instinctively adjusted the aperture and focus. I had just knelt down when a huge butterfly, almost completely red, suddenly sped into view, and without thinking I pressed the shutter release.

That evening the weather was uncommonly warm. Mo Lao was still in high spirits. We drove to a well-known French restaurant in Monterey and had a most delicious seafood dinner. Mo Lao and I shared a bottle of chablis, and we drank it all up.

We went home on Highway 1, which runs along the Pacific coast. Hsi-hu sat beside me while I drove, and did not say a word. The two girls were both asleep in the arms of their grandfather. To our left the ocean spread out like a great net—we just cut along its edge. Indistinctly I heard Mo Lao, seated in the rear, lowly humming a tune:

"Swallows fly in pairs; by the painted railings, the people are quiet, and the evening wind is faint."

I followed with:

"I remember the gate and lanes in those years; the scene is vaguely familiar. . . ."

IV.

After the pictures were developed I was surprised by my own unexpected stroke of genius. Those with the willow in the background were nothing special. They generally expressed a melancholy mood. But that lucky shot of Mo Lao and the red monarch butterfly—heavens! I suddenly felt excited, as if I had found my long-sought answer. Wasn't this it? Wasn't this exactly it? For a moment my historian's instincts were aroused. The contrast in the picture was so strong: a reddish-orange monarch butterfly, its spread wings about to close—this small creature, which had flown three thousand miles, had by coincidence extended its three pairs of legs to prepare for a rest. On the other hand, Mo Lao's head—his silver strands of hair glistening in the light of the setting sun— was stopped just as it was being raised. And both of them were so tired, ordered by some mysterious force to be framed in a De Chirico-style painting![3]

Soon afterwards, I began to include the history of Mo K'uang-shih, my father-in-law, as one of my research topics.

Of course the first step was to find all the firsthand materials I could. This was not difficult, because many of Mo Lao's contemporaries had published their memoirs and the periodicals Mo Lao edited in his youth had survived up to now in fragments. There were also microfilmed newspapers and documents relevant to my research in our library, so reconstructing the events of Mo Lao's life was not difficult.

I organized the materials very quickly and reviewed the various theories regarding China's modern history. Three simple points were adopted as the basis of my study:

1. Mo Lao was a typical example of a modern Chinese intellectual involved in politics.

2. The experience of the model, politically involved Chinese intellectual was tragic.

3. The crux of this tragedy lay in contradictions that the intellectuals themselves had no way of transcending. To summarize, these included:

—The ambivalent attitude toward "authority" expressed during the creation of political power.

—Vacillation in the quagmire of what Karl Mannheim[4] called the utopian mentality and real politics, while having to give up the intellectual's role as social critic.

—The psychological complex of xenophobia and iconoclasm brought about by the dual pressure of western industrial civilization and traditional culture.

After I finished this tentative plan, my psychological tenseness seemed to relax slightly. Yet I still felt vaguely that, if it were only for presentation at the annual conference, this had already met the requirements of a solid paper. But I could not help asking myself: Wasn't I unconsciously applying worn-out academic formulas merely by setting up a framework like this for my paper? This misgiving made me hesitate: I dared not start writing too hastily. Finally I decided to have Hsi-hu act as a reader. I drafted a main outline following my plan, sealed it in an envelope, and left it on Hsi-hu's dresser table. The next day it returned to my desk with a note attached:

"I don't see my father in his flesh and blood."

Hsi-hu's reaction naturally deepened my apprehension. Although she was a very special reader, and though I well knew that those who write history nowadays do not write for readers outside academic circles with no knowledge of history or basic training in behavioral science, I could not but consider Hsi-hu's reaction. The paths of historical development were one thing—any second-rate historiographer could handle it. But interpretation and analysis of the logic of historical development placed historical events and figures in a broader perspective. This was another matter. This was the only important mission that my education had prepared me for. I was a person who worked in the direction pointed out by his education, a young, energetic scholar who had published two important works. Yet my wife said to me: You're merely playing word games! Although she was no historian, she was Mo Lao's daughter. Didn't Mo Lao's intellectual life and political activities, and all his major choices and decisions of the past thirty years, affect her life directly, and weren't they reasons why Hsi-hu became Hsi-hu? What right did I have to oppose this instinctive, direct reaction? Wasn't this simply a resounding slap on my historian's mouth?

Under this kind of attack, I resolved to look through all the works I had published. Reading them again, I had to admit that I found myself in an extremely embarrassing situation. My writing was mechanical, practiced, but had no vitality. My reasoning and analyses were rigorous, logical, well-organized, but lacked any original ideas. For the most part, my theoretical framework was the mere dutiful application of the ideas of a few social historians who were then popular in academic circles. All I did was to add a decorative outer coat to them.

I felt that the ground beneath my feet was slowly shifting, that the construction project I had toiled to build was sinking. Again I picked up that photograph of Mo Lao and the monarch butterfly and examined it closely. Then I simply shook all the photographs of butterflies that had accumulated over the past few years out from my drawer and spread them out on the table. The contrast produced here was so clear, so obvious. Except for this most recent one, all that the photographs showed me was a variety of butterfly corpses. They were all images of cold death. One by one I reexamined the entries in the diary I had kept over the past few years. Without a doubt, what was recorded here was merely the slow process of my advance toward death.

It was already deep into the night, and I was still in a daze, facing a table covered with butterfly corpses. Without my knowing it, Hsi-hu had been standing behind me. Her hair brushed lightly against my cheeks. She said softly:

"I think P'ing-p'ing has a fever!"

We gave P'ing-p'ing some liquid aspirin and held her in our arms until her temperature dropped and her eyes closed. It was already dawn when I went to sleep, completely worn out. This was probably the soundest I had slept in several years.

V.

After almost four months of hard labor, I finally finished Mo Lao's oral history. Mo Lao, who was nearly eighty, had a surprisingly good memory. I checked the documents I had collected and discovered not only that Mo Lao's recollections supplemented them with many details, but even that his memory of less significant dates, place names, and relationships between events was seldom mistaken. This made me marvel at the sense of history possessed by an intellectual of Mo Lao's generation.

After I revised my original draft, Mo Lao gave some of his close friends who were either directly or indirectly involved in his personal history a few copies to look over. Everyone encouraged us to publish it. I sought Hsi-hu's opinion. She said her father should be the one to decide. As for Mo Lao? He just said:

"It doesn't matter whether it's published or not. After all, it's all about things of the past. But I do want to ask you one question. These past few months I've let you ask enough questions, right?"

Of course I already knew what he wanted to ask, and it seemed that he already knew that I knew. He continued:

"Don't use high-sounding talk to put me off. Why are you young people interested in old folks like us?"

I was silent for a long time. I didn't know how best to answer this question. Mo Lao spoke again:

"Ai! I probably can't blame you for this, since in fact there is nothing better for you to do, right?"

It was the middle of March. The monarch butterflies, which stay along sunny California's coastal belt, had completed their annual winter sojourn. In the season when floral fragrance fills the air, they started their journey homeward. And during this spring season in a foreign land where ten thousand flowers bloomed, our first son came into the world. Mo Lao chose for him a strange sounding name—Nai-chan, which probably takes its meaning from the lines "Then I see my house, / I exult and run to it."[5] Sharing in the festive air created by the newborn baby's cries filling the house, Mo Lao, who was sitting in front of the hallway in the warm sunlight, suddenly said to me:

"These butterflies are really strange. How do they know it's time to go back?"

I had originally intended to answer by citing one entomologist's theory. The words were on the tip of my tongue, but for some reason I couldn't get them out. So I just made up a bit of nonsense:

"It's probably already spring where they are headed."

NOTES

1. Literally, "Mo the Venerable." Here it is used as a proper name.
2. Aleksandr (Ivanovich) Herzen (1812–1870), Russian journalist and political thinker who was exiled for his ideas about revolution. After six years of exile he returned to Russia in 1842, but left again in 1847. He settled in England in 1852.
3. Giorgio De Chirico (1888–1978), Italian painter, one of the founders of the "metaphysical school." In metaphysical painting representational but bizarre imagery was used to disquiet the viewer. For this reason De Chirico is regarded as a forerunner of the Surrealists.
4. Karl Mannheim (1893–1947), sociologist who taught in Germany until the rise of Adolf Hitler. He believed that social conflict was caused by differences in individual ways of thought and in personal criteria of truth. To Mannheim, these differences were more important than economic inequality and class consciousness.
5. "Nai-chan" means "Then I see." The lines are from "Returning Home" by T'ao Ch'ien (365?–427).

OU-YANG TZU   (1939–   )

Poor eyesight has prevented Ou-yang Tzu (pen name of Hung Chih-hui) from concentrated reading and writing in recent years. Accordingly, she is forced to give up a writing career dating back to her undergraduate years at National Taiwan University, when she published one exquisite story after another in noted journals. But no reader seriously interested in Taiwan fiction of the late fifties and early sixties could fail to recognize her gift as a writer who finds thwarted passions and ungovernable irrationality a rewarding subject for proper study. Although she is often assailed by didactic critics for her nonchalance toward social or political causes, the value of her art asserts itself by baring the truth about the limit of reason, by charting the psychic forces that paralyze the mind and the will. Selected for this anthology, "The Net" is a powerful reminder of the plain fact that neither religion nor ethics can hope to resolve the dilemmas of the human heart in conflict with itself. Ou-yang Tzu holds a B.A. (1961) in English from National Taiwan University, and an M.F.A. (1964) from the Writers' Workshop of the University of Iowa. Though she is restrained by her health from engaging in creative writing, occasionally she delights us with an essay or a translation, which she finds less strenuous. Her first collection of stories is That Long-Haired Girl (Na ch'ang-t'ou-fa ti nü-hai-tzu, Taipei, 1967). Later she revised seven pieces in that volume and reissued them together with her new writing under the title Autumn Leaves (Ch'iu-yeh, Taipei, 1971). An early version of "The Net" in English is included in Lucien Wu's New Chinese Writing (Taipei, 1962). The present translation, however, is based on the new edition and for this reason represents not only a change in content but in language as well. Ou-yang Tzu now lives with her family in Austin, Texas.

The Net

Translated by the author

Her bag in one hand and a baby bottle in the other, Yü Wen-chin stepped out of a drugstore on Heng-yang Road in downtown Taipei. A wave of hot air assaulted her as soon as she was outside the air-conditioned store.

It certainly was clumsy of the maid, she thought, to drop the bottle and

185

break it while feeding Pao-pao.[1] She wished the maid would be more careful in the future. How she would have liked to stay home on a hot humid afternoon like this, instead of coming downtown to buy a baby bottle!

Slowly she walked along the street toward the bus station. She stopped now and then to do some window shopping. Although Wen-chin never did enjoy coming to this part of the city, she found it not at all unpleasant now that she was here to look around a little.

"Yü Wen-chin!"

Hearing her name called, she halted in the middle of a step. A look of surprise flitted across her face. Yet she did not turn around at once. For a few seconds she stood completely still, not moving a muscle. Then suddenly she flushed.

"Yü Wen-chin!"

She turned around. A young man about her age, twenty-five or so, in a clean white shirt and a pair of dark brown pants, was elbowing his way through the crowd and coming toward her. He was tall and good looking, although a little on the thin side.

"Ah, T'ang P'ei-chih!" she uttered. Joy appeared on her face. She literally beamed.

The man came up to her and stopped. He too was smiling happily. For a minute they just stood facing each other on the crowded street, smiling, rejoicing, speechless with exultation.

"But when—when did you come to Taipei?" Wen-chin asked, looking at her friend tenderly.

The man seemed surprised at her words. His smile faded somewhat, and he eyed her with an uncertain look upon his face.

"About two weeks ago," he said.

"Visiting your sister?"

"Yes."

With watery eyes Wen-chin looked him up and down several times. She was beside herself with joy.

"It's been three years," she said, laughing a little, "and you haven't changed a bit!"

"Neither have you," T'ang P'ei-chih said.

At this moment Wen-chin remembered she was holding the baby bottle in her hand. She moved the hand a little toward her back. As she was doing so, she had a feeling that T'ang P'ei-chih had already noticed the bottle.

"Why don't we go to some place where we can sit down and talk," he suggested.

"Yes, of course," she said.

They started to move on. Wen-chin slipped the bottle into her bag when she thought T'ang P'ei-chih wasn't looking.

They entered an ice cream shop and each ordered a glass of fruit juice. Wen-chin felt effervescent, bubbling over with happiness. She just couldn't keep from smiling.

"You've been in Taipei for two weeks," she said, "and you didn't even let me know!"

"But I did!" he exclaimed.

"You did?" She was surprised. "How?"

Again, an uncertain expression came upon his face. Then he smiled, faintly, self-consciously.

"Why, don't you remember?" he said, not looking at her. "I did write you a letter."

"A letter? When?" she asked, puzzled. "Why, I didn't—"

"And you answered my letter," he cut in, hastily, as if for some reason he did not want her to finish her sentence. Then all of a sudden he reddened. "You did answer my letter, didn't you? You told me you couldn't make it because it was—it was—your—"

He faltered, stopped, and looked down. Wen-chin grew pale. For a few minutes they sat silent, stiffly, awkwardly.

"Yes, maybe—" she said softly, as if murmuring to herself. "I did receive your letter—"

Then words failed her. She said no more. All the while T'ang P'ei-chih kept his eyes lowered, a forced smile upon his face.

Five minutes later Wen-chin picked up her bag.

"It's getting late," she said and stood up. "I'd better go now."

Suddenly T'ang P'ei-chih raised his eyes and looked at her, painfully, appealingly. It seemed as though he wanted to say something, to plead with her about something. Yet he said nothing. Wen-chin saw suffering on his face.

He did not offer to take her home.

Wen-chin was exhausted when she finally reached home. She closed the front door and leaned against it for a while, resting, trying not to think. Then she went to the kitchen, took the bottle from her bag, and put it in the cabinet where the maid stored Pao-pao's things. She then left the kitchen and went to the bedroom.

At the bedroom door she paused, and stood eyeing the neatly made double bed as if seeing it for the first time in her two years of marriage. But soon she looked away and stepped quietly to the far end of the room where a crib was standing. Carefully she raised the mosquito net and peeked inside the crib. Pao-pao was sound asleep, his tiny mouth half open.

Staring at the baby, Wen-chin wondered why she would much rather T'ang Pei-chih didn't know she was now a mother. She was almost sure though that he had seen the bottle. It was surprising that despite her

marriage to Ting Shih-chung, and the fact that they hadn't seen each
other for three years, things had remained the same between her and
T'ang P'ei-chih. The bond was still there, tying them together. And then,
in spite of themselves, they still couldn't help hurting each other because
both of them were so highly sensitive and understanding.

Wen-chin had often imagined what it would be like if instead of Ting
Shih-chung she had married T'ang P'ei-chih. She did not think it would
have worked, because they knew each other too well and they had too
much in common. Strange though it might sound, they were simply too
close to be able to live together as husband and wife.

With Ting Shih-chung it was quite different. He had really made her
happy by taking her for granted, and by willingly accepting all her
sacrifices. She felt secure with him, and was sure of herself as long as she
could cling to him. Since their marriage two years ago, she had given
herself up to him, offering him everything—her body, her mind, her will.
Ting Shih-chung had never hesitated to accept these offerings, taking
them as though they were his inborn right. Wen-chin found contentment
in her surrender, and drew immense gratification from the realization
that she had lost herself for the sake of someone she loved.

This kind of contentment and gratification was exactly what T'ang P'ei-
chih was unable to give her. Never, never could she be at ease with T'ang
P'ei-chih, because each of them was so eager to sacrifice for the other but
at the same time would refuse to accept the slightest sacrifice in return.
Wen-chin remembered how, because T'ang P'ei-chih loved music, she
would go on talking about Beethoven and Mozart. On the other hand,
knowing she loved literature, T'ang P'ei-chih would try hard to change
the subject to Tolstoy or Romain Rolland. They just could not quite fit
together in this manner; the easiest way for them was to do or to talk
about something that did not really concern either of them. They would
choose words carefully in conversation, and take great pains to decide
whether they should do this or do that. "Would I hurt him by so doing?"
"Wouldn't he feel bad if I said this?" She remembered burdening herself
with such questions all the time.

And yet, those had been in many ways the most wonderful days of her
life—the days when they were together as college students. On entering
the classroom every morning, she would always meet his gentle smile.
His eyes would glow tenderly at the sight of her, as if saying to her, "Oh,
friend, my friend, here I am." And then she would feel happy all day long,
even without exchanging a single word with him.

Her married life had gone smoothly enough. She loved Ting Shih-
chung dearly and felt she could not live without him. And yet the shadow
of her intimacy with T'ang P'ei-chih was there, always there, deep down
in her soul. It had never occurred to her that she was being spiritually

unfaithful to her husband. They were so different, these two men; they could not be compared. Besides, she scarcely looked upon T'ang P'ei-chih as a man. It could have been the same if he were a woman. Although it might not be honest to say that she never desired him, she had sensed from the start that things would not turn out that way between them. And then he never had actually asked her to marry him anyway.

Daylight was beginning to fade and the room grew darker. Wen-chin heard a mosquito buzzing around. She closed the mosquito net over the crib. The clock struck half past six. It was time for Ting Shih-chung to return.

She was dimly conscious of something awakening within her. For two years she did not seem to have really existed. She had not been living her own life, because Ting Shih-chung, ever full of energy and eager to protect her, would consider and arrange everything for her. He loved her tenderly and possessed her completely. And she had been pleased to give herself up like this, thinking it a great privilege to be so wanted by a man.

But now, after two years' hibernation, her will was suddenly stirring, awakening. How T'ang P'ei-chih had avoided looking at her! What a painful expression he had upon his face! She knew very well that he was suffering from the realization that he had hurt her. Words had never been of much use between them; they understood each other without the need for talk.

From outside the house came the noise of a motorcycle, and she knew that her husband was back. A minute later the front door opened.

"Wen-chin!" His voice was clear and cheerful.

She did not move, nor did she reply.

"Wen-chin!"

Still she did not answer. The steps drew nearer; Ting Shih-chung appeared at the bedroom door.

"Are you there?" he said, coming into the room. "It's dark here. Why didn't you turn on the light?" He switched the light on. Wen-chin shielded her eyes against the dazzling light. She did not look in his direction.

"Oh, I wasn't aware it was dark," she said nonchalantly. "Pao-pao is asleep." She still did not look at him.

"How is our little one today?" he asked, toning down his voice so he would not wake the baby. "He has been a good boy, hasn't he?" He came over and put his arm around her. Then he walked with her closer to the crib, raised the mosquito net, and peered complacently at the baby.

"Look how beautiful he is," he said, squeezing her. "I have never seen a baby like him."

She was silent.

"I mean it," he said. "This baby is different. He is just different!"

Wen-chin felt like crying. She loved Ting Shih-chung so much. She would die without him. And yet, at the same time, her newly awakened self was asserting itself, wanting to be set free.

After supper, they sat around as usual in the living room. Shih-chung was in his armchair, reading the evening paper. Now and then, however, he would raise his head and talk to Wen-chin. He told her how he had outwitted a colleague with whom he was competing for a promotion. He told her how his boss was impressed with the way he handled a fastidious client. Wen-chin sat quietly across from him on the sofa, not paying much attention to him. Shih-chung either did not notice or thought nothing of her unusual silence.

"Shih-chung," she said, at last.

"Yes?" He raised his head.

"I want to ask you something."

"What is it?"

"I've been wondering if you opened a letter addressed to me."

"Which letter?" he said, surprised. "You know I open your mail. I didn't think you minded."

"It was from a friend of mine, T'ang P'ei-chih."

"Who is T'ang P'ei-chih?" Shih-chung asked. He made a face and pretended to be jealous. "Is it he, or she? A secret admirer?"

Wen-chin took a hard look at him.

"And you answered the letter, didn't you?" she said.

"Oh, that one!" he said. "Now I remember. Sure, the name was T'ang. It was last Saturday, I believe. You weren't home when the postman delivered the letter. So of course I opened it, and then answered it to spare you some trouble."

"You should at least have told me!" Wen-chin felt dryness coming into her voice. "Where is the letter?"

"The letter? What do you need it for?" he said. "Of course I threw it away."

Threw it away! Of course he threw it away! Wen-chin was at once overcome with bitterness. How easy it is for him to say so! And how light hearted he appears! Yet I have to suffer for it. T'ang P'ei-chih, too, has to suffer for it . . .

"But don't worry, I remember what it said," Shih-chung assured her. "It wasn't long, just a page, saying that he had come to Taipei from Ping-tung, to visit a sister or a brother. By the way, why didn't you ever tell me you have friends living that far down in the south? Anyway, he asked if you would meet him on Monday, at his sister's or brother's home. This friend of yours—he's kind of rude, isn't he? He should have come to see us at our home, instead of ordering you around. Now, of course you remember last Monday happened to be our second anniversary. So I answered in your name that you couldn't make it, but just might drop in to see him some other time."

"And you signed my name," she said, frostily.

"Certainly," he said. "Why, anything wrong?"

She made no reply. Poor, poor friend, she thought. Surely T'ang P'ei-chih could tell it was not her handwriting; he must have guessed who had written the letter. What he hadn't dreamed of was that after nearly a week she could still be ignorant of the whole matter. If he had thought of such a possibility, she was sure he wouldn't have said a word about having written to her. It was too late when he realized she knew absolutely nothing, and he saw that he had hurt her. And so, in desperation T'ang P'ei-chih tried to conceal his perception of the truth; he would rather sacrifice himself by pretending not to understand her, not to have even noticed that the letter wasn't written by her, than let her know that he had guessed how her husband had been dominating her. Poor, poor P'ei-chih. How he must be feeling sorry for her!

Wen-chin raised her eyes. Shih-chung was again absorbed in the evening paper. The cigarette in his hand was burning close to its butt. Suddenly she felt he was strange to her, almost as if she had never had anything to do with him. Yet in reality they were in love; she did not know how she could live without him. How very odd it was. He was now leaning forward to reach the ashtray. He looked so handsome; big eyes, dark brows, firm lips. And he had such self-assurance. Oh, how she would love to rest in his strong, protective arms. He was more precious than life. She could always count on him to take good care of her. There was no need, no need whatsoever, for her to bother about anything at all. Whereas T'ang P'ei-chih could only make her suffer. She, too, could only make him suffer. Always suffering, fearful that the other might be hurt. And they'd get hurt anyway.

"What else did he say?" she asked.

"What? Oh." Shih-chung frowned a little. "Can't remember any more." Then he seemed to have thought of something. "Ah, yes. He did ask if you are happy."

"If—I am happy?"

"Yes. And so I answered him, 'My dear friend, I am the happiest woman in the world. We just had our first baby, a boy. He is so cute, looks just like my husband. If only you knew how happy we are!'"

Wen-chin winced. Oh my goodness, she thought, so P'ei-chih knew about Pao-pao all the time! She felt sick and disgusted.

"Well, what do you think?" Shih-chung lifted his brows proudly and smiled. "Wouldn't you have written the same yourself? You see, I know you perfectly. I can read your mind."

Can you? she thought. An ironical smile came to her lips. For two years she had never once tried to analyze herself. She had no thoughts of her own. She had come to rely on Shih-chung so much, and had let him do all the thinking for her. Now she didn't even know whether she herself was happy. Oh, how unfair, how very unfair it was!

Poor dear P'ei-chih! she thought. How could you ask me if I am happy? How could you ask me a question so difficult to answer? Wen-chin was sure, though, that she would have replied just the same, in the affirmative. But what right had Shih-chung to speak for her? What right had he to decide for her whether she was happy or not?

Wen-chin leaned back in the sofa and closed her eyes. She felt very unhappy. Shih-chung was her support; she certainly could not afford to lose him. But that other face, so strained with pain and full of sadness, haunted her. She cared for P'ei-chih just as she cared for herself. Yet it was to Shih-chung that she owed all she had. For two long years she had allowed Shih-chung to do anything he liked with her, and now it was as if she had also left P'ei-chih at his mercy. Yet P'ei-chih was proud—he had always been. This was the essential cause of his suffering.

Then it occurred to her that she was being very selfish, for to think about P'ei-chih was to think about herself. How could I expect to be paid for my sacrifices? she thought with self-reproach. Then there was the fact that she loved her husband. She loved Shih-chung very much indeed, and was eager to dedicate her whole self to him. But I can't help it, I just can't help it, she thought in agony. Oh, dear P'ei-chih, my poor, poor friend . . .

In the ecstasy of their reunion, after three years' separation, she had had to leave him abruptly without even concealing the pain he had caused her. Oh, poor, poor friend! Shouldn't I go see him? Yes, I must see him, I must. But what's the use? He'd just look at me, and I at him. Then I'd say, "Oh, my friend, I am awakened! Now I know I love myself more than my husband!" And how would he take it? What would he think? "Here she comes again to sacrifice herself, poor friend! But I won't have it, I won't have it!" What more could I do? What more could I say?

"Wen-chin."

She opened her eyes. Shih-chung was smiling at her. He had on his face the kind of tender look that she knew only too well. He rose from the armchair and came to sit down with her. He put his arm around her, squeezed her, and started to kiss her. Wen-chin jerked her body and tried to stand up.

"Wen-chin," he whispered, "let's go to bed."

"No, not now," she said, pushing him away a little. "It's feeding time again."

"But the maid just fed him," he said, not letting her go. "I saw her feeding him."

He pushed her down a little and started again to kiss her, passionately.

He was holding her so tight she could hardly breathe. Still she struggled.

"No, don't, please, don't, not tonight," she protested. "I was just thinking—just thinking—"

Shih-chung pretended not to hear her. Still kissing her, he managed to unzip her gown, unclasp her brassiere, and began to caress her breasts. Then suddenly he was up on his feet and, carrying her in his arms, he started for the bedroom.

Wen-chin struggled harder.

"Let—me—go!" she screamed.

Shih-chung was taken aback. He loosened his grasp, let go of her, and looked at her in amazement.

Tears were streaming down her cheeks.

"I was just thinking—" she uttered sobbing, "it might be better for us to separate—for a few days, I mean—"

"What? To separate!" Shih-chung was astonished. "What do you mean, to separate?"

Wen-chin kept on sobbing, unable to say a word.

A look of annoyance came over his face. Suddenly he was cold toward her.

"I think I know what you mean, all right," he said, shrugging. "You mean you don't love me any more, right? So you don't love me any more. But what does that matter? It's all right with me; you may do as you please."

He turned away and strode heavily into the bedroom. A moment later he came out with a pillow and a blanket in his arms. He unloaded them on the sofa without so much as a glance at her.

"Don't worry," he said, "I'll sleep here on the sofa tonight. Lock the door if you like."

No sooner had he finished these words than a frightened expression seized her face. She stopped sobbing at once. For a minute she stared at him, mouth half open, eyes full of panic. Then she moaned. Holding out her hands and rushing toward him, she fell all at once on her knees.

"Oh, Shih-chung," she cried, panting, clutching his legs. "Don't—don't forsake me, please, don't—don't leave me—"

Again tears streamed down her face, and she was shuddering all over with sobs. Nearly on all fours on the floor, she began to press her face desperately against his feet. Her body kept writhing inside her unzipped gown, and her hair, long and dishevelled, was all over the place.

For a moment Shih-chung stood petrified, then he bent down, took her gently in his arms and helped her to her feet. She rested her full weight upon him and put her arms around his body. "Don't, please, don't forsake me—" she repeated, again and again, and wept miserably. Shih-chung patted her lovingly on the back.

"Now, Wen-chin, don't be silly," he said tenderly. "How could I ever forsake you, you silly child?" He put his cheek against hers.

She felt very weak, and stayed paralyzed in his arms.

"It was rude of me, Wen-chin," he said kindly. "Frankly, I am very ashamed of myself. You look so pale. Are you sure you're all right? Not sick or anything? You must be awfully tired. I'll let you have a good night's sleep, this I can promise you. I should have been more considerate—"

"Oh, please, Shih-chung, please!" Wen-chin hugged him with all her might, and burst out in another flood of tears. "No, Shih-chung, I'm not sick at all. Not tired either. Don't you see? I'm just fine, just fine. Please, Shih-chung, please love me. It was selfish of me, please forgive me, please. But I do love you. Don't you see? I really do love you. Don't leave me alone, please. Don't forsake me. I was just testing myself. To find out if I could live without you. No, I can't. I can't live without you. I knew it all along. So please don't leave me, please. There is no me, but you and me. I am nothing, I do not exist—" She panted for breath, totally exhausted.

"Now, now, my love," Shih-chung said, "of course I know you love me. I wouldn't want to leave you for the world." He patted her on the back, as if comforting a little girl who had hurt herself by accident.

"What a child," he murmured.

By and by she calmed down. She ceased weeping, closed her eyes, and rested her head on his shoulder.

"You know, Shih-chung," she said feebly, "it's just that I was a little jealous of you. I felt I love you more than myself."

Shih-chung seemed amused and laughed a little. Then he squeezed her and planted a kiss on her forehead.

"But now, I don't feel jealous of you any more," she continued murmuring. "I am very happy. I am glad that I love you more than myself." She was smiling. At the same time, one more tear fell down her cheek.

"Now, my dear wife," he said, softly. "Why don't we do the talking tomorrow. Let's go to bed."

Wen-chin opened her eyes wide.

"And you, with me?" she asked.

"Certainly," Shih-chung said, smiling.

He held her by the waist and they went together to the bedroom. Wen-chin was weak and could hardly stand on her feet. But she had told him the truth. She was truly happy.

NOTE

1. "Pao-pao" literally means "precious," a common form of address for Chinese babies. Here it is used as a proper name.

WANG CHEN-HO (1940–   )

Comic strains have characterized much of Wang Chen-ho's early writing,
such as "An Oxcart for Dowry" (Chia-chuang i niu-ch'e, 1967; included in
Chinese Stories from Taiwan). *To be sure, as evident in the present selec-*
tion, "The Story of Three Springs," his fictional world teems with comic
moments. But such moments rarely translate into a full-bodied comic
work. For, almost alone of his contemporaries, Wang depicts a life that is
comically conceived but tragically understood—a life of forced compro-
mises and forfeitures. His characters lend themselves to the categorization
of the predator and the prey. When cornered, his mock-hero extricates
himself from the predicament by making virtues of docility and yielding.

Like Ch'en Ying-chen and Huang Ch'un-ming, Wang is deeply con-
cerned about the bankruptcy of Chinese virtues under Western impact.
He is troubled by the Chinese practices of sprinkling their conversation
with English phrases, of abbreviating their given names in initials, or of
adopting outright a Western name. "Hsiao Lin in Taipei" (Hsiao Lin lai
Taipei, 1973) lampoons what he regards as excesses of Western adulation
by transliterating in Chinese one Mr. T. P. Ku as "Kicking-in-the-Ass Ku."
Aside from three volumes of stories, Wang has written a number of one-
act plays. His works are discussed in Chinese Fiction from Taiwan: Critical Perspectives.

The Story of Three Springs[1]
Translated by Jane Parish Yang

—for B. L.—

When she was about eighteen, she went to a fortune-teller with some of
her sworn sisters. The fortune-teller was from far away, and all of his
clients testified that his judgment of the past and predictions of the future
were extremely accurate. She couldn't remember all the details now, only
that one sentence, and she was able to remember it because in it latent
seductive powers awaited release: "Miss, you'll have a life of peach blos-
soms,[2] marriages galore. Three stars will with Beauty mate, busy with
carnal pleasures your whole life through." Fearing that she didn't understand, the fortune-teller wildly gesticulated with hands and feet to help
explain every line, every word.

195

"Miss, you'll enjoy the pleasures of three husbands in your life. One, two, three. No more, no less. Exactly three."

After they had gone a safe distance from the fortune-teller's booth, her sworn sisters competed with each other in teasing her.

"Ah-chiao, so a husband for you is like a shoe—as soon as one is worn out, you replace it with another. What a deal!"

That prophecy had now come true, twenty-five years later—three husbands, not one more and not one less. It was as if she had made a pact with that fortune-teller.

Preparations for Ah-chiao's third marriage were already being made for summer. The ceiling fan whined overhead. The dormitory was empty, since all the bus attendants had left for work. Ah-chiao sat under the fan picking over sweet potato greens, carefully stripping the stems piece by piece. No one did that where she came from, but city folk were picky. Ah-chiao was wearing only a slip, but she wasn't afraid anyone would come in because this place was off limits to men. Perspiring as she sorted the greens, she finally finished and replaced them in the small rattan basket. Just as she was about to take them back to the kitchen, she suddenly spotted a figure entering the dormitory. Before she could see clearly who it was, the figure had already appeared in front of her.

"Ah-chiao, how are you? Haven't seen you for ages."

"Uh—," she was too frightened to speak. Her face was expressionless and her mouth agape—she didn't know what to say. Ah-chiao's mouth was slightly larger than average. She had only to part her lips and immediately two deep V-shaped creases would run down from her nostrils to her lips. The creases made her look as if her face was wreathed in smiles. Thus, even though she was in fact scowling, she would give the impression that she was being seductive, with her head tilted slightly to one side. Maybe this was why she lived a "peach blossomed" life.

When the coffin of her first husband, Ah-yüan, was being lowered into the ground, she had wailed "My husband, my master!" But below the coarse hemp hood of her mourning gown were those lips of hers, spreading out in a broad grin. Out of curiosity, her relatives walked over to her on the pretext of comforting her, and peered under the hood to determine whether she was in fact crying or laughing. Her Aunt Liang even suggested that a doctor be called immediately, since she though Ah-chiao had probably become so distressed that she didn't know the difference between crying and laughing anymore.

But, before the unexpected visitor, she was really smiling this time, her mouth gaping wide open. The visitor was Mr. Ying, an inspector for the Highway Bus Bureau. Perhaps because he had been an inspector for too long, it became his habit to drop in on people when they were least prepared. This time was no exception. He hadn't bothered to knock, though this was a dormitory for single women.

"Ah-chiao, long time no see. You look better each time I see you. Is your son still in the army?" Inspector Ying was from her hometown, and had moved to the city some five or six years ago. Last year, when Ah-chiao and Skinny Kao had called it quits, she had ended up coming to the city and earning her keep doing house chores for Inspector Ying's family. Later, when the old amah in the bus attendants' dormitory got sick and quit her job, Inspector Ying had recommended Ah-chiao to fill the post. While she was working as a maid in his house, no matter how shabbily she was dressed, she had never felt as embarrassed as she did now. Now that she was earning a government salary, her status was different. People like to save face, just as a tree wants to keep its bark intact. Facing a man with only a slip on was certainly not appropriate. Making an excuse that she was going to get some tea, she retreated to the bedroom to put on a dress, and then returned to offer her guest some tea. With an extra garment on, Ah-chiao suddenly came to life and responded to whatever she was asked in her most ladylike manner.

But after half an hour, she was lost for words again. Perhaps she could use another piece of clothing. Fortunately, Inspector Ying finally got around to the point of his visit. She was speechless. Her throat burned as if she had just swallowed a mouthful of stir-fried red peppers, her mouth gaping wide open with that "smile" of hers. Ying took her reaction to mean that she was pleased but too shy to speak. As a result, he rambled on buoyantly with a torrent of words.

For a long time after Inspector Ying left, Ah-chiao remained slouched against the chair, motionless, bathed in sunlight, as if she were immersed in a tub of bubbling hot water, not daring to move an inch for fear of scaldinig her skin. When the bus attendants returned, one by one, she was still in this dazed state. At dinner, an attendant named Tsung, her eyebrows arched, complained that the sweet potato greens were over-cooked. She also had other derisive remarks for Ah-chiao's ears. Ah-chiao, however, ate her meal in silence, as if she hadn't heard a thing. Ordinarily she could be expected to bang the table and shoot back a caustic remark or two.

After everyone had gone to sleep, Ah-chiao lay quietly on her canvas bed and went over in her mind everything Inspector Ying had said. She came to her senses and finally realized that Ying wanted to introduce a boyfriend to her. She was, of course, long familiar with the meaning of "boyfriend." Almost every night the bus attendants discussed almost nothing else but "boyfriend." She was, however, a woman over forty, and she felt a bit uneasy to hear herself mentioned in one breath with, Ugh! a "boyfriend," as if she were guilty of trying to turn back the clock of life. It was in this mood of misgiving that she began to analyze the nuances of Inspector Ying's words concerning, of course, her future spouse.

Ah-chiao's "boyfriend" was fifty-one this year. That seemed a bit too old, but maybe it was better that way, because older people weren't as vigorous and thus were easier to control. Ah-yüan, her first husband, had worked as a carpenter and was every inch as tough as a nail. If she talked back to him at all, fists would rain down on her in an instant. She couldn't recall what year it had been when she had told him not to use such language as "fuck your mother" and other curses on New Year's day, so that they would have good luck in the years to come. No sooner had she finished speaking than one of his legs landed on her chest. Badly hurt and bruised, she took to bed. Afraid that her condition would be found out, she made up some excuse not to visit her parents' home the second day of the New Year.[3]

With Skinny Kao, the businessman, it was a different matter: they stayed together two days and separated for three. Even on the days they were together, he was always on the go. They really didn't have enough time to nurture mutual affection. But though they had their share of arguments, at least they never came to blows. Skinny Kao had a wife and family and could have dropped her at any time to go back to them. But he didn't, and probably it was for that reason that she was willing to offer herself to him without reservation. Even so, in the end they still went their separate ways. The saying that "loving couples don't live to grow old together" was true after all.

The "boyfriend" Inspector Ying introduced was a Mr. Ou, who was on the payroll of a county government office. It seemed that he was head of some section. His position would be an honor for her. Besides, he wanted to take her formally as his wife. His two sons were already married and independent. The older one was apparently doing business in Japan and the younger one worked in a sugar refinery. His family was truly simple, with few house chores to take care of. Well, Ah-chiao thought, I might as well meet him and see what happens.

They arranged to meet at Joy-at-the-Threshold, a Japanese restaurant, at 7:30 p.m. sharp. She hurried to fix dinner for the attendants, then changed into a blue dress with a purple mosaic pattern made from the nice fabric Skinny Kao had given her. She looked lucky from head to toe.

Ah-yüan had died at thirty, run over by a car. Everyone said he had died in his prime because of his inauspicious features—ears stuck out, nostrils stuck out, teeth stuck out. If these three things stuck out, then it was small surprise that he died stuck out in the road. Skinny Kao went bankrupt and his property had been auctioned off. His inauspicious facial features were to blame—at least that was the opinion of those who knew

him. He was skinny, so his bones were exposed; his forehead was con-
cave, so his eyebrows were exposed; his cheeks were low, so his cheek-
bones were exposed. With these three things exposed, prosperity and
honor were hard to hold. This time Ah-chiao was determined to pay
special attention to facial features.

They sat in a quiet corner of the restaurant, separated from the other
tables by Japanese-style carved screens. A lantern hung overhead, a faint
flush flooding over them through the pinkish shade. Mr. Ou sat in this
reddish glow, his face reflecting the rosy tint of the lamplight, an auspicious appearance indeed. Seeing him in this light, respectably dressed in
a western suit, Ah-chiao was ecstatic. Of all the men she was acquainted
with, not one had ever worn a western business suit. Not even Skinny
Kao. Mr. Ou's forehead was bald and shiny, as if rubbed with oil. It was
said that those with high bald foreheads were sure to get rich. No need to
work, and there would be plenty of food. She wished all his hair would
hurry and fall out to guarantee his lasting good fortune.

Mr. Ou sat opposite Ah-chiao, with Inspector Ying to one side. Having
introduced the two principal parties, Ying busied himself with helping
Mr. Ou read the menu, turning to Ah-chiao for suggestions. Ah-chiao
laughed nervously, her mouth as wide as usual, as if she were dining with
a foreigner and didn't know how to answer. Seeing her "smile," Inspector
Ying thought that she was satisfied with everything and didn't ask for any
further suggestions. After ordering, Inspector Ying quietly disappeared.

"Say, where has Inspector Ying gone?" Ah-chiao spoke up for the first
time, her eyes boldly fixed on Mr. Ou. Her dark plump hand unconsciously slipped down from the table to her legs. She was afflicted with
varicose veins and had put on long thick stockings for this occasion, in
spite of the hot weather. She should be safe, she thought, because she
was sitting opposite Mr. Ou where he couldn't see her legs.

"Oh, yes. I wonder where has he gone?" Mr. Ou smiled, speaking in a
tone which suggested that he had discovered Inspector Ying's absence
just now.

They started to talk, each sentence so formal that it sounded as if it had
come out of a conversation textbook. At the beginning of each sentence
was tacked on the phrase "Inspector Ying told me that . . ." or "Inspector
Ying mentioned that . . .", as if they had made a special trip to the
restaurant just to discuss Inspector Ying.

When the food was being served, Inspector Ying suddenly reappeared
on the scene. As soon as they saw him coming, their conversation abruptly halted, as if they were gossiping about his personal affairs. They
talked as they ate, only now it was Inspector Ying and Mr. Ou who did the
talking. They talked a lot, mostly about current events, worlds apart from
Ah-chiao's life. She seemed lost, her mouth agape, like a child listening in

on adult conversation. Still, she was happy. After all, Mr. Ou had studied in school and knew a lot of things. If this introduction led to marriage, Mr. Ou could take care of the letter-writing to her son and daughter so she wouldn't have to bother other people. She thought of her son, Chün-hsiung, stationed in Kaohsiung on military duty. She thought of Ts'ai-o, her daughter, working as a maid in a hotel in Wan-li township. She wondered how they were getting along now, since she hadn't heard from them for ages. Troubled by these thoughts, her lips involuntarily parted even wider.

Mr. Ou was in the heat of analyzing some current event and was about to finish when he suddenly noticed Ah-chiao's "smile." Mistaking that as her interest in his argument, he hurriedly repeated himself two or three times for her benefit. After that, he did his best to dig up all the topics he was familiar with to discuss with Inspector Ying. He expounded enthusiastically, as if he were giving a campaign speech.

A steaming dish of freshly shelled shrimp was brought to the table. Since the shrimp had been soaked in cornstarch, they were glassy and slippery. Mr. Ou picked up a large one with his chopsticks, dipped it in catsup, and was about to deposit it in his mouth when the plastic chopsticks slipped from his hand and dropped under the table. The shrimp landed squarely on Ah-chiao's chest, leaving a large spot of catsup. Her breast looked as if it had blood on it, speared by Cupid's arrow sent by Mr. Ou. Ah-chiao gasped; her face went pale. She grabbed a handkerchief to wipe the spot, her heart sinking. Inspector Ying called a waiter to bring a wet washcloth. Mr. Ou sat on one side speechless, like a naughty child awaiting punishment. He wrung his hands, murmuring "I'm sorry" over and over again.

The wet washcloth arrived. Ah-chiao prudently broke into a real smile. "Oh, don't bother. I'll take care of it when I get home. It's just an old dress. Really, it's not worth the bother."

The next day Inspector Ying showed up carrying a present from Mr. Ou. Opening it, she found some material from Hong Kong to make a ch'i-p'ao.[4] Ah-chiao felt overjoyed as she stroked the smooth shiny brocade. She had seen others wear this kind of fabric but had never touched it before. Unfortunately, there were only two yards, only enough for plump Ah-chiao to make a one-piece western-style dress.

About one month later, Mr. Ou and Ah-chiao became husband and wife. With Ah-yüan she had had an eight-month engagement. She flirted with Skinny Kao four or five months before they started living together. But now, with Mr. Ou, it had taken only one month. One gets more impatient as one gets older.

By the time Mr. Ou was ready to make a formal proposal, two items of news concerning the practical aspects of marriage were circulating. A sixty-five-year-old woman was engaged to be the second wife of a Mr. Ou, owner of a soy sauce shop. The betrothment money was $52,000.⁵ A fifty-seven-year-old procuress married a stationery store merchant. Because her "market value" was less than others, the asking price was a little lower, only $45,000. Ah-chiao naturally listened attentively to all of these gossips, and held off giving a straightforward answer to Mr. Ou's proposal. She would always change the subject, and she mentioned that some owner of a ready-made garment shop had sent a matchmaker over to propose to her.

"He said he'd give $40,000 for the betrothment, and what's more, I would have the key to the counter cash box."

Then her tone of voice would change. Shrugging her shoulders, she would break into a smile. "But if the person isn't honest and likes to fool around, I wouldn't take him even for $100,000! Don't you agree?" This pronouncement carried an implication that she was interested in Mr. Ou for his trustworthiness despite the fact that he wasn't wealthy.

But the next time, she would change her tune again. Who says fickleness is limited to young women?

"There's a Mr. Chang who also came with a matchmaker," she would say. "Everything about him is acceptable, except he can't come up with reasonable betrothment money."

She certainly wanted both the man and his money. According to what the fortune-teller had said, this would be her last marriage, so all the more reason to ask for a decent betrothment price. If she let this golden opportunity slip by, she would never get another. She had no hope of getting a high price like $52,000 or even $45,000. After all, not every woman her age could be as highly sought as the two exceptional ladies in the news, although it was a fact that she was more experienced in marriage. So she decided to settle for $30,000.

Originally, she was going to hold stubbornly to this figure, or else Mr. Ou could look elsewhere. Why so impatient? Hadn't someone paid $52,000 for a woman over sixty? Later, however, she heard through the grapevine that Mr. Ou's younger son, Shun-ch'eng, had mocked her and strongly opposed bringing her into the family as his step-mother. Worse still, she also heard that Mr. Ou had indicated to someone that he didn't care about the outcome of his proposal one way or the other. After fuming about it for a while, she gave in and expressed her willingness to negotiate.

In the end, Mr. Ou's final offer was to have his $20,000 savings account transferred to her name. It took Ah-chiao more than three days arguing with herself before she finally told Inspector Ying, "Well, I'll put the matter in your hands, sir."

They decided not to make a wedding announcement or send around engagement cakes,[6] as was the custom. And they didn't want to celebrate in the restaurant. Instead, they would prepare a banquet at home for one table,[7] just for close friends and relatives. Ah-chiao had no objection to the new frugality ethic.

Around 10:30 p.m., the weather suddenly changed. Luckily, the guests had all gone home. The rain came pouring down and lasted more than two hours. About midnight the rain grudgingly let up and then ceased altogether. By that time Ah-chiao had finally finished her bath and changed into a new nylon nightgown. She sat in front of the new vanity table facing the mirror, pinning up her newly coiffured hair into a net. All the bus attendants routinely did this before they went to bed, just as they mechanically punched tickets when passengers got on the bus. She looked at herself in the mirror, and discovered that her cheeks were flushed bright red. Ah-chiao wasn't going to drink much, but tonight everyone kept toasting her, a sip here, a sip there, and before she knew it, half a bottle of Red Dew wine had thus gone into her stomach. With her hairnet in place, Ah-chiao slowly turned around.

"Say, who was that woman sitting across from me?"

"The one in the long gown sitting next to Chang, the department chief?" Mr. Ou returned with a smile. He was lying on the couch and smoking, his belly covered with a bright red Japanese blanket. The newly replaced tatami mats had a yellowish sheen, and the air was filled with the fresh pleasing scent of dried straw. The freshly papered walls sparkled like snow. The brocade quilts and embroidered pillows were piled neatly on the redwood double bed. The sheets were a bright orange. Everything in this room was as new as the hearts of the newlyweds.

"That's right. She was the one." The hem of her nightgown was accidentally pulled up to her knees. She quickly lowered it to cover her legs. She had no stockings on and this wasn't the appropriate time for her varicose veins to show.

On the other side of the plywood partition was the bedroom of Shun-ch'eng and his wife, Pao-chen. Just a minute earlier, she had heard Pao-chen washing the dishes. Now it was quiet. Probably everyone was in bed.

"That was Third Aunt." Mr. Ou lowered his voice as much as possible, as it was almost midnight. Besides, this was their wedding night and anything they said would attract interested eavesdroppers. Even a simple statement like "I'm going to the toilet" could be converted into a lascivious statement by word of mouth. His daughter-in-law Pao-chen, for instance, was gifted with the ability to transform anything ordinary into the fantastic. Fortunately he had always quoted the maxims of Chu Pai-lu,[8] such as "Gossiping women are the media of licentiousness and thievery," to remind her not to meddle in other people's business. But still he didn't want to take a chance, particularly tonight.

Ah-chiao snorted softly. "So that's Third Aunt!" Her voice had a hint of contempt. "No wonder she was always trying to put me down."

Mr. Ou motioned to her to lower her voice.

Ah-chiao pretended not to understand his signal and continued to rattle along with an innocent look on her face. She said Third Aunt always looked at people out of the corner of her eyes. When Ah-chiao had toasted her, she had pretended to be flustered and refused to accept the compliment, as if she didn't want Ah-chiao to have the honor.

"If she can't drink, well, there's nothing to it. But what's the meaning of repeating 'Wait 'till next time'? Humph. That double-talking bitch! She was obviously putting a curse on us so that we won't live out our lives together. Humph. Next time indeed! Till I marry again was what she meant!"

"She didn't mean that."

"Well, I hope not." Ah-chiao was absolutely certain there was no next time, since the fortune-teller had told her that she would have only three husbands in this life, no more.

She snorted again, and enumerated Third Aunt's faults at the banquet one by one. She had asked Ah-chiao her previous husband's name and occupation, and the name and occupation of the one before that. She did this kind of residence check right in front of Department Chief Chang, Inspector Ying, Shun-ch'eng, and Pao-chen! If Inspector Ying hadn't changed the subject, Third Aunt might even have taken notes to file away for future reference on how often Ah-chiao had slept with her previous husband and the one before that.

Ah-chiao chose her words dispassionately, as if she were relating how unfilial a neighbor's child was to his parents. She prattled on effusively, as if the affair was no concern of hers and she had no cause to get angry. Her cheeks seemed more than ever to be crinkled in a beneficent smile, emanating from her very heart. Mr. Ou was in an embarrassing situation: he could neither confirm nor refute what Ah-chiao had said about his Third Aunt. All he could do was let Ah-chiao carry on, at times adding a noncommittal word or two himself.

"Why did you invite her?"

"She's the only remaining elder in the family. There was no excuse for not inviting her. She's always had a sharp tongue. Better just ignore her."

Someone seemed to be moving around in Shun-ch'eng's room and Mr. Ou immediately stopped talking. Having finished his cigarette, he stood up and undressed. He hadn't taken a bath yet. Afraid that he would catch a cold, he hadn't dared take off his clothes until he had sobered up. Ah-chiao, eyes riveted on Mr. Ou, didn't speak, either.

A moment later she stood up and declared: "A relative like this is like a chicken who only shits and doesn't lay eggs. If you want my advice, don't have anything to do with her anymore!" She raised her voice as she spoke, enunciating the last few words as if she were giving a military order and wanted everyone to hear it distinctly.

What could Mr. Ou say? He bowed his head and silently unbuckled his pants. His palms were sweaty and he had a hard time loosening his belt.

Mr. Ou usually went to the bathroom from the time he got home from work to the time he sat down to dinner, about five or six o'clock. He suffered from constipation and had to squat there for as long as half an hour. The drawstring on his shorts was a bit short, leaving only a short section to be drawn and knotted at the waist. If he were careless and stood with his legs too far apart, the drawstring would slip back without warning into the eyelet at the waist. He had been thinking of asking Pao-chen to buy the kind of shorts with an elastic waist. Today, around 5:40 he had gone to the bathroom as usual. He must have taken an inordinate amount of time there, for Inspector Ying, tired of waiting outside, urged him to hurry in a loud voice. The drawstring to Mr. Ou's shorts had thus been spirited into the eyelet. Frantic, Mr. Ou pulled the whole drawstring out and tied it tightly around his waist, then pulled up his suit pants. Once outside, he was dragged off by Inspector Ying to the wedding ceremony. Naturally, he had had no time to attend to this business again. Later, busy with the banquet, he had completely forgotten about it.

Now it was the belt that was stuck, perhaps because perspiration had soaked the leather. Mr. Ou became frantic and gave a hard tug. With a flourish the suit pants dropped to the floor along with his undershorts, guilelessly baring his sallow skinny rump, the white cotton drawstring still around his waist.

Fortunately, Ah-chiao was not unfamiliar with the sight of a naked man. Without the slightest hint of a blush, she gave a short grunt and walked over to help him get out of his pants. She then picked up the undershorts, scrutinizing them coldly as if she were a nurse examining the shorts of someone with venereal disease.

"Cheap things are always like this. The belt is never long enough." She looked at him out of the corner of her eyes, then her voice raised slightly. "Doesn't Pao-chen know how to sew? If she were willing to make you a pair, this wouldn't happen!"

Her tone of voice seemed to imply that Mr. Ou's grievance was all due to his daughter-in-law's unworthiness. Mr. Ou felt it was necessary to say a few words in Pao-chen's defense. They were only separated by a plywood partition. If Pao-chen had overheard! But how could he say anything in earnest with all this naked sincerity exposed to Ah-chiao? Nevertheless, Mr. Ou still wanted to get in a few words. When he was about to speak, Ah-chiao drew near and reached out to untie the drawstring at his waist, her nimble fingers at times tenderly grazing the skin below his bellybutton.

When she was married to Ah-yüan there had been a relative, probably the wife of Sixth Brother, who had taught her on the sly twelve ways to domesticate a husband. Of utmost importance was the necessity to over-power the mother-in-law and tame the husband. On her wedding night, when they sat down to dinner the first thing she did was to reach for the chicken head. There's an old saying: "Chew the hen's head and you're taking the mother-in-law's head!" Little did she know that the mother-in-law was no one to be fooled. No sooner had Ah-chiao picked up the chicken's head than the old lady blocked Ah-chiao's chopsticks in midair. A knowing smile flashed on her lips as she reminded Ah-chiao: "It's simply improper to have the daughter-in-law gnaw the bones of the chicken head on her very first day. Here, this piece is a meaty one. Take it!" She picked up the tailbone and practically tossed it into Ah-chiao's bowl.

Today there was no mother-in-law to contend with, only a Third Aunt. Ah-chiao was sure that Pao-chen would spread around her stinging re-marks about Third Aunt. That, Ah-chiao was certain, would stop her from sticking her nose into Mr. Ou's affairs. Now all she had to deal with was her husband. Would he be any problem?

The next day her facial expression was deathly blank. Only her two enormous breasts, unrestrained by a bra, bounced rhythmically from side to side with each step she took, like two electrically powered mill stones hanging down from her shoulders. Mr. Ou, by contrast, was the one who showed embarrassment, as if he was the one who had lost his virginity. He walked with an unusual gait, as if he hurt somewhere.

He was wounded, indeed. He had never thought he would turn out to be this useless. So many precious evenings had passed, and yet Mr. Ou was still unable to summon his masculinity. Ah-chiao kept after him relentlessly, pressing him until he felt like crying. A conscientious prac-titioner of the arcane art of virility-strengthening by way of scrotum-massage, Mr. Ou now found himself cut down to size. He tried every other method imaginable, but pathetically there was no ripple of move-ment. Finally, Ah-chiao resolutely raised one of her huge breasts and stuffed it into Mr. Ou's mouth. That seemed to work a little, but not long enough for the final consummation. Near daybreak, Mr. Ou broke into tears. Ah-chiao hurriedly coaxed him to sleep, leaving whatever there was to be said for tomorrow.

Never having experienced such a situation before, she became a bit panicky, too. She asked all around for some medicine for restoring viril-ity. Someone tipped her off that T'ien Hsi-t'ang ginseng pills from Hong Kong were quite useful for that purpose. She immediately bought some, and had Mr. Ou take a dose every four hours or so. If he forgot to take them to work, she would take a pedicab down to the district government office building and have him suffer the embarrassment of downing one in front of his colleagues before she would return home. Day after day passed, but Mr. Ou's potency showed no sign of returning. His constipation, however, became worse.

Suddenly she recalled that Skinny Kao had taken a kind of red pill before they had intercourse. He said it was imported from Japan. After taking it, his performance was always remarkable. It would be embarrassing for her to make inquiries at the drugstore, so she pleaded with Mr. Ou to go instead. Unable to refuse her, Mr. Ou agreed to ask around when he went to Taipei on his next business trip, for he was too embarrassed to ask around where he was known.

True to his word, Mr. Ou returned with a bottle from his trip to Taipei. However, it was an American brand. Ah-chiao was so overjoyed when she saw it that, to put it crudely, she had to tighten her buttocks to keep from letting out a joyful fart. After her marriage, she kept her job as cook for the bus attendants. She didn't want to give that up. As soon as she had prepared their evening meal that day, she rushed home and the moment she arrived she got hot water ready for Mr. Ou's bath. After bathing, Mr. Ou checked his watch, took the pills, and waited quietly with Ah-chiao, their eyes fixed on the new wall clock someone had given as a wedding present. He counted the passing of each second, each minute out loud, as if making a countdown for a satellite takeoff. That evening, his satellite took off on schedule and smoothly slipped into its orbit as planned with no mishap.

Ah-chiao was so ecstatic she blossomed!

Two weeks later, Mr. Ou returned to his old self. To his utter disgust, the American pills no longer worked.

Ah-chiao searched for another wonder drug even more earnestly. Finally she obtained a prescription from a woman from her hometown and hurriedly made a copy. Carrying it back home, she scurried about gathering all the ingredients together: some polygonum multiflorum, epimedium, foxglove, atractylis lancea, ligusticum root, and things like that. She also bought a white eel to simmer with the rest of the ingredients. In the middle of the night she woke Mr. Ou up to make him finish the whole brew along with the eel.

The next morning when she got up, Mr. Ou was still sound asleep. Without waking him, she headed for the dormitory to start work. She had just put the rice in the pot for the congee when Pao-chen's oldest son came rushing into the dormitory in a panic.

"Grandfather's taken ill! Mother says for you to hurry home."

His illness was serious but not fatal. Perhaps the medicine had been too strong, just as too much excitement is harmful to heart-attack patients. Mr. Ou's weak, aging constitution wasn't up to this strong supplement. His whole throat had been scorched dry. He could open his mouth but no sound came out, as if he were speaking on the other side of a thick glass window. They brought in a doctor to give him some medicine and a shot, but his voice, like a maiden in ancient times, refused to come out.

This went on for more than a month, but Mr. Ou still couldn't speak. His son, Shun-ch'eng, sent for many doctors of western medicine whom he knew, including Director Hsü of the Provincial Hospital. None could give an explanation for his dumbness. Ah-chiao, waiting on him nearby, sneered coldly every time she saw Shun-ch'eng bringing the doctors to the house. She silently cursed them—what are those shitty doctors coming here again for?

Having encountered such a mysterious protracted illness, Ah-chiao didn't miss a single opportunity to visit temples to burn paper money, and certainly didn't forget to get a packet of joss-stick ashes to bring back to steep in water for Mr. Ou to drink. The mystical fire-tempered medicine could surely dispel evil influences and hasten his recovery, she thought. Once when Shun-ch'eng caught her doing it, he raced over, grabbed the glass out of her hand, and dumped its contents onto the floor. "You've already harmed Father to this point, isn't that enough for you? You still make him drink this filthy water! Besides, Father has always looked down on herbal medicines and fire-tempered ashes. He's been to school and works for the district government. He's no country hick who believes in this nonsense."

Since her husband's dumbness showed no signs of improvement, Ah-chiao could say nothing in reply, but the way Shun-ch'eng insulted her was deeply imprinted in her heart, and she awaited her revenge. "I'll take my revenge, no matter how long I have to wait," she promised herself.

Later someone told her that the juice from celery stalks could ease the inflammation and restore the voice. Ah-chiao waited until Shun-ch'eng had left for the office, then stealthily squeezed out some celery juice into a large bowl and mixed it with brown sugar. She saw that Mr. Ou wasted no time in downing it. The next day Shun-ch'eng found out, probably having been informed by Pao-chen. He didn't make a scene, though, probably because he, too, held out a thread of hope for this herbal concoction.

About ten days later Mr. Ou got his voice back. That day there wasn't a second from morning to night that Mr. Ou wasn't talking, as if he were fearful that if he hesitated an instant he might not be able to speak again. Or perhaps he was simply trying to make up for not being able to speak for over a month. Anyway, he behaved like a student who, after goofing off the whole summer, spends the whole day before school registration making up a summer's worth of calligraphy assignments!

But Mr. Ou's virility was like water over the dam, never to return again.

As time went by, Ah-chiao became more uninhibited. In the beginning she had remained somewhat on guard against Shun-ch'eng and Pao-chen. She even kept her anger to herself about their not referring to her as "Mother," though her heart was wrenched and torn by jealousy. Her new assertiveness was due to the fact that she was responsible for the recovery of Mr. Ou. If it hadn't been for that celery juice, would he have gotten his voice back? Gradually her grievances against Shun-ch'eng and Pao-chen spilled out in one great rush, like an overflowing garbage pail being dumped out. On his part, Shun-ch'eng felt that respectable gentlemen do not quarrel with women, so he turned a deaf ear to Ah-chiao's taunts. Pao-chen, not wanting to embarrass her husband and father-in-law, was also not willing to confront Ah-chiao. Gradually, Ah-chiao tired of finding fault with the two. It was no fun picking a fight if one's opponent didn't fight back.

Mr. Ou thus became the unfortunate target of Ah-chiao's jeers, being mocked bluntly as "The Ball-less One" or "The Limp-stick." Sometimes she would pointedly complain that if she had married that ready-made garment merchant back then, she wouldn't have come to this—a passionate woman with no one to show her passion to. Or she at least should have followed the example of that old procuress, charging a betrothal price of NT$45,000. That way, she wouldn't have labored in vain. There were times when she would even be more straightforward: she would tell her husband that even so-and-so was older than he was, but so-and-so never missed a shot—both his wife and his concubine were kept contented and pregnant.

Of course she no longer felt the need of hiding the coiling varicose veins on her legs from Mr. Ou now. When he saw them, he would choke, his heart stuck in his throat. Later, Mr. Ou didn't dare look down any more. This became a habit, and from then on no matter what he was doing, Mr. Ou always craned his neck up high, his eyes raised, as if he was intoning some martial verse about marching forward, fearless of the danger ahead. Even going over reports in the office with his bifocals on, he would hold his head up high, eyes on the ceiling. For this his colleagues gave him the nickname "Mr. Cobra."

Mr. Ou received his salary on the fifth of each month. When he brought it home, he would give a third of it to help Pao-chen with the household expenses. He gave half of the remaining amount to Ah-chiao, and kept the rest for pocket money. This went on without incident for three or four months, but suddenly one Sunday Ah-chiao unexpectedly protested.

"People raise children to have a source of support in their old age. Now you're simply reversing this practice. Not only don't you demand a penny of their money, you're actually giving them yours! Is this what you raised your children for?"

"Since I can take care of myself, why should I make it more difficult for Shun-ch'eng?"

"Humph. That's very considerate of you indeed! But if you didn't have any income, I wonder if Shun-ch'eng would feel so kindly toward you, or simply let you starve to death."

"I just give him a little sum. Why make such a fuss?"

"Just 'a little sum' is it? It comes to seven or eight hundred dollars. I slave all month and get only four or five hundred. And you say it's only 'a little sum.'"

No matter what she said, Mr. Ou wouldn't agree to stop helping Pao-chen with the monthly expenses. He didn't say so explicitly, he just changed the subject whenever Ah-chiao brought it up.

That evening when Mr. Ou turned out the light and felt his way into bed, Ah-chiao gave him a hard shove and pushed him off the bed. She next cast down his pillow and quilt after him, as if she were throwing out trash.

"You ball-less thing! You're not fit to sleep on the bed. Unfit to sleep on the bed . . . "

Each word resounded louder than the last. Mr. Ou wanted her to lower her voice and not create a scandal. But Ah-chiao, on the assumption that "the more disgraced her husband became in public, the more power she would have over him in private," raised her voice on purpose to an earsplitting level.

There was really nothing Mr. Ou could do with her. He didn't have the strength to begin with, so he just stood by silently, letting her tantrum run its course, her abuse sprinkled with "ball-less" and "you useless thing."

But Ah-chiao wouldn't let him remain silent. "Tell me, is there anything about you that's useful? You're afraid of your own children. You're nothing more than a sack of garbage. Humph. What do you have to say for yourself? Tell me, what part of you, inside or out, is useful? Tell me!" How he wished his dumbness would recur at times like this! Even if it were only for a minute, it would be wonderful.

By the time Mr. Ou crawled onto the bedstead, the cocks were already crowing in the morning. She had him caress her buxom chest to massage away her anger, and wouldn't allow him a second's rest. Mr. Ou hadn't slept a wink the whole night. He yawned incessantly while he was at work, prompting his colleagues to poke fun at him, saying he hadn't slept well because of his "overtime assignments."

He gave all his salary to Ah-chiao next month. She only gave him about two hundred dollars allowance for cigarettes, reminding him he'd better quit smoking because she might cancel the allowance next month. Out of Mr. Ou's salary three hundred dollars were to be sent immediately to her son, Chün-hsiung, who was serving in the army. One hundred dollars was to be sent with equal dispatch to Ts'ai-o, her daughter, with a letter saying that if she disliked her husband, she should divorce him! So long as one is a woman, why worry about not getting a husband? Ah-chiao had wanted to add: Just look at your mother, what have I lost? Isn't my present husband a respectable gentleman with a western business suit? She wanted to advise Ts'ai-o to take similar steps, but she couldn't bring herself to say so in front of Mr. Ou.

Naturally Mr. Ou wasn't willing to write down what she said. What person in his right mind would encourage his children to get a divorce? But Ah-chiao wouldn't yield an inch. Recalling his disgrace at having been shoved out of the bed, Mr. Ou finally gave in.

Ah-chiao had always had her dinner with the bus attendants, if only because it was free of charge. But after she took charge of finances, she often returned home to eat dinner. Every time she was at the table, she pointedly found fault with the food. In the name of her love for Mr. Ou, she would point out how hard it was for him to make a living outside, and that he couldn't go on without meat. After that, she would go out and buy five or six dollar's worth of red-cooked pork for herself and Mr. Ou. When the grandchildren whined that they wanted to eat some pork, too, Ah-chiao's features froze and she scolded them, saying, "Children shouldn't eat rich food!" Pao-chen sat silently nearby eating her dinner. Although she didn't say a word, her face flushed and blanched intermittently, as if under a spotlight. Seeing that Pao-chen wasn't about to take her on, Ah-chiao was somewhat disappointed and chagrined.

After that, whenever Ah-chiao came home to dinner, Pao-chen would herd the children into their bedroom and wouldn't let them out. But Ah-chiao would still have her points to make:

"Humph. She feeds you with only what's fit for a pig. What an insult!"

"What are you fussing about? You don't give her any help. Where's the money to eat meat and fish every day?"

"Humph. She doesn't have the money to feed you, but she has money to buy her own food to feed her children behind our backs. What kind of a section chief are you? So easily taken in!"

Ah-chiao would harangue on and on like this. At times Mr. Ou would get angry and talk back to her. He would point out that since Pao-chen wasn't answering back, why should she keep prattling on so? He would also remind her that Pao-chen, like herself, was raised with the affection and care of her parents, and for this reason shouldn't be picked on, just as she herself wouldn't like to be picked on. Chu Pai-lu was certainly right in saying that "One who runs a household with a ruthless hand will come to an early end."

"Humph. It's Pao-chen who's the cunning and ruthless one. 'Dogs that bark don't bite'" Ah-chiao's mouth was agape, the two creases from her nose to her lips were etched in a smile. Even when enraged, she always appeared ecstatic, as if naturally addicted to bickering.

One Monday morning some time later, Ah-chiao solemnly announced that she and Mr. Ou were going to cook separately. Mr. Ou listened to her announcement in silence. He didn't go to the office that day, either, fearful his colleagues would again poke fun at him, saying he had had another "overtime assignment." They couldn't have guessed that he had again slept on the floor half the night.

Shun-ch'eng, stunned at first at the announcement, suddenly became enraged. "This is all your doing, you old hag, trying to break up our household, you—" Before he could finish, Mr. Ou had rushed over to box him soundly on the ears.

"Call her an old hag, but she's still your step-mother."

Her hands on her hips, Ah-chiao curled her lips in a sneer.

Later, Mr. Ou regretted what he had done. He had never before hit his children like that. He kept wanting to find a chance to explain, but Ah-chiao kept a close watch on him that day, not letting him slip away to be alone with Shun-ch'eng.

The next afternoon Shun-ch'eng and Pao-chen moved into the Restoration Sugar Refinery's dormitory. Ah-chiao was a bit disappointed, for she hadn't expected to get rid of her enemies this quickly. It was unfortunate, because she still had all sorts of tricks up her sleeve that she wouldn't have a chance to show off now. But she was very good in making use of her talents. The day after Shun-ch'eng and Pao-chen moved out, wherever she went, she would complain: "They don't want to spend money on their aging father, so they've moved out! Young people these days are really something! They carry an abacus around their necks, calculating everything. Now all the burden falls on me, taking care of the house as well as going to work."

Once Shun-ch'eng and Pao-chen were gone, the house seemed deserted. Mr. Ou felt terribly lonely. Recalling the times he had spent with Shun-ch'eng and Pao-chen, and the fun he had had with the grandchildren, he fell silent, sitting woodenly on the sofa, his eyes glazed over as if in a trance. He saw himself in front of the grandchildren, explaining to

them the meaning of Chu Pai-lu's maxim on managing the household:
"Rise at dawn, sprinkle and sweep the terrace . . . keep the house and
yard sparkling clean . . . " He had also offered advice to Pao-chen and
Shun-ch'eng, urging them not to be greedy about money, or drink too
much.

As soon as Ah-chiao saw him lost in thought like this, she would busy
herself serving him tea and fruit, speaking to him tenderly as if she had
graduated from a training school for new brides. She would comfort him
by saying:

"Chün-hsiung's about ready to leave the army. When he gets back, we
should find him a wife, then the house will be a bit more lively. Chün-
hsiung's an obedient child, just wait and see! He'll be more filial to you
than anyone else could be!"

As the days passed, Mr. Ou gradually got used to his feeling of loneliness and desolation. But Ah-chiao, on the other hand, became more and
more demanding, wanting him to quit smoking and stop writing letters to
Shun-ch'eng. She even limited his toilet time to ten minutes. Sometimes
when he was unusually constipated and went over the time limit, Ah-
chiao would rap on the door to the toilet, causing whatever little bit he
was laboriously squeezing out to be sucked back in. From then on Mr. Ou
learned his lesson and didn't dare defecate at home anymore. Instead, he
tried to perform mightily in the office rest room. The toilet was filthy and
reeked of urine. When he came out, the foul stench hung around him and
wouldn't go away. Mr. Ou thus gained another nickname: Mr. Stink.

He would force himself to hold off on Sundays, waiting until Monday to
defecate. On those days he didn't dare move around too much, for when
he did, his belly would puff up and send out farts in protest. Lately he
hadn't gone out visiting on Sundays, all because of this. His only hobby
was, as in the past, to read over the newspaper carefully. But while he
read selectively before, he now became interested in the ads as well,
especially the colorful columns run by the dubious sex clinics. He would
savor such phrases as "Turn Impotency to Potency" or "Men, Your Opportunity to Restore Virility is Now!" and commit them to memory.

Early one Sunday, Ah-chiao had Mr. Ou write Ts'ai-o, asking how
divorce proceedings were coming along and whether or not she needed
her mother's help. Having sealed the letter in the envelope, Ah-chiao
took it out to mail.

It was the end of October. Autumn was in the air. A slight chilliness
pervaded the morning, and the sunlight was like a glass of tepid water one
swallows medicine with.[9] Plump Ah-chiao still felt hot in her short
sleeves, perspiration beading her forehead. Having mailed the letter, she
cut over to the market and bought over a catty of pig intestines to make an

herbal soup known for its cooling effects. Her back was already sopping with perspiration as she struggled out of the crowded market. She chose shaded parts of the street to walk along, thus taking three times as long to get home. Reaching the lane to her house, she spied Mr. Ou and Shun-ch'eng talking outside, shaded by the banyan tree. They appeared solemn, with Shun-ch'eng constantly looking about as if standing guard. Scurrying into an obscure shaded corner and waiting for them to finish their conversation, Ah-chiao pricked up her ears to hear what they were saying, but to no avail. If only she had returned earlier, she thought. Her biggest worry had been letting the two of them have a chance to be together.

Shun-ch'eng finally left when the sanitation truck entered the lane. Mr. Ou waved him away anxiously as if trying to hurry him. No sooner had he turned back into the house than Ah-chiao sauntered in carrying the pig intestines. Holding the morning paper high above his head, Mr. Ou resembled a cobra arching its neck to the tune of some distant flute. Behind him was a large window, tightly shut to seal off the cool autumn breeze. The dark green curtains were pulled half shut, allowing only part of the sunlight in. Sitting in the green shade of the curtain, he appeared submerged in a pond overgrown with algae. Spying Ah-chiao, he nodded and acknowledged her with only "You're back," then lapsed into silence again, as if the deep green water had blocked his windpipe.

Ah-chiao exhibited the pig intestines wrapped in lotus leaves to Mr. Ou: "I bought over a catty of pig intestines to make the soup!"

"Uh." A grunt, then silence again. Mr. Ou continued reading the paper, savoring the colorful clinic ads.

Having cleaned and chopped the pig intestines, Ah-chiao changed her clothes before going into the living room. She looked around and found it needed some cleaning up, so she took up a broom to sweep the floor. Since Pao-chen and her family had left, the morning cleaning fell on her shoulders, but she never complained. Perhaps she had heard Mr. Ou reciting Chu Pai-lu's maxim so often that after a while even she came under its influence. Ah-chiao didn't know who this mysterious Chu Pai-lu was, but thought that since Mr. Ou invoked his name every day he must be some powerful deity.

Taking up the broom, she first opened all the windows to let light in. The breeze carried in the urgent tune of the sanitation truck churning out its gay music, *ding, ding, ding.* Ah-chiao remembered that the garbage pail in the kitchen needed to be taken out now, since it would be another week before the truck would come again. A draft of the autumn air blew in. Mr. Ou suddenly sneezed, a spray of saliva the size of a bowl wetting the paper.

"Don't open all the windows at once!" Covering his mouth, he sneezed again, this time spraying his hand with saliva. Embarrassed, he quickly pulled out a handkerchief to wipe it off.

"Am I right in saying you're just useless? Only a little breeze!" She closed the windows half-way and turned around, opening her mouth several times as if trying to say something. She swallowed hard several times to hold it back, but what was in her mind was as difficult to repress as urine in a bulged bladder. So in the end she broke loose:

"Wasn't Shun-ch'eng just here?"

"So you know!" This time instead of sneezing, he farted twice.

"What made him bother to come over? Didn't he say he wouldn't come here anymore?"

Mr. Ou stuffed the handkerchief back into his pocket and swallowed, as if preparing to deliver an oration. He said Shun-ch'eng wanted to go into business and urgently needed some capital. He had come over to ask Mr. Ou to help him out. He spoke casually, as if it were some trivial matter.

"And what did you tell him?" Ah-chiao glared at Mr. Ou to make sure he wouldn't come up with a lie.

"We ought to help him out. Of course, I have to ask you first. The savings account is in your name anyway."

Ah-chiao didn't say a word. She resumed her sweeping with a flourish, and savagely attacked the small six by six living room. Dust arose all over. Mr. Ou hated dust, often telling his grandchildren that it contained germs. Once dust was inhaled into one's body, it was easy to come down with some illness. He hurriedly pulled out his handkerchief again, selected a corner not wet from his sneezing and tightly covered his mouth. Seeing him act like this, Ah-chiao purposely raised up a cloud of dust. Afterwards, she straightened up, and plunked the broom to the floor. "You can save your breath. Not a penny from me for your baby boy! May the Thunder God take care of him some day."[10]

The transition from her throwing down the broom to her speaking spanned less than twenty seconds. The alacrity of her movement, like some woman sword fighter, was startling and allowed one no way to duck out of the way.

Sitting silently on the sofa, Mr. Ou appeared in a trance, as if some of his acupuncture points had been touched by the lady swordsman and he had been temporarily rendered speechless.

"This was agreed upon beforehand. This money is mine to use as I see fit. You have no say in it any more. If you don't remember, I'll bring Inspector Ying in!"

"Ai-ya, it's not such a big deal—"

Not letting him finish, Ah-chiao cut in. "This was agreed on beforehand. Since it's mine now, there's no way for you to want it back. Anyway, I want to save this money to get Chün-hsiung a wife. If you want to give it to that short-lived boy of yours, you'll have to take it over my dead body."

Unwilling to hear any more, Mr. Ou became angry. "All right then, don't help him. But don't curse him. Can't we have some decency in our house?" His head was held high, like a cobra poised to strike.

The sanitation truck's chimes sang out urgently. If she didn't take out the kitchen garbage, it would have to wait another week. Without retorting, she turned into the kitchen, eyebrows arched, her haughty appearance enough to scare even spirits and ghosts.

Carrying the plastic garbage pail into the living room, Ah-chiao stopped short, cocked her head and poked her free hand at Mr. Ou's face.

"Look, the son you raised yourself, and he doesn't give a shit about you. Decency? What a laugh! Don't you ever try again to snatch away money for my coffin and give it to someone else![11] You're really useless!"

"What do you mean, useless?" Mr. Ou abruptly stood up, the late autumn sunlight filtering through the window and reflecting off his face, as if he were an old nag confined to its stall.[12]

"Tell me just one thing here or at work that you can do. Mr. Ball-less— shall we talk about decency some more? What a joke!" Without looking back, Ah-chiao started for the door with the garbage in hand.

Another draft of autumn wind blew into the room. The sanitation truck chimes continued to urge the people to hurry out with their garbage. *Ding-ding-ding, bring out the garbage.* No more joyous sound than this.

After dumping the garbage, Ah-chiao carried the empty pail back into the parlor. Mr. Ou snapped the paper open in midair, his veins popping out on his fingers as he vigorously pointed to a large clinic ad.

"I'm going to Taipei on business Friday and look these people up. This time I'll look them up! You just wait and see! Am I really all that useless? I won't let you call me Mr. Ball-less my whole life, that's for sure!"

Illiterate, Ah-chiao stared at the newspaper as if she were the White Snake facing Fa-hai's magic spell against spirits, full of fear as well as respect, unable to speak.[13] When she finally found something to say, Mr. Ou had already left the room. That newspaper which had momentarily cast her under its spell lay against the table leg.[14] The pages rustled back and forth in the wind, happily dancing about. Ah-chiao seemed to recall that Mr. Ou had farted noisily, as he shouted just then. Maybe he had gone to the toilet. Since he was so angry today, she decided not to rush him, just in case he really was in the midst of evacuating his bowels.

She picked up the newspaper and laid it flat on the table, scanning it at the same time, but she couldn't find the place Mr. Ou had just referred to. She would have to take it to show someone to see what mysterious element it contained. She shrugged, her eyes coming to rest on the Chu Pai-lu maxim hanging on the wall. She couldn't make out even one word of it, but was familiar with what it meant. Maybe it was true that the educated could really practice what they preach, not to mention that Mr. Ou had a deity like Chu Hsi on his side. Maybe he really could make the flat round and the round flat. Who knows? She appeared worried and heaved a sigh. She was afraid that one day she'd lose her hold on the money and Mr. Ou, and according to the fortune-teller, this was her last marriage. Suddenly she remembered that someone had mentioned that spirits and ghosts were equally afraid of a fierce person. A smile instantly brightened her face as if she already had a plan. She decided that Mr. Ou's toilet time should still be limited to ten minutes. She shouldn't make any allowances.

Ding-ding-ding. The sound became fainter. The sanitation truck was moving away.

NOTES

1. Reference to the three marriages of Ah-chiao.
2. A man or woman fated to encounter an unusual number of love affairs or marriages in his or her life is said to be under the influence of the "Peach Blossom Star."
3. In traditional China, a wife returned to her parents' home for a visit on the second day of the New Year.
4. Tight-fitting Chinese sheath with a high mandarin collar and side slits.
5. The figures are in New Taiwan currency. The exchange rate was roughly one American dollar to forty at the time of the story.
6. Flat round cakes filled with sesame paste sent to relatives and friends on announcement of an engagement.
7. Usually for ten or twelve people.
8. A scholar of the early Ch'ing, Chu Pai-lu (1617–1688) was the author of *Maxims to Order a Household (Chih-chia ke-yen)*. Here and elsewhere in the story, Chu's sayings do not always appear in complete quotations.
9. Chinese herbal medicine pills are supposed to be swallowed with lukewarm boiled water.
10. Reference to a folk belief that thunder is an expression of Heaven's anger. An unfilial son or daughter is therefore a likely target for a thunderbolt.
11. Money for one's coffin: an exaggerated way to indicate one's savings are not to be squandered without a specific and urgent purpose.
12. Reference to a line from "*Yu-t'u pu-t'ung,*" a poem by Ts'ao Ts'ao (A.D. 155–220), Chinese warrior, statesman, and poet. The complete line: "though the old thoroughbred is confined to its stall, / its ambition soars a thousand *li*" (*lao-chi fu-li/ chih-tsai ch'ien-li*).
13. Legend has it that a white snake in West Lake in Chekiang Province assumed the form of a beautiful woman to seduce men and eventually cause their

death by imbibing their energy. The most famous version of this legend is the subject of a Ming story "Eternal Prisoner under the Thunder Peak Pagoda" (*Pai-niang-tzu yung-chen lei-geng-t'a*) in which the Buddhist monk Fa-hai finally subdues the snake by magic spells.

14. In the story cited above, various Taoist charms were used to dispel the white snake, but to no avail.

CHANG HSI-KUO

(1944–   )

Chang Hsi-kuo has a Ph.D. (1969) in electrical engineering from the University of California at Berkeley and is at present Chairman of the Electrical Engineering Department at Illinois Institute of Technology. However, to the Chinese readers in Taiwan and abroad, he is better known as a prolific writer of tsa-wen essays, novels of manners, and, more recently, science fiction. Though he has made his home in the United States since the seventies, he takes a trip to Taiwan almost every other year. In view of his interest in the effect of Taiwan's growing economy on the lifestyle as well as the value concepts of its people, his frequent visits are as important to him as field trips are to the sociologists or anthropologists. His close observation of social manners has resulted in the creation of the first prototype of the homo economicus *in Taiwan fiction. The* Chess Champion *(Ch'i-wang, 1975) depicts a new species of Chinese who feels no compunction in trading Confucian ethics for material gains. As can be seen in "Red Boy," Chang Hsi-kuo is no less attentive to the fate of his compatriots in the United States. The trials and frustrations the "Red Boy" undergoes are metaphorically the collective experience of overseas Chinese torn by the opposing claims for partisan allegiance from a divided China. His novella "Earth" (T'i, 1967) is included in* Chinese Stories from Taiwan, *and his works are discussed in* Chinese Fiction from Taiwan: Critical Perspectives.

Red Boy

Translated by Jeannette L. Faurot

LETTERS: 1

Dear Son:

We received your letter of May 18. When your father finished reading it he was so angry he started trembling all over, and for a long time he could not even talk. You really should not have written a letter like that; it broke your father's heart. You know that I do not write to you very often, because of my eyes. It is usually your father who writes, but this time he is really angry.

There are some things I must say to you. The whole family loves you

218

and cares about you very much. You have always been your father's favorite. Do you remember how hot it was on your 20th birthday, and how your father still insisted on going to Tainan to see you because he was afraid you would be lonesome all by yourself? You have always been the most well-behaved and obedient of our children, and you were also good at your studies. Unlike your sister Yün, you never gave us cause to worry. But I feel that you have been changing ever since you left home. I know that it is difficult to live abroad, but you must think of our hopes for you, and work hard at your studies so that you can become a famous physicist. That would be an honor for us all.

Every time we get a letter from you I always read it carefully and discuss it with your father. He always writes you words of instruction and encouragement, and he also got you a subscription to the airmail edition of the *Central Daily News,* for fear you might be homesick. We are not opposed to your concern for national politics; we know that you have always loved your country. But these are problems that you have no way to solve. The biggest personal regret your father has is that he studied the humanities, with the result that we now have very little money and nothing to show for ourselves. That is why he insisted on you and your brother studying science and engineering, so that you could become useful men and avoid stepping into that trap. We have sacrificed a lot for your education, and now you say you want to throw away your degree. This is too great a heartbreak for your father. Even if you do not care about a splendid future for yourself, you should still think about how your parents had to scrimp and save to support you.

The reason my eyes are bad is because of all the worries of the past few years. Your father also has his chronic liver ailment. How can you bear to break your parents' hearts? After we got your letter I cried and cried, and for the rest of the day I could not see anything. This morning I am a little better, so I am making this effort to write to you in the hope that you will listen to your mother's advice and work hard. Do not write any more discouraging things to upset your parents.

Last week I sent you a can of shredded dried meat. Let us know when you receive it. Take special care of yourself, as you are alone in a foreign country.

Wishing you happiness,
Mother

May 27, 1971

Dear Brother,

This morning I got a letter from home, after having just phoned you long distance last night. As I said to you then, I don't object to your not

wanting to study physics. The longer a person stays in America, the less
interest he has in a degree. I can understand your mental confusion
completely. But Dad and Mother's hopes are so high for you, you really
should do everything to apply yourself to your studies for their sake, so
that you can bring honor to the family after you get your degree. I myself
am not Ph. D. material, and now that sister Yün has made such an unfortunate marriage, all the family's hopes rest on you alone—this is a responsibility you cannot ignore. There are lots of "snakes among the dragons"
there in the city of G, and plenty of unsavory organizations. You are young
and impulsive. Don't be taken in by other people, or do something on a
whim that you will regret for the rest of your life. As I said last night, after
this semester is over you should come and stay at my place for a while. I
know Ch'eng, the manager of the Chinese restaurant here—I have already talked with him about this, and he says there wouldn't be any
problem getting you a summer job. Once you break away from that
political action group and think about it calmly and quietly, maybe you
will change your mind. If your thinking still hasn't changed after summer
vacation, it won't be too late to make a decision then. You know that I
have always been on your side, and my suggestions to you now are all for
your own good. I hope you will come as soon as vacation starts.

Wishing you well,

Your elder brother,
Wei

June 3, 1971

To my Fellow Student Kao Ch'iang:

Last week I attended the National Affairs Symposium that you sponsored. I heard a lot of provocative discussion, and was deeply moved by
it. From childhood we have cultivated selfish, indifferent, individualistic
attitudes, and have never seemed able to rid ourselves of such states of
mind. Now, for the first time, we have a chance to understand that we
must stand up and fight for a more beautiful future. Your work is very
significant, and I have the greatest respect and admiration for you all. I
am sending $10; though it is a small amount, it may show that I am sincere
in my support.

Wishing you progress,
A Stranger

July 1

Dear Ch'iang,

It has been a long time since I've written you. One reason is that I have
been getting ready for my Ph. D. orals as well as working on experiments,

and I'm just too busy with my work; but another reason is that I have gradually discovered that our ways of thinking have grown very far apart. I've thought of writing you several times to talk about things, but I never managed to do it. The day before yesterday I received the magazine *Spring Sprouts* which you sent. I read it all at one sitting, and it has stirred up a flood of thoughts which I can't adequately express in words.

You have gone to a lot of trouble to put out a mimeographed publication like that, and of course I respect you very much for it. But I can't completely agree with the way you are doing things. You praise the Chinese Communists and glorify their successes in building up the mainland, but whose achievements are these after all? Are they the achievements of the Chinese Communists? Or are they the achievements of the eight hundred million Chinese people? You are always talking about how "The Chinese People" do this and that, but you yourselves have never shed one drop of blood or lost one drop of sweat to build China. You have harsh criticism for the various policies on Taiwan, but you yourselves have never put forth an ounce of effort for Taiwan. So what right do you have to criticize Taiwan? By what right can you share in China's accomplishments?

If you truly support the Communists, nothing is stopping you from going to the mainland to join their ranks in the work of reconstruction. If you truly want to change Taiwan, there is nothing preventing you from going back there to work for reform. If you can't do either, but just engage in a lot of empty talk in a foreign country, I think you are not only doing nothing to help the situation, but you are even exposing your own indecision, and just talking big.

Though I've criticized you a lot, I really don't have any solution myself. It is easy to criticize others, but hard to do something oneself. I hope you don't mind my speaking so frankly.

Wishing you well,

Chi-kang

Oct. 8

Dear Ch'-iang,

I have received the third issue of *Spring Sprouts*, which you sent. In return I have sent you a copy of the "Study Newsletter," which we publish here. We can't compare with G—there aren't many people here who are politically aware. Most the the Chinese students here are still at the stage where they read swordsman stories, work on producing a "China Night," and take part in Bible study groups. Speaking of Bible study groups, there is a Brother Kung here who is a deacon in a local church, and he has quite an ability to draw people in. The Bible study group, surprisingly enough, usually has several dozen participants, and is much stronger than our organization's study group. My criticism of them is that they use God's name to carry on a matchmaking service. But they really have brought together several couples.

Last semester Hsiao Li-hsing transferred here from Harvard. He is very enthusiastic, and he showed such a willingness to work that this semester he was voted president of the Chinese Students Organization. But he moved too quickly. He suddenly pulled toward the left, and most of the members couldn't keep up—in fact he stirred up a lot of resentment among some students, who are threatening to set up another organization. I had already criticized Hsiao Li-hsing's blind leftism at a work review meeting. Recently we have adoped a "go-slow" policy, and have been using various methods of persuasion to win people's trust. This way of "persuading but not pressuring" has already produced some results. We will be going to New York to take part in the China Unification Conference. Will you be going? Talk to you later.

Wishing you Victory!

Chung Kuei-ching

Oct. 11

Dear Brother,

Yesterday Lin P'in came here to attend a conference, and I found out from him what you have been up to in G. He happened to bring along an issue of your publication *Spring Sprouts.* How could you get mixed up with those people, and publish such an outrageous magazine? Have you ever considered what kind of effect this might have on Dad? He will be retiring in two more years. If he loses his job in the next two years, he will not be eligible to get his pension, and the whole family's livelihood will suddenly collapse. You are really awfully stupid, totally out of touch with reality! Right now Dad and Mother don't know, but when they find out they will be furious and worried to death. I hope you will rein in your horse before you get the to edge of the cliff, and get out of that organization as fast as you can. I will be in the city of G on the 5th of next month and I will discuss this with you in more detail then.

Best wishes.

Your brother,
Wei

DOCUMENTS: I

[Airmail dispatch from G City, Nov. 16:] Yesterday (the 15th) the Anti-Communist Patriotic Alliance of G held a large gathering in the Activities Center of G University, under the leadership of our patriotic students

Fang Hsing-hua, Ch'en Hsing-ya, and others. Before the meeting began, two Communist agents who have infiltrated the area, a certain Kao and a certain Wang, tried to force their way into the hall and disseminate propaganda leaflets; but when this was discovered by the patriotic student Li Te-sheng and others, they were quickly restrained. The two agents, Kao and Wang, scurried away like rats to their holes, amid the angry jeers and general indignation of the crowd. After this event, the emotions of the students were raised to an even higher pitch, and in addition to passing unanimously a "Declaration of the G City Chinese Students Anti-Communist Patriotic Alliance," they rose reverently at the close of the proceedings to sing the national anthem, and under the leadership of Fang Hsing-hua shouted "Long Live the Republic of China!"

LETTERS: II

Nov. 30

Dear Brother,

You are really getting more and more outrageous in your behavior! You even got your big name in the paper! Fortunately the writer had some compassion, and your name was only elliptically represented, so Dad and Mother probably won't be able to guess that it was you. Just think, the one who was a "Model Youth" of Chien-kuo High School ten years ago is now a "Communist agent"! I break out in a cold sweat thinking about it. When things have gone that far you really should hold back a bit. Also, if you are spending so much energy on such activities, how are you going to keep up with your schoolwork? What is your thesis director going to think? Several months ago you promised me you would finish your degree. How could you join up with that political action group again, with your promise still ringing in my ears? Let's make a gentleman's agreement. You finish your degree for me, and don't participate so much in political activities (I'm not saying to *stop*), and I will do all I can to help you keep this from Dad and Mother. I am not trying to interfere with your political beliefs. Everything I am saying is because I want to help you. Don't get into trouble again!

Best wishes,

Your brother,
Wei

Dec. 5

Dear Son,

We have received all your letters. Recently several scholars have returned here to lecture. Your mother and I were deeply moved; we wonder when we will see you returning home with your studies completed. There are some communist sympathizers now posing as students overseas while they are actually working for the enemy and stirring people up. You must be especially careful not to be duped by them. Your mother's eyes have been troubling her again these days, and my health is far from what it used to be. Sometimes my back aches so much I cannot sit for very long. Your sister Yün has had another quarrel with Li Wu, and for the past few days she has been staying here. Nothing is going as one would wish. Your report card is our one source of comfort. I hope you will continue to work hard to bring honor to the family. Now that it is getting colder, be careful about what you eat and drink, and keep warm at night. I have sent some vitamin pills. Take them often, and when you do, take them with warm water. You must maintain a regular schedule in your daily activities.

Wishing you success in your studies.

Father

Dec. 6

Dear Ch'iang,

I haven't been in touch with you for a long time. Everything here is the same as before. Since we have had too few readers for our "Study Newsletter" we have changed to publishing it on an irregular basis. The students still aren't willing to discuss politics, but the last time we showed a film a lot of people came. The Bible study group is as strong as ever. I have the attitude that "if you don't go into the tiger's den, you won't catch the tiger," so I've taken part in their gatherings a few times, and had a few arguments with Brother Kung. This man is about as tolerant as one can be, and no matter how I try to provoke him, he never gets angry. He is really something.

The Bible study group has its good points—everyone is very friendly, and each week everyone contributes some food to have a big feast, on the pretext of having a meeting. Whenever someone gets sick, all the brothers and sisters look after him. Even though there is something artificial about it, still it is an expression of human warmth. When Chinese students are abroad they have emotional needs, for, after all, they are only human. The Bible study group does exactly that—it fills everyone's inner needs. Religion really does have a great power to anesthetize. The people in the Bible study group don't care anything about the universe outside their group. Talking to them about politics is like "playing a zither before an ox."

When I mentioned this insight to Hsiao Li-hsing, he accused me of "sentimentalism." I think that fellow is a bit egotistical, using Chairman Mao's quotations all the time to criticize people. Actually, all he knows is how to recite the words of the *People's Daily* writers—he is nothing but a tape recorder. He always thinks that because he came from Harvard and took part in the Protect Tiao Yü T'ai movement[1] there, he is a cut above everyone else. He always sets himself up as leader, and criticizes everyone else for separating themselves from the masses. He said something about how the masses were water, and it was wrong for us not to be in the fish's position. It seems to me he is the one who has really separated himself from the masses. When I wanted to work from within the Bible study group, I got this horrendous lecture from him. I was so angry I didn't want to stay in the political study group any longer. I've heard that you used to know him pretty well—what kind of a person was he then?

Wishing you victory!

Chung Kuei-ching

DOCUMENTS: II

Comrades:

Recently the revolutionary situation has been very good. However, in our final revolutionary struggle with the counterrevolutionary forces, just as we were about to win the great victory, there arose among us a poisonous weed, who silently carried on his plot to destroy the revolution and undermine the mass movement. This poisonous weed is none other than Kao Ch'iang, who has until now been one of our closest comrades-in-arms. Some of you may find it strange—isn't Kao Ch'iang one of our hardest-working comrades? Wasn't he considered a Communist Agent? How could he be a poisonous weed?

Kao Ch'iang was indeed an enthusiastic worker in the past. But since the spread of the Great China Unification Movement, Kao Ch'iang has not been able to cast off the baggage of his outmoded thinking. He has fallen behind; he cannot keep up with the masses. The glory of being labeled a Communist Agent muddled his brain. He was falling behind, but he was never willing to admit it, and instead accused others of going too fast. He is clearly a right-wing opportunist, but insists on calling others blind leftists. Leaving aside the fact that he has been spreading poison among his own friends, he has also put forth the idea in public meetings that the revolution is useless, thus severely dampening the revolutionary will of the masses. He is also busy organizing a splinter group, shamefully plotting to create a party within a party. When Wang Chien-kuo went to New York to participate in the Unification conference, Kao took that opportunity to gather a few adherents to his side, and set himself up in opposition to Wang. Furthermore, he confiscated the correspondence and documents, and refused to give any to Wang. These counterrevolutionary, counter-mass-line plots may deceive others, but they will not deceive the broad masses. The eyes of the masses are as bright as snow. We must root out this poisonous weed, Kao Ch'iang, and denounce his rotten crimes.

We hereby announce that Kao Ch'iang and his fellow travelers have been repudiated by the broad masses. The words and actions of that handful of bad elements by no means represent the will of the masses!

We extend to you a Revolutionary Salute!

Headquarters
The G City Revolutionary Uprising
Headquarters

Urgent Announcement from the G Protect Tiao Yü T'ai Action Committee:

Recently someone has distributed an anonymous letter under the name "G City Revolutionary Uprising Headquarters" in an attempt to sow discord among the members of our organization. Our organization does not have a "Revolutionary Uprising Headquarters." The words and deeds of a minority cannot represent our organization. We want to make one point clear: criticism and self-criticism are methods we use frequently and continually to discipline and strengthen one another. Rumors from outside are all untrue.

The G City Protect Tiao Yü T'ai
Committee

Jan. 7, 1972

Letters: III

Jan. 28

Dear Ch'iang,

I received your letter. I am very sorry that such a great misunderstanding has occurred. I remember that when the Protect Tiao Yü T'ai movement first began, everyone worked together with one mind for China's national sovereignty. I would never have imagined that when we started the China Unification Movement people not only wouldn't unite but would even split up into four or five factions. You said that some people are moving too fast, and I agree. Now that we are trying to drum up support for China Unification after having worked on the Tiao Yü T'ai

movement for a year, the reaction of the masses is like a used-up tooth-
paste tube—you can't squeeze out any more enthusiasm. Here, too, we
are like a pan of loose sand. If Hsiao Li-hsing were willing to be a little
more humble, things might be better. But all he knows how to do is put
labels on people. Anyone to the right of him is a "compradore Ph.D.,"
anyone to his left suffers from "leftist juvenilism"—as though he were the
only one who received the true word from Mao Tse-tung. A lot of enthusiastic students got out because of the way he did things. I'm not clear
about the inside story of your conflict with Wang Chien-kuo. But if my
hunch is right, you must have a problem in leadership over there too. The
first thing everyone learns is how to grab for power, and nothing gets
done. It is really frustrating.

I am getting more and more fed up with politics, and I go to the Bible
study group a lot. Don't laugh at me. I really don't believe in all that. But
it is a place to go on weekends for a good meal, and you can meet some
nice girls—I am going after one now. She goes to Bible study every week,
and that's why I am so diligent about going. What worries me most is that
our ways of thinking are so different. I will have to find a way to gradually
convert her. Yesterday I gave her a Little Red Book, and she gave me a
New Testament in return. Oh well, we can exchange them, and read each
other's. Talk to you later.

Wishing you happiness,

Chung Kuei-ching

Jan. 29

Dear Brother,

I have heard that you have locked horns with leftists there in G, and
that they have opened fire on you. You really puzzle me. One minute you
seem to me a fanatical leftist, and the next minute you are laying out new
boundaries on the right. You really are a bit too versatile. But at least it is
good that you got out of the leftist camp. Maybe things will quiet down in
the future. As I told you before, meddling in politics is a dirty business;
you can't come out of the mud and not be tainted.

We are expecting another child soon. Your sister-in-law will give birth
in September. This is the last one. No matter whether it is a girl or a boy,
we aren't planning to have any more. Our company laid off several dozen
people. One whole research division was completely dissolved, and even
old-timers who had been here more than ten years had to leave imme-
dately, so morale in the company is not good. There is no feeling of
security when you work for Americans. If they lay me off, I plan to go

back to Taiwan to look for work. I certainly won't stay here and take any more of this.

Best wishes,

Your brother,
Wei

Feb. 5

Dear Mr. Kao,

Ch'en Chi-kang has already left this school. When he left he instructed me to take care of his correspondence, which is why I have been so presumptuous as to open and read your letters to him. Ch'en and I shared an apartment for the past two years, and we got along well together. Since you are a good friend of his, I need not worry about telling you his whereabouts, but please keep it in strictest confidence.

Three months ago Ch'en went to the mainland. When he went, only a few people knew about it. You are probably well aware that he was not at all a leftist. When the Protect Tiao Yü T'ai movement began, we all participated enthusiastically. Later, when nothing happened in the movement, and various leftist and rightist splinter groups formed, Ch'en became very discouraged. The fact that he did not pass his Ph.D. orals was also a great blow to him. For a while he wanted to look for work, but right now it is not easy for someone in hydrodynamics to find a job. Later he decided to go back to the mainland. We debated several times whether he should go back. He himself was rather confused. Even on the night before he was to leave, he had not completely made up his mind. I have read all the materials you sent to him, and I can understand very clearly all his hesitation and suffering. I really respect his courage. A lot of people talk very prettily about how one should "serve the people," but do they do it themselves? They love the material pleasures of America, and while they shout about revolution, they are busy raking in the money. Every time I run into these people, I can't help thinking of Ch'en Chi-kang. I think he is a much better person than those leftists who are all talk and no action.

As for myself, I have chosen the opposite path from Ch'en. During summer vacation this year, after I finish my degree, I will go back to Taiwan. Although the direction I have chosen is different from Ch'en's, we are both completely sincere, and we have both been through a bitter struggle. I can see from your letters to Ch'en that you are also a sincere man, and that is why I have presumed to write so much; I hope you are not offended.

When you send publications in the future, please address them to the

P.O. Box of the Chinese Students Organization. Thank you.
   Best wishes,

Wang Fu-ch'eng

Feb. 28

Dear Ch'iang,
   We have decided to get married on March 4, and we hope you will be able to attend. We are sending an announcement and a map. Please note that the church and the reception hall are not at the same place. If you come a day early, please look for me at my present address, and I will find a place for you to stay.
   Ch'i-fang's and my marriage is really the Lord's work. Pastor Sung will be in charge of our wedding, and Brother Kung will give a testimonial. My heart is now filled with joy and peace. In the past three years I have never been so happy. This is all the Lord's gracious will.
   May the Lord be with you.

Chung-kuei and Ch'i-fang

Feb. 29

Dear Brother,
   You said that you have been feeling depressed recently, that you aren't interested in politics any more, and that you feel there is nothing you want to do. Things have a way of reversing when they reach an extreme; maybe you were too active before, and it would be good just to get some rest. During this trip of President Nixon's to Communist China, I saw on TV that life over there is still very hard and they have no freedom of speech or movement. It made me feel very sad.
   Your sister-in-law has got quite a case of morning sickness. She is constantly eating sour plums, pickles, and chocolate bonbons. A few days ago she suddenly caught cold and was sick for three days, and since she wasn't supposed to take medicines it really worried me. I've heard that the more severe the morning sickness, the more likely it is you will have a boy, so I am secretly happy about it. If we do have a boy, Dad and Mother will be very pleased.
   The situation at our company has improved—everyone got a raise, and I got the biggest one of all. One good thing about America is that if you have ability you will gain people's recognition. The reason I like America is because of their way of treating everyone equally. When you go to work later on you will undoubtedly feel the same way.
   Best wishes,

Your brother,
Wei

March 18
Dear Son,

We have not received a letter from you in a long time—why is that? Your mother and I are very concerned. If you are too busy with your studies, at least send us a postcard to relieve our worries. Recently your brother Wei has also been writing less often. Since Mei-lan is pregnant he has to work even harder. Mei-lan will be giving birth in September. If you still have not started school by then, you should go and help out— that is your obligation as a brother. I hope Mei-lan will have a boy this time; then our family will have someone to continue the line and burn incense to our ancestors. Your sister Yün has already passed the Ministry of Foreign Affairs interpreter's examination, and may be sent abroad. But she is worried about leaving the children behind. Li Wu is already openly living with that devil of a nurse. That man is really detestable, completely untrustworthy, just like Nixon. Your mother weeps day and night about Yün's situation, and I can do nothing to console her. You should write soon so that she will not have additional worry.

Wishing you progress in your studies,

Your Father

March 30
Dear Brother,

What's wrong with you, not writing home for several months? I tried to call you long distance yesterday, but the phone company said your line was disconnected because you owed them too much on your phone bill. Do you have financial problems? Or has some new problem come up? You are really too much—a man in his twenties who still indulges in this kind of moodiness. When are you going to grow up? I would really like to come to G to see you, but your sister-in-law is not well and I can't leave her. Please call me as soon as you get this letter, and also write to Dad and Mother.

Best wishes,

Your brother,
Wei

Documents: III

June 25, 1972
United States Federal Bureau of Investigation to Mr. Wei Kao:[2]

We have received all your letters directed to this bureau. In regard to your request that the FBI attempt to locate Mr. Ch'iang Kao, the result of our investigation is that Mr. Kao has not registered as an alien for the past two years. At the moment it is not clear whether Mr. Kao is staying in the United States illegally, or whether he has already left the country. The Bureau will follow established procedures in continuing the investigation. Since large numbers of people are reported missing each year, the FBI cannot investigate every case in detail. If we receive any news about Mr. Ch'iang Kao we will inform you immediately. In the meantime, we ask for your patience.

Sept. 23, 1972

United States Federal Bureau of Investigation to Mr. Wei Kao:

We have received your letter of Sept. 15. The Bureau is still in the process of investigating the whereabouts of Mr. Ch'iang Kao.

Nov. 18, 1972

United States Federal Bureau of Investigation to Mr. Wei Kao:

We have received your letter of Nov. 7. The FBI has no way of ascertaining whether your brother is dead or alive. Because of limited manpower, the Bureau is no longer able to continue investigating the case of your brother's disappearance. Please accept our apologies.

NOTES

1. The "Protect Tiao Yü T'ai Movement" is a consciousness-raising student movement that first erupted in the U.S. in January 1971. Reverberations of this patriotic sentiment, however, were felt almost immediately in Hong Kong and later in Taiwan. In essence, it is a protest against the State Department's decision (April 9, 1971) to return the Chien-kuo (*Senkaku*, in Japanese) Islands, about 100 kilometers northeast of Keelung, to the jurisdiction of Japan in 1972. Tiao Yü T'ai is the biggest of this group of eight islands.

Though at variance with nearly every other political issue in their foreign policy, the People's Republic of China and the Republic of China on Taiwan were in perfect accord regarding the territorial claim of China on these islands.

2. Because this and the following two documents were issued by the FBI, accordingly Chinese names are given in Western nomenclature rather than in the Chinese system, in which the family name precedes the given name. Thus, Wei Kao is Mr. Kao.

LI YUNG-P'ING (1948–)

Born and raised in Sarawak, Li Yung-p'ing came to Taiwan to study English literature at National Taiwan University, where he took his B.A. in 1967. Driven by homesickness, he tried to recall his childhood in the South Seas through the medium of fiction. His first attempt, "The La-tzu Woman" (La-tzu fu, 1968), epitomizes the mise-en-scène and the ethos of his imagination, which are to recur frequently in his later writing. "The Rain from the Sun" is one of three related but independent stories under the serial heading "Legends of Chi-ling" (Chi-ling chi). Its title is meta-phorically ambiguous. On the one hand, it refers to the tropical showers which are so hot that they appear to have come direct from the sun. On the other hand, it denotes the stultifying atmosphere and blinding pas-sions that drive some Chi-ling residents to the brink of madness and depravity. What is unique in Li Yung-p'ing's fiction is his ability to elicit intense human drama out of the moral chaos in a self-contained legendary world. His work offers a dramatic foil to the staple of tendentious writing in recent Taiwan fiction.

Li Yung-p'ing received his Ph.D. in comparative literature from Wash-ington University in 1982, and is currently a member of the English Department at National Sun Yat-sen University in Kaohsiung. Most of his publications appear in the United Daily (Lien-ho Pao). *A fastidious writer with a penchant for revision, he is taking his time to add finishing touches to his published stories before gathering them in an anthology. "The Rain from the Sun" won the first prize in* United Daily's *fiction contest in 1979, and is accordingly included in* United Daily Prize-winning Stories in 1979 *(Lien-ho Pao liu-pa-nien-tu tuan-p'ien-hsiao-shuo-chiang tso-p'in-chi, Taipei, 1979). Li's work is discussed in my article "The Tropics Mythopoetized" cited in the Preface.*

The Rain from the Sun

Translated by Candice Pong and Robert Eno

Hsiao Lo[1] walked home under the scorching sun. His gaunt chest was bare and he cursed Heaven for the heat. His mother was sitting on the doorsill with her head bent, carefully picking out unhulled grains from a

232

pan of rice. She heard him kick open the wooden gate of their bamboo hedge fence, and spoke without lifting her eyes from her chore.

"Hsiao Shun's wife from next door just came by with the news. Liu Lao-shih is back in town."

Hsiao Lo stood in the shade of the doorway and glanced at his mother, then, turning away, he stared out over the white glare on the pond in front of the house.

"Mother, you're missing two of your buttons."

She set the pan of rice down on the ground and closed her blouse over her old, vein-streaked breasts, fastening it with a hairpin that she plucked from her head.

"For the next day or two you're going to stay home and wait this out," she said. "You stay away from that demon. If you go on with your evil deeds, I swear I'll knock my head against this door and die before your eyes!"

Hsiao Lo sat down on the doorsill, close to his mother. "Heaven damn this heat! It's enough to make your sweat turn cold. A month since the last rain!"

The old woman turned around and looked closely at her son. "Don't you go on cursing Heaven! Sooner or later, lightning will strike you down after all you've done." She reached over and felt his chest. "What's wrong with you, breaking out in a cold sweat on a hot day like this? Go fix yourself a bowl of hot ginger broth and drink it right now. It's good for cold sweat."

Hsiao Lo went into the kitchen, filled a ladle with water and poured it over his head. His mother, coming in after him with the pan of rice, saw him hunched over the half-full jar, his arms braced against the rim, looking down into the muddy water with a vacant stare.

"Look at you!" she scolded. "Your face is green as a corpse!" She set the pan on the stove and went to the cupboard to look for ginger. Hsiao Lo raised his head and yanked off the undershirt draped across his shoulders to wipe his face with it, slowly making his way back out. As he walked into the courtyard he passed a bitch dozing in the shade, and he gave her a kick in the chest.

"Mother, I feel sick. The smell of ginger makes me want to throw up. Fix it for me later."

The old woman shook her head in resignation. "Back to your evil ways again, eh?"

The young wife of their neighbor came into the kitchen, her breast exposed, nursing the baby in her arms. She was grinning as she spoke to Hsiao Lo's mother. "I was just passing by and decided to drop in to see you. Why is that dog yelping so piteously?"

The bitch was tied up in the courtyard, and now lay whining in the shadows. She was curled up, licking her belly with her long red tongue, and looking furtively at the man standing above her.

Hsiao Lo's mother took a ham bone from the cupboard and threw it out into the courtyard. "He's been out dog-snatching again. Who knows where he got this one."

Hsiao Lo came back into the kitchen. He ignored the two women and walked directly to the iron pot used for cooking pig slop. He heaved it onto the stove and began to fill it with ladlefuls of water. Without a word, he proceeded to pile a big stack of wood in the belly of the stove. Hsiao Shun's wife watched as he took a dagger from a hidden compartment in the cupboard. She carried her little son out into the courtyard and peered down at the dog.

"What a fine-looking bitch," she chuckled, looking back at Hsiao Lo's mother. "Her fur's so black and so slick. Looks young, too. I'd say she hasn't had any pups yet."

The old woman heard her but said nothing. She carried out a pan of bean sprouts, sat down on the doorsill, and began to snap the ends off with her fingers.

Hisao Shun's wife looked up at the sky. "A month since it last rained, and nothing but blue sky for days. Anyway, I can't say I'm not happy to see at least some dark clouds gathering up there."

"Auntie," raising her voice, she called out to Hsiao Lo's mother, "the weather's changing."

The old woman kept on snapping beans as if she were not listening. "It's about time, too," she muttered to herself. "Heaven couldn't be so blind as to let the sun dry up all the pepper plants in the gulch."

Down in the courtyard Hsiao Lo tossed a ladle of water on the whetstone and crouched down with the dagger in his hands. Hsiao Shun's wife stood in the shade and watched him sharpening it. Her child, sucking heartily at her breast, giggled with delight and suddenly bit down on her nipple.

"Auntie, it's really something. Have you heard of a baby growing teeth in the first year! It's a sure sign he'll grow up to be the scourge of his mother." She slapped the child affectionately on the cheek.

"No comparison with the dog thief I've got in my house," said the old woman from the doorsill. "When I carried him, he kicked and jolted in my belly. And that first month of lying-in, he bit and chewed whenever I suckled him. Finally, by the time he was two, he had grown the sharpest teeth I've ever seen. It was as if I'd been his enemy in some previous life and now he'd returned to get even with me."

Hsiao Lo thrust the sharpened dagger into his waistband and turned to his mother. "I was a bad seed from the very start, born with a worm in my brain. Sooner or later it'll eat up my soul and drive me crazy, and then you can rest easy, Mother."

His mother kept her head bent over the bean sprouts. After a while she looked over to Hsiao Shun's wife. "See what a good son I've raised. He's got sharp teeth now, and his arms are thick and brawny. Even his own mother can't hold him down. Running after that hoodlum Sun Ssu-fang from dawn to dusk, calling him his brother! Tagging behind him wherever he goes, whoring and gambling. And the night of the Kuan Yin parade in Wan-fu Lane,[2] he was teamed up with Sun Ssu-fang again in his evil ways. And now Liu Lao-shih's come back! Let him settle the account himself."

The stove began to spit and crackle as the water in the pot boiled over. Hsiao Lo hunched over and fed more wood into the burner. His sweat poured down, glistening on his swarthy body. He mopped his forehead with his undershirt as he watched the fire.

Hsiao Shun's wife came to the kitchen door and spoke to the old woman. "Strange, wasn't it, that we had a rainstorm the first time Liu Lao-shih ran away from the asylum in the city and came back to Chi-ling. It's a month ago. And it hasn't rained since."

Hsiao Lo's mother got up and carried her pan inside. She went into the main room where the Kuan Yin altar stood. She wiped her hands before she lit three joss sticks and placed them before the statue. "A lot of the men in our town and those from the gulch went to Wan-fu Lane that evening to see the parade. When Liu Lao-shih's wife was dragged into the whorehouse and raped by a gang of drunks, not one of these men came forward to raise a finger and stop Sun Ssu-fang and his foul deed. They suddenly turned into a flock of gaping geese—just stood there gawking. The poor little thing Ch'ang-sheng hanged herself the next morning. If Heaven has eyes, these men will surely be punished."

Hsiao Lo didn't say a word. He took a length of hemp rope from the cupboard and stuck it in his waistband. Averting his eyes from his mother's stare, he picked up a hemp sack and sauntered out to the court-yard. It was four o'clock and the sun's rays slanted into the house. Hsiao Lo's long thin shadow was cast across the courtyard and up onto the opposite wall, where his head and neck hung at an angle to the rest of his body. It looked as if it were the very image of the Death Messenger in the temple processions, swaying on tall stilts, shaking his big rushleaf fan and dangling his tongue.[3]

The pot of water on the stove was at full boil, filling the kitchen with hot, moist air. Hsiao Shun's wife pulled her nipple from her son's mouth, coaxing him to turn around and watch Hsiao Lo sport with the dog. Hsiao Lo hissed and shook the sack at the dog. The bitch huddled at the foot of the courtyard wall and watched him with stealthy, gleaming eyes. The baby had nestled his cheek against his mother's breast and was watching

Hsiao Lo's caper with amusement. Suddenly, he opened his mouth and burst out crying, his tiny fists pawing at his mother's bosom.

"Stop teasing it," Hsiao Shun's wife pleaded with Hsiao Lo, trying to calm her child. "It's sickening to watch."

Hsiao Lo took another step towards the dog, gave the sack a hard jerk and stamped his foot on the ground. The bitch was aroused. Slowly she struggled to her feet and snarled at Hsiao Lo, baring her fangs. This finally drew a grin from Hsiao Lo. He sprang forward, and in two quick steps had swung the sack over the bitch's head. A quick yank and the sack was closed. Then he whipped the hemp rope from his waistband, wound it around the top of the sack, and pulled it into a tight knot.

"Heaven is watching!" The old woman had stuck her head out of the kitchen door and saw what her son was doing.

The baby had stopped crying. His arms were wrapped around his mother's neck; he chuckled with delight now, and watched Hsiao Lo throw the heavy sack to the ground and give it a kick.

"Show some mercy and kill her with a club. One good blow will do it! Look how she's kicking and jumping in there. If you want her to suffocate to death, you'll have to wait an hour or two." Hsiao Shun's wife carried her son over to the sack and nudged it with her foot.

Hsiao Lo removed a cigarette butt he had placed behind his ear and lit it inside the stove belly. He went back out and squatted down at the edge of the courtyard, dragging on his cigarette as he watched the sack turn and twist in the sun. Hsiao Shun's wife frowned disapprovingly as she stood looking at him.

"You'd better mend your evil ways. Didn't your mother tell you yet? Hsiao Shun came home a while ago and said that a stranger came to town at noontime. He said he's got a sack over his shoulder and something heavy's in it. His face is so hairy that he looks like a wild man from the mountains, and they can't see his mouth, or his nose, or even his eyes. So no one knows who or what he is. And when he came into town he went straight to the k'u-lien tree[4] in front of the county granary and sat down under it. Doesn't pay attention to anyone—just sits there hugging his sack, and he's been sitting patiently since noon. As soon as the news that Liu Lao-shih was back in town was reported, some of the men who had a bad conscience for what they did all rushed home and huddled inside like they'd seen a ghost. But then they got restless sitting around doing nothing, so now they've all slipped into the woman Chu's teashop across the street from the granary. Hsiao Shun said you're not to go out for the next couple of days, because who knows, that crazy man might have a butcher's cleaver hidden in that sack."

"A bad seed like me is bound to be struck down by lightning sooner or later. Why should I be scared of his butcher's cleaver?" Hsiao Lo tossed away his cigarette and stood up. He grabbed a pole which they kept for carrying buckets and walked toward the middle of the courtyard. His mother's voice came from inside. "There's lightning above and the King of Hell below. He's got a ghost in his conscience. There's no use worrying about him."

Hsiao Shun's wife pressed her baby's head against her bosom, standing to one side and watching without a word.

Hsiao Lo moved his hand over the writhing sack and groped around for the dog's head. Then he lifted the pole high and struck down hard. A stifled moan came from the sack. The bitch's hind legs jerked the sack taut twice and quietly Hsiao Lo struck it again.

Hsiao Shun's wife took her hand away and sighed. "You really did a clean job. Last time Hsiao Shun killed one, he pounded away a dozen times, only to find the dog was still kicking around in the sack."

Now the sack collapsed into a lifeless lump. Hsiao Lo went up to it and turned it over with his foot. Blood began to seep out slowly. He squatted down, deftly undid the rope and dragged the bitch out. Her skull was split in two.

Hsiao Lo's mother stuck her head out through the kitchen doorway. "Are you sure you want to watch such evil with your baby in your arms?" she called out to Hsiao Shun's wife.

Hsiao Shun's wife was watching Hsiao Lo draw the sharpened dagger from his waistband. It flashed with a cold brilliance. "It's already dead!" she shouted back without turning her head. "My son didn't see him kill it."

Hsiao Lo held the dagger in one hand and grasped the dog's neck with the other. He ran the tip of the dagger over the throat for a moment, then he slit open the gullet with a single, measured stroke. He stood back a few steps as a stream of blood gushed out. He watched for a while, then he went back to the stove and poured several ladles of boiling water over the dead dog. The bitch lay on her back, her legs pointed up toward the red evening sun. Her eyes were open and shone like glass beads, blank with astonishment. Somehow, her expression resembled that of a dead five- or six-year-old child.

Hsiao Lo wiped the bloodstained dagger on the dog's fur, and gave the cutting edge one or two skims on the whetstone. Then he split the dog open from her throat straight down through her belly in one smooth cut. He tossed the dagger aside and wedged his right hand into the cleavage. He flicked his fingers through the length of the gash, then yanked the sides open with both hands. He thrust his hand inside and began to dredge out the dripping innards. Hsiao Shun's wife walked over with her hand covering her son's face. She crouched halfway down and ran a finger over the dead dog's teats. She squinted back at Hsiao Lo and chuckled.

"The little brat! Her nipples were just starting to get big. Another six months and she'd have found herself a mate to make her a real bitch."

Hsiao Lo got a basin and filled it with hot water. He rinsed out the belly of the dog. Then he flayed the carcass and chopped it into pieces. "I'll stew her up with pepper and sauce," he said to Hsiao Shun's wife. "You can have a bowl of it tonight." She giggled and stood up, hiding her mouth in her baby's cheek and giving it a smacking kiss. "I don't want any," she replied, pushing her nipple back into the baby's mouth. She started to walk toward the kitchen door, but suddenly turned to look back. "Last time that bastard Hsiao Shun forced me to eat some, it made me feel sick for days. Every time I went out I felt as if all the dogs on the street were glaring at me." She chuckled again and said, "Dogmeat really does something funny to you! It makes your whole body itch with a burning sensation."

Hsiao Lo put the meat into the pot and left it stewing on the stove. Suddenly a fit of dizziness seized him and he felt everything falling away. His legs became shaky. He reached out and grabbed the edge of the stove to brace himself, then slowly sank down onto a stool. He stared out into the sunlit courtyard, where the dog's innards lay in a pool of blood. But he could not shake off the sudden memory of Liu Lao-shih wielding that blood-soaked cleaver.

That evening, two days after the night of the Kuan Yin Festival, Liu Lao-shih had gone crazy because his wife had hanged herself. He sprang out of Wan-fu Lane to search out his wife's rapists in East Market Street. Hsiao Lo was hiding in the thatched privy behind the woman Chu's teashop opposite the county granary. Peeking over the wall, he watched that deranged man bolt silently into the kitchen next door, grab Sun Ssu-fang's wife and, without a word, slice off her nipples. The woman Chu had bolted up her shop. She dragged Hsiao Lo out from the privy and shoved him into the teashop. She had made him stand behind the door and watch through the slats.

The street was seething with people. A crowd of idlers had gathered in front of Sun Ssu-fang's house. With nothing better to do after dinner, they jostled around the house with their mouths hanging open and watched Liu Lao-shih spring out of the house holding a bloody cleaver in his hand. He strode off toward West Market Street, silent as before, and they all fell in behind him, pushing and shoving each other as if afraid to lose sight of an angry demon. After a while the clamor died away, and the only person left on the street was Liu Lao-shih's mother. The old woman was down on her knees in the middle of the street, her face turned toward the retreating crowd, sobbing loudly. Hsiao Lo had run out the back of the teashop and fled home. He had lain under his quilt retching all night. His mother made him two bowls of ginger broth, but he vomited it back up, all over the old woman's face.

"If you don't clean up the courtyard, the neighbors will see all the blood and think we're running a murderer's den." His mother had sent Hsiao Shun's wife away and come back into the kitchen. Her son was staring out into the courtyard, sweat pouring from his torso. She went up to him and felt his chest. "Your skin feels cool. Breaking out with a cold sweat on a hot day like this! I told you to go fix yourself some ginger broth. What harm could it do you? If you come down with sunstroke in this kind of weather, well, don't expect me to listen to you groan and moan all night." She felt for the ginger in the cupboard and looked hard at her son again. "And you're going to stay home for a few days. Keep you from stirring up that madman and getting chopped up by that cleaver."

"Stop nagging me, Mother." Hsiao Lo yanked the drenched undershirt from his shoulder and pulled it over his head. "Vengeance will fall on the evildoer, debts will fall to the debtor. I'm just going to take a look at him, he's not going to cut me into pieces just for that!" He turned his back to the old woman and quietly slipped the bloodstained dagger under his shirt. Then he fed more wood into the belly of the stove and put a cover over the pot stewing the dogmeat with pepper and sauce. "Watch the fire, Mother. I'll clean up the courtyard when I get back."

Hsiao Lo stepped out the gate. The blinding white sun of noon had burnt itself into a disk of raw luscious crimson, ready to sink. It looked as if it had permanently suspended itself over the horizon at the edge of town. A hot, arid wind suddenly rose, twisting out from nowhere. It pierced the undershirt that clung to his skin, and, cooled by the damp sweat, sent a shiver creeping up Hsiao Lo's spine. He turned his back to the sun and began to walk. Next door, Hsiao Shun's wife sat on her doorsill, her breast bare as she suckled her child. Her lips parted in a grin when she saw Hsiao Lo go by. Hsiao Lo felt a wave of nausea. He clutched at his chest, squatted down by the gutter, and belched out two mouthfuls of gastric spittle. He didn't care who saw.

It was quiet down the alley. Women in their thinnest clothing sat out on their doorsills, waving large rushleaf fans. The young ones suckled their babies, the old ones culled their rice. From time to time, they looked listlessly at the sky and watched the dark clouds that had been gathering overhead since midday. Dogs sprawled silent in the shade, their red, slimy tongues jerking as they panted for breath. Nobody stirred when Hsiao Lo went by. Both the women and the dogs stared at him with lazy, vacant eyes.

It had been hot the day of Kuan Yin's birthday, the nineteenth day of the sixth month. The heat had been just as oppressive as it was today. By noon Hsiao Lo had drunk himself sick. For a while he had managed to hold up by hugging his chest, but he soon gave up and vomited his bellyful of meat and wine all over the street.

Earlier that day, altars had been moved out in front of all the shops along East Market Street. At noontime the women came out carrying incense urns. Overhead the sun seemed to be pouring on them like molten iron. They lit their joss sticks, bowed before the altars and solemnly prayed that Kuan Yin protect and bring peace and prosperity to every household in Chi-ling when she came around for her annual ceremonial parade through the town.

Hsiao Lo grabbed a short bench from the woman Chu's teashop and sat outside under the eaves. He fanned his chest and watched the street gradually fill up with the men from the gulch. They had come in for the festivities of the day and were scurrying in and out of Wan-fu Lane, poking their heads in here and there with eyes agog.

"Lecherous louts! Coming into town and making a beeline for Wan-fu Lane on today of all days!" Sun Ssu-fang staggered over with a bottle of wu-chia-p'i wine[5] in his hand, cursing the heat with every step. He was about to pull off his undershirt when he lurched and fell against the woman Chu, who had just come out of her shop carrying an incense urn.

"Why don't all of you go home and stay there until you sober up!" she snapped. "This place stinks of your vomit!" Just as she said this, she caught sight of someone in Wan-fu Lane that made her change her tone of voice. "Well, well, today's a great day indeed!" she smirked, "Liu Lao-shih has let his woman out."

Sun Ssu-fang followed her gaze. "And what a smooth, white piece of meat! To have it all wasted on that coffin-maker!"

The woman Chu set the incense urn down gently on its stand, and gave Sun Ssu-fang a dark, cryptic look over her shoulder. "Don't cross that coffin-maker. You know what they say about him, 'He's slow to boil, but when he does, he cracks the pot.'"

Hsiao Lo felt another surge rise inside his chest. He tore over to the gutter and vomited until his stomach was empty. This sobered him up a bit, and when he looked up from the gutter her saw Liu Lao-shih's wife, Ch'ang-sheng, coming out of Wan-fu Lane, walking in the sun down East Market Street with a basket on her arm. She wore a simple blouse with a high collar, and her trousers were of the same material: a small flowered pattern on a plain white background. Her eyes narrowed against the sun. The men on the street all turned their heads to watch her as she passed by. A lustful gleam came to their eyes as they looked her up and down.

Four young punks, about fourteen or fifteen years old, came scrambling out of Wan-fu Lane. They fell in behind Ch'ang-sheng and followed her

on tiptoe, grinning mischievously. As they came up under the k'u-lien
tree in front of the county granary on East Market Street, they let out a
shrill whistle and swooped around her. They pantomimed the men who
bore Kuan Yin's sedan chair in her yearly procession through town: they
dipped and swayed with shouts of "heigh-ho, heigh-ho!" Just as they were
working themselves to a frenzied pitch, they caught a glimpse of Hsiao Lo
bearing down on them like a mad demon, and they scattered.

Hsiao Lo drew a bill, crumpled beyond recognition, from his waistband, and, flourishing it in his hand, sidled up to Ch'ang-sheng. "Mistress
Liu," he simpered, crouching, "you dropped some money." Ch'ang-
sheng's face flushed red but she kept on walking with her eyes down. For
a while Hsiao Lo trailed stupidly behind her, but he noticed all the shop
women lighting incense in the sun so he stuffed the bill back into his
waistband. Slowly he caught up with Ch'ang-sheng. "Don't you know
today's Kuan Yin's birthday? How come Brother Lao-shih's still squatting
in his shop making coffins?"

Ch'ang-sheng's face went pale as she turned around to look at Hsiao Lo.
Hsiao Lo felt a quiver go through his heart, and he sobered up a little
more. He retreated, taking a slow step back, and at the same time he said
to her, "Mistress Liu. A busy street in broad daylight. You've nothing to
be afraid of."

A string of firecrackers, the fuse lit, was thrown from the eaves of one of
the shops. It fell without a sound right in front of Ch'ang-sheng's feet.
Then it broke into a burst of explosions. Hsiao Lo's head shot up. He saw
one of the four young punks hiding under the eaves behind a post. The
boy was craning his neck and grinning at Ch'ang-sheng. He held a stick of
incense in his hand, the tip glowing fiery red.

"You filthy little runt! If you've got any hair on your prick, I'll pull it
out!" Hsiao Lo sprang toward the boy, raising his fists. Another string of
firecrackers came shooting out into the street. Ch'ang-sheng stood with
the basket on her arm, at a loss as to what to do and pale as could be. As
Hsiao Lo charged after the boy, cursing, the little wine left in him surged
to his head. He tore off his undershirt, baring his gaunt chest, and ran up
and down the street, wildly chasing after all the young punks in the
street. The uproar reached every shop in the street, and every other
young lout hurried out to join in, carrying firecrackers and a stick of
burning incense. A score of half-grown boys followed close behind Hsiao
Lo, tossing firecrackers every which way, goading him with shouts of
"Welcome Boddhisattva Kuan Yin, Goddess of Mercy!"

"Hsiao Lo!" Hsiao Shun walked up to him and shook him hard. "Has
the Death Messenger snatched your soul away?"

Hsiao Lo raised his head and gazed at Hsiao Shun.

"Look at you! Your face is as green as a corpse!" said Hsiao Shun, loosening his grip. He looked up at the sky. "The weather had better be turning. If it doesn't rain soon, the folks down in the gulch might as well go hang themselves in front of Kuan Yin."

Hsiao Lo suddenly began laughing idiotically. "That lunatic Liu Lao-shih, has he really come back?"

"He's still sitting there under that k'u-lien tree in front of the granary, taking his nap." Hsiao Shun went up a few steps toward home, but suddenly turned and eyed Hsiao Lo inquisitively. "That night after you and Sun Ssu-fang got drunk, why didn't you just go and sleep it off? Why did you run into Wan-fu Lane and bring this evil curse on all of us?"

That day Sun Ssu-fang had gotten drunk on wu-chia-p'i. At first, his pock-marked face flushed bright red. As he drank into the evening it turned a grayish green, and a steady stream of curses poured from his lips toward the sky.

He led a bunch of hangers-on staggering into Wan-fu Lane, cursing and coughing. "What has the world come to? Here comes the mother whore leading her flock to worship Kuan Yin, choking the street with their incense!"

Hsiao Lo leaned against Red Spring's door. His bellyful of wu-chia-p'i was acting up. He felt his bloodshot eyes fill with water. Then he became aware of bursting firecrackers, and when he looked up, all of Wan-fu Lane seemed ablaze. Those four filthy young punks from East Market Street were scampering barefoot into the lane, screaming, "Welcome the Boddhisattva! Welcome!"

"I'll get you, you little—" Hsiao Lo started toward them, cursing, but the wine surged to his head again. He spun around twice then fell sprawling in the middle of the lane, raising howls of laughter from all the men gathered under the eaves of the brothels watching the Kuan Yin parade.

A firecracker rocket shot up into the dark sky. Hsiao Lo craned his neck to watch it. Half of the sky was aglow with an umbrella of red petals. Seconds later they dissipated like meteors, into the vast night.

Hsiao Lo was crawling to his feet, knees still weak, when his eyes fell on the sedan chair bearing Kuan Yin. He fell back to his knees, staring, in a trance. There, seated in the darkness of the pitching, tossing sedan chair, he was sure he saw Ch'ang-sheng, so demure, so beautiful, her eyes half closed.

Those four young punks came scampering up to Hsiao Lo and dragged him over under the eaves, twisting his arms.

"You drunken devil! Just after downing a few cups of cat piss,[6] you go spewing filth in the middle of the lane and blocking Kuan Yin's holy procession. What gall! You're just begging us to spit on you!"

Ch'ang-sheng was dressed in her simple blouse and trousers, a print of tiny flowers on a white background. She was kneeling demurely before her husband's coffin shop next to Red Spring's brothel. She held joss sticks up to her brow. With an expression of extreme reverence she followed her mother-in-law in paying homage to Kuan Yin, Bestower of Children. The Boddhisattva was dressed in snow-white robes, and in her arms she held a rosy-cheeked infant, upon whom she gazed with half-lidded, rapt eyes, her face filled with compassion.

Slouched against the door of the coffin shop, muttering curses, was Sun Ssu-fang, his face green with drunken stupor.

"The Boddhisattva is going to show us her magical power!" cried Hsiao Lo. He ripped the undershirt from his body, exposing his gaunt chest.

Out in the middle of the lane, an old shaman⁷ stood soaked in blood, a sword gripped tight in his hand. His eyes were half shut as if in a trance. Blood slowly seeped from his navel onto his black robe, which was already dyed a deep crimson. He displayed it dripping before Kuan Yin's eyes.

"The Boddhisattva has revealed to us her magical power!" cried Hsiao Lo. He staggered up to the shaman, reached out his hand and rubbed some blood from the old man's navel: laughing foolishly, he smeared it on his own face. His cry was echoed by the onlookers under the eaves of the brothels. It grew into a roar: "The Boddhisattva has revealed to us her power!"

Hsiao Lo stood up in the lane and tried to steady himself. His eyes, blurred with the wu-chia-p'i wine, glanced over the crowd of men jostling under the long row of eaves. Their faces were strangly contorted. Suddenly overcome by the rank stench of blood, his heart faltered and everything began to fall apart. He went reeling down and toppled squarely before Kuan Yin's sedan chair.

The four runts pounced on him without warning and dragged him away, spitting, "You drunk! Blocking the holy sedan chair again. Just wait till we open our pants—we'll piss on you, one at a time!"

The sky whirled, the earth churned. Hsiao Lo could feel the worm that was gnawing at his brain, turning round and round, spiraling down. The din of firecrackers and the roar of the crowd no longer reached his ears. His eyelids twitched with spasms as he tried to open his eyes. Vaguely, he saw Ch'ang-sheng's mother-in-law sprawled in front of Red Spring's door. The faces under the eaves began to bloat and balloon before his eyes, spinning around him, crowding toward him as if they were going to devour him.

"The Boddhisattva has given us a sign!"

With a great leap Hsiao Lo butted his head against the door of the brothel run by Red Spring. It flung wide open. In the hall, perched on her altar, sat the statue of Kuan Yin, head bowed, eyes lowered, mute and withdrawn. The light from two red candles shone on her compassionate face, so peaceful and yet so mysterious.

The door to Red Spring's room was half ajar. The red embroidered quilt on the bed was covered with slime. Sun Ssu-fang, his swarthy back glistening, was sprawled over Ch'ang-sheng's snow-white breasts. He was biting her nipples in wild abandon, nipples that had never suckled a child. A final surge rose inside his chest, and Hsiao Lo fell into a crouch beneath the altar. The vomit rose in one rush after another; he felt as if his insides were being dredged out. He stared up toward Kuan Yin, as his violent retching echoed through the stale air. The noise of the crowd and the firecrackers outside rose back to a clamorous din. All of Wan-fu Lane seemed to have lost its soul. And like the turtledove's bloody mourning cry, deep in the midnight woods, came Old Mother Liu's shriek, "Heaven will smite! Lightning will strike! Thunder will roar!"

A group of young boys were running and hollering on East Market Street when they saw Hsiao Lo at the other end, walking toward them with glazed eyes. They came to a braking halt, and slowly jostled each other across the street to the front of the preserved fruits shop. They stared at Hsiao Lo, choking with mischievous laughter. An old woman came out of the shop. She glared at them angrily. "Vengeance will fall on the evildoer, debts will fall on the debtor. Now that Liu Lao-shih's back, the whole lot of you will have to pay!" She glanced up at the sky, then bent down to pick up the tray of orange peels that had been left drying in the sun. "The Boddhisattva has eyes," she muttered, as she carried the tray back inside.

The boys snuck up after Hsiao Lo and tiptoed behind him. As the k'u-lien tree came into view, the youngest one sidled up by Hsiao Lo and tugged at his pants. "Brother," he whispered, "don't go up there. That demon Liu Lao-shih is waiting for you."

Hsiao Lo looked over his shoulder. At the end of the street, the sun was still suspended over the horizon. The street was bathed in red. Over by the granary everything was quiet, except for the cawing of the black crows[8] that wheeled about the branches of the k'u-lien tree. The tree, scorched by the sun for the past month, stood gaunt and lonely. A thin veil of golden dust now hung over it. Bent at the waist, it hunched toward the sinking sun, seeming to stare at it vacantly. Beneath the tree sat the napping man, his arms wrapped around his knees, hugging a sack to his chest.

The woman Chu came out of the teashop. She stood under the eaves complaining loudly about the heat. She craned her neck to look at the sun, then looked up at the mass of dark clouds gathered overhead.

"The weather's turning. If it doesn't rain soon, we might as well put a torch to the town and burn it all down." She emptied the basin of muddy water that she had brought out with her onto the ground in front of her shop. She had already noticed Hsiao Lo standing in the middle of the street, looking as if he had lost his soul. His bloodshot eyes were blurred, but he kept them fastened on the man beneath the tree.

"So, you too know when vengeance is near!" she scolded. As she turned back, she saw the men huddled inside her shop looking out into the street.

"Big, brave bunch of he-men, all of you! You've done your evil deeds, and now your hearts are ghost-ridden. One look at you fine fellows makes a woman feel sick."

The old fortune-teller walked across the street carrying a cup of tea. He kept his eyes on the ground as he slowly made his way, but glanced up to study the man sitting beneath the tree. "Liu Lao-shih committed murder and went crazy. The constables took him and locked him up tight. How could they let him escape a second time? It just doesn't stand to reason! And then, this man here doesn't look crazy at all. I think he's just a drifter passing through."

"If it *is* that crazy demon," said the woman Chu, "so much the better. As long as you've got a clean conscience, why should you care? Could it be, old sir," she laughed coldly, "could it be that you, too, were watching the parade in Wan-fu Lane that night?"

The fortune-teller's face stiffened. He looked over and spoke gravely. "I was watching them greet Kuan Yin from my doorstep. Not a drop of blood ever touched me. I'm white as innocence itself, and my conscience is clean." He uncurled a finger from around his cup and pointed at Hsiao Lo. "This little lout got himself drunk and went with Sun Ssu-fang and his gang. It's they who sinned, who brought us disaster, who summoned the plague demon to descend on us. It's they who dragged every frightened innocent in town into their evil mess!"

The old man's words brought the customers in the teashop shuffling to the doorway. They craned to look at Hsiao Lo, and then peered over at the man beneath the k'u-lien tree. The sun beyond the town was growing redder and redder as it sank. From the woman Chu's teashop, the empty street in front of the county granary appeared to be spread with a thin veil of golden dust. The shadow of the man joined the shadow of the tree and they slanted across the street, stretching over toward the teashop. Women from shops next door carried out stools to sit under the eaves. They fanned themselves with large rushleaf fans. The young ones bared their breasts and suckled their babies. Their listless eyes were all turned toward the k'u-lien tree across the street. An arid gust of wind suddenly twisted through the air. The shadow of the k'u-lien, long and scraggy, softly caressed the heart of Chi-ling Town. The women looked up at the dark, heavy clouds assembling swiftly in the sky. They listened to the ceaseless, mournful cawing of the black crows above the granary.

One of the men in the teashop stood holding his own porcelain teacup from home. He peered out from the doorway a long while, then burst out, "Vengeance will fall on the evildoer, debts will fall on the debtor. That cleaver of Liu Lao-shih's surely will not fall on an innocent body!"

"When Liu Lao-shih went crazy," said another man, shaking his head, "and took to the street killing people, who of us didn't wish to see every one of those louts chopped down. Who'd have thought that the victims would be two women—the whore Red Spring and Sun Ssu-fang's wife?"

The woman Chu snorted. "Why, you're actually eager to see Liu Lao-shih come back and wreak his vengeance. Don't tell me you two didn't play your parts that night!"

She walked to the back of her shop and filled a basin with water to splash on the ground under the eaves. Hsiao Lo's lone shadow was still stretched across the street. She went over to him and grabbed him by the arm. "Don't you know what's good for you?" she chided. "Standing out in the middle of the street attracting attention! If you could see how wretched you look standing out here! If that man were really Liu Lao-shih, he would've chopped you to pieces long before this!"

Without a word, Hsiao Lo followed her into the teashop. He sat down behind a table near the door. The fortune-teller casually walked outside and stood under the eaves sipping his tea. Again he peered across the street and studied the man sitting beneath the tree, then turned his grave face back to look at Hsiao Lo thoughtfully. The woman Chu brought out a cup of freshly brewed tea and set it in front of Hsiao Lo. She studied him. "Why didn't you stay put at home? Why come running here and create a spectacle for these men?"

Hsiao Lo drew out the dagger from under his shirt. He placed it down softly on the table and sat staring at the half-dried dog blood smeared on its blade.

One of the men from the gulch sitting behind him suddenly heaved a sigh. "This weather! If it doesn't rain now, I'm going to tie up my wife and kids tomorrow, drag them to Kuan Yin's temple, and chop them to pieces. That'll open the Boddhisattva's eyes!"

"If she won't open her eyes," answered another, "there's nothing you can do to make her. Even if you took a torch to the main temple on West Market Street, she wouldn't if she doesn't want to."

The woman Chu walked over and filled their cups with hot water. "You two just forget about slaughtering your families and burning down the temples. If your consciences are clean you don't have to worry about the ghost of Ch'ang-sheng going down to the gulch to search you out."

Suddenly, thunder rolled overhead. The woman Chu stood in the mid-

dle of her shop, holding herself very still, head tilted to listen. It came
from far above the seven heavens, rolling and grumbling, like someone
being throttled. The whole town of Chi-ling paused, as if its heart had
stopped beating. In front of the granary the street lay silent and empty.
The crows, perched on the k'u-lien tree, flew up in confusion, flapping
their wings and cawing with mounting urgency.

It was dark inside the teashop; the lamps had not been lit. The rays of
the setting sun, heavy and silent like molten gold, filtered down the street
from beyond the town and cast themselves upon the shadowy faces of the
men inside. The townsmen and the men from the gulch all laid their cups
gently on the tables. They looked out and saw the red sunset grow deeper
and dimmer. They cocked their ears, gauging the sounds from the
heavens above.

A streak of lightning slithered out from behind the k'u-lien tree like a
long, white snake. A moment later they heard the muffled roll of thunder
come across the sky. Soon the sky above the granary was crossed with
streaks of lightning, splitting the heavens asunder at last. Waves of thunder chased each other across the sky, rearing and pitching over Chi-ling
Town.

"It's turned at last!" exclaimed the woman Chu, tossing aside the kettle
and striding out under the eaves. All down the street, from the north end
to the south, not even a single shadow of a man was in sight, except that of
the one sitting beneath the k'u-lien tree. Beyond the town, the blood-red
sinking sun ignited the western sky. It hung just over the horizon, glaring
back through the center of town to the k'u-lien, gaunt and lonely.

A hot gust of wind twisted silently over the street, scattering the dark
evening air, sweeping up the rustling yellow leaves lying in front of the
granary. The woman Chu shivered, and turned to look at Hsiao Lo. He
had lifted his head, and was staring out with fathomless, empty eyes. A
bolt of lightning sliced the sky in two; the dagger on the table gleamed a
cold blood-red. One by one, the men inside the teashop came out and
huddled under the eaves. They sipped their tea and watched the white
snakes slithering across the crimson sky. Another gust of wind twisted
down the street. Fat drops of rain began to fall pattering down.

On either side of the teashop the women rose from their stools to stand
under the eaves of their shops. The younger ones were still suckling their
babies, and the older ones held their rice pans closely to their bosoms.
Quietly, they all watched the torrents of rain coming down.

The man beneath the tree rose to his feet. He looked up at the flock of
crows frantically beating their wings, seemingly bewildered by the wind
and rain. They scattered toward the west, a burst of black specks in the
brilliant awesome sunset.

The man they feared to be Liu Lao-shih shook off the raindrops and wiped his hairy cheeks with the back of his hand. Throwing the sack over his shoulder, he walked out into the street, tucking his chin down on his chest.

Hsiao Lo felt for the dagger. He slipped out of the teashop and onto the street like a kite broken loose from its string.

The two of them stood in the middle of the street. The man slowly looked up at Hsiao Lo. The wind howled past the granary. The k'u-lien, hunched toward the sun beyond the town, soughed as it scattered its yellow leaves over the ground beneath it. On one branch sat a lone crow. Its mournful cries mingled with the sound of the wind and rain.

Slowly the man turned around, shrugged the sack on his shoulder, and heedless of the rain he began to walk away down the long street.

Hsiao Lo stood in the street alone, blankly staring after the man's retreating back. He looked over to the side. The woman Chu was still standing at the door of her shop, looking at Hsiao Lo quietly through the rain. Under the row of eaves across from the granary, men and women stood lost in a trance, hypnotized by the great torrent of rain. Hsiao Lo felt a vast emptiness growing in his heart. At last, he deposited the dagger back under his shirt and he, too, turned toward the blurry red sun beyond the town. Then, tucking his chin down on his chest, he began to walk home. The empty street glistened with the rain and the sunset. It stretched on and on, broken only by the gaunt and lonely shadows of the two men.

NOTES

1. The Chinese nomenclatural system needs a word of explanation here. "Hsiao Lo" literally means "Little Happiness." "Lo" is a given name. When a surname or a given name is prefixed by *hsiao*, it is intended as a familiar form of address. Another character that is prefixed by *hsiao* is Hsiao Shun. Like Hsiao Lo, a number of proper names in the story are invested with either ironic or symbolic significance. Thus "Wan-fu Lane" is "Lane of Myriad Blessings"; the town, "Chi-ling," means "Auspicious Tomb." The coffin-maker Liu Lao-shih can be translated as "Liu the Honest One."

2. Wan-fu Lane is the red-light district of Chi-ling Town. The woman Red Spring, mentioned later in the story, is one of the prostitutes residing in the lane. Kuan Yin is the Boddhisattva Kuan Yin, worshipped in China as the Goddess of Mercy and Progeny. Legend has it that she once became a prostitute in order to redeem the sinners from this lust-ridden world.

3. The *wu-ch'ang* is a personification of the Buddhist doctrine of impermanence. In popular belief, it is thought of as a messenger demon of death under Yen-lo, the King of Hell. Hence the translation.

4. A lofty tree, *Melia japonica*, with bipinnate leaves; a native of East Indies, it grows in hot climates. Also known as Pride of China and the Chinaberry.

5. A millet wine soaked in the bark of the spicy plant *Acanthopanax spinosum.*

6. Vulgar expression for liquor or wine.

7. A familiar figure in popular Buddhist-Taoist ceremonies, the *chi-t'ung* (here translated as "shaman") is believed to be capable of communicating directly with the deities on behalf of ordinary mortals. The rituals he performs are usually violent and bloody, often involving physical self-affliction in a demonstration of his supernatural, divinely endowed prowess.

8. A symbol of ill omen in Chinese superstition.

TUNG NIEN

(1950–   )

The kind of abject poverty which inflicted so much suffering on Chung Li-ho's characters in the fifties has not surfaced in Taiwan fiction in the seventies. This does not mean that Taiwan has become an "affluent society" equal to the United States or Western Europe. But in fairness it must be said that with industrialization the majority of the people have enjoyed a standard of living unparalleled in recent Chinese history. However, concomitant with material improvement are problems of alienation and social discontent, generating from awakened aspirations and frustrated desires. Such problems become all the more acute when the person in question is a country youth relocated in a cosmopolitan city like Taipei and hoping to find employment. Tung Nien's "Fire" in this anthology is thus a realistic portrait of a good-natured young man from the countryside who vents his anger at an indifferent society by destruction and self-immolation.

Tung Nien (pen name of Ch'en Shun-hsien) has worked as a marine radio operator and has made good use of his experience in a number of stories. In 1978 he was invited to visit the United States for three months under the auspices of the International Writing Program at the University of Iowa. His stories are collected in The Rainy Little Town *(Lo-yü ti hsiao-chen, Taipei, 1977) and in* Fire *(Ta-huo, Taipei, 1979). He is at present an art editor at Lien-ching Press.*

Fire

Translated by Nathan K. Mao and Winston Yang

As the ancient wall clocks struck three times in one home after another, the waning moon, slanting against the western sky, dropped behind a cluster of tall buildings. Without a speck of light, the sky was so somber that when blazing flames shot up from the roof of a dark building, the sight seemed exceptionally frightening. In any case, this was deep in the night, and residents in the neighborhood all seemed to be in peaceful and profound slumber.

Hsiao San's[1] father was a carpenter who worked on a fixed salary at a factory. He made just enough to support his family of five. Hsiao San's mother wanted to supplement the family income by taking a job, or at

250

least by working part time, but her health was simply too poor. For his three children's tuition, Hsiao San's father often had to work overtime at night or moonlight in the neighborhood. Regardless of how hard the father worked, the family always lived from hand to mouth and was strapped for funds. And the family's debts were gradually mounting.

Hsiao San's eldest brother finally graduated from college and completed his military obligations. A few days after leaving the army, the Investigation Bureau of the Ministry of Justice notified him to report for work as he had passed his job-qualifying examination.

On a hot, summer afternoon, he returned from Taipei, and he was perspiring heavily. His father said kindly to him, "Eldest, why don't you go to the beach for a soak?"

Ta Ko[2] did not like swimming, and would rather cool off by sitting in the shade under a tree, but because of Hsiao San's proddings, he went to the beach.

They had a good swim. They swam from the islets by the shore to the outer sea, and they returned when no more outlying islets could be seen. They lay on the beach, which was filled with people. Nearby were more than two dozen senior high school students, a few of whom had just taken the joint college entrance examination. They had probably not done well, because they were griping about this and that. Ta Ko was in a very good mood; never had he felt better. He was thinking how his family would soon see better days, and reflected upon how hard he had worked for his degree. Hsiao San was also in a good mood, because he had just taken the joint entrance examination for Taipei's senior high schools and he had done well. After a short break, Ta Ko said he had to go home to pack his belongings. Hsiao San had already had enough of a good swim and did not care to sunbathe on the hot beach anymore, so he also wanted to leave.

Just after they had changed their clothes and were ready to leave for home, they saw a high school student and a younger boy who were having a squabble. The latter was either fifteen or sixteen, about the same age as Hsiao San, but his speech and mannerisms were those of an older hooligan, and he was very intimidating. The high school student lost his restraint and slapped him once on the face. Suddenly the younger boy pulled a knife from his pocket and released the shining switchblade. Terrified, the high school student quickly hid behind Ta Ko.

"Little brother," Ta Ko said amiably, "ai, don't fool around with the knife. What if– . ."

"Mother's—,[3] what does this have to do with you? You think you are tall and strong?" Waving his knife, the boy roared, "Get out of my way, or you'll catch it."

Embarrassed, Ta Ko very much wanted to step aside, but the high school student followed him closely, either behind him or circling around him. No one saw exactly how it happened, but in the confusion that ensued, the boy missed his target and stuck the blade into Ta Ko's back.

Thus Hsiao San's brother died. This tragedy grieved Hsiao San's father to no end. The sudden worsening of the family situation made it impossible for Hsiao San and his father to go on with their plan. His father had always insisted that his sons should finish their college education before going to work, but this was no longer possible.

Hsiao San came to Taipei, not as a result of having passed the entrance examinations—for under those circumstances he would rather have failed—but to make a living.[4] He apprenticed at a beef-cake shop on Eight Virtues Road. Old and childless, the shopkeeper and his wife treated him rather kindly, so for two years he was well fed and became big and strong. His slightly dark skin and unshaven face made him look as if he were twenty-five or twenty-six when he was only seventeen or eighteen years of age.

Business slackened, and the cake shop finally closed. But soon, through an advertisement posted on a sidewalk billboard, Hsiao San found a job as an apprentice at a small ironworks factory. So he lived on Wen-chung Street, just to be close to where he worked.

It was a three-story building. The first floor was a beauty salon for women; the second and third floors, partitioned into more than ten cubicles, were rented to students and factory workers. Hsiao San lived on the third floor with a colleague as his roommate. After work the two would sometimes go to a movie together, or they had midnight snacks at some sidewalk food stalls. He enjoyed this kind of life very much, until one day his colleague left for military service. All alone, after work he'd still go to a movie or have some midnight snacks from time to time, but he felt something was missing.

His work was undemanding. All day he was expected to stand beside an iron-planing machine shaped like a bull's head. Since the machine was automatic, he had to do nothing else but insert pieces of iron between the iron pinchers, turn the machine on and let the scraper smooth the surfaces. The job was so easy that he became bored with it after a while. Going to work was a painful chore, yet returning home after work wasn't any better either. For a while he looked forward to weekends. He would go home every weekend and his mother would cook some meat and make a bowl of good soup for him, even though dinner was still skimpy. At home when he ran into his old schoolmates he felt inferior to them. Not able to combat the feeling of inferiority, he fabricated all sorts of excuses, including that he had to work overtime, and gradually stopped going home. Nonetheless he sent home what remained of his salary at the end of each month. In the beginning, he tried his best to send the even amount as printed on the remittance slip,[5] to the extent of straining his own budget. For this reason he was always close to the point of starvation. No one asked him to do that; he did it willingly. He was a good boy. Yet he was not exactly like those unreflecting "good boys" who took their suffering in stride and never rebelled. Even when they had occasional grievances, they merely blamed their fate. He greatly resented his fate, and as he had only a junior high school education he couldn't exalt his thinking to a higher level of abstraction. Therefore his rebellion was substantively aimed at his tangible surroundings, and his solid physical build contained instantly combustible rage.

The room he rented was the smallest one on the top floor. Situated on the end of a balcony, it was a storage room adjacent to the toilet and the shower. It was so tiny that it could barely hold one wooden bed. Because people went to the toilet and the shower all the time, he always kept his door tightly shut. Sometimes when it got too stuffy in his room he would sit on a high-legged round stool in a corner on the balcony and watch the crowd moving to and fro in the alley. Or he would simply study the structures of his neighbors' doors and windows across the street. He was such a gloomy and eccentric fellow, his neighbors in the same building never said hello to him, and, for his part, he made no effort to greet them. It seemed he never entertained any idea of getting to know anybody, either. Moreover, the tenants moved in and out, and no one would know where they were from or where they were moving to.

Now the situation suddenly changed. It was no longer a question whether he cared to know who his neighbors were: the knowledge was forced upon him. Next to his room lived five young bricklayers; from their speech, manners, and boisterousness he gathered that they, like himself, were young people. Directly across from him lived three or four girls who pandered their charms at a disreputable place disguised as a coffeehouse. Every night after eight or nine the bricklayers either played rock music and hit songs at the highest possible volume, or else they wrestled one another, making a lot of noise, banging the wooden beds and walls. Sometimes this lasted until midnight. When they were drunk, they were even more crazy. As for those girls, if they did not spend the night with their patrons, they'd come home around one or two in the morning. Drunk or sober they would argue boisterously or gossip incessantly. He was deeply disturbed by these people, not to mention the noise of running water that might occur any time from the toilet and the shower. He was never able to get a sound sleep.

His landlord did not live on the premises, so there was no one to impose any discipline. When tenants couldn't take the noise any longer, they simply moved out, one after another. From time to time he thought about moving out too, but he was afraid he couldn't find a room as cheap as the one he had. All he could hope for was that after he worked a little longer he would get a pay raise from his boss. As for his awful neighbors, he hated as much as he feared them; the long-haired bricklayers greatly outnumbered him, and the prostitutes usually associated with thugs. These were the facts. At one time he lost his temper, and he yelled at them from his room as loudly as he could. What he received in return was momentary peace and quiet, after which everything quickly returned to normal—only the next morning he noticed one of his slippers outside his door was missing. For a good many days in a row he hoped his missing slipper would return. In the end, however, not only did the missing slipper fail to turn up, but the remaining slipper also disappeared as well. He was quite upset over that pair of missing slippers for a few days, even though they cost only NT$10.00.[6] He did not buy new ones, and made a point of trying to retrieve his old ones. He even took the risk of crawling into the bricklayers' and the prostitutes' rooms—all to no avail. In any case, a little clue left him fully confident that he would eventually find the slippers. He discovered that the girls had only one pair of slippers in their room. Thus, he reasoned that they'd be wearing his slippers during the day or after midnight—at times when he wasn't around.

For several successive days he went to bed late in order to check on the girls. Any time anyone came home and opened the door, he'd stick his head out from his door to see who it was. Finally, one night he caught one of the girls.

"Hey, lady," he roared after the girl in anger, "those slippers are mine!"

The girl was startled by his roar. Placing both hands on her chest, she looked at him, in surprise.

"Those slippers you're wearing are mine," he repeated, pointing at her feet. "I've been looking for them for days, and there they are, on your feet."

"What?"

"What, what? The slippers you're wearing are mine. Which one of you stole them?"

"Oh, I didn't know," the girl said, hurriedly removing her slippers. "I just moved in."

Upon learning that she had just moved in, Hsiao San instantly felt apologetic about his own rudeness. He not only assumed a polite tone, but let her wear his slippers until she changed into someone else's. He was especially nice to her, because he had a good impression of her even before their first meeting. The reason was simply this: without any particular hobby to occupy himself with, and without any method to block out the noise of the bricklayers and the girls, he had developed, in time, the ability to distinguish the identity of each speaker from their conversations. In fact, apart from not being able to tell what they looked like, he was very familiar with the voices, personalities, and the names of his neighbors. The newcomer's name was Ai Yüeh. She had had a tenth-grade education. On two occasions she cried bitterly because she had been forced to drink beyond her capacity by her clients. She bared her sufferings by singing a Taiwanese song or a popular sentimental song in Mandarin. Hsiao San was deeply moved, as he listened on the sly in the next room.

From then on any news of the girl became the major diversion in his humdrum existence. He was very willing to go to bed late to wait for the girls to come back, and to listen to their banter. And almost without fail they would mention her in their conversation. Those jealous of her would mock her; those who cared for her would teach her how not to hurt a client's feelings while succeeding in avoiding unnecessary harassment. It seemed she was quite popular at one of those coffeehouses. She came home every night and stayed home Saturdays and Sundays.

Recently he began to pay even more attention to what went on across the hall. Whenever a door was opened he would stick out his head and look around—with the same anxiety he experienced when he was looking for his slippers. Finally, he felt he couldn't hold his feeling in any more and started writing her a love letter. He tore up what he wrote again and again, until he gathered enough courage and dropped whatever he had written in the mailbox. But he got no reply. He felt embarrassed and ashamed for days on end. However, there was no difference that he could detect in the way the girls acted or talked toward one another. So he wrote her another letter. He reiterated how he admired her, how sympathetic he was toward her, and how he had made a vow to get her out of bondage. This time he received her reply in a note which was slid directly into his room under his door. That night he was so ecstatic he couldn't sleep. After work he stayed up waiting for her until twelve o'clock. But she did not come home that night.

"Ai Yüeh is not coming home tonight?" one of the girls said.

"No," another girl said. "Maybe she's spending the night with the guy who writes her every day."

"Oh, really, who could that be? Very mystifying indeed."

"It's either Hsiao Chang or Hsiao Lin. Humph, they're really head over heels for her."

When he thought of Hsiao Chang or Hsiao Lin, of a taxicab racing toward such and such a hotel on such and such a street, he felt so anguished that he lost all zest for life. He lay like a corpse on a hard, cold bed, staring at the darkened ceiling. At first he entertained some hope, thinking that she must have been so intoxicated by her client that she did not know what she was doing. He hoped that the taxi had a long distance to go—far enough for her to sober up—then she would think of him and rush back. Anyway, he kept waiting and waiting. Next door's clock struck to tell him that it was four in the morning. Whatever should have happened must have already taken place. His hopes were dashed. He swore he'd never speak to her again. Yet, he couldn't resist switching on the light and taking her letter out from under his pillow to read once again. Word for word, again and again he slowly digested her feelings. In doing so he forgave her instantly, although not totally. Something kept gnawing at his heart, making him feel melancholy. But out of this rose a feeling of warmth toward her, an understanding from shared suffering. He crawled out of bed and wrote her a letter, pretending that he knew nothing about what happened during the night and that he was merely replying to her letter. It was nicely written, the sheet wet from his tears.

For three successive nights Ai Yüeh did not come home at night. Then she was home every night. She was not a diligent writer; her handwriting was ugly and her diction crude. But as long as she wrote him, he was happy.

Their first date was at Hsiao Mei Ice Cream Parlor, and they ordered some fruit. They went back to the same place three more times, but because it cost more than he could afford, later he stopped going there. For her part, she also seemed reluctant to go out with him during her work hours, as it would reduce the tips she got from drinking patrons. Since they couldn't meet in the evenings and he must work during the day, they really couldn't have a decent date until Sunday. Sometimes he was tempted to have a real go at it and loosen his purse strings in order to take her downtown to see a movie or to go on a picnic in the mountains. But all she wanted to do was chat a bit with him in his dingy room, usually on Sunday mornings. Afterwards, she would disappear for the rest of the day.

Because of jealousy he often wanted to forget her completely. Moreover, each time he saw her, he discovered that she had become more dissolute, as could be seen by the fact that she no longer complained about her bitter life when drunk. Instead, she used dirty words freely and continuously. Yet, whenever he saw her, he would forgive her for all these blemishes and treat her as he would a maiden.

With someone to care about, life was more pleasant. His serious attitude and efficiency so impressed his employer that he was given a more responsible job and a salary raise. Even though the increase was not much, this small extra income enabled him to become a more decent lover. He and the girl saw each other so often that he had an illusion about happiness. After he had mastered a trade, he thought, he would have a family and be established in a job, just like everyone else, so long as he continued to work hard. Ever since he had this hope he forgot he was still under twenty-one, and treated her like she was his wife. His feelings toward her became much stronger, particularly after one incident.

The incident happened unexpectedly. One Saturday night she staggered into his room in a drunken stupor. She was like a rape victim. He was so frightened and tense that when she started to gyrate her body, he, bending over her and trembling, showered his liquid of lust upon her body. This caused her to sober up immediately, and, without a word, she got up, dressed, and started smoking at the head of the bed. He too had calmed down a great deal. He held her hand and sat next to her, intending to do it all over again. But she seemed to be interested only in smoking. After she finished her cigarette, she left.

From then on, he never heard her voice again or saw even a shadow of her. From the talk of her friends, he learned she had moved away and had changed her place of employment. He continued to write to her, hoping that someone would transfer his letters to her. Those letters stayed cold in the mailbox. Thus, no matter how deeply apologetic he was or how much he loved her, she gradually faded from his memory. This somewhat idealized version of his first love left its painful marks on his innocent heart, and he felt as though he had recovered from a major illness that had enfeebled him to such an extent that he wasn't capable of feeling anything.

When he had regained his normal ability for feeling and thought, he was badly scorched by the memory of his affair with Ai Yüeh, so much so that he was driven to smoldering anger. One night, he could no longer bear the commotion from the next room and he pounded on the plywood partition.

"Hey," he screamed, "I need to go to sleep."

A peal of laughter came as a response. The people next door also pounded on the wall as hard as they could. "What are you yelling about?"

"Shit!" Dashing out of his room he pushed into their room through the unbolted door and confronted them angrily: "You people have no heart! You know what time it is? If you don't need to go to bed, I do. I've got to go to work tomorrow. Don't push me too far just because there're so many of you. I'll fight you with my life."

He stood by the door, nearly filling up the space of the doorway. His daring life or death rage stunned them. Startled and dumbfounded, they either sat on or stood by their beds. No one spoke a word. When he saw a knife attached to a wooden club by the beds, he became scared. He apologized, explaining how he was an insomniac and how he had lost his self-control. After he said that, he dragged his trembling legs out of their room. He nearly leaped into his own room and cautiously bolted the door. Out of fear, he took a pair of pliers with him to bed.

"Motherfucker!" someone shouted in anger. "It was already too much that he pounded on the partition. He even barged in! This, this simply shows he never gives a shit about us. We must teach him a lesson."

"Well," someone else put in. "I told you guys before. Don't overdo it. We really made so much noise that no one could sleep."

"God damn it! Why must he, a young buck, go to bed so early?" another one was heard saying. "Don't we all have to get up early every morning to work?"

With the exception of the fair-minded one, the rest of the group continued to complain, but since it was very late, they soon settled down. Hsiao San breathed a sigh of relief and put down his pliers. He thought he would buy them some fruit after work the next day just to make friends with them.

He actually did buy some fruit the next day, but something else happened. Just after he had taken his bath and returned to his room, someone knocked twice on his door—very hard. After a little hesitation he stuck his head out and looked. A capless old policeman was standing outside the room directly across from his. He heard another policeman yelling. Thinking that the policemen were there to check on the residency papers, he took out his mobile residency declaration and put it on the table. To save money, he didn't have his hair cut as often as he should, so his hair always looked a bit too long. For this reason he did not care to meet the policemen,[7] and stayed put in his room. It seemed that the two policemen hadn't come to check the residency papers, but he still did not know what was going on. As he tried to eavesdrop, his neighbors were being taken away by the police.

They returned home late. When he detected their footsteps, he was about to open his door to greet them, but before he did that, someone knocked on his door hard, yelling, "Get out!"

"What for?" he asked curiously as he opened the door. They were all in the hallway; they all looked angry and drunken. What surprised him the most was that their hair had been cropped. "What for?" the one who just asked him to come out said, "Look at our hair."

"What about your hair?"

"Fuck your mother! Yesterday you pounded on the wall and barged into our room, yet we didn't do a thing to you. Weren't we nice enough? Why in your mother's name did you tell the cops to catch us gambling?"

"Tell the cops about your gambling? Oh, no, I didn't." He realized that it was a serious matter and he became extremely nervous. He raised his voice trying to explain, but because the misunderstanding had come so suddenly and sounded so absurd, he couldn't help laughing.

"You asshole, you'd better stop laughing. Soon after we started our mahjong game I saw you pass by our door and look us all over."

"My heavens! I was on my way to take a shower," Hsiao San explained immediately. "I took a look only to see if all of you were back. You see, when I got off work today I bought two bunches of grapes especially for you guys. Yesterday I overdid it and I felt sorry about it. Now all I want is to offer you my apology and see if we could become friends; and if I want to be your friend, why would I betray you to the police? Moreover, I didn't see you gamble. As a matter of fact, I like you to gamble, because gambling doesn't make as much noise as your hard rock."

"Shut your trap and stop acting. Screw the grapes! Your mother's—. What's wrong with hard rock? What's wrong with relaxing a bit after a day of work? It's none of your fucking business, just as our mahjong game is none of your goddam business!"

"Really, it's no big deal for us to be caught gambling and fined a few dollars," another person said. "What really made me mad is that they cut off our hair. How can we meet people with this short hair?"

"Oh, please calm down, listen to me."

"You go to hell," the leader slapped Hsiao San in the face. "'Calm down' my ass!"

Hsiao San was shocked and momentarily stunned by the slap. They were so puny and he was so big. His humiliation gave him the illusion that he could calm them down, so he violently retaliated with a punch, which immediately got him in a confused scuffle. The scuffle lasted only a short while, but he was already covered with the wounds inflicted by clubs and other weapons. At last, all he could do was flee to his room for his life. He forced the door shut, then collapsed on the floor, completely exhausted.

The girls who lived directly across from his room woke him. Two girls were quarreling and calling each other names because of their jealousy over one patron. One girl was thoroughly drunk, cursing and crying at the same time. He had no interest in them. To his alarm he discovered his face was covered with blood, his mouth and nostrils were filled with the strong stench of blood, and his body was stiffening. He could not move. He felt something wrong with his chest and he had trouble breathing. When he breathed, bubbles of foamy blood gushed out of his nostrils. In addition, he was chilled all over and felt dizzy. Then suddenly he was frightened by the thought of his brother. After that knife had been stuck into his back, his brother ran, with the knife, toward home. After taking two or three steps, he uttered his last words, "My God, save me!" Now his brother's trembling desperate cries once again reverberated in his ears. At the same time, he remembered the last exchange between the brick-layers: "Enough? That asshole! We'll show him something more spectacu-lar." At this his fear was replaced by extreme grievance and rage. A terrible suicidal thought was born in his heart. He wanted to burn every-thing away. He gave this idea much thought and debated with himself. He thought of that clear, refreshing sea coast, the azure waves, and the pleasant sounds they made; he thought of that noisy bull-headed planing machine, and that crazy prostitute Ai Yüeh. Then he thought of his poor parents. He believed that when they saw his miserable, pitiful condition, they'd shed tears of sorrow. Thinking of his parents, he finally broke into tears.

He had been lying on the floor. As a matter of fact, he couldn't do anything but lie there. It was late at night; not even the sounds of cars could be heard. He groped along the wall of the hallway toward the kitchen. He closed the door and the window. Before closing the window he looked outside. Not too far away was one street lamp, and its gradually dimming light in the darkness created a silver hue amidst the lanes and rows of houses. It stood by itself in desolation and in sadness, much like how he felt. He turned on the girls' gas burner and his own little gas burner; like poisonous snakes, they hissed immediately. Not giving a second look, he staggered back to his own room. He used a wet towel to clean off the bloodstains on his face, and put on some clean street clothes and shoes. He wanted to polish his shoes, but he had neither the time nor the energy. The gas smell was getting strong. He struck one match, then another, still another.

The flame was getting higher and higher. In the chasm between buildings, there were rumbling noises and hollow sounds of explosions. The fire created a red hole in the sky and made the dark night even darker with its whirling smoke. Police cars and clanking fire engines came from everywhere, and the shrill police sirens awakened the residents who lived in the nearby blocks. Light came out of all windows, people ran in the streets, and the curious gawked at the fire. When they saw that ball of frightening, strange-looking fire, they shook their heads and sighed. Firefighters in black uniforms climbed to rooftops everywhere, like phantoms. Water spurted out of their rubber hoses and spread across the sky like a fountain jetting its water, surrounded by wild fire. That water fell on the desolate streets under the streetlights like glistening teardrops.

NOTES

1. Literally, "Little Third," referring to the third one of the siblings; here it is used as a proper name.
2. Literally, "Eldest Brother"; here used as proper name.
3. A profanity.
4. Presumably, Hsiao San must have matriculated into one of the colleges in Taipei, but now he came to the capital not for study but for work.
5. The money order form provided by Taiwan's postal offices prints the remittance amount in columns, such as $100, $200, $1,000 and so forth, presumably for

the convenience of their customers. Thus, instead of writing down the dollar figure, all the customer has to do is to circle the amount he wants to send.

6. The exchange rate is roughly one US dollar to NT$40.00.

7. Regarding the hippie style of living as a form of Western decadence, the Taiwan government in the early seventies was most unhappy with the sight of long-haired and unconventionally dressed young men and women. One common penalty meted out to the men for breaking any law was to give them a free crew cut.

CHANG TA-CH'UN
(1957–   )

The pathos evoked in Chang Ta-ch'un's "Birds of a Feather" revives memories of Pai Hsien-yung's (1937–   ) celebrated Taipei jen *(Taipei, 1971; English translation by the author:* Wandering in the Garden, Waking from a Dream, *Indiana University Press, 1982). However, unlike Pai's characters, who are fond of taunting the Taiwanese for their "rusticity," the Shantungnese soldier in Chang's story is free of such provincial chauvinism. Chang and Pai belong to two generations of Taiwan writers. Not only do Pai's* ta-lu jen *(mainlanders) subsist on dreams of their hometowns, but the fervent hope of eventual repatriation is the very* raison d'etre *of their exile. Sobered by more than thirty years of harsh political reality, the old serviceman from Northern China entertains no similar expectation. And it is precisely his attempt to cure his homesickness by making his chicken coop a proxy home that generates the story's profound sorrow.*

The youngest of the authors in this anthology, Chang Ta-ch'un is uniquely equipped to ponder the fate of the aging ta-lu jen *in the context of Taiwan's acquisitive society. A Shantungnese born and raised on the island, Chang speaks Taiwanese and is for this reason a bona fide native. Yet the loneliness of his parents' generation haunts him with such tenacity that in the end it becomes his personal solitude. "Birds of a Feather" is executed with admirable restraint. While his ancestral lineage with the mainland affords Chang compassionate insights, his awareness of contemporary values checks his sentimental impulses and redresses the balance of economic fact and familial piety. Chang Ta-ch'un's stories are gathered in* Birds of a Feather (Chi-ling t'u, *Taipei, 1980). A graduate of Fu-jen University, he is now in the employ of* China Times (Chung-kuo shih-pao). *His reportorial experience has found its way into his stories of crime and violence in the underground world.*

Birds of a Feather

Translated by Hsin-sheng C. Kao

I.

I hung up the phone and walked out of Platoon Command Headquarters. Outside, the bright, clear sky, untainted by clouds, extended all the way to the eastern reaches of the horizon, where a continuous line of low structures of red brick and grey tile marked a small town. The rich fields that stood between me and the town were a fertile green. In the distance several figures were heading my way along the ridges between the paddies. The sun splashed down from straight overhead. I squinted my eyes and saw that my watch was pointing exactly to twelve—twelve o'clock on the very day that I had been stationed for two whole months on this long beachhead.

The figures on the ridges drew even closer, and they turned out to be farm children from the town. I turned around and walked toward the trees of the windbreak. The cackling of chickens burst from within the windbreak. There in the woods, where motes floated in myriad rays of sunlight, I could make out the faint outlines of chicken-wire fences and chicken houses, and also the strong body of a man, the muscles of his left arm swelling, his chest, shoulders, head, and face dripping countless coin-sized drops of light and dark shadow nonstop as he moved about.

Already the four squad leaders had come out, each from his own base of operations, to greet me with a salute.

"The order has been given! Division Command phoned: The war game 'Operation Golden Wind' is to begin. We need to break camp immediately. Within six hours, all personnel and equipment should be in the trucks and every installation in our present defense area should be restored to its original condition." I paused a while, then when I raised my eyes, there emerged from the woods stout Ts'ai Ch'i-shih. He came to a stop, standing in the sunshine, clutching under his left arm his huge red-feathered, black-tailed rooster. It was like a statue, its head and comb erect, its entire body marked with spots of sunlight, the feathers between its neck and breast flapping in the howling wind from the sea.

"Special attention!" Still staring at the rooster's bright curved beak with a pointed tip, I added: "Except for individual and group equipment, no other items may be brought along."

They nodded their heads. Ts'ai Ch'i-shih drew yet a few steps closer behind them. Yu Huo-yao of the Third Squad, as if having suddenly remembered something, thrust out his chest and said: "Reporting to the Platoon Leader! What about the chickens? The chicken fences . . ."

"The chicken fences have to be gotten rid of, the chickens . . . you are to deal with them yourselves." I couldn't help but turn around and cast a glance over the small town, those farm children all squatting out there together. "Sell them!"

The day when I left Headquarters to report here, I met Ah-ch'ing, the youngest among that group of children on the ridges between the paddies. He was squatting in a ditch; he caught one earthworm without fail every time he reached his hand out. I saw he had a plastic bag stuffed into

his waistband, inside of which were twenty or thirty crickets, grasshop-
pers, leafhoppers, and other such insects.

"They'll die of suffocation, kid." I commented without a second
thought, having stopped to look.

"Doesn't matter, they're going to be fed to Uncle Ts'ai's Big Belly."[1] He
didn't even bother to turn his head, but concentrated on searching in the
ankle-high rice seedlings.

"What? Fed to whom?"

"Ai-ya! . . ." He very impatiently turned around, pointed to the west
side of the windbreak and said: "Didn't I say Uncle Ts'ai's Big Belly?" So
saying, he bent over again and paid no further attention to me.

It was only after I took charge of the troops that I became aware of the
fact that my comrades were raising chickens in the woods. I got to know
Ts'ai Ch'i-shih, who seemed unable to carry on a conversation without
making reference to his hometown in the mainland. I got to know the boy
Ah-ch'ing. And, of course, I also got to know these some thirty chickens,
each of which was given a name and a serial number by their master, Ts'ai
Ch'i-shih. Among Ts'ai's birds was one rooster whose back towered a full
foot and a half above the ground when it stood erect. He was therefore
called "Big Pillar."

The four squad leaders ran past Ts'ai Ch'i-shih to go back to give out the
orders. As if he had not seen them, he walked forward a few steps and let
go with his arm. Big Pillar immediately spread both its wings and flew for
about ten feet in the direction Ts'ai's arm was pointing. As the rooster
touched the ground, it stirred up a cloud of yellow dust. Ts'ai Ch'i-shih
then brought his legs together and gave me a military salute: "Reporting
to the Platoon Leader! Do you want . . . want us to sell the chickens?"

"Hurry back to where you belong and do what your squad leader tells
you."

He said nothing more, but saluted me with a brisk "Check," then raised
his arm, gently calling: "Here!" At this, Big Pillar hopped a couple of
paces, leapt with its whole body, and flew back to Ts'ai Ch'i-shih's arm.
Gently brushing the dust off its neck and wings, Ts'ai marched away in
huge strides. The shining black feathers of the tail, clustered thickly
under the back of his arm, waved gently like a flower in vigorous
bloom.

The fellows of this group had arrived here six months earlier than I had.
Not wanting to waste either manpower or local resources, in their spare
time after making patrols and standing guard they had put themselves to
work at the simplest form of production—raising chickens. In the woods
of the windbreak, an area some 1,800 meters in breadth and 10-odd
kilometers in width, they built chicken houses. Some of the men, particularly serious about their project, even had chicken-wire fences installed

on all four sides. And there were others who were more ambitious: they frequented the neighboring small towns to study the ways the farmers constructed their chicken houses, in order to improve their own. With the passing of time, however, the spare-time project became more for pure amusement than for profit. Of course, there were those whose sole purpose in raising chickens was to make money. As Yu Huo-yao was always saying: Someday, when he got discharged from the service and returned home, this chicken money would indeed become handy when he married and raised a family.

Yet Ts'ai Ch'i-shih differed from the others, just as his chicken fence was different from those of the others: there was no wire; rather all the fencing was hand-woven of selected pine branches, sealed inside and out with yellow mud. When the conversation turned to the subject of that fence, his comrades would laugh at him: it was made that way so that his chickens wouldn't be hurt by fence wire. Of course the jokes did not stop there. Either explicitly or implicitly, he and his chickens had become a source of amusement for the others. But no matter how vulgar and crude the language became at times, Ts'ai Ch'i-shih just grinned slightly, showing a row of somewhat tarnished gold teeth.

The third night after I reported in, a billowing sound, either from the sea or from the trees, swept over from the woods of the windbreak. Taking advantage of the bright moon, which lit up half the sky, I strolled leisurely to have a look at each of the sentry boxes. Before I stepped out, however, Deputy Platoon Leader Liu told me: "If between the base of operations and the sentry box you happen to see someone, the chances are it is Ts'ai Ch'i-shih—his chicken houses are there and he doesn't leave them, even at night." Perhaps Liu was concerned that I might be alarmed by some unexpected noise, but be that as it may, I walked straight to the area where the Second Squad was stationed.

At first I heard heavy footsteps pacing back and forth, followed by a gruff but muffled voice quietly muttering a few scolding words, and then all was quiet again. Tracing the last dying echo of the sound that reverberated in the air back to its source, I stealthily drew closer and leaned against a pine tree. Next to the tree was a ramshackle old bicycle.

The trees in the clearing were rather sparse, and there in the middle of a mud-walled enclosure stood an extremely large chicken house. I saw a man in a T-shirt and shorts, his short-cropped hair shining silvery in the moonlight, his back toward me, his arms wrapped around his chest. Suddenly he pointed to the ground in front of him, saying in his strong Shantung accent: "What do you think this is? Your old home? You want to eat white rice? Seems to me that you've already forgotten who you are. What's wrong with what you've got?" So saying, he bent over to lift a package of something, and dashed it to the ground. There arose the cackling of chickens.

I moved forward, and there on the ground was a split-open package of feed with a medium-sized black chicken standing to the side.

"Just wait until your Brother Ah-ch'ing comes back, I'll ask him to feed you shit! If you're still so choosy, Idiot Number Two, if you're still so choosy it'll serve you right to starve you to death! Now beat it and get to sleep!" The man raised his arm, and the black chicken beat its wings and leaped into the chicken house. Heaving a long sigh, the man squatted and began gathering one handful after another of the chicken feed, putting it back into the feed trough.

When he realized there was someone behind him, he turned his head quietly while his body remained motionless, his left hand reaching ever so slowly toward a firewood hatchet by the door frame.

"You must be Ts'ai Ch'i-shih!"

"Yes?" He briskly stood straight up, his hatchet in hand, his eyes beaming and alert. Then after one or two seconds, he threw down the hatchet and ran toward me: "Platoon Leader?" He opened the door for me, mumbling some words of apology.

I pointed to the cot in the chicken house, "Do you always sleep here at night?"

"Yes, Sir."

"From now on, go back to the base to sleep!"

"Report to the Platoon Leader, I'd never neglect my duties . . ."

"Go back to base to sleep!"

"Yes, Sir."

He saw me off at the fence, his dark, expressionless face glistening in the moonlight. Even when he stole a look at me, there was no trace of grievance in his eyes, only the soft glow of moonlight. In an instant, even I forgot—forgot my reason for making him go back to the base.

II

At two-thirty in the afternoon, the job of checking the defense installations was finally completed. I handed over a detailed list of damaged items to the administrative master sergeant, relaxed a bit, and prepared to go have a look at each squad. One foot out the door and I felt the sunshine penetrate me, giving me a feeling of satiated heaviness as if the sun had been hanging forever at the same spot without even the slightest movement. The group of children previously so boisterous had been driven away by Deputy Platoon Leader Liu. The only one left was little Ah-ch'ing, who sat alone under a ch'ieh-tung tree[2] by the rice field, his hands pressed against his cheeks as he stared at me from afar.

At the opening into the windbreak were Yu Huo-yao and two others, all wearing broad-brimmed rainhats and unbuttoned white shirts that revealed their bare chests, their hands motioning profusely in argument. Next to them stood two motorcycles, a bamboo chicken cage resting on each rear seat. Taking notice of my approach, Yu Huo-yao lowered his head with a frown and waved his hand: "Forget it, forget it! I'll accept your price, but the weight has to be accurate!" This said, he lifted the whistle from where it hung on his chest and blew it sharply. Immediately ten comrades emerged from the woods, each holding two long skewers to which were tied chickens, thrashing and flailing their wings.

I took a detour at the Fourth Squad's defense area, then returned to my round of inspection. Some of my comrades were busy tearing down chicken houses, others were tying up the chickens. And among their loud laughter and conversation, there was nothing but talk of how to spend their chicken money. I judged by their speed that there should be no problem in handing over the base by five o'clock as planned.

Passing by the Second Squad, I saw that Ts'ai Ch'i-shih's mud wall had been completely leveled, his pine branch fence neatly folded. The chicken house was only yet half done with, but the thirty-some chickens had been divided into seven or eight iron coops. He was occupied trying to pry loose a long nail in direct sunlight.

"Busy all by yourself, eh?"

He turned around suddenly, his balding head slick with grease and sweat, which covered his whole face. He wiped a bit with his hand: "It's okay! Too many people could ruin my work." As he spoke, he noticed that a long nail had come out crooked; he took up a hammer to straighten it. He examined it several times to see if it was straight, and, satisfied, put it aside.

"Two chicken buyers have come from town; you are going to see them in a little while, huh?" I said these words only after gathering all my courage, for it was all too clear to me that an unusual bond existed between Ts'ai and his chickens.

He stopped with the work in his hand and, looking over his chicken coops, replied to me with a grin: "Yes, Sir."

I took my leave, but after walking only ten steps or so, I couldn't help but turn and take one last look at him. He was still standing there in a daze, his hands crossed over a small branch, his face half buried in his T-shirt sleeves, looking much like a chicken suspended in midair. The crowing of a cock came from behind him, and though I knew it must be Big Pillar, from where I stood it seemed as if it were Ts'ai Ch'i-shih who had cried out.

Everything was still in an uproar outside the woods. Two chicken coops had already been packed half full. Some of the more vicious birds had fought one another early on, and shreds of brightly colored feathers flew out constantly from the bamboo holes. Yu Huo-yao, sidling himself into the cushioned seat of a motorcycle, was shouting loudly to two squad leaders something to the effect that it would be convenient to do the counting all together; his listeners nodded in agreement. The chicken buyers removed their hats and cooled themselves by fanning the hats with a noisy rattle. Ah-ch'ing also drew near, gathered up a fistful of feathers, and crinkled his nose as he smiled at me saying: "A shuttlecock!" Suddenly, a white wing pushed out from the coop and flapped about furiously, unable to withdraw back inside through the tight bamboo hole, leaving the bird's neck exposed for another grey cock to peck at fiercely. Ah-ch'ing ran up to me and pulled at one of my trouser legs. His other hand held a plastic bag full of bugs. He suddenly thrust up that bunch of chicken feathers:

"A shuttlecock!"

Another fierce fight broke out among the chickens.

One day upon returning to Command Headquarters after checking the guard posts by the harbor, I met Ts'ai Ch'i-shih, who, having done his sentry duty, was feeding insects to the chickens, together with Ah-ch'ing. The black chicken named Idiot Number Two flapped its wings, swooped down off its roost, knocked two chicks out of the way, snatched up a grasshopper, and gulped it down.

Ts'ai Ch'i-shih then threw down the plastic bag, stepped forward, and picked up Idiot Number Two by the neck, slapping it on the beak: "Starved blind, you little bastard? Do you know who they are?" Waving a pointing finger after the chicks that had run off: "Yellow Flower is your little daughter, and Pearl is your sister-in-law, see? How come you don't recognize them? What did I teach you? 'Even the fiercest tigress will not eat her own cubs,' huh! Damn you, little terror! You're at home now, and if you can't make your grandma love you, your uncle care for you, someday when you leave home who the hell is going to watch out for you? Why don't you do some good while you're still young? Taking from others! You little bastard . . ." Having spoken, he tossed Idiot Number Two to the brown dirt, raising a cloud of dust. Immediately it rushed over to the foot of the wall and cocked its head, looking at him.

Ts'ai picked up a few black feathers that had fallen to the ground. Walking toward me, he forced a bitter smile: "He really knows no discipline! He'd be impossible if I didn't scare him up a bit, I'm afraid!" His fingers twisted the feathers back and forth, spinning them like flower petals; then crouching down to Ah-ch'ing, with his chin held high he said: "I'll tie a shuttlecock for you." Seeing that he seemed to deliberately want to hide something, we took up the topic of the shuttlecock and began to talk. He told me that the best feathers for a shuttlecock are those from either side of the chicken's tail, where they are relatively straight with just a slight curve; the down around a chicken's neck is also long enough, but when the shuttlecock is struck, it won't soar as high nor have strength in its rebound. He also mentioned that he had been able to hit a shuttlecock very well since he was four years old, and that he could tie his own from the time he was seven.

"That was when I was back home." He slowly stroked the beard stubble under his chin: "At thirteen I left home, and on the day of my departure my brother fought with me over a shuttlecock. I got a sound thrashing, too! Oh . . ."

Ah-ch'ing moved quietly to the base of the wall and was gently petting Idiot Number Two's spine.

"You, you got no relatives here?" I asked.

He stared at Ah-ch'ing: "Let's see, how many years is it now?"

His large, rough hands on his waist, he stood there, his body tilted to one side. As dusk drew near, it grew dark within the woods much faster, and what light did filter through from the sky was no longer discernible. However, I could clearly see the many folds of his skin, from his earlobes down to his chin and neck, as if his skin had been piled up and released countless times and now just hung there flaccidly. Big Pillar gave a low crow, flew out of the chicken house and thrust out his neck, then sprang to the top of the wall. He stood steadily facing the other side of the woods, where the western sky was tinged with a faint red. It was the source of the light that filtered through the woods.

III.

After the chicken merchant had forced the white chicken wing back in through the hole in the bamboo cage, he smiled at me, tipping the rainhat on his short, unkempt yet slick hair as a kind of greeting. He then shouted to his partner, mounted his motorcycle, and, while still busy starting the engine, asked Squad Leader Yu: "Will four more cages be enough?"

"That'd be plenty!" Yu Huo-yao counted the money, then began to count it all over again, then suddenly, as if he just remembered something, he added: "Let's see! Wait, wait a second, make that six cages." He turned toward us explaining: "There's all of Ts'ai Ch'i-shih's family." A surge of laughter rose from the side.

"Be in the trucks on time." I kept them in line: "Keep track of the time for me!"

"Yes, Sir." Unrestrained cheerfulness welled up from the corners of Yu Huo-yao's mouth.

The two others also looked very happy, but not quite as happy as Yu

Huo-yao. Just as I was about to leave, I overheard one of them saying:
"When I was feeding them, I never thought the money would roll in like
this! Looking at each, one after the other . . . "

"If we had been able to feed for another six months or a year, there'd
have been five hundred or even a thousand more catties, then I'd even
have enough money to raise children!" Yu Huo-yao moistened his
fingertip with saliva: "How many catties for you?"

"What?"

"How many catties for your squad? Let's weigh the big birds first."

I still vaguely remember that dusk which had swiftly turned dark
within a short period of conversation. In those vast deep woods only the
sound of Big Pillar soaring up and down could be heard. Ah-ch'ing,
realizing that Ts'ai Ch'i-shih was angry, had crept home quietly.

"Here!" Ts'ai Chi'i-shih called, raising his copper-dark arm, and Big
Pillar landed on his elbow with a jump and a beat of his wings. Like a
hunter holding a falcon, Ts'ai stood up straight: "Big Pillar is really very
smart. He can stand guard to watch the house without being as menacing
as a dog. The old folks in my hometown used to say that chickens are
nightblind, that they need either a dog or a goose to guard them; but I
don't believe it, Platoon Leader, just look at him! Big Pillar cuts a figure
just like a hawk!"

"For sure!" But as I reached out my hand to stroke Big Pillar's neck, it
swiftly dodged its head and poised its sharp beak at my fingertips. "It
really is quite sturdy! How much does it weigh? Seven, eight catties?"

Taken somewhat aback at first, Ts'ai's expression froze: "Reporting to
the Platoon Leader, my chicken . . . isn't to be weighed!" Then, appearing apologetic, he laughed somewhat drily: "This one, I've never
weighed, never once weighed."

Now it was my turn to feel embarrassed, as if I had forced him to do
something he had no desire to do. I could only offer vacant words: "Oh!
. . . That's right . . . Big Pillar, what an interesting name, Big Pillar."

"Interesting, huh!" He led me into the chicken house, put the chicken
on its roost, and lit a candle. In the flickering light of the candle, the cot,
now shifted somewhat further back in the interior, revealed itself. I
though of what Second Squad Leader Ch'en had told me: Ts'ai was still
constantly sneaking back to his chicken house to sleep and returning to
the base in the early hours of the morning; yet he never missed his guard
duty. Ts'ai pulled out a bamboo stool for me to sit on, while he himself
stood away inside, as if to hide the cot. "Big Pillar, that's my nickname
alright. I was called that in my hometown. In those days . . . but, well,
what's the use of bringing up corny old stories, what's the use indeed."

He moved forward to toy with the candlewick and trimmed off a spark,

which flew into his huge shadow cast on the wood-frame wall. To the side
of the shadow was a row of hand-carved clothes hangers, and there, his
knapsack with a feather sewn onto the shoulder strap.

"You'd better be heading back to the squad, it's getting on mealtime." I
finally broke the silence. As I got up, "Big Pillar" Ts'ai stretched his neck a
bit. "When I get the chance, I'll chat with you again. We could chat about
our old hometowns, how about it?"

"Yes, Sir, I certainly will."

Walking out of the mud-walled enclosure, I turned back again but
couldn't see even the least bit of candlelight leaking out. I called out:
"Ts'ai Ch'i-shih!"

"Present!" And he came rushing out.

"Oh, by the way, if you prefer to sleep here at night, then by all means
sleep here; no need to run back and forth."

He grinned, showing his tarnished gold teeth: "Yes, Sir! Thank you,
Sir!" He then raised his hand, to make a gesture at once like a salute and
yet not like one, waving two circles in the air. As a breeze blew through,
he appeared to be limping a bit, his T-shirt stuck tight to one side of his
body, the other side blowing free.

First there was the sound of a motor. Then *chop, chop, chop*, Ts'ai Ch'i-
shih was cutting down his chickenhouse. Big Pillar's beak was pecking
tap, tap. I slowly opened my eyes; there was the shiny black telephone
sitting in the sunlight that slanted in from the west window. Orders:
Operation Golden Wind. Someone shouting: "Ts'ai—Ch'i—shih." "In my
hometown, I was called 'Big Pillar,'" his words were still ringing in my
ears. I put on my hat. My watch was pointing to four-thirty. I walked out.

"Ts'ai Ch'i-shih! . . . Your chickens! . . . " It was Yu Huo-yao.

A motorized three-wheeled handcart was parked in the middle of the
yellow dirt road between the woods and the rice fields.

"Hurry up! It's almost sundown!" The slick-haired chicken merchant
appeared quite impatient. "Well, do you want to sell them or not?"

Ts'ai Ch'i-shih picked up a towel and wiped his hands, walking slowly.
Little Ah-ch'ing threw down the things in his hands and bounced over
from the ch'ieh-tung tree.

"What's the matter?" The sturdy figure blocked the opening to the
woods, his shadow slanting across the ground to some length, with the
head cast right at the chicken merchant's feet.

"The chickens! Do you want to sell them or not?" He took a few steps
forward, the shadow's head climbing up his ankles even as he tread down
upon it.

"Sell? . . . The chickens?"

"Of course, what else?" Yu Huo-yao stuffed a bundle of money into his pocket: "The boss, Mr. Chu, has been waiting for quite some time, so hurry up, hurry up. He has other things to do after this! . . . Look, Platoon Leader is also here. Everybody's waiting."

"Sell?" Draping the towel over his shoulder, he didn't budge. Ah-ch'ing pulled at one of his trouser legs: "So many, many feathers, shuttlecocks, shuttlecocks!"

"How about this, I'll give you a special deal: egg chickens, thirty dollars per catty; meat chickens, thirty-five; the small ones, not figured by the catty, each chick . . . "

"No weighing, none of them are to be figured by the catty. I'll sell! Okay . . . but not by the scale. My chickens are to be counted by the head! No matter what the size, every one, two hundred dollars each. The hardships I've gone through in raising them can't be measured on a scale, cannot . . . Two hundred dollars is a bargain. I . . . "

"What? Two hundred?" Boss Chu raised two fingers, waving them back and forth: "Are you kidding me, mister?"

Ts'ai Ch'i-shih took up his towel to wipe his face, the shadow of his head traveling to the other's groin. He gently pushed Ah-ch'ing aside with his huge palm: "Originally I hadn't planned on selling them at all, not unless I found a proper buyer." The blue sinews snaking in his forehead, a pearl of sweat oozing out to drip into the dirt, he continued: "I'm not putting the squeeze on you for money!"

"All right, all right, thirty-five a catty, the same price for all of them." Chu was wearing his rainhat. Yu Huo-yao, astonished at his offer, fidgeted his fingers in his pocket and looked as if he wanted to say something but swallowed it down.

"No bargaining, two hundred!"

"He's kidding me!" Chu pulled a long face toward us on his side, and said to Yu Huo-yao: "Squad Leader Yu, I don't want this guy's chickens. What airs! As if his birds are a kind of golden geese! Let him kill them himself for food, and I'll bet he'll get diarrhea! . . . Mister! I don't want to buy them. You keep them, just keep them!"

"Uh . . . can't we calm down and talk this over, Boss Chu?" Yu Huo-yao said, drawing his hand out and patting his trouser pocket, then tapping Boss Chu's shoulder.

"I don't want them! What a lunatic!"

Ts'ai took one step forward, his shadow now covering Chu's entire body: "Let me tell you, Ts'ai Ch'i-shih is not to be had at any cheap price!"

The motor started up, drowning out Ts'ai's voice, then raising a cloud of dust-yellow smoke as the cart drove off to the south down the main road.

Ts'ai shouted out once again: "I'm not to be had at any cheap price!" he then turned and rushed back into the woods, emerging a little while later pushing his ramshackle bicycle, which he immediately mounted to ride away.

"Ts'ai Ch'i-shih!" I blocked the path of his bicycle: "What are you doing? We'll soon be on our way. Don't make trouble!"

"If I may report to the Platoon Leader, I'm okay." He looked at me, his eyes appearing extremely peaceful, like the moonlight of the other night. "Honestly, Sir, I wouldn't . . ."

I made way and he mounted his bicycle. Ah-ch'ing ran to meet him but tripped over Ts'ai's raised leg, and immediately burst into tears. Ts'ai quickly dismounted. Unable to console Ah-ch'ing, he crouched there worrying, as a steady stream of sweat dripped down all over him.

After crying for a while, Ah-ch'ing suddenly stopped and gasped: "A shuttlecock! . . . Big Belly's shuttlecock, I want it!"

Ts'ai didn't respond but only squeezed Ah-ching's shoulder firmly with his huge palm, then turned to pick up the bicycle from the ground, and rode off along the field ridges, his back disappearing from view, merging into the silhouette of the little town. While here, the feathers that littered the ground were already covered with dust.

IV.

The first group of troops being sent to take over arrived at Command Headquarters at five o'clock sharp. After handing over some official papers, Deputy Platoon Leader Liu led some of them around on a tour. I made use of the free time to make a few phone calls to check up on each squad's progress in its assigned preparations, and received word that all equipment would be completely organized at five-thirty and the men would be in the trucks at five forty-five and ready to depart at six o'clock sharp.

"Squad Leader Yu!" I added: "How is he? Is everything okay?"

"Reporting to the Platoon Leader, everything is okay. He just went out to buy a bundle of incense, a few packs of sacrificial paper money, very normal for him." As soon as he finished, I could hear him cover the receiver on his end while he laughed to himself.

"Have you notified Second Squad Leader Ch'en yet?"

"I've already informed him, and he said he'll take special note of it." The muffled laughter of others near the telephone could be heard again.

I hung up, but I still had a feeling that the matter had not been settled. Looking out the window, I saw that the ubiquitous little Ah-ch'ing was still around. Deputy Platoon Leader Liu and his group, however, were laughing and chatting as they returned from their tour. I went outside, the heat of the sun was more tolerable now, as it had already sunk halfway below the flat roofs of the Headquarters and slipped among the treetops of the windbreak.

"Platoon Leader Huang, I'll tell you something funny: you should have left these chicken houses to us." A lieutenant handed me the list of damaged items, and I was just about to reply when a figure came running out of the woods. I recognized Squad Leader Ch'en, carrying on his shoulders two military knapsacks, one of which clearly bore on its shoulder strap the imprint of a feather:

"Reporting to the Platoon Leader!" Ch'en said.

I made a gesture with my hand to the people lined up opposite us, and Deputy Platoon Leader Liu led them inside.

"What happened?" I asked.

"Ts'ai Ch'i-shih has dug a huge pit in the woods, and taken the chickens, along with their cages, everything—and smashed them all to bits with a wooden club! . . ."

Not waiting for him to finish, I ran as fast as I could to the woods.

Legs spread, Ts'ai stood there, steady as ever, the long shadow of his body falling into the depths of a large rectangular pit. Therein lay six or seven iron cages, tossed around in every direction and utterly smashed, a scene of mutilation beyond recognition. Chicken feathers were scattered everywhere. Then, just when I decided that I couldn't bear to look any further, I saw him turn around, holding Idiot Number Two in his hand. He said, as if he hadn't seen me: "This time it's not your fault! Little bastard, even if you were cruel, even if you were greedy, I want you to die bravely, you little bastard. Don't complain now . . ." Having spoken, he broke its neck with a crack, threw it into the pit, and raised his arm, saying:

"Come on over here!"

"Ts'ai Ch'i-shih!" I shouted as I firmed my fist. The list of damaged items was crumpled into a ball.

Big Pillar sprang to its original position, from I do not know where, fluttered the feathers of its entire body, erected its brilliant red comb, and lifted its head, and then stayed motionless. Ts'ai Ch'i-shih said nothing, only stroking lightly all its shimmering feathers. A teardrop rolled down from the corner of his eye, flowing all the way down the folds of skin on his neck and then vanishing completely.

The moonlight of that night, perhaps of many nights hence, appeared, penetrated the tiniest cracks in the woods, and what fell on the human body was no longer coinlike bits of shining daylight, but rather a vast expanse of untinted clarity.

"Do you still remember?" Ts'ai Ch'i-shih leaned against a pine tree with his eyes closed. Tucking Big Pillar under one arm, he stroked the feathers of its neck with his free hand while he murmured as if in a dream: "On the day of departure, you still fought with Idiot Number Two over a shuttlecock, and your father hung you up and gave you a sound caning. Oh Big Pillar, a man can only be had for good price! It just can't be argued . . ."

Again, the sound of another "crack!" I looked away.

"Go pay back the life you owed someone!" He sighed and threw the rooster into the pit, where it landed with a dull thud. Turning around, he picked up a bag of chicken feed and threw it into the pit. Three bloody claw marks showed clearly on his left arm.

"Ts'ai Ch'i-shih!"

He glanced at me, then as if some important thought had just occurred to him, he suddenly jumped into the pit to pluck a bunch of feathers from either side of Big Pillar's tail. Putting them in his breast pocket, he jumped back out and grabbed a shovel to start filling the pit with dirt.

After the hole was filled, he got into his military uniform and put his hat on properly. He then took three sticks from his bag of incense and lighted them, together with a bundle of sacrificial paper money, while chanting: "Little guiding spirit, please honor my prayer, and lead the whole family of them back to . . ."

I came out first. Each truck was already positioned in its proper place. Two new soldiers were still covering their mouths, laughing over Ts'ai and his chickens.

"Who dares laugh again? Slap your mouths shut!"

The wind within and without the woods of the windbreak quieted down suddenly, as the sun sank to the corner of the sky from whence the winds came.

Ts'ai Ch'i-shih came walking in the breeze toward the road. Under the ch'ieh-tung tree, he fondled Ah-ch'ing's hair lovingly, took the bunch of feathers from his breast pocket, and stuffed them into Ah-ch'ing's tiny hand, saying: "Learn to make your own shuttlecocks!"

Then, as the trucks' engines started up, he ran over to me and told me quietly: "Reporting to the Platoon Leader! I'm okay, except, my price wasn't cheap!"

I watched him turn and get into a truck, which left its tire tracks behind as it sped off to the north, its two small red taillights shining persistently through the churning smoky fog. I started my jeep, and in the smoky fog before me there seemed to be a number of fluttering dark forms, kicking yellow dust as they touched ground.

Was it Big Pillar and his family?

NOTES

1. "Big Belly" (*Ta-tu-tzu*) is nearly homophonous with "Big Pillar" (*Ta-chu-tzu*)—Ts'ai Ch'i-shih's pet name for his black-tailed rooster—hence the boy's playful mispronunciation.

2. *Ch'ieh-tung* tree, also called *ch'ung-yang mu* or *ch'iu-feng*, is the Chinese name for *Bischofia javanica*, which grows mostly in tropical areas.

INDEX OF AUTHORS

Where the author is identified by a pen name,
his or her real name is given in parentheses.

277

INDEX OF TITLES

The date of first publication is given in parentheses following the title.

279